Survey Research Methods

Survey Research Methods

Earl R. Babbie

University of Hawaii

Wadsworth Publishing Company, Inc.
Belmont, California

Designer: Gary Head

Cover: Richard Forster

Editor: Ellen Seacat

Technical Illustrator: Carl Brown

ISBN 0-534-00224-2

L. C. Cat. Card No. 72-95060

Printed in the United States of America

    5 6 7 8 9 10—77 76 75

To
Sam Stouffer
Paul Lazarsfeld
Charles Glock
and the Old Turks

Preface

Survey research is probably the best known and most widely used research method in the social sciences today. Its use in the academic world grows daily. It is now taught and used in departments of sociology, political science, psychology, business administration, public health, and geography to name a few. Increasingly, social science graduate students are encouraged to conduct surveys to satisfy thesis and dissertation requirements for original research. Undergraduate classes frequently conduct surveys, and faculty members publish reports of hundreds of surveys every year.

Outside the academic world, almost everyone has heard of public opinion polls, election predictions, consumer market studies, and censuses. To some extent, everyone in the United States at least has been affected by surveys. Politicians launch or scuttle campaigns and dreams on the basis of voter surveys. Manufacturers mass-produce or discontinue products on the basis of market research findings. Federal aid programs often hinge on the results of population surveys in distressed cities and states. In addition to professional survey research activities, nonprofessional surveys are conducted frequently. Social clubs poll their members on club policies and picnic dates. Libraries and cafeterias poll their users about desired services and hours. Radio stations invite listeners to call in votes on community issues.

Such widespread use and acceptance of survey research would seem to indicate that the technique is easily learned and used. Everyone who has read the report of a public opinion poll in his local newspaper is likely to feel he could conduct a poll of his own. After all, anyone can ask questions and count the answers.

Why This Book Emphasizes Logic and Skills

This book is addressed to three problems related to the misconception that survey research is simple. First, the faddish popularity of survey methods has inevitably resulted in a large number of bad surveys. Sometimes survey techniques are used poorly; often surveys are conducted when some other research method would have been more appropriate. Hopefully, by discussing the logic and skills of survey research in some detail, the text will help raise the quality of surveys conducted.

Second, the widespread overuse and misuse of survey methods has led to the wholesale rejection of survey research by many people, including a growing number of young social scientists. In this regard, it is hoped that the book will indicate that survey research can be an extremely useful method of scientific inquiry in certain situations. Used correctly and in appropriate situations, surveys can provide needed information that could not feasibly be obtained by any other method.

Third, the assertion that a given survey was poorly conducted presupposes an established body of scientific standards against which to evaluate survey activities. Unfortunately, this is not really the case. To be sure, in some aspects of survey research, such as sampling and the statistical manipulation of data, some very rigorous standards do exist. But in other aspects, such as the wording of questions and the codification of responses, the standards are not as clearly defined. Such standards that do exist are generally not formalized, and, moreover, they tend to be transmitted as an oral tradition from researcher to student-apprentice. However, beginning researchers who do not have access to this apprenticeship system may not understand even the informal standards. This book attempts to point out such informal standards and to place them within the logical context of scientific inquiry.

The general orientation for this text is reflected in the title, *Survey Research Methods.* As a survey methods instructor and as a survey consultant, I sorely felt the need for a single volume that would provide students and other prospective researchers with a practical guide to survey research. Books and essays discussing the theoretical logic of scientific inquiry are plentiful enough, but typically they do not specify how scientific norms are applied in practice. At the other extreme, a handful of "survey cookbooks" are available, providing step-by-step guidelines for making surveys, but their utility diminishes rapidly as the researcher's field situation differs from those discussed directly in the texts. Whenever a researcher faces a field problem not covered by the "cookbook," he will probably be at a loss. This book attempts to provide a solution to such a problem.

This text focuses on the *logic* and the *skills* of survey research. Relatively little attention is given to statistics, since several excellent statistics texts are available. In covering the various aspects of survey design and analysis, I have used the following format. First, the theoretical logic of, say, sampling is discussed. The reader should understand the basic logic of selecting a sample of respondents whose answers can be taken to represent the population from which they were selected. Then the most typical methods of sampling are discussed step by step. At this point, the reader should understand not only *how* to select a conventional sample but also *why* conventional sampling methods follow from the theoretical logic of sampling. Then a variety of practical problems frequently faced by researchers in the field are introduced, and the typical methods for dealing with those problems are discussed within the context of the logic of survey sampling. Here, the reader should understand why the solutions suggested offer the best correspondence with sampling logic and ideal sampling methods. While it will not be possible to consider all the practical problems that readers may eventually face, it is hoped that they will understand the logic of sampling in practice sufficiently well to permit them to arrive at good solutions of their own. Even when the research situation does not permit a *good* solution, the reader should be able to evaluate the significance of his actual decision in regard to the conclusions to be drawn from his study.

No survey fully satisfies the theoretical ideals of scientific inquiry. Every survey represents a collection of compromises between the ideal and the possible. The primary goal of this text is to help readers arrive at the best possible compromises. *Perfect* surveys may not be possible, but *good* surveys can and should be done.

This book may seem rather elementary. It focuses almost exclusively on *basic* logic and skills. For example, relatively little attention is given to scaling techniques, whereas much attention is devoted to constructing simple indexes. Similarly, the discussions of survey analysis focus primarily on percentage tables. There are two reasons for this orientation. The existing methodological literature already covers advanced techniques rather fully, while the more basic techniques have not been treated as extensively. More important, a firm grounding in the basic logic and skills of survey research is a prerequisite for fully understanding the more advanced techniques. Thus, if the reader can fully understand the logic of analysis through percentage tables, I feel he will be better equipped to undertake correlations, regressions, factor analysis, and so forth. At present, unfortunately, many students leap directly into more complicated forms of analysis without really understanding the logic of research in general.

How This Book Can Be Used

This book is aimed at a rather broad audience: anyone interested in conducting a survey or in using and/or evaluating the results of a survey. More specifically, it is aimed at three distinct audiences: methodology students, beginning researchers, and research consumers.

First, *Survey Research Methods* is intended for undergraduates taking their first course in research methods. While a number of instructors prefer to emphasize survey research in the general course, other methodologies may be covered in addition. Hence, this book is published in softcover to allow for a flexible use of materials. The organization of the material grew out of my own classroom experiences in teaching survey methods, and an early draft of the text was tested in that setting. In addition to the materials in the body of the text, most chapters are accompanied by a list of additional readings that might be used for more detailed examinations of specific topics.

Second, the book is intended as a practical and realistic guide for the beginning researcher who has had little or no previous experience in survey research. The book dwells on the likely problems, decisions, and compromises that are the day-to-day substance of field research. I have attempted to provide the broadest possible range of examples from my own research and consultation in a wide variety of research projects and research conditions and from the experiences of colleagues and other researchers. I hope that the number of examples will increase the likelihood that a researcher will find guidance in the text. At the same time, I have sought to present such examples within the basic logic of scientific inquiry. Rather than asking the reader to memorize specific techniques—even a broad variety of techniques—I ask that he understand why those particular techniques are recommended and used. Thus, when the researcher must compromise or approximate, he should be in a position to know what he is compromising and what the effect of compromise is likely to be.

Finally, I hope that consumers of survey research will find in this book a methodological grounding to aid them in enlightened, critical evaluation. I hope I have presented a sufficiently complete picture of the practical realities of field research to improve the perspective of the more casual survey critics. By discussing honestly the merits and possible uses of survey research, I would hope to convert some critics into enlightened supporters. But no less importantly, I discuss the disadvantages, shortcomings, and misuses of survey research in the hope of helping some of its more overzealous supporters to become a bit more critical.

Acknowledgments

I was extremely fortunate to have had the opportunity to learn survey research in essentially an apprenticeship setting under the tutelage of Charles Glock. At a time when faculty members are accused of exploiting students, Charlie consistently treated me as a junior colleague. I was encouraged to take on projects of my own and became more independent, although I was always able to turn to Charlie for more advanced guidance. I feel a debt to Charlie Glock that cannot be discharged by the standard acknowledgment in a preface. While I have subsequently learned things about survey research that Charlie did not teach me, I am still somewhat embarrassed to call this book my own.

At the same time, I am indebted to a number of other teachers and colleagues. Foremost among these is Rod Stark, who served as my big brother during the early years at Berkeley. Later at Berkeley, I had the good fortune to meet Gertrude Selznick, who forced me to look ever deeper into the logical grounding of survey analysis, and our comparing notes on empirical research gave me a much better understanding of what scientific inquiry was all about. Other teachers and colleagues who have improved my own understanding of survey research as science include George von Bekesy, Lin Freeman, Dave Gold, Ren Likert, Bill Nicholls, Jay Palmore, Steve Steinberg, and Charlie Yarbrough. And I am especially grateful for the detailed and thoughtful comments of three reviewers of the manuscript: Andy Anderson, Joseph Spaeth, and Billy J. Franklin.

By the same token, I should acknowledge my debt to the many researchers with whom I have worked in a consultative capacity. Some have taught me new techniques; some have reviewed and commented on early drafts of this text. Among them are Jim Dannemiller, Dave Ford, Dennis Hall, Dave Johnson, Jan LeDoux, Heung-soo Park, Dinny Quinn, Francoise Rutherford, Yongsock Shin, Dave Takeuchi, Chuck Wall, and Choon Yang.

Despite all this, the textbook itself would never have materialized without the help of several people involved in the manuscript itself. Jack Arnold, Steve Rutter, and Rod Stark organized and provided important editorial inputs from Wadsworth. Barbara Higa undertook an extensive bibliographic project. Pat Horton did yeoman service in helping me find time to write and in typing the rather lengthy manuscript.

Because of her special expertise in data collection and general experience in survey research, my wife, Sheila, was asked to coauthor the book, and she played an important role in the initial organization of it. Shortly after writing began, it became impossible for Sheila to devote sufficient time to the book, but she continued to serve as an active consultant, confidante, and critic.

Contents

Part One   The Scientific Context of Survey Research

This book is addressed to the subject of scientific research. It has the dual purpose of assisting readers in the execution of scientific research of their own and in the understanding of scientific research conducted by others. Although the book focusses on a particular research method—survey research—it should be read within the general context of science. Whereas survey research employs specific techniques peculiar to that particular method, each of those techniques may be seen to fit into the general norms of scientific inquiry.

Although science has been with us for centuries and countless books have been written on the topic of scientific research, it remains a somewhat enigmatic subject for nonscientists and beginning scientists. The purpose of Part One of this book is to provide an overview of the logic of science so that the specific techniques of survey research may make more sense later in the book. Three chapters are addressed to this topic.

Chapter One considers the basic logic of science. It begins with a discussion of the traditional image of science—an image I believe is generally misleading and inappropriate in the context of actual scientific research. My purpose in this regard is not to debunk, but to make science relevant and realistic.

Science in practice is neither mystical nor pure. Like all human activities, scientific research is a compromise between the ideal and the possible. It is often guided, in practice, by emotion, error, and irrationality. Nevertheless, scientific research is importantly different from other human activities, and I shall attempt to elucidate those differences in Chapter One.

Chapter Two is addressed to the even knottier topic of *social* science. This is a topic about which a great deal has been written in recent years. Some writers insist that social science is every bit as "scientific" as natural science, while others debunk such a notion. Still others see social research as progressing toward, but not yet achieving, the status of science.

I shall suggest that this is a meaningless question. Just as it is impossible to provide a definitive statement of what science *really* is, it is similarly impossible to state whether social science is or is not scientific. Instead, we shall consider the differences and similarities between the social and natural sciences and explore the implications of those for the logic and techniques of social scientific research.

Chapter Three is devoted to a specific examination of survey research. The chapter begins with a consideration of the history of the method and then turns to the ways in which survey research fits into the general norms of science and social science.

The ultimate purpose of these three chapters, then, is to prepare the reader to understand the logical bases which underlie the specific skills and techniques of survey research. It is hoped, of course, that the reader will also become better grounded in the basic logic of science per se. This is especially important since, as noted above, all scientific research is a compromise between the ideal and the possible. The bulk of this book is addressed to such compromises.

We shall begin by examining what ought to be done under ideal circumstances. Then we shall consider what compromises are most appropriate when the ideal cannot be achieved. Unless the reader fully understands the basic logic of science, he will be unable to understand why one compromise is accepted in lieu of another. If he does understand this logic, when he sets about conducting his own research, he will be able to achieve the best possible compromises under actual field conditions.

Chapter One

The Logic of Science

"Science" is a household word. Everyone has used it at one time or another, yet images of science differ greatly. For some, it is the same as mathematics, for others it is white coats and laboratories, others confuse it with technology, and still others equate the term with difficult high school or college courses.

Science is, of course, none of these things per se. It is difficult to specify exactly what science *is,* however. This chapter begins by summarizing the image of science that is frequently presented to students in introductory science courses. Then we shall examine a counterimage of science that is gaining popularity. Finally, I shall attempt to outline the logical components of science as it is practiced.

1.1   The Traditional Perspective

Introductory courses in scientific disciplines often present an image of science that makes it appear straightforward, precise, and even routine. While I shall criticize this perspective later in the chapter, it provides an excellent starting point.

Scientific Theory

Scientists, we are told, begin with an interest in some aspect of the world around them. They may be interested in knowing how blood pressure is regulated in the body, why one strain of rice is hardier than another, what determines the paths of comets, what causes cancer. The subject matter is then rigorously examined and structured in highly abstract terms.

The scientist identifies all the phenomena relevant to the subject under study. On the basis of existing knowledge, he may interrelate those phenomena into a network of causal relationships. In this fashion, he develops a *theory,* a set of interrelated, logical propositions that explain the nature of the phenomenon under study.

To test the validity of his theory, he then presumably derives *hypotheses,* predictions about events. Often, these hypotheses are of an *if-then* form. If Event A were to occur, then Event B would follow. Since this relationship is warranted by the general theory, the failure of Event B to follow Event A would call into question the validity of the theory itself.

Operationalization

Theories are by nature abstract and general. Hypotheses, while more specific, are also typically somewhat abstract. Thus, hypotheses must be converted into *operational terms.* The scientist must specify which real world phenomenon would constitute Event A and which would constitute Event B.

If the scientist's hypothesis concerned the effect of temperature on the growth rate of a certain plant, he would specify the manner in which both temperature and growth would be measured; that is, what *operations* would be equated with those concepts. Having specified those operations, he would describe an experiment that would test his hypothesis, including the duration of the experiment, the frequency with which temperature and growth would be measured, specifying whether temperature is to be artificially controlled (and how) or whether natural variations are to be noted, how the measurements are to be recorded and analyzed, and so forth.

On the basis of his hypothesis, he might predict growth rates that should correspond with different temperatures and might specify the relative correspondence between predicted and observed growth rates that would constitute a confirmation or rejection of his hypothesis.

Experiment

Finally, the operations specified are undertaken. The data are collected and manipulated as prescribed, and the hypothesis is thereby tested. If the hypothesis is confirmed by the experiment, then the general theory from which the hypothesis was derived is also partially confirmed. If the hypothesis is not confirmed, the general theory is called into question. Whatever the outcome, the scientist presumably publishes his findings, the world becomes a little better place to live, and he starts thinking about other topics of interest.

While imagination and brilliance would seem called for in the construction of theories, little or none seems necessary in the collection and analysis of data. With everything specified in advance, technical assistants could presumably conduct and interpret the experiment.

Summary

Since the scientist operates in accord with rational and objective procedures, his conclusions are presumably of a higher quality than the subjective impressions and prejudices of the layman. The scientist deals with facts and figures, and, we are told, figures do not lie.

1.2   The Debunking of Science

In recent years, some students have been given an image of science and scientists that is quite different from the traditional perspective presented above. This more iconoclastic view of science has a number of dimensions.

First, it is pointed out that scientists are motivated by the same human emotions and are hindered by the same human frailties as are other human beings. Scientists, we are told, frequently select their subjects of study on the basis of personal biases, and some may devote all their energies to "proving" some pet hunch. Rather than objectively framing and executing experiments, their research is a continuing search for data to substantiate a prejudice.

Similarly, the cults and cliques of the scientific world have been held up to public view. It has been pointed out that a scientific paper submitted for publication may be judged more on the basis of the researcher's academic credentials (degrees, school, and the like) than on the intrinsic merits of the paper itself. A journal editor trained under Professor X may reject all papers submitted by students of Professor Y.

Moreover, it is frequently pointed out that "accepted ideas" in scientific disciplines are very difficult to challenge. A research paper presenting a radically new perspective on an old and presumably settled issue may never see the light of publication.

On another topic, we are told that "grantsmanship" has replaced scholarship in science, that many researchers evaluate a prospective research project in terms of the likelihood of foundation funding rather than in terms of its possible contribution to understanding. In these terms, a researcher may be judged by the number of research assistants he employs rather than by the quality of his research findings.

Since so much scientific research is conducted within universities, it is relevant to note the growing criticism of the "publish-or-perish" norm attributed to most contemporary academic departments. In a word, an academic researcher must abide by the "nonscientific" norms of the contemporary scientific community in order to obtain the resources needed for the conduct of research.

These criticisms of present-day science have been further fueled by a number of candid research biographies published in recent years by noted scientists.[1] Increasingly, practicing scientists have attempted to present honest accounts of their research projects, to place their findings in proper perspective, and to provide better guidance to aspiring researchers. Since these accounts have pointed to errors, oversights, and other practical problems, many of the contemporary critics of science in general have taken these as inside admissions that science is bunk.

The recent debunking of science is probably a healthy turn of events. For too long, science has been regarded as a mystical enterprise and scientists as infallible superhumans. If science is a rational and objective activity, then it should withstand objective and rational evaluation. Those aspects that do not survive such a critique probably should not remain a part of science per se.

The main danger in the present criticism is that it may provide an easy way out of the difficulty of understanding science. For a student, it is much simpler to dismiss all science as ritualistic nonsense than to learn statistics or the logic of scientific research. It is easier to regard all science as bad than to become a good scientist.

I am, of course, biased on this topic. I believe that science is a distinctive human activity. While many activities that may be called "scientific" are not so, in my opinion, many scientific activities are importantly different from other human activities, and understanding those differences is extremely important.

The primary problem here lies with the inaccuracy of the traditional perspective of the scientific method as it is conventionally presented to beginning science students. Science in practice does not correspond to the traditional image of science, but, at the same time, it need not be as bad as its severest critics contend. The following section aims at describing *science in practice* as distinguished from the traditional perspective. Then we shall turn to those features that make science distinct from other human activities.

1.3   Science in Practice

Whereas the traditional perspective suggests that the scientist moves directly from an interest in some phenomenon to the derivation of a theory, this is seldom if ever the case. His initial interest in the phenomenon often stems from some previous empirical research, perhaps some anomalous findings generated by his own research or the work of some other researcher. Thus, he may begin with a very specific discovery—that a given event is usually followed by another or that two variables are empirically related to each other—and he then sets out to develop a more general understanding of why that is the case.

---

[1]See, for example, James Watson, *The Double Helix* (New York: The New American Library, 1968) and the collection of research biographies in Phillip Hammond (ed.), *Sociologists at Work* (New York: Basic Books, Inc., Publishers, 1964).

Theories are almost never the result of wholly deductive processes. They are more typically the end result of a long chain of deductive and empirical activities. At one point, the scientist may have a tentative explanation for an empirical relationship; he may test it partially through the collection of more data, use the new results to modify his explanation, collect more data, and so forth. Theory building, then, involves an interaction of deduction and observation.

It follows, therefore, that theories are seldom confirmed at a given point in time. There are relatively few "critical experiments" in science—experiments upon which the whole theory stands or falls. Instead, evidence built up over time lends support to a continually modified theory. Eventually, some form of the theory may become generally accepted, but we can seldom point to a given time at which it was "proven" or accepted. Moreover, all theories continue to undergo modifications. No scientist has or will ever discover Truth.

Operationalization of concepts is never as clear-cut as the traditional image of science suggests. While this will be discussed in greater depth in Chapter 7, it should be noted here that most scientific concepts lend themselves to a variety of different empirical interpretations. Thus, the researcher typically specifies tentative operationalizations of those concepts, and the results of his experiments are used to evaluate those operationalizations as much as for testing hypotheses.

Even where concepts are operationalized in a reasonably acceptable fashion, experimental results are seldom conclusive in an absolute sense, even with regard to specific hypotheses. Typically, a hypothesis is confirmed or rejected *to a certain extent*—but seldom completely. As noted above, theories are normally accepted on the basis of a *weight of evidence* over several experiments. If a large number of empirical observations are better explained by a given theory than by any other available theory, that theory will probably be accepted.

Finally, the impression that empirical testing is a routine activity is wholly incorrect. The traditional image of science suggests that brilliance is required in the derivation of theories and in the design of experiments but that the execution of the experiment itself is pretty dull and unimaginative. In practice, the execution of an experiment, the collection of empirical data, requires countless critical decisions. Unexpected situations arise. Bizarre observations are recorded, suggesting measurement errors. Data may be lost or falsified. The operationalization of concepts is never completely unambiguous and must be further specified during the experiment. Each of these situations requires decisions that will influence the outcome of the experiment and, by extension, the evaluation of the hypothesis and the theory from which it may have been derived.

This is an important point in the context of the present volume. Many of today's students have served, or know others who have served, as research workers in scientific projects. Most can attest to the disparity between the project design and the day-to-day work on the project. Especially in the case of a poorly supervised project, the research worker may take a rather jaundiced view of the scientific-sounding description of the project as reported in an academic journal. Such a student may conclude that all science is "unscientific."

I emphasize this point for two purposes. First, I would stress (and will do so throughout the volume) that the quality of a research project can depend importantly on the seemingly mundane decisions and activities that go into the collection and processing of data. The project director who does not involve himself in such activities runs a serious risk of directing a meaningless project. At the same time, however, the implications of such decisions—even sloppiness—are not always easily apparent. What might seem a sloppy procedure to the layman might in fact be insignificant to the ultimate worth of the data. Making good decisions and evaluating the implications of bad ones depends on a well-founded understanding of the logic of science as a distinctive activity. It is this latter topic to which we will now turn.

1.4   What Is Science?

At base, all science is aimed at understanding the world around us. There are three major components of this activity: description, the discovery of regularity, and the formulation of theories and laws.

First, the scientist observes and describes objects and events appearing in the world. This may involve the measurement of velocity of a falling object, the wave length of emissions from a distant star, or the mass of a subatomic particle. Such descriptions are guided by the goals of accuracy and utility.

Second, the scientist attempts to discover regularities and order among the sometimes whirling, buzzing chaos of experience. In part, this may involve the coincidence or correlation of certain characteristics or events. Thus, for example, the scientist may note that air pressure correlates with altitude or that the application of a force to an object results in a modification of its velocity.

Third, the scientist attempts to formalize and generalize the regularities he discovers into theories and laws. Examples of this would be Newton's law of gravity and Einstein's general and special theories of relativity. Theories and laws, then, are general, logical statements of relationships among characteristics and events that provide explanations for a wide range of empirical occurrences.

It should be noted that nonscientists pursue these same three goals. All of us observe and describe the world around us. We seek to find regularities: the office worker may find that arriving late for work results in a reprimand. We seek to formulate laws and theories that will provide overall guidance in everyday life, such as religious perspectives holding that adherence to religious teachings will result in worldly and/or otherworldly rewards.

To emphasize this point, it may be useful to note the similarities in the respective activities of a careless scientist and a racial bigot. Both make observations about the world and may report those observations to others. For example, the scientist observes that members of a given primitive tribe enjoy relatively good dental health; the bigot observes that a given Jewish shopkeeper has cheated him in a business transaction. The scientist tentatively concludes that the primitive tribe's diet may be responsible for their dental health, while the bigot concludes that the shopkeeper's religion was responsible for his unethical business practices.

Both the scientist and the bigot seek new observations to reflect on their tentative conclusions. The scientist checks the dental health of other primitive tribes having similar diets, while the bigot keeps an eye on Jewish shopkeepers. It is important to note that both the scientist and the bigot are *selective* in their subsequent observations. In his attention to diet, the scientist may overlook different tribes' climatic environment, economic structure, and so forth. The bigot, in turn, will overlook shopkeepers' education, social class, and so forth. Moreover, both the scientist and the bigot may tend to ignore, temporarily perhaps, certain observations. The scientist may ignore the good dental health of tribes having radically different diets from the one that interests him, while the bigot may temporarily discount disconfirming observations as the products of extraneous variables or inaccurate observations. The scientist may disregard reports of a tribe having the diet in question plus bad teeth assuming they are the result of bad field work. The careful scientist, of course, would deal with such cases ultimately. The bigot will discount reports of an honest Jewish shopkeeper as inaccurate.

When they face up to disconfirming observations, both the careless scientist and the bigot will seek other observations that will bring the initial observation into line with the developing theory. In the case of a tribe having good teeth but a different diet, the scientist may intensify his field work in an effort to discover that the tribe's diet is more similar to the one in question than initially appeared. Confronted with a dishonest non-Jewish shopkeeper, the bigot may engage in a search for a Jewish great-great-grandfather.

Despite empirical anomalies, the scientist in question may end up with a theory relating a certain diet to dental health, and the bigot will end up with a theory that Jews are dishonest. Both theories will be apparently substantiated by empirical observations and logical explanations.

The above comparison is aimed at making two points. First, there is no magical difference between scientific and nonscientific activities. We have seen two rather similar lines of inquiry. Second, and related to the first point, the activities of "scientists" vary in their "scientific" quality. It makes more sense to speak of more or less scientific activities than to dichotomize between scientific and nonscientific. Thus, a particular line of inquiry conducted by a professional physicist may in fact be relatively unscientific, while a plumber may conduct an inquiry of the highest scientific caliber.

In the remainder of this section, we shall turn our attention to those characteristics that make a given activity more or less scientific. We shall attempt to understand the ideal characteristics of science, realizing that no given activity is ever fully in accord with those ideals, whether conducted by a professional scientist or a layman.

Science Is Logical

Science is fundamentally a rational activity, and scientific explanations must make sense. Religions may rest on revelations, customs, or traditions, gambling on faith; but science must rest on logical reason.

Logic is a difficult and complex branch of philosophy, and a full delineation of systems of logic is well beyond the scope of this textbook. Perhaps a few examples will illustrate what is meant by science being logical. For example, a given event cannot, logically, cause another event that occurred earlier in time. The movement of a bullet cannot cause the explosion of the gunpowder propelling it. Thus science takes a different approach from the *teleological* views assumed by some religions. For example, some Christians believe that Jesus was destined to be crucified, and that this destiny thereby caused him to be betrayed and tried. Such a view could not be accepted within the logic of science.

In the logic of science, it is impossible for an object to have two mutually exclusive qualities. The flip of a coin cannot result in both a head and a tail. By contrast, we might note that many deeply prejudiced people argue that Jews are both "clannish" (refusing to mix with non-Jews), and "pushy" (forcing themselves in with non-Jews). Faced with such an assertion, the scientist would suggest that either one or both of the characterizations of Jews are untrue or that the two characteristics are being defined in such a way that they are not mutually exclusive.

Similarly, a given event cannot have mutually exclusive results. Thus, getting a college education cannot make a man both wealthier and poorer at the same time. It is possible for a college education to result in wealth for one man and poverty for another, just as some Jews might be described as clannish and others pushy, but contradictory results or descriptions fly in the face of logic and are intolerable to science.

All this is not to say that science in practice is wholly devoid of illogical assertions. Many readers will already realize that physicists currently regard light as both particles and waves, even though these are contradictory descriptions of the nature of light. This particular contradiction exists in science since light behaves as particles under some conditions and as waves under others. As a result of this situation, physicists continue to use the two contradictory conceptualizations as they may be appropriate in given conditions. Nevertheless, such a situation represents a strain for the logic of science.

Moving somewhat beyond this "common sense" notion of logic, there are two distinct logical systems important to the scientific quest, referred to as *deductive logic* and *inductive logic*. Beveridge describes them as follows:

Logicians distinguish between inductive reasoning (from particular instances to general principles, from facts to theories) and deductive reasoning (from the general to the particular, applying a theory to a particular case). In induction one starts from observed data and develops a generalization which explains the relationships between the objects observed. On the other hand, in deductive reasoning one starts from some general law and applies it to a particular instance.[2]

The classical illustration of deductive logic is the familiar syllogism: "All men are mortal; Socrates is a man; therefore Socrates is mortal." A researcher might then follow up this deductive exercise with an empirical test of Socrates' mortality. This is essentially the approach discussed as the "traditional perspective of science" early in this chapter.

Using inductive logic, the researcher might begin by noting that Socrates is mortal and observing a number of other mortals as well. He might then note that all the observed mortals were men, thereby arriving at the tentative conclusion that all men are mortal.

Deductive logic is very old as a system, dating at least to Aristotle. Moreover, this system was predominant in Western philosophy until the sixteenth or seventeenth century. The birth of modern science was marked by the rise of inductive logic in a variety of scientific contexts. Increasingly, the general conclusions derived from careful observations contradicted the general postulates that represented the anchoring points of many deductive systems.

In astronomy, for example, Ptolemy accounted for observed variations from this model by developing an *epicyclical* model in which stars and planets rotated—in circles—around points in space which, in turn, rotated around the stationary earth in circles. As further variations were noted, the system was made more and more complicated in order to retain the key beliefs of circular motion and a stationary earth.

Copernicus attacked the Ptolemaic system by suggesting that the sun, rather than the earth, was the center of the universe. This radically new perspective was derived on the basis of observed celestial motion rather than from an initial commitment to the earth as the center of the universe. Copernicus, however, did not challenge the assumption of circular motion. "The

[2]W. I. B. Beveridge, *The Art of Scientific Investigation* (New York: Vintage Books, 1950), p. 113.

later astronomer, Kepler, said that Copernicus failed to see the riches that were within his grasp, and was *content to interpret Ptolemy rather than nature.*"[3] Kepler, on the other hand, was determined to interpret nature—in the form of the voluminous empirical data that he inherited from the Danish astronomer, Tycho Brahe. As Butterfield goes on to tell us:

> *We know how with colossal expenditure of energy he tried one hypothesis after another, and threw them away, until he reached a point where he had a vague knowledge of the shape required, decided that for purposes of calculation an ellipse might give him at any rate approximate results, and then found that an ellipse was right.*[4]

This example should illustrate the rise of inductive logic in science. Similar dramas occurred in other fields of inquiry during the fertile sixteenth and seventeenth centuries. A century or so later, the inductive, scientific research of Charles Darwin clashed with yet another tradition.

It should not be concluded from the foregoing historical account that deductive logic is inherently incorrect or that it is now outmoded. An exercise in deductive logic is as good as its internal consistency and the truth of its beginning assumptions. And inductive logic, on the other hand, is only as good as its internal consistency and the accuracy of its observations.

In practice, scientific research involves both inductive and deductive reasoning as the scientist shifts endlessly back and forth between theory and empirical observations.

Science Is Deterministic

Science is based on the assumption that all events have antecedent causes that are subject to identification and logical understanding. For the scientist, nothing "just happens"—it happens for a reason. If a man catches a cold, if it rains today, if a ball seems to roll uphill, the scientist assumes that each of these events is susceptible to rational explanation.

As we shall see in the following chapter, this characteristic of science presents a special strain for the social sciences in competition with common sense about social behavior. While the layman may say that he performed a certain act, voting for a political candidate, simply because he decided to do so, the social scientist would probably argue that the vote was determined by a variety of prior events and conditions. The decision to vote might be

---

[3]Herbert Butterfield, *The Origins of Modern Science* (New York: The Macmillan Company, 1960), p. 24, emphasis added.

[4]Ibid, p. 64.

attributed to the man's social class, region of the country, and so forth, even though the man himself might deny the influence of such factors.

Several caveats should be entered in this regard, however. First, scientists do not know, nor do they pretend to know, the specific causes of all events. They simply assume that such causes exist and can be discovered. Second, science accepts multiple causation. A given event may have several causes, the voting decision may have resulted from a number of different factors. And one event may have one cause, while a similar event may have a different cause. Two men may vote for the same candidate for different reasons, but it is assumed that reasons exist in each case.

Finally, much science is based on a *stochastic* or *probabalistic* form of determinism.[5] Thus, Event A may result in Event B 90 percent of the time, or 70 percent of all Republicans may vote for a given political candidate, while only 23 percent of the Democrats do so. In this sense, then, political party affiliation would be said to determine voting behavior, even though the determination was not complete. (Other factors might be introduced to explain the discrepancies.)

Science Is General

Science aims at general understanding rather than at the explanation of individual events. The scientist is typically less interested in understanding why a given ball falls to earth when released from a height than in understanding why all such balls tend to do so. Similarly, the scientist is less interested in explaining why a given man voted as he did than in understanding why large groups of people voted as they did.

This characteristic of science is related to its probabilistic determinism. It is conceivable that we could completely explain the reasons lying behind a given event—why a given man voted for Candidate X. The scientist might conceivably discover every single factor that went into the voting decision. If he were successful in this, then presumably he could predict the voting behavior of identical persons with perfect accuracy. In the long run, however, such a capability would not provide much useful information about voting behavior in general. First, it is doubtful that the scientist would ever find another person with exactly the same characteristics. More important, his discoveries might help him very little in understanding the voting behavior of people with other characteristics. The scientist, then, would be happier with less than 100 percent understanding if he were able to understand voting behavior in general.

---

[5]The reader should be warned that this issue is far more complicated than suggested here, and there remains a good deal of disagreement in the scientific community on it. Some scientists argue that there is a probabilistic element in all real-world phenomena. Others argue that the universe is totally determinate but that our sciences are not yet sufficient to understand that determinate system. Still others use the terms "deterministic" and "probabilistic" as antithetical.

This is the sense in which the scientist and the historian differ in their approaches to the same subject matter. The historian aims at understanding everything about a specific event, while the scientist would be more interested in generally understanding a class of similar, though not identical, events. By the same token, the psychologist and the therapist would differ in their approaches to human behavior. The psychologist would examine schizophrenic behavior among several individuals in an effort to arrive at a general understanding of schizophrenia, while the therapist would take advantage of existing general knowledge in an effort to help a specific individual.

Generalizability, thus, is an important characteristic of scientific discoveries. The discovery that red balls fall to earth at a given acceleration is less useful than the discovery that balls of all colors do so. Similarly, it is less useful to know that balls fall with a given acceleration at sea level, than to know that the acceleration of all falling balls can be determined from their altitude.

Science Is Parsimonious

As the previous sections indicate, the scientist spends much of his effort in the attempt to discover the factors that determine types of events. At the same time, he attempts to discover those factors that do not determine the events. Thus, in determining the acceleration of a falling object, we discount its color as being irrelevant.

More generally, the scientist attempts to understand the reasons for the events, using as few explanatory factors as possible. In practice, of course, the number of explanatory factors taken into account typically increases the degree of determination achieved. One political scientist may achieve a certain degree of explanation of voting behavior through the use of only two factors, say party affiliation and social class. Another might achieve a more complete understanding by also taking into account such other factors as race, region of upbringing, sex, education, and so forth. Frequently, the scientist is forced to choose between simplicity, on the one hand, and degree of explanation on the other. Ultimately, he tries to maximize both. In part, this accounts for the elegance of Einstein's famous equation: $E = mc^2$.

Science Is Specific

It was noted above that science is general in that it aims at discoveries and laws that have general applicability. Most general concepts are subject to a variety of interpretations, however. Thus, while the social scientist may wish to explain the sources of prejudice in general, he will always realize that there are many different forms of prejudice. In designing, conducting, and reporting his research, therefore, he will be precise in his methods of measuring such a concept.

In conducting a research project on the topic of prejudice, then, the scientist must generate a *specific* operationalization of the concept prejudice: for example, agreement with several questionnaire statements that seem to indicate prejudice. In reporting his research, he will be careful to describe his operationalizations in detail so that the reader will know precisely how the concept has been measured. While a given reader may disagree with the operationalization, he will at least know what it is.

Often the generalizability of a given discovery is substantiated through the use of different operationalizations of the concepts involved. If a given set of factors results in prejudice as measured in a number of different ways, the researcher (or the scientific community) may conclude that those factors result in prejudice *in general,* even though prejudice itself is not susceptible to a single measurement that would be accepted by everyone.

Science Is Empirically Verifiable

Science at its most elegant results in the formulation of general laws or equations describing the world around us. Such formulations, however, are not useful unless they can be verified through the collection and manipulation of empirical data. A general theory of prejudice would be useless unless it suggested ways in which data might be collected and unless it predicted the results that would be obtained from the analysis of those data.

There is another way of viewing this characteristic, however. In a sense, no scientific theory can ever be *proved.* Let's consider the case of gravity. Physicists tell us that a body falls to earth because of the general attraction that exists between physical bodies and that this relationship is affected by the mass of the bodies involved. Since the Earth has a vast mass, a ball thrown out a window will move toward the Earth.

Such an explanation of gravity is empirically verifiable. A researcher can throw a ball out a window and observe that it falls to earth. This does not prove the truth of the theory of gravity, however. Rather, the researcher specifies that if the ball does *not* fall to earth, then the theory of gravity is incorrect. Since the ball is, in fact, observed to behave as expected, the theory of gravity *has not been disconfirmed.*

Thus, when we say that a scientific explanation must be subject to empirical testing, we mean, more precisely, that the researcher must be able to specify conditions under which the theory would be disproved. As he consistently fails to disprove the theory, then, he may become confident that the theory is correct. But it is important to realize that he will never have proved it.

Pursuing the above example, another theorist might note that the experimental ball was of the same color as the ground to which it fell. He might

suggest, therefore, that bodies of the same color are attracted to each other
—for whatever reason he might devise. The initial experiment, then, would
lend confirmation to both of the competing theories. The second theory,
however, suggests a method of disconfirmation. If a ball differing in color
from the earth were thrown out the window, it should not fall to earth. To
do so would disconfirm the second theory. An appropriate second experiment
would, hopefully, result in an empirical disconfirmation of the color-attrac-
tion theory.

Science Is Intersubjective

It is frequently asserted that science is "objective," but
such an assertion typically results in a good deal of confusion as to what
"objectivity" is. Moreover, it has been noted increasingly in recent years that
no scientist is completely objective in his work. All scientists are "subjective"
to some extent—influenced by their personal motivations.

In saying that science is "intersubjective," I mean that two scientists with
different subjective orientations would arrive at the same conclusion if each
conducted the same experiment. An example from political science should
clarify this.

The tendency for intellectuals in America to align themselves more with
the Democratic Party than with the Republican Party has led many people
to assume that Democrats as a group are better educated than Republicans.
It is reasonable to assume that a Democratic scientist would be happy with
this view while a Republican scientist would not. Yet, it would be possible
for the two scientists to agree on the design of a research project that would
collect data from the American electorate relating to party affiliation and
educational levels. The two scientists could then conduct independent studies
of the subject, and both would discover that Republicans as a whole have a
higher educational level than do Democrats. (This is due to the fact that the
Democratic Party also attracts a larger proportion of working-class voters
than does the Republican Party in America, while businessmen are more
attracted to the Republican Party.) Both scientists—with opposite subjective
orientations—would arrive at the same empirical conclusion.

Clearly, scientists often disagree among themselves. They may offer
grossly different explanations for a given event. Such disagreements, however, typically involve questions of conceptualization and definition. Thus,
one social scientist may report that religiosity is positively related to prejudice, while another disagrees. The disagreeing scientist will, in all likelihood,
suggest that either or both of the variables have been incorrectly measured.
He may conduct his own study, measuring the two variables differently, and
report a negative relationship between them. If the first researcher had reported the design and execution of his study in precise and specific details,

however, and the second were to replicate that study exactly, he should arrive at the same finding. This is what is meant by the *intersubjectivity* of science.

Science Is Open to Modification

It should be clear from the previous section that "science" does not provide a set of easy steps to the attainment of Truth. Two scientists, both adhering to the previously discussed characteristics of science, may arrive at quite different explanations of a given phenomenon. At a given time, moreover, there may be no way of evaluating their relative merits. If the two explanations contradict one another, presumably both cannot be correct. Either one or both will later be proven incorrect, or else it will be discovered that the two explanations are not mutually exclusive after all.

Countless "scientific" theories of the past have subsequently been disproved and replaced by better ones. Current theories will eventually be replaced. More basically, we shall probably never discover Truth in any area of inquiry.

In an important sense, science does not even seek Truth, but rather utility. Scientific theories should not be judged on their relative truth value, but on the extent to which they are useful in understanding the world around us.

In the final analysis, the characteristics of science that have been discussed above provide a set of guidelines that enhance the utility of discoveries and theories. Inquiries that seek to adhere to these characteristics will, in the long run, produce more useful discoveries than inquiries of another sort. Thus, one man may be able to predict the weather more accurately on the basis of his "trick" knee than all the scientific meteorologists in the world. But, in the long run, the scientists will contribute more to our general understanding of the nature of the weather.

Summary

This chapter began with a review of the traditional image of science, primarily as a set of steps that inevitably lead to Truth. This view was balanced against a more recent, critical view of science, which suggests that scientists are not much different from laymen.

In the bulk of the chapter, I have attempted to show that while scientific inquiry is not cut-and-dried, is not infallible, it is importantly different from other human activities. While scientists are surely subject to all the frailties of other men, science provides a set of guidelines that can enhance the utility of their research.

While this chapter has been addressed to science in general, the following one will focus specifically on *social science*. We shall see that social science is bound by the same rules as other types of scientific inquiry. At the same time, however, its special subject matter presents special problems—and special opportunities.

Additional Readings

Beveridge, W. I. B., *The Art of Scientific Investigation* (New York: Vintage Books, 1950).

Butterfield, Herbert, *The Origins of Modern Science* (New York: The Macmillan Company, 1960).

Irvine, William, *Apes, Angels, and Victorians* (New York: Meridian Books, 1959).

Kaplan, Abraham, *The Conduct of Inquiry* (San Francisco: Chandler Publishing Co., 1964).

Kuhn, Thomas S., *The Structure of Scientific Revolution* (Chicago: The University of Chicago Press, 1962).

Watson, James D., *The Double Helix* (New York: The New American Library, Inc., 1968).

Whitehead, Alfred North, *Science and the Modern World* (New York: The Macmillan Company, 1925).

Chapter Two   Science and Social Science

One of the livelier academic debates of recent years has concerned the "scientific" status of those disciplines gathered under the rubric of the *social sciences*—typically including sociology, political science, social psychology, economics, anthropology, and sometimes fields such as geography, history, communications, and other composite and specialty fields. Basically at issue is whether human behavior can be subjected to "scientific" study. Whereas the previous chapter has pointed to the confusion that surrounds the term "science" in general, it should come as no surprise that academicians have disagreed about the social sciences.

Opposition to the idea of social *sciences* has risen both within the fields and outside them. Within the fields, the movement toward social science has represented a redirection and, in some cases, a renaming of established academic traditions. Increasingly, departments of government have been replaced by departments of political science. There are today few university departments of social studies, while sociology departments abound.

In many cases, the movement toward social science has represented a greater emphasis on systematic explanation where the previous emphasis was on description. In political science, it has meant a greater emphasis on explaining political behavior rather than describing political institutions. In anthropology, it has represented a lessening of the emphasis on ethnography. The growth of such subfields as econometrics has had this effect in economics, as has historiography in history. Some geographers have moved from the enumeration of imports and exports to mathematical models of migration. Quite understandably, professionals trained and experienced in the more traditional methods of these fields have objected to the new orientations.

Outside the social science departments, similar opposition has come from the physical sciences: from physicists, biologists, chemists, and so forth. Sometimes informed by the traditional image of science discussed in the previous chapter, the physical scientists have often objected that the "scientific method" could not be applied to human social behavior.

All too often, the advocates of social science have fueled the debate through the blind emulation of the trappings and rituals of the established sciences. This has taken many forms: a fascination with laboratory equipment, often inappropriate uses of statistics and mathematics, the development of obscure terminology, and the wholesale adoption of theories and terminology from the physical sciences.

For the most part, these errors would seem to have grown out of an acceptance of the traditional image of science and a lack of understanding the logic of science in practice. Would-be social scientists have too often attempted to reach understanding through methods that do not work even for the physical scientists. The result frequently has been ridicule from physical scientists, professional colleagues, and laymen.

It is the firm assumption of this book that human social behavior can be subjected to "scientific" study as legitimately as can atoms, cells, and so forth. This assumption must be understood within the context of the earlier discussion of science in practice, however. From this perspective, there would seem to be no significant difference between the physical and social sciences.

Like physical scientists, social scientists seek to discover regularity and order. The social scientist looks for regularity in social behavior. He does this through careful observation and measurement, the discovery of relationships, and the framing of models and theories.

2.1   The Search for Social Regularities

Measuring Social Phenomena

The first building block of science is measurement, or systematic observation. There is no fundamental reason why social scientists cannot measure phenomena relevant to their inquiry. The age and sex of social actors can be measured. Place of birth and marital status can be measured in a number of different ways, varying in accuracy and economy.

Aggregate social behavior can be measured systematically as well. The political scientist can determine the election-day voting behavior of the entire electorate or of individual precincts. The amount of traffic over a given section of highway can be measured at different points in time.

Attitudes may also be measured, although this is a point of broad disagreement. For example, anti-Semitic prejudice can be measured by determining individual acceptance or rejection of beliefs and perspectives representing such prejudice. Religiosity, political liberalism and conservatism, authoritarianism, and similar variables can be measured in similar fashion.

Attitude measurement is frequently challenged as "unscientific"; and, while later sections of this chapter and of subsequent chapters in this book are addressed to this issue, a word or two of comment is in order here. It must be recognized that all such measurements (*all* measurements, in fact) are arbitrary at base. The social scientist cannot unequivocally describe one person as "religious" and another as "irreligious." Rather, he will describe people as *relatively more or less* religious. This is by no means unique to *social* science, however, as evidenced by the "hardness scale" used by physical scientists, the Richter scale for earthquakes, and so forth.

Ultimately, all scientific measurements must be judged on the basis of their utility for inquiry, rather than on the basis of absolute Truth. The social scientist can never hope to describe a person as "religious" in an absolute sense any more than the chemist can ever describe a given element as "hard." The religiosity/hardness of a given person/element has meaning only in relation to other persons/elements.

It may be charged that social scientists continually revise their measurements of variables and that two social scientists at a given time differ in their methods, but this is not unique to social science, either. The openness of all science demands continual change.

Discovering Social Regularities

There is a tendency to regard the subjects of the physical sciences as more regular than those of the social sciences. A heavy object falls to earth every time it is released, while a man may vote for one candidate in one election and against him in the next. Similarly, ice always melts when heated, while seemingly religious people do not always attend church. While these particular examples are generally true, there is a danger in going on to discount the existence of social regularities altogether. The existence of observable social norms denies this conclusion.

Some social norms are prescribed by the formal institutions of a society. For example, only persons of a certain age or older are permitted to vote in elections. In American society, men are drafted into the armed forces, but women are not. Such formal prescriptions, then, regulate, or regularize, social behavior.

Aside from formal prescriptions, other social norms can be observed. Registered Republicans are more likely to vote for Republican candidates than are registered Democrats. University professors tend to earn more money than unskilled laborers. Women tend to be more religious than men.

Reports by social scientists of such regularities are often subject to three types of criticism. First, it may be charged that the report is trivial, that everyone was aware of the regularity. Second, contradictory cases may be cited, indicating that the observation is not wholly true. And third, it may be argued that the people involved could upset the observed regularity if they wished.

The charge that many of the social scientist's discoveries are trivial or already well known has led many would-be social scientists to seek esoteric or obscure findings that would prove that social science is more than pretentious common sense. This is inappropriate from a number of standpoints. To begin, there are so many contradictions in the broad body of "common sense," that it is essential to systematically weed out the existing misconceptions. Even where a proposition is unchallenged by laymen, it is necessary to test it empirically.

Many social science methodology instructors begin their classes by revealing a set of "important discoveries" that have come from social science, derived from studies conducted by Samuel A. Stouffer during World War II.[1] These "discoveries" include findings that (1) Negro soldiers were happier in Northern training camps than in Southern ones, (2) soldiers in the Army Air Corps, where promotions were rapid, were more likely to feel that the promotion system was fair than were those in the Military Police, where promotions were very slow, and (3) more educated soldiers were more likely to resent being drafted than those with less education. Once students have begun to dismiss the "important discoveries" as obvious, the instructor then reveals that each of them was disproven by the studies and explains why the observed relationships are susceptible to logical understanding, though requiring greater sophistication.

In short, "documenting the obvious" is a valuable function of any science, physical or social. This is not a legitimate criticism of any scientific endeavor. (Darwin coined the term "fool's experiment" in ironic reference to much of his own research.)

The criticism that given generalizations from social science are subject to disconfirmation in specific cases is not a sufficient challenge to the "scientific" character of the inquiry either. Thus it is not sufficient to note that a given man is more religious than a given woman. Social regularities represent probabilistic patterns, and a general relationship between two variables need not be true in 100 percent of the observable cases.

Physical science is not exempt from this challenge. In genetics, for example, the mating of a blue-eyed person with a brown-eyed person will *probably* result in a brown-eyed offspring. The birth of a blue-eyed offspring does not challenge the observed regularity, however, since the geneticist states only that the brown-eyed offspring is more likely and, further, that brown-eyed offspring will be born in a certain percentage of the cases. The social scientist makes a similar, probabilistic prediction—that women overall will be more likely to appear religious than men. And with an adequately tested measurement device, he may be able to predict the percentage of women who will appear more religious than men.

Finally, the charge that observed social regularities could be upset through the conscious will of the actors is not a sufficient challenge to social science, even though there does not seem to be a parallel situation in the physical sciences. (Presumably an object cannot resist falling to earth "because it wants to.") There is no denying that the religious, right-wing bigot

---

[1]Samuel A. Stouffer, *et al.*, *The American Soldier* (Princeton, N. J.: Princeton University Press, 1949).

could go to the polls and vote for an agnostic, left-wing radical black if he wanted to upset the political scientist studying the election. All voters in an election could suddenly switch to the underdog so as to frustrate the pollster. By the same token, workers could go to work early or stay home from work and thereby prevent the expected rush-hour commuter traffic. But these things do not happen sufficiently often to seriously threaten the observation of social regularities.

The fact remains that social norms do exist, and the social scientist can observe those norms. When norms change over time, the social scientist can observe and explain those changes. Ultimately, social regularities persist because they tend to make sense for the actors involved in them. Whereas the social scientist may suggest that it is logical to expect a given type of person to behave in a certain manner, those people may very well agree with the logical basis for the expectation. Thus, while the religious, right-wing bigot *could* vote for the agnostic, left-wing radical black candidate, he would consider it stupid to do so.

Creation of Social Theories

Social scientists have not yet developed theories of social behavior comparable with the theories developed by physical scientists. Of course, there have been countless theories of social behavior dating back centuries, but none of these is seriously defended as adequate. This observation must be made in the context of the history of many, now inadequate, theories pertaining to the physical world, however. The ultimate demise of the Ptolemaic theory of epicycles does not deny the scientific standing of present-day astronomy. Nor even does the knowledge that contemporary theories in physics will eventually be supplanted deny the scientific status of that field.

Nevertheless, at present, the social sciences do not have formal theories comparable with those existing in other fields. In part, this is due to the fact that systematic "scientific" methods have not been applied to social behavior for as long as they have been applied to physical phenomena. And at the same time, the reluctance to admit the susceptibility of social behavior to scientific study has limited the resources made available for the development of social sciences.

In addition, however, this textbook grows out of the conviction that the scientific development of the social sciences has been seriously handicapped by a misunderstanding of the logical nature of science in general. A commitment to the traditional image of science, as opposed to an understanding of science in practice, has had this effect. In view of this, we shall turn now to a discussion of the characteristics of social science, parallel to the discussion in Chapter 1, which dealt with science in general.

2.2   The Characteristics of Social Science

Social Science Is Logical

The social sciences aim at the rational understanding of social behavior. This is not to say that all social behavior is rational, however. Some social behavior is irrational, some nonrational; but the social scientist himself should be relatively rational in understanding all forms of behavior.

The social scientist is bound by many of the same logical constraints as the physical scientist. A given event cannot cause another event that occurs earlier in time. A given object cannot have mutually exclusive characteristics, and a given event or characteristic cannot have mutually exclusive results. And both deductive and inductive logic are appropriate to social science, as discussed with regard to science in general in Chapter 1.

Social Science Is Deterministic

Like physical scientists, social scientists assume that events occur for reasons, that things do not "just happen." Every event or situation has antecedent determinants.

This characteristic of social science seems often at odds with common sense, as some earlier discussions in this chapter have indicated. The social scientist may conclude that a group of people behave in a certain fashion because of a number of prior events and conditions: for example, the voting behavior of the religious, right-wing bigot in an earlier discussion. In this sense, the conditions of religiosity, prejudice, and right-wing political orientations *determine* the man's voting behavior. This is not to deny that the man in question *could* vote for the agnostic, left-wing radical black candidate; he is simply unlikely to do so.

The deterministic posture of the social sciences represents its most significant departure from the more traditional, humanistic examinations of social behavior. Whereas the humanistically oriented observer might consider the soul-searching and agonies by which a given man will weigh the relative merits and demerits of a given action, arriving at a considered decision, the social scientists would more typically look for the general determinants of such a decision among different aggregates of persons. Where the humanist would argue that the decision reached by each individual person represented the outcome of an idiosyncratic process, the social scientist would say it could be fit into a much simpler, general pattern.

Social Science Is General

As already indicated, social science is aimed at the observations and understanding of overall patterns of events and correlations. The utility of a social theory or social correlation is enhanced by its generalizability. The larger the scope of phenomena it explains, the more useful it is.

Thus, a theory of voting behavior that applies only to whites is less useful than one that applies to voters of all races. A theory of religiosity that applies only to Christians is less useful than one that applies to people of all religions —or people with no religion at all.

While the social scientist often begins with an attempt to explain a rather more limited range of social behavior or the behavior of a limited subset of the population, his goal is normally to expand the explanatory power of his findings to other forms of behavior and other subsets of the population.

Social Science Is Parsimonious

Like the physical scientist, the social scientist attempts to gain the most explanatory power out of the smallest number of variables. In many cases, the additional consideration of new variables adds explanatory and predictive power, but it also results in a more complicated model. And, in practice, the addition of more variables often reduces the generalizability of the explanation, since certain variables may have one effect among members of one subset of the population and a different effect among those of other subsets.

It should be noted that the parsimonious character of social science, like its deterministic posture, opens it to criticism from those holding a more humanistic view. Whereas the humanist would tend to explore the depths of idiosyncratic factors resulting in a decision or action on the part of a given social actor, the social scientist consciously attempts to limit such inquiry.

The social scientist, then, might attempt to explain overall voting behavior, through the observation of, say, three or four variables. The humanist would object that each of the voters had many other, individual, reasons for voting as he did, that the limited number of variables did not adequately explain the depth of decision making for any of the subjects under study. The problem here is that the social scientist has an importantly different goal from that of the humanist. He is consciously attempting to gain the greatest amount of understanding from the smallest number of variables. Neither the scientist nor the humanist in such a case is more correct than the other; they simply have different goals. We must fully understand the scientist's goal, however, in order to recognize that this criticism is not a valid one.

Social Science Is Specific

The social scientist, like the physical scientist, must specify his methods of measurement. Perhaps this is especially important in the social sciences, since they deal with concepts more vaguely defined in common discourse. While the physicist defines "acceleration" more rigorously than the layman, the scientific definition is not greatly at variance with the common understanding of the term. Concepts such as "religiosity" and "prejudice," however have such varied meanings in common language that their rigorous definitions are not readily apparent.

While the social scientist can subject such concepts to rigorous scientific examination, he must clearly specify the nature of the measurements being made in each instance. And his definitions will be evaluated on the basis of utility—their contribution to generalized explanation and understanding— rather than on the basis of absolute Truth.

Social Science Is Empirically Verifiable

To be useful, social scientific propositions and theories must be testable in the real world. Thus it is useless to assert that religiosity is positively associated with prejudice without suggesting ways in which the two variables might be measured and the proposition tested. As in the physical sciences, the social scientist must be able to describe empirical conditions under which a given proposition would be judged incorrect, ways in which it might be disproved.

Religious beliefs, such as the existence of God, for example, are not susceptible to empirical verification. Similarly, the assertion that members of a religious or racial group are disloyal "in their hearts" even when they appear to act in a loyal manner is not subject to empirical verification. The same would be true of propositions predicting human social behavior in the event that the sun did not rise on a given morning.

Social Science Is Intersubjective

To the extent that a given social scientific examination has been described in adequately specific detail, any other social scientist— of whatever personal persuasion—should be able to replicate the examination with similar results. Contrary social scientific findings are more the result of disagreements over the most appropriate research design than over the results to be obtained from a given design.

This is as true of research into highly emotional topics such as religion, politics, and prejudice as in the study of the acceleration of falling objects. In practice, of course, researchers seldom conduct studies that they believe to be designed incorrectly. The conservative social scientist, for example, is unlikely to define conservatism in a way that is likely to make conservatives appear evil.

Social Science Is Open to Modification

No social theory is likely to survive indefinitely. Either a growing weight of disconfirming evidence will bring it down, or a newer, more parsimonious, replacement will be found. In any event, no social science finding can be expected to withstand the long-term test of time.

In practice, of course, the social scientist deals with phenomena that also come under the purview of ideology: religious, political, and philosophical. And ideologies are less open to modification than science. When the social scientist explains religiosity in terms of background variables, he challenges basic religious beliefs about moral behavior, religious reward and punishment systems, and so forth. When the political scientist concludes that the working class in America is more authoritarian than the middle class, he challenges left-wing political ideology. And the deterministic posture of the social sciences in general flies in the face of a philosophical free-will image of man that has a long history in Western civilization.

The danger is that individual social scientists may be so personally committed to particular ideological stances that their commitment will prevent them from maintaining the openness of their science. Thus, the committed left-wing political scientist may be unwilling to consider, undertake, or accept research activities which might lead to the conclusion that the working class is more authoritarian than the middle class.

As found in earlier discussions, this situation is not unique to the *social* sciences. Physical science inquiry has challenged and continues to challenge accepted ideological belief systems. And individual physical scientists have been handicapped by ideological commitments that reduced the openness of their scientific activities.

2.3   Methods of Social Scientific Research

Although the present textbook is addressed specifically to a single method of social research, it will be useful to place that method in the context of the others available to the social scientist. In part, this is done to suggest that the examination of a given social phenomenon is often best accomplished through the use of several different methods. This seems an especially important point to make at a time when survey research is so rapidly gaining popularity. While survey research has special advantages, we shall see throughout this book that it has shortcomings as well and that it is not the appropriate method for studying certain topics. The social researcher who limits himself to a single method, survey or other, severely limits his ultimate ability to understand the world around him.

At the same time, it is important to realize that all methods of social research are guided by the general characteristics of science as outlined in this and the previous chapter. It will be useful, therefore, to examine the relative strengths and weaknesses of each method in that regard.

The Controlled Experiment

In many ways, the controlled experiment represents the clearest example of scientific research. While there are many variations in experimental design, we shall limit our attention to the before/after design with a single control group.

Let's assume for the moment that a researcher is interested in methods for reducing racial prejudice. Assume further that he tentatively believes that antiblack prejudice might be reduced by a greater awareness of the important roles played by blacks in American history. To test this hypothesis, he might locate or even produce a motion picture documenting black American history. This film would represent the *stimulus* for the experiment.

Next, the researcher would select two groups of subjects. In practice, he would probably ask people to volunteer for the experiment; and, if he were a university researcher, the chances are that his subjects would be university students. The single most important consideration in the selection of subjects would be the creation of two *matched* groups, that is, two groups of subjects as similar to each other as possible. This might be accomplished through conscious matching of characteristics (sex, age, race, and so forth), or the researcher might assign subjects to the two groups on a random selection basis.

One of the groups would be designated the *experimental group* while the other would be designated the *control group.* Both groups would be given some test to measure their initial levels of antiblack prejudice. For example, they might be asked to complete a questionnaire calling for agreement/disagreement with a number of statements reflecting antiblack prejudice. Hopefully, both groups would achieve about the same overall score on this test.

Then, the experimental group would be shown the film documenting black American history. The control group would not be shown the film. Subsequent to the showing of the film, both the experimental and control groups would be retested for antiblack prejudice. The researcher's hypothesis would be confirmed if the experimental group were found to be significantly less prejudiced than the control group upon retesting.

The role of the control group in such an experiment is critical. It serves the function of isolating the experimental stimulus as the single source of change among the experimental subjects. If the initial test and the retest were separated by a long time span, it is possible that the experimental subjects might become less prejudiced due to factors lying outside the scope of the experiment. The film might be irrelevant to the observed reduction in prejudice. If this occurs, then the control group should also decline in prejudice between the initial test and the retest. The hypothesis would be confirmed only if the experimental group declined in prejudice *more* than the control group. Similarly, the control group helps the researcher to guard against the effect of the experiment per se. It is possible that the act of testing and retesting would make the subjects more sensitive to the purposes of the study. While they might appear relatively prejudiced in the initial test, it might have the effect of alerting them to the fact that the researcher wanted to discover how prejudiced they were. Since few people wish to be identified as prejudiced, they might be more wary in responding to the retest questionnaire—attempting to answer in such a way as to avoid appearing prejudiced. Again, however, this factor should operate equally for the control and experimental groups, and their differential decline in observed prejudice would be the test of the hypothesis.

The isolation of experimental variables is the key advantage of the controlled experiment. It has several disadvantages as well, however. First, the controlled experiment typically provides no useful descriptive data. If 20 percent of both the control and experimental groups agree with a certain prejudiced statement, this tells us nothing about the percentage of the larger population who would agree with it, since the subjects are not typically selected through random sampling methods from that population. And to the extent that they are drawn from a special subpopulation—such as students —their descriptive value is reduced further.

Second, the controlled experiment represents an artificial test of the hypothesis. The relevance of the experiment to the real world is always subject to question. Following the above example, let's assume that the documentary film appears to reduce antiblack prejudice significantly when administered as part of a scientific experiment in a special laboratory, with the subjects aware that they are participating in an experiment. This would not necessarily mean that the film would have a similar effect if administered to a mass audience over television or in local theaters.

Finally, the findings may not have generalizable applicability to other segments of the population. Conceivably, the film would reduce prejudice among college students—if subjects were drawn from among students—but have no impact on nonstudents. A nonexperimental example will illustrate this possibility. For years, it was believed that while the working class was more prejudiced against blacks than the middle class or the upper class, anti-Semitism was believed to increase with increasing social class. The basis for this conclusion was largely a series of prejudice studies conducted among college students. Students from higher-class families were consistently found somewhat more anti-Semitic than those from relatively lower-class families. This finding, however, was due to the fact that the students studied all came from a relatively narrow range of higher-class families. Thus, upper-class students were slightly more anti-Semitic than were the upper-middle-class students. Subsequent studies among the general population, however, indicated that the working-class respondents were more anti-Semitic, just as they were more antiblack.

The shortcomings of the controlled experiment can be reduced through research sophistication, varying the experimental design, and replication among greatly differing groups of subjects. Moreover, it can be especially valuable when combined with other research methods directed at a single research topic.

Content Analysis

Some research topics may be susceptible to the systematic examination of documents: novels, poems, government publications, songs, and so forth. For purposes of illustration, let's suppose that the researcher is interested in examining changing official Soviet attitudes toward the United Nations. He might limit the time span of the study to the years 1950 to 1970, and he might decide to accept editorials in *Pravda* as his indication of official policy.

He would then obtain copies of all *Pravda* editorials during the period under question, or he might establish a sampling design that would select, say, every tenth editorial. Each such editorial would then be examined and scored in terms of whether it was favorable to the UN or critical of it—or that it had no relevance to the UN. This activity would require a systematic scoring method. He would be forced to specify what types of references to the UN would be regarded and scored as favorable and what types of references would be regarded and scored as critical. Conceivably, he might want to weight references differentially in terms of the relative strength of support or criticism. In such a case, he would need to specify the manner in which differential weights were assigned.

Having scored the editorials, he might then aggregate those scores in such a way as to characterize different periods of time. Perhaps he would combine the scores assigned by calendar year. He might then report that 20 percent of the 1950 editorials were generally favorable to the UN, that 22 percent of those in 1951 were favorable, and so forth. The pattern of differences over time would represent the official Soviet attitude toward the United Nations.

While these data would serve a useful descriptive purpose, the researcher might wish to go beyond description to explain the observed fluctuations in official Soviet attitude toward the UN. Let's suppose that he believed Soviet attitudes were largely determined by the amount of criticism the Soviet Union received from other members of the UN: when other members criticized Russia on the floor of the UN, Russia, in turn, became more critical of the UN itself.

The researcher might examine this possible explanation through an additional content analysis: of speeches and debates in the UN. He would decide what forms of communication within the UN best reflected the hypothesized stimulus and would examine and score either all or a sample of them in terms of anti-Soviet criticism. Scoring methods would again have to be specified, and the scores assigned would be aggregated for the same periods of time used in the initial study. He would then compare the two patterns of fluctuations to determine whether anti-Soviet criticism was typically followed by anti-UN pronouncements in *Pravda*.

Content analysis has the advantage of providing a systematic examination of materials that are more typically evaluated on an impressionistic basis. A news reporter, for example may read through *Pravda* editorials over time —making a mental note of those mentioning the UN and perhaps noting those editorials expressing either strong support or strong criticism—and develop a general impression of the fluctuations in official posture. Through systematic content analysis, however, the researcher guards against the inadvertent biases he may build into the examination. He may begin with a suspicion that the Soviet was relatively pro-UN during a certain period, and he could unconsciously pay more attention to favorable editorial contents during that period, while generally discounting the negative ones discovered. By adhering strictly to a preestablished sampling and scoring system, he would lessen the influence of his own preconceptions.

Content analysis, like all research methods, has its weak points. First, the type of documents selected for examination may not provide the most appropriate reflection of the variable under study. In the above example, it is possible that editorials in *Pravda* do not provide the best indication of official Soviet attitude toward the UN. Possibly the public speeches of selected government officials would be more appropriate. Or, Soviet pronouncements on the floor of the UN itself might be more appropriate. And in most such cases, the researcher is not in a position to determine which source represents the best focus of the study. This difficulty could be alleviated somewhat, of course, by examining different sources systematically, and determining whether each source provides the same conclusion.

Second, scoring methods almost always have an arbitrary element. Some editorial comments on the UN might be sufficiently ambiguous as to make scoring difficult if not impossible. Other comments might be regarded as favorable by one observer and critical by another. The researcher can possibly reduce this problem by seeking independent evaluations from other researchers experienced in the particular subject matter. To the extent that several independent observers would agree on the scoring of given editorial comments, the utility of that scoring system would seem greater. Ultimately, there is no way to insure that editorial comments are being correctly scored in any absolute sense. In lieu of this, however, the researcher must be as specific as possible in creating, executing, and reporting the scoring system. At the very least, those reading his research report must know precisely *what* the scores represent, even though they might disagree with the appropriateness of the scoring system used.

Analysis of Existing Data

There is a danger in equating scientific research with the collection and analysis of *original* data. In fact, some research topics can be examined through an analysis of data already collected and compiled. The classic example of this may be found in Emile Durkheim's study of suicide.[2] Interested in discovering the primary reasons for suicide, Durkheim conducted his comprehensive inquiry without collecting a single original datum. Rather, he tested a wide range of hypotheses through the examination of published suicide rates for different geographical areas. For example, he examined differential rates of suicide among Protestants and Catholics by comparing the rates in predominantly Protestant areas with those for predominantly Catholic areas. He examined the effects of climate by comparing rates in warm areas with those found in cooler areas.

The analysis of existing aggregated data has the great advantage of economy. The researcher does not need to pay costs of sampling, interviewing, coding, experimental subjects, and so forth. This form of social research faces two important disadvantages, however.

First, the researcher is limited to data that have been collected and compiled, and those data may not adequately represent the variables of interest. A healthy dose of ingenuity frequently can help to resolve this problem, however. When Samuel Stouffer wished to examine the effects of the Depression on the family in America and elsewhere, he considered a variety of possible indicators of an hypothesized breakdown of traditional family norms.[3] Divorce rates provided one indication, but Stouffer went well beyond that to consider rates of interreligious marriages, civil as opposed to religious ceremonies, marriages performed outside the home states of the couples, and so forth. Durkheim exhibited a similar ingenuity in the examination of suicide.

The second problem involves what is called the *ecological fallacy*. Whenever the researcher correlates variables generated from aggregated data, it is difficult to determine a direct relationship between the variables ultimately under examination. For example, while Durkheim found suicide rates consistently higher in predominantly Protestant areas than in predominantly Catholic areas, he had no way of determining whether the Protestants were committing suicide. Conceivably, Catholics living in predominantly Protestant areas had the highest suicide rates of all. Or, while Stouffer found more "impulsive" marriages during the Depression years, he had no way of determining that those involved were the most affected by the Depression. Again, an ingenious and logical examination of the data can help to reduce this danger, and the reader is encouraged to seek guidance in the two volumes cited above.

---

[2]Emile Durkheim, *Suicide: A Study in Sociology*, translated by George Simpsen (New York: The Free Press, 1951).

[3]Samuel A. Stouffer, *Social Research to Test Ideas* (New York: The Free Press, 1962), pp. 134–153.

Case Study

The case study represents a comprehensive description and explanation of the many components of a given social situation. A community study such as W. Lloyd Warner's examination of "Jonesville" would be an example of the case study approach.[4] In this instance the researcher seeks to collect and examine as many data as possible regarding the subject of his study. In the case of a community study, he will learn about the history of the community, its religious, political, economic, geographical, and racial makeup, and so forth. He will seek to determine the social-class structure of the community—who are its most prominent and powerful citizens, and who are at the bottom of the pile.

In short, he will seek the most comprehensive possible description of the community and will attempt to determine the logical interrelations of its various components. What was the impact of the lumber mill closing in the early 1930s? How did the 1940 reform mayor change the power relations in the community?

It is important to realize that this approach to social research differs radically from the others considered so far in terms of scientific objectives. Whereas most research aims directly at generalized understanding, the case study is directed initially at the comprehensive understanding of a single, idiosyncratic case. Whereas most research attempts to limit the number of variables considered, the case study seeks to maximize them. Ultimately, the researcher executing a case study typically seeks insights that will have a more generalized applicability beyond the single case under study, but the case study itself cannot assure this.

For example, a given case study may indicate that the influx of unskilled foreign laborers into the community had the effect of generally moving the indigenous laborers upward occupationally, with many of them assuming supervisory jobs over the new migrants. This discovery might lead the researcher to assume that he has uncovered a general principle of occupational mobility, that a similar change would occur in most communities experiencing an influx of unskilled foreign laborers. The single case study could in no way confirm this hypothesis, however, and further studies in other communities would be required for that purpose.

Participant Observation

The term "participant observation" refers to a method of data collection. The researcher seeks to become a member of the social event or group under study. He may join in a peace march as a method of obtaining

---

[4]W. Lloyd Warner, *Democracy in Jonesville* (New York: Harper & Row, Publishers, 1949).

data about its other participants. Or he may join a religious group he wishes to study.

In practice, the participant observer may or may not reveal his research role, and this decision has important methodological and ethical implications. If he openly admits to other participants that he is conducting a scientific study of the group, his presence may very well affect the phenomenon he wishes to study. Awareness that their actions may be reported in print may affect the actions of participants. On the other hand, if the participant observer conceals his research activities and pretends to be a typical member of the group, he will be subject to ethical questions regarding the deception. Since research situations and purposes vary so greatly in this instance, it is not possible to provide a general guideline, but the reader should be aware of the issues involved.

Like the researcher conducting a case study (as the participant observer may be doing), he will attempt to collect the maximum amount of information. By immersing himself in the actual social events in progress, he will be in a position to obtain a far greater depth of knowledge than is possible for, say, the content analyst or the experimenter. At the same time, however, the participant observer will find great difficulty in maintaining systematic research procedures. It will be humanly impossible to observe and record everything that happens; thus, the participant observer must select his data. The *attempt* to observe and record everything may result in unconscious biases forming the basis for selection. Thus, for example, he may begin forming the conclusion that black students are becoming more active in the direction of peace-march activities, and may unconsciously become more attuned to noting instances that will support that conclusion. Ultimately, the primary danger will be that he cannot tell the reader his criteria for selecting and reporting observations, so that the reader will not be able to evaluate the appropriateness of the criteria used.

We shall return to a brief consideration of these research methods in the conclusion of Chapter 3, which examines survey research per se. After describing the nature, strengths, and weaknesses of survey methods, we shall compare survey research in those regards with the other methods described above. The conclusion to be reached in that later discussion can be revealed here, however. The best social research format is usually one that involves the use of different methods focused on the same topic.

Summary

In this chapter we have considered the possibility of applying the methods of scientific inquiry to social behavior. While we have noted some special considerations involved in such an application, we have found no fundamental obstacle to social science. The characteristics of science in general can be brought to bear on the study of society, though this cannot be accomplished through an emulation of the traditional image of science.

We have also seen that social researchers may draw upon a variety of research methods to assist them in observing and understanding social behavior. The following chapter is addressed specifically to survey research as another method of social research. We shall soon see that the basic characteristics of science in general apply equally to survey research in particular.

Additional Readings

Campbell, Donald T., and Julian C. Stanley, *Experimental and Quasi-Experimental Designs for Research* (Chicago: Rand-McNally & Co., 1968).

Durkheim, Emile, *The Rules of Sociological Method,* translated by Sarah Solovay and John Mueller; edited by George Catlin (New York: The Free Press, 1962).

Lerner, Daniel, (ed.), *The Human Meaning of the Social Sciences* (New York: Meridian Books, 1959).

Franklin, Billy J., and Harold W. Osborne (eds.), *Research Methods: Issues and Insights* (Belmont, Calif.: Wadsworth Publishing Co., Inc., 1971). pp. 1–117.

Wallace, Walter, *The Logic of Science in Sociology* (Chicago: Aldine-Atherton, Inc., 1971).

Chapter Three

Survey Research as a Method of Social Science

This textbook is addressed primarily to the logic and skills of a particular research method: survey research. Before continuing, it would be appropriate to describe briefly the components of a typical survey, although we shall see later that survey methods can be applied in a much wider variety of topics and designs.

Assume that the researcher is interested in studying certain attitudes among students at a state university. A sample of several hundred or more students is selected from the total student body. A questionnaire is constructed to elicit information (for example, attitudes) relevant to the researcher's subject of inquiry. The questionnaires are then administered to the sample of students, either in face-to-face personal interviews or in a self-administered format, perhaps conducted through the mail. The responses given by each student in the sample are then coded into standardized form that can be recorded in a quantitative manner. Each student's coded responses are then transferred to IBM-type data cards and then perhaps to magnetic tapes. The standardized records for all students are then subjected to an aggregated analysis to provide descriptions of the students in the sample and to determine correlations among different responses. The descriptive and explanatory conclusions reached by this analysis are then generalized to the population from which the sample was selected, in this case to the entire student body.

3.1 A Brief History of Survey Research

Survey research is sufficiently similar to other methods of research as to give it a rather lengthy history. In particular, surveys are very much like censuses, differing primarily in that a survey typically examines a *sample* from a population while *census* generally implies an enumeration of the entire population. Censuses, of course date back at least to the ancient Egyptian civilization, when it was deemed useful to the rulers to obtain empirical data describing their subjects.

The political functions of survey research have continued to the present day, of course, with the continuation of censuses, the appearance of political polls conducted on behalf of candidates, and the uses made by political sociologists. One of the first political uses of the attitudinal survey appeared in 1880. A German political sociologist mailed questionnaires to some 25,000 French workers to determine the extent of exploitation by employers. The rather lengthy questionnaire included such items as:

. . . does your employer or his representative resort to trickery in order to defraud you of a part of your earnings?
If you are paid piece rates, is the quality of the article made a pretext for fraudulent deductions from your wages?[1]

The survey researcher in this case was Karl Marx. While 25,000 questionnaires were mailed out, there is no record of any being returned.

The sociologist Max Weber is also reported to have employed survey research methods in his research on the Protestant Ethic. In addition to his comparative historical examination of economic development, he also studied Protestant and Catholic factory workers to provide confirming data at the individual level.[2]

For the most part, however, contemporary survey research is a product of American researchers in this century. The present state of the method has resulted from important developmental work in three separate sectors of the society.

First, the continuing work of the United States Bureau of the Census has been important in the fields of sampling and data collection. While the Census Bureau is best known for its decennial enumeration of the entire population, the great majority of this agency's activities are devoted to a continuing series of sample surveys, providing up-to-date demographic and economic data between enumerations. The Census Bureau has played a singularly important role in the development of standardized definitions for sampling and methods for implementing those definitions in the field. And at the same time, the data generated by the Bureau have constituted an invaluable resource for the development of sampling designs in specific surveys. (Chapter 6 will illustrate this point in detail.)

The second source of development is to be found in the activities of commercial polling firms such as those organized by George Gallup, Elmo Roper, and, more recently, Louis Harris. These firms have generated a continuing source of funds to support the development and use of survey methods,

---

[1]T. B. Bottomore and Maximilien Rubel (eds.), *Karl Marx: Selected Writings in Sociology and Social Philosophy* (New York: McGraw-Hill Book Company, 1956). See page 208 for questions cited.

[2]Paul F. Lazarsfeld and Anthony R. Oberschall, "Max Weber and Empirical Research," *American Sociological Review* (April 1965), pp. 185–199.

particularly in the areas of product marketing and political polling. Thus, during periods when funds were not available to support academic survey research, the commercial polling firms were able to continue experimentation with sampling methods, question wording, data-collection techniques, and other aspects of survey research. More recently, the commercial polls have proven an invaluable source of data for secondary analysis, and numerous academic books and articles have been published reporting more detailed analysis of data collected initially for descriptive, commercial purposes.

The scientific refinement of survey research, especially sophisticated methods of analysis, has been largely the product of a few American universities. More specifically, it represents the efforts of two men and, later, a scattered group of survey research centers. Samuel A. Stouffer and Paul F. Lazarsfeld must be regarded as the pioneers of survey research as we know it today.

Stouffer's pioneering work largely represented attempts to apply empirical methods of social research to social problems, beginning with analyses of the effects of the Depression in America, and in the collection of data regarding the status of black Americans during the 1930s.[3] With the advent of World War II, Stouffer directed the Information and Education Branch of the Army of the United States, bringing together a group of rising social scientists to examine issues relevant to the successful prosecution of the war.[4] Then, during the McCarthy era of the early 1950s, Stouffer conducted national surveys to examine the effects of the anticommunist crusade.[5]

Across all these studies and countless others, Stouffer attempted to develop scientific methods of empirical research appropriate to the examination of social phenomena. All these efforts flowed from a sound scientific training under the British statisticians Karl Pearson and R. A. Fisher and a native ingenuity. Stouffer's legacy remains in currently used study designs, sampling methods, questionnaire designs, the logic of analysis, and so forth.

Paul Lazarsfeld came to America from a European intellectual background. Like Stouffer, he was interested in the study of relevant social phenomena such as leadership, communications, economic behavior, and the professions. In the examination of such topics, however, Lazarsfeld, like Stouffer, continued the development of rigorous techniques for applying empirical methods to social issues. In the area of political behavior, Lazarsfeld felt it important to examine voting as a *process* rather than a single event. To do this, he designed and executed panel studies involving the reinterviewing of a given set of respondents at different times during the course of a political

---

[3]An excellent overview of Stouffer's work may be found in the posthumously published book by Samuel A. Stouffer, *Social Research to Test Ideas*, (New York: The Free Press, 1962).

[4]See Samuel A. Stouffer, *et al.*, *The American Soldier: Studies in Social Psychology in World War II*, vol. I–IV (Princeton, N.J.: Princeton University Press, 1949 and 1950).

[5]Samuel A. Stouffer, *Communism, Conformity, and Civil Liberties* (Garden City, N. Y.: Doubleday & Company, Inc., 1955).

campaign, thereby following changes in voting intentions over time. Not content with description, however, Lazarsfeld combined this effort with a careful examination of the demographic and social factors associated with observed changes.[6]

While Lazarsfeld's contributions to the development of survey research have been too many to enumerate here, and the list continues to grow as of this writing, three seem especially important. First, Lazarsfeld's career has overlapped with the technical development of mechanized data-processing equipment, first cardpunches and sorters, then computers. He must be given primary credit for seeing the potential of such equipment for analytical social research and for starting social scientists on the road to realizing that potential.

Second, Lazarsfeld used the potential of mechanized data-processing equipment in elucidating and formalizing the *logic* of survey analysis. Whereas Stouffer's ingenuity permitted him to suggest reasons for observed relationships in his own research, it was Lazarsfeld who formalized those reasons into a logical model of such relationships and showed how the model could be implemented in practice.[7] (This topic will be discussed in more detail in the consideration of the "elaboration model" in Chapter 15.)

Lazarsfeld's third major contribution to survey research has been in development of the permanent research center supporting survey methods, beginning with the organization of the Bureau for Applied Social Research at Columbia University. Like Stouffer's Army research group, the Bureau brought together and trained a legion of bright young social scientists, but the Bureau was able to survive peacetime. Similar institutions subsequently organized include the National Opinion Research Center at the University of Chicago, the Survey Research Center (later expanded to the Institute for Social Research) at the University of Michigan, and the Survey Research Center at the University of California in Berkeley.

While the four institutes mentioned above have been the most important in the development of survey research methods, similar institutes now exist on university campuses across the country and around the world. Such institutes serve a number of functions. First, while academic departments often provide classroom instruction in survey methods, it is typically in the survey institutes that students receive practical, apprenticeship training, often working as research assistants. Second, countless surveys are conducted by such institutes, funded by government and foundation grants or on behalf of commercial clients. Similarly, they provide consultation and services to other researchers using survey methods. Finally, such institutes play an important role in methodological development in survey research. Thus, while an individual researcher conducting a particular research project might be reluctant

---

[6]Paul F. Lazarsfeld, *The People's Choice* (New York: Columbia University Press, 1948).

[7]See Patricia Kendall and Paul F. Lazarsfeld, "Problems of Survey Analysis," in Robert Morton and Paul Lazarsfeld (eds.), *Continuities in Social Research: Studies in the Scope and Method of "The American Soldier"* (New York: The Free Press, 1950).

to experiment with alternative data-collection techniques, an organized research unit is able to do so over the course of several studies.

Before concluding this short history of survey research, some mention should be made of the role played by professional associations. Over the years, professional associations whose members frequently employ survey methods have provided forums for discussing new techniques and empirical findings through their association meetings and professional journals. Perhaps the two primary associations in this regard are the American Sociological Association and, more recently, the American Political Science Association.

At the same time, the American Association for Public Opinion Research (AAPOR) has served as the primary association relevant to survey researchers, bringing together academic, commercial, and government practitioners. And the *Public Opinion Quarterly*, published by AAPOR, is the key journal for survey research.

Subsequent chapters of this book will trace the history of certain components of survey research. Against the backdrop of this brief overview, however, it would be appropriate to move to an examination of the place of survey research within the general context of science.

3.2 The Scientific Characteristics of Survey Research

As noted earlier, survey research is but one of many research tools available to social researchers. It bears repeating that survey methods are not appropriate to many research topics nor do they necessarily provide the best approach to topics to which they might be reasonably applied. Nevertheless, survey research can be used profitably in the examination of many social topics and can be especially effective when combined with other methods.

More important, perhaps, I firmly believe that survey research provides the best teaching example for instruction in social science methodology. The student who fully understands the logic and skills of survey research will be excellently equipped to learn and to use other social research methods. My basis for this belief is that survey research is like a crustacean: all the bones are on the outside. In subsequent chapters we shall carefully examine all the approximations, compromises, and other shortcomings of survey research. As will be discussed shortly, survey research serves a pedagogical function in that those shortcomings are made clearer than in other social research methods, thereby permitting more considered evaluations of their implications.

Survey Research Is Logical

Survey research is guided by all the logical constraints discussed in the two preceding chapters. In practice, moreover, survey data facilitate the careful implementation of logical understanding. While this topic will be explored in much greater detail in Chapter 15, an example would be appropriate at this point.

In a study of church involvement among Episcopalians, Glock and his colleagues[8] discovered that lower-class churchwomen were more actively involved in the church than were those of higher social status—involvement decreased steadily with increasing social class. In the context of a deprivation theory of church involvement—people who were denied prestige and status in the secular society would be more likely to involve themselves in church life as an alternative source of gratification—the researchers suggested that this observation merely reflected the greater deprivation of lower-class women. By extention, it was suggested that among those women who enjoyed a degree of secular status gratification, social class would not affect church involvement. The data at hand indicated whether or not the respondents had ever held office in a secular organization. The logical argument set forth, then, suggested that among those women who had held secular office, class would not affect church involvement. This expectation was tested empirically and found correct.

The format of survey research often permits the rigorous, step-by-step development and testing of such logical explanations. Through the examination of hundreds and even thousands of survey respondents, moreover, it is possible to test complex propositions, involving several variables in simultaneous interaction.

Survey Research Is Deterministic

Whenever the survey researcher attempts to explain the reasons for and sources of observed events, characteristics, and correlations, he must assume a deterministic posture. And where the survey format permits a clear and rigorous elaboration of a logical model, this clarifies the deterministic system of cause and effect.

Moreover, the availability of numerous cases and variables permits the survey analyst to document more elaborate causal processes. He may go beyond the initial observation of a correlation between an independent and a dependent variable to examine the role played by several intervening variables. Thus, returning to the above example, we note that social class does not directly affect church involvement among Episcopal women, but rather it has this effect through the intervening variable of secular gratification. Lower-class women are less likely to be elected to offices in secular organizations, for example, with the result that lower-class women, as a group, are

---

[8]Charles Y. Glock, Benjamin B. Ringer, and Earl R. Babbie, *To Comfort and to Challenge* (Berkeley: University of California Press, 1967).

more involved in the church. But if they *do* gain secular gratification, their social class has no affect on church involvement.

Survey Research Is General

Sample surveys are almost never conducted for purposes of describing the particular sample under study. Rather, they are conducted for purposes of understanding the larger population from which the sample was initially selected. Thus, the Gallup Poll may interview 1,500 American voters for the purpose of predicting how some 70 million will vote on election day.

Similarly, the explanatory analyses in survey research are aimed at the development of generalized propositions about human behavior. The survey format promotes this general scientific aim in two special ways. First, with a large number of cases studied in a given survey, the analyst can replicate findings among several subsets of the survey sample. If he finds an overall correlation between religiosity and prejudice, he may easily determine whether this relationship occurs equally among men and women, Protestants and Catholics, whites and blacks, among different social-class groups and so forth. The replication of a finding among different subgroups strengthens the assurance that it represents a general phenomenon in society.

Second, the careful reporting of the methodology of a given survey promotes replication later by other researchers and/or among other samples and subgroups. In this fashion, the generalizability of the findings can be tested and retested.

Survey Research Is Parsimonious

Because the survey researcher has a large number of variables at his disposal, he is in an excellent position to carefully examine the relative relevance of each. Like all scientists, he would like to obtain the greatest amount of understanding from the fewest number of variables. He is not required to guess at the most relevant variables in the initial design of the study, however (or at least not as much as researchers using other methods). Since the survey format lends itself to the collection of many variables that can be quantified and processed by machine, the survey analyst can construct a variety of explanatory models and then select the one best suited to his aims.

Survey Research Is Specific

In the context of this scientific characteristic, the crustacean-like nature of survey research is most important. Ironically, this characteristic also opens survey methods to the greatest amount of criticism.

The survey conclusion that religiosity and prejudice are positively related to one another will be based on specific operational definitions of both religiosity and prejudice. Each of the variables must be constructed from specific responses to specific questionnaire items, coded and scored in a specified manner. Since all these details would be spelled out in the research report, the critical reader would be able to discover that respondents described as "very religious" were those who agreed to five specific questionnaire items. He might then object that such a criterion did not fully capture the meaning of "religiosity" as he himself—and by extension, others—understand the term. He might then conclude that the general conclusion was unfounded.

In one sense, this would be a valid response. The conceptualization and measurement of variables lies at the heart of science in practice. And if variables are not conceptualized and measured appropriately, observed correlations among such variables may not be meaningful. Thus if an independent observer disagrees with the measurements, he might logically disagree with the general conclusion.

What is too often overlooked in this situation is the ease with which the critical reader can arrive at and perhaps document his disagreement. Since the survey analyst has described precisely how his measurements have been developed and made, the reader knows precisely what they represent. The superficiality and approximations involved in all scientific research are simply more apparent in surveys.

By way of contrast, let's consider the researcher who may have studied the relationship between religiosity and prejudice by immersing himself as a participant observer in one or more religious groups. Such a researcher might report that his observations suggest a negative relationship between religiosity and prejudice. In his report, he could give a qualitative description of the manner in which he distinguished religious from irreligious persons, prejudiced from unprejudiced ones. Probably such qualitative descriptions would appear much closer to the depth of meaning these terms have in the common language usage.

Unfortunately the independent observer would have no way of knowing precisely how these descriptions were employed in practice. Nor would there be any way of judging the extent to which the researcher's bias, perhaps unconscious, in favor of the negative relationship might have affected his designations of persons as religious/irreligious and prejudiced/unprejudiced. This is not to say that the researcher's observations and designations were in fact biased or that his conclusion was incorrect. Very importantly, however, neither the researcher nor the independent observer would be able to make determinations in these regards. (It should be noted, of course, that participant observation in practice varies in rigor and specificity. The point is that the survey researcher is forced by the method itself to be explicit.)

Scientific research aims at ever more sophisticated and more useful conceptualizations and measurements; but, at every step along the way, the methods used must be made specific. Survey research, by its very nature, lends itself readily to this.

Conclusion

The other characteristics of science are equally relevant in the context of survey research. Where science must be empirically verifiable, survey research provides one method of empirical verification. And the comments made in the preceding sections illustrate the manner in which the survey format lends itself to intersubjectivity.

Finally, survey research methods facilitate the openness of science. Since survey research involves the collection and quantification of data, such data become a permanent source of information. A given body of survey data may be analyzed shortly after collection and found to confirm a particular theory of social behavior. If the theory itself undergoes modifications later, it is always possible to return to the set of data and reanalyze them from the new theoretical perspective. This would not be as easily possible in the case of less rigorous and less specific research methods.

3.3 A Comparison of Survey and Other Methods

The preceding sections have already made a number of comparisons between survey research, on the one hand, and other social scientific research methods on the other. It has been pointed out that a comprehensive inquiry would profit from the use of different methods focused on the single topic. Three additional points should be made in this respect.

First, the logic of the controlled experiment can provide a useful guide to the logic of survey analysis. Where the experimenter isolates the experimental variable through the use of matched groups, the experimental and control groups, the survey analyst seeks to accomplish this by *controlling* for variables after the fact. As an example, the experimenter may assure that both the experimental and control groups have the same sex distribution, to avoid the possible influence of that variable on the experiment. The survey analyst accomplishes this either by checking to assure that subgroups in his sample have the same sex distribution or by testing the observed relationship separately among men and women. The logical goal of isolating relevant variables by ruling out the influence of extraneous ones is the same for both methods, however.

Second, the coding of survey responses is essentially an instance of content analysis. Frequently, this survey researcher will ask open-ended questions that solicit a response in the subject's own words. Such responses, however, must always be codified into *types* of answers. Thus, it might be necessary to code a given set of responses as being either generally supportive of the enactment of a certain law, or generally opposed to such enactment. In this respect, survey researchers can learn importantly from the experiences and methods of content analysts.

Third, survey interviewing can profit from the experience of participant observers. Methods of gaining rapport, maintaining neutrality, and observing accurately are important to both activities.

3.4   Is Survey Research *Really* Scientific?

In view of the mass of criticism that has been lodged against social scientists in recent years, against survey researchers and particularly sociological practitioners of survey research, perhaps I may be permitted to conclude this chapter on a rather chauvinistic note. A few years ago, Allan Mazur published an article entitled "The Littlest Science."[9] In that article, Mazur addressed himself to the question of whether sociology could call itself scientific. As the title of his article suggested, he concluded that this was just barely justifiable. Not surprisingly, the article brought an immediate and often heated response.

Mazur, along with most of his positive and negative reviewers, would agree that there can be no ultimate answer to the question of whether a discipline such as sociology is or is not a science. As Chapter 1 of the present text indicates, any definition of science must be arbitrary; thus there can be no absolute answers. At the same time, the question is worth consideration even if it cannot be answered.

It is my view that future researchers may one day look back upon this era and conclude that the use of survey research by sociologists and other social scientists was a critical period in the development of science in general. This tentative expectation is not merely the megalomaniacal pipe dream of a survey researcher who is coincidentally a sociologist by training. The comments of two other researchers illustrate the basis for my expectation.

Daniel Suits, an economist addressing a conference of government researchers and planners in Honolulu, recently varied from customary academic terminology and spoke not of the "hard sciences" (for example, physics, chemistry) and the "soft sciences" (for example, sociology, political science), but rather distinguished between the "hard sciences" and the "easy sciences." His point was that physicists can engage in scientific research rather easily by virtue of their subject matter, while sociologists have a much more difficult row to hoe.

Martin Trow has traced some of the implications of this situation in a

---

[9]Allan Mazur, "The Littlest Science," *American Sociologist* (August 1968), pp. 195–200.

different context.[10] Addressing himself to the uses of survey methods in the field of education, Trow noted an interesting anomaly. He observed first that the educational setting is nearly ideal for survey research: the prospective subjects are articulate and familiar with questionnaires, they are easily enumerated and sampled, and questionnaires can be administered under controlled conditions in the classroom. Why, then, Trow asked, have most educational surveys been so trivial and unsophisticated? His answer was that conditions have been *too* good. Educational researchers have never been forced to cope with imperfect research conditions, and since they have never been forced to make compromises and approximations in the design and execution of surveys, they have never had to come to grips with the basic logic of scientific survey research. Having not had to vary from the obvious ideal, they have not had to fully understand why it was considered ideal.

Trow's point is, I think, of far more general significance. The very adversities that face the social sciences demand the creation of a more sophisticated logical system of understanding. Moreover, survey research, because of its specificity of operation, may provide the most useful vehicle for dealing with those adversities in a rigorous and systematic manner. Some additional examples may clarify this further.

When the chemist wishes to study the properties of hydrogen, he is unlikely to concern himself very much with sampling techniques. One hydrogen atom is like any other, and any such atom will suffice for the study. The sociologist, on the other hand, cannot study any convenient individual or group of individuals. While the chemist can generalize his findings to all hydrogen on the basis of studying only convenient atoms, the sociologist must develop a more sophisticated understanding of the logical concept of generalizability as well as operational methods for achieving it. It should be noted, of course, that other scientists than sociologists face problems of sampling—geneticists for example—and sociologists have found guidance in the work of other disciplines. Nevertheless, the problems of sampling and generalizability are at their greatest in the study of social behavior. And survey research provides an excellent vehicle for the development of useful methods and, by extension, fuller understanding.

The act of measurement provides another example. Consider the sociologist attempting to measure something like religiosity. There is no clear ideal conceptualization from which to work. Nor is there any easy measurement operation available to approximate such an ideal. If he attempts to employ survey techniques, the sociologist of religion finds the problem is even more basic than that. He may discover that one questionnaire item elicits a religious response from a respondent while another item elicits an irreligious response. Moreover, a slight variation in the wording of a given item will affect the responses obtained.

---

[10]Martin Trow, "Education and Survey Research," in Charles Y. Glock (ed.), *Survey Research in the Social Sciences* (New York: Russell Sage Foundation, 1967), pp. 315–375.

Similarly, the sociologist finds that the mere presence of the researcher can affect his subject of study. Asking a respondent to report an attitude may result in a greater crystallization of that attitude than existed prior to the inquiry. It is as though a metal bar would stretch or shrink in length whenever the physicist came by to measure its length. Clearly, the situation faced by the sociologist demands a very sophisticated understanding of what conceptualization and measurement entail.

The multiplicity of relevant variables, as well as the complex and probabalistic nature of causation in social behavior provide further demands for more sophisticated understanding of what science really is. And the list of examples could go on.

It is worth noting in this context that the "easy sciences" are not quite as straightforward as many might imagine. Physicists realize, for example, that they cannot simultaneously measure an object's location and its velocity; measuring one quantity affects the other. Medical scientists are forced to utilize sugar pills in tests of new drugs because some patients seem to improve when they believe they are receiving a powerful new drug and/or because medical researchers often tend to see more optimistic developments in those patients whom they believe are receiving the new drug. At the same time, we find nuclear physicists asserting that particles moving in a given direction and experiencing no additional forces will *probably* continue moving in that direction.

The fact that social scientists face all these problems simultaneously calls for an extremely sophisticated understanding of the logic of scientific inquiry. If social scientists can come to grips with the situation they face today, it seems likely that all science will benefit. And, as indicated repeatedly above, survey research provides an excellent method of taking on the challenge.

Additional Readings

Glock, Charles Y., *Survey Research in the Social Sciences* (New York: Russell Sage Foundation, 1967), pp. ix–xxi.

Lazarsfeld, Paul F., "Introduction" to Samuel A. Stouffer, *Social Research to Test Ideas* (New York: The Free Press, 1962), pp. xv–xxxi.

Part Two   Survey Research Design

The eight chapters comprising Part Two of this text are addressed to the several aspects of survey design and execution. We shall examine the activities that result in the possession of a body of data for analysis and will consider the decisions that the researcher must make in terms of the multitude of options available to him.

There is a tendency to regard the analysis of survey data as the most challenging and exciting part of the enterprise and to regard the design of a survey and the actual collection of data as less exciting. I would have to confess to feeling this way, and I suspect most other survey researchers would agree. It is during analysis that one begins to gain an understanding of the subject matter at hand and is in a position to share findings with colleagues.

It is a mistake, however, to assume that study design is less challenging than analysis or that it requires less brilliance and ingenuity. Quite often, in fact, ingenuity is required in survey analysis only because of its lack in the design and execution of the study. And while the researcher may find satisfaction in being able to overcome design problems through clever analytical manipulations, he should still be embarrassed that the problems even existed, and, moreover, he will often find that no amount of ingenuity can solve many of those problems.

As a researcher becomes more competent in the various aspects of survey design, he will come to the realization that design requires the same logical problem-solving abilities as survey analysis. In this respect, it will become equally exciting and challenging.

Chapter 4 describes the various study designs available to the researcher. The intent here is to familiarize the reader with the range of options and to help him determine which of those best suits a particular research aim.

Chapters 5 and 6 are addressed to survey sampling. The first of these deals with the logic of sampling, while the latter presents examples to clarify the implementation of that logic in practice.

After sampling, we shall turn to conceptualization and instrument design in Chapter 7. Here we shall deal with the process through which the survey researcher refines his concepts and develops questionnaire items to measure them. Chapter 12, in Part Three of the book, returns to this issue as it must be faced during survey analysis.

Chapters 8 and 9 focus on the techniques of data collection in mail surveys and interviews, respectively. Chapter 10 picks up from that point and deals with the different methods available for converting completed questionnaires into manipulable, quantitative data.

While Chapters 4 through 10 represent an approximate chronology of a survey project, Chapter 11 is not placed in that context. It considers an often overlooked component of professional survey research: pretesting and pilot studies. We shall discuss the various techniques by which the researcher can test the several aspects of his study design before committing his major resources in the field and how he may evaluate the results of such tests. Chronologically, this activity overlaps the others discussed in Part Two.

Chapter Four

Types of Study Designs

While the term "survey research" refers to a particular type of empirical social research, there are many different kinds of surveys. One might include under this term censuses of populations, public opinion polls, market research studies of consumer preferences, academic studies of prejudice, epidemiological studies, and so forth. Surveys may differ in their objectives, cost, time, and scope. Moreover, a variety of basic designs may be included under the term "survey."

This chapter begins with a brief discussion of the possible objectives of survey research. Then it examines the concept "unit of analysis." Finally, it presents an overview of the different strategies available to the researcher in the pursuit of his goals.

4.1   Purposes of Survey Research

There are probably as many different reasons for conducting surveys as there are surveys. A politician may commission a survey for the ultimate purpose of getting him elected to office. A marketing firm may conduct a survey for the purpose of selling more Brand X soap. A government may conduct a survey as an important basis for the design of a mass transit system or for the modification of a welfare program.

While the variety of such purposes is too great to begin enumerating here, three general objectives crosscut these many concerns: description, explanation, and exploration. While a given survey may (and usually does) aim at satisfying more than one of these objectives, it will be useful to examine them as distinct for present purposes.

Description

Surveys are frequently conducted for the purpose of making descriptive assertions about some population: discovering the distribution of certain traits or attributes. In this regard, the researcher is not concerned with why the observed distribution exists, but merely what that distribution is.

The age and sex distributions reported by the Bureau of the Census are examples of this. Similarly, the Department of Labor may seek to describe the extent of unemployment among the American labor force at a given time, or at several points over time. And the Gallup Poll may seek to describe the percentages of the American electorate who will vote for the various candidates for President, the distribution of attitudes regarding the Indochina War, the distribution of attitudes toward sex education in the schools and toward fluorides in the water. The percentage of a population likely to purchase a new commercial product would be still another example.

The sample survey provides a vehicle for discovering such distributions. The distribution of traits among a carefully selected *sample* of respondents from among the larger population can be measured, and the comparable description of the larger population is inferred from the sample. (Chapter 5 discusses the logic of such inferences.)

In addition to describing the total sample (and inferring to the total population), the researcher often describes subsamples and compares them. Thus, the Gallup Poll may begin with a report of the voting intentions of the entire electorate, and then describe Democrats and Republicans, men and women, voters of different ages, and so forth, separately. While the descriptions of different subsets may be compared, the primary purpose here is description rather than explanation of differences. (Such comparisons, however, provide an intermediary step between the logic of description and the logic of explanation, as will be discussed further in Chapter 13.)

Explanation

While most surveys are aimed, at least in part, at description, many have the additional objective of making *explanatory* assertions about the population. In studying voter preference, for example, the researcher may wish to explain *why* some voters prefer one candidate while other voters prefer another. In studying unemployment, the researcher may wish to explain why part of the labor force is employed while the remainder is not.

An explanatory objective almost always requires *multivariate* analysis: the simultaneous examination of two or more variables. Preferences for different political candidates might be explained in terms of such variables as party affiliation, education, race, sex, and region of the country. By examining the relationships between candidate preferences and the several explanatory variables, the researcher would attempt to "explain" why voters pick one or the other candidate. (The logic of explanation is dealt with at length in Part Three of this book.)

Exploration

Survey methods can also provide a "search" device when the researcher is only beginning his inquiry into a particular topic. For example, a group of researchers recently were planning an exhaustive study of the nature, sources, and consequences of student radicalism on a university campus. While they had many ideas on these subjects, they were wary that they might have overlooked some additional components of the situation. If a large study were based solely on their preconceptions, it would run the risk of missing some critical elements.

The survey research method provided one technique for resolving this difficulty. A loosely structured questionnaire was constructed, and about 50 students who differed in their political orientations were interviewed in depth. No attempt was made to select a representative sample of students, nor were data collected in a standardized form. Rather, the students interviewed were encouraged to speak freely about their political views and their attitudes toward student radicalism.

These interviews resulted in a largely revised research design for the main study. Respondents did indeed mention factors relevant to student radicalism that the researchers had not initially anticipated. Certain political orientations that had earlier seemed contradictory now made more sense. These additional factors were subsequently taken into account by the main research design.

Before leaving this topic, it is important to note some of the things that the study did not accomplish. It did not answer the basic research questions that prompted the planning of the study. It did not adequately elucidate the nature of student radicalism, nor did it satisfy the researcher's curiosity regarding the sources and the consequences of student radicalism. The manner in which the data were collected clearly precluded such results. The exploratory study, however, did raise new possibilities, which were later followed up in the more controlled survey.

These, then, are the three basic objectives on which survey research can be brought to bear. As noted at the outset, most studies have more than one such objective (sometimes all three), but they provide useful organizing principles in the design of surveys. Before turning to the specific types of study designs available for meeting those objectives, we should take a moment to introduce a basic, but often confusing, term: the "unit of analysis."

4.2   Unit of Analysis

Survey research provides techniques for studying almost anything. The *things* under study in a given survey are the *units of analysis.* Typically, the unit of analysis for a survey is a person, but there is no reason why this need be the case, and it often is not. Data are collected for purposes of describing the individual units of analysis; those descriptions are aggregated and manipulated in order to describe the population represented by the units of analysis.

In a survey of voter preferences for Candidates A and B, each voter sampled and surveyed is the unit of analysis. Each is described in terms of the candidate he favors. Then the several preferences are aggregated to describe the population of voters in terms of the percentages who favor the two candidates. In an unemployment survey, members of the labor force are the units of analysis. Each is described as being either employed or unemployed. These individual descriptions are then used to describe the whole labor force in terms of the unemployment rate.

While units of analysis are typically people, they might be families, cities, states, nations, companies, industries, clubs, governmental agencies, and so forth. In each instance, the individual units of analysis would be described, and those descriptions would be aggregated to describe the population they represent. For example, the researcher might collect data describing cities in the United States. Each city might be described in terms of its population size; all American cities might then be described in terms of the mean population. Or additional variables describing the cities might be introduced to explain why some cities are larger than others.

A given survey, of course, may involve more than one unit of analysis. A household survey of a particular city may be aimed at providing the following information: the percentage of residential structures that are in deteriorating condition, the racial distribution of heads of households, mean annual family income, the unemployment rate, and the age-sex distribution of the resident population. In these examples, the units of analysis would be, respectively, residential structures, households, families, members of the labor force, and residents.

Units of analysis for a given survey may be described on the basis of their components. Thus, cities could be described in terms of their unemployment rates or their racial compositions. Surveys might even be conducted for purposes of providing those descriptions. But if the object of the study is to describe cities and to aggregate those descriptions for the purposes of describing all cities, then the city is the basic unit of analysis for the study. At the same time, units of analysis may be described in terms of the groups to which they belong. Thus, an individual may be described in terms of the number of people in his family or whether his residential structure is deteriorating.

The applicability of survey methods to various units of analysis may sometimes confuse the beginning researcher and result in the selection of an inappropriate unit of analysis for a particular line of inquiry. In particular, the dangers of the *ecological fallacy* should again be noted.[1]

---

[1] For a more comprehensive discussion of this topic, see W. S. Robinson, "Ecological Correlations and the Behavior of Individuals," *American Sociological Review* (June 1950), pp. 351–357.

Let's suppose the researcher is interested in exploring the possible relationship between race and crime: are blacks or whites more likely to engage in criminal behavior? The appropriate unit of analysis for this inquiry would be the individual person. Samples of black and white respondents might be studied and their respective crime rates computed and compared.

Given the availability of certain municipal data, however, the researcher might be tempted to approach the problem in a different way. He could easily obtain overall crime rates for major American cities, and he could also find data reporting the racial composition of those same cities. In analyzing such data, he might discover that crime rates were higher in cities containing a higher proportion of blacks in their populations. He might conclude, therefore, that blacks have higher crime rates than whites. This line of inquiry, however, is subject to the ecological fallacy in that the researcher has no assurance that the crimes committed in predominantly black cities *were committed by blacks*. It would be conceivable that the highest crime rates occur among whites living in predominantly black areas. Such a misinterpretation would not have been possible had the researcher employed the correct unit of analysis.[2]

Whatever the nature of the data used to describe the units of analysis, it is important that they be identified in advance. Otherwise the sample design and the data collection methods may prohibit the analysis appropriate to the study. Whenever more than one unit of analysis is involved in the study, this consideration is all the more important. One final example should clarify matters.

In a household population study of a given city, the researcher may decide to collect his data through interviews with the heads of a sample of households, but he wishes to make assertions about residential structures, households, families, and persons. Data about the structures could be collected by asking relevant questions of the respondent (How old is this house?) and through observation (How many stories in the structure?). Data about the household might also be collected through interviewing (How many families live in this house?) and through observation (What is the race of the head of the household?). The respondent might be asked for data to describe the families living in the household (What are their annual incomes?) and the individual persons in that household (What is the sex and age of each person?).

In a complex study such as this, with several units of analysis, special care must be taken in the organization of the data for analysis. If the researcher

---

[2]It should be recognized that sometimes the researcher is simply not in a position to conduct an inquiry utilizing the most appropriate unit of analysis. In such cases, an ecological analysis might represent the only feasible approach to the topic at the time. Durkheim's famous study of suicide is an example of an excellent case in point; for a discussion of the ways in which Durkheim avoided the ecological fallacy, see Hanan Selvin, "Durkheim's *Suicide* and Problems of Empirical Research," *American Journal of Sociology* (May 1958), pp. 607–619. Another example would be Samuel A. Stouffer, "Effects of the Depression on the Family," in Samuel A. Stouffer, *Social Research to Test Ideas* (New York: The Free Press, 1962), pp. 134–153.

wishes to determine the percentage of residential structures that are in deteriorating condition, each structure should be described only once in the computation regardless of the numbers of families or persons living there. If he wishes to determine the percentage of the population who live in deteriorating structures, a given structure should be entered in the computation as many times as there are people living in it. If five people live in a given deteriorating structure, each person should be described as living in a deteriorating structure, and all the person descriptions would be aggregated to describe the city's population.

The safest course to be pursued in a complex survey such as this would be to create separate data files for each unit of analysis. In this example, the researcher should create a structure file, a household file, a family file, and a person file. Each file would contain all the data relevant for analysis with that unit of analysis even though the data might have been collected about some other unit of analysis initially. Thus, each person file might contain an indication of the race of the head of the household to which that person belongs. Once the unit of analysis for a given computation was determined, the researcher could easily make the computation through the use of that data file.

4.3   Basic Survey Designs

Having specified the objectives of his survey and the units of analysis, the researcher has several different designs to choose from. In this section, we shall discuss cross-sectional surveys, longitudinal surveys, and the use of cross-sectional surveys to approximate longitudinal ones. The following section will discuss variations of these basic designs.

Cross-Sectional Surveys

In a cross-sectional survey, data are collected at one point in time from a sample selected to describe some larger population *at that time.* Such a survey can be used not only for purposes of description but also for the determination of relationships between variables at the time of study.

A Gallup Poll to determine voting intentions would be a cross-sectional survey. It is worth noting that respondents in such a poll are typically asked: "If the election were held today, who would you vote for?" The results are appropriately reported: "If the election were held today, Candidate X would win in a landslide." A survey to determine the unemployment rate would also describe a population's unemployment as of the time of study.

By the same token, a cross-sectional survey of the relationship between religiosity and prejudice would report that relationship as of the time of study. The researcher might report that religious people were more prejudiced than irreligious people, but he would recognize that the relationship might change later on. A subsequent survey might find quite a different relationship. (Generally speaking, however, such relationships tend to persist longer than simple descriptions.)

Longitudinal Surveys

Some survey designs permit the analysis of data over time: either descriptive or explanatory. Data are collected at different points in time, and the researcher is able to report changes in descriptions and explanations. The primary longitudinal designs are trend studies, cohort studies, and panel studies.

Trend Studies: A given, general population may be sampled and studied at different points in time. While different persons are studied in each survey, each sample represents the same population but at different times. A good example would be the Gallup Polls conducted over the course of a political campaign. At several times during the course of the campaign, samples of voters would be selected and asked who they will vote for. By comparing the results of these several polls, we might determine shifts in voting intentions.

In the ongoing study of prejudice in America, surveys have frequently asked respondents whether they felt that black and white children should attend the same schools. Over the years, the percentages favoring integrated schools has consistently increased. These data permit the researcher to note trends in attitudes toward integration.

It should be noted that trend studies often involve a rather long period of data collection. Typically, the researcher does not himself collect all the data used in a trend study, but conducts a secondary analysis of data collected over time by several other researchers.

While the above comments have been limited to descriptive trend studies, there is no reason why a researcher might not examine trends in relationships among variables. One example might be the relationship between religious affiliation and political preference. Traditionally, Catholics and Jews in America have been more likely to vote for the Democratic Party than have Protestants, but the researcher might examine this relationship over time.

Cohort studies: Trend studies are based on descriptions of a *general* population (such as American voters) over time, although the members of that population will change. Persons alive and represented in the first study may be dead at the time of the second, and persons unborn at the time of the first study may be alive and represented in the second. Or, a trend study of attitudes among students at State University will reflect a different population of students each time a survey is conducted.

A *cohort* study focuses on the same specific population each time data are collected, although the samples studied may be different. As an example, we might select a sample of students graduating from State University in the class of 1970 to determine their attitudes toward work. Five years later, we might select and study another sample drawn from the same class. While the sample would be different each time, we would still be describing the class of 1970. (If we studied the graduating class of 1975 the second time around, we would, of course, have a trend study of graduating classes rather than a cohort study of the class of 1970.)

A different type of cohort study would be the following. At one point in time, the researcher might sample from among all Americans in their twenties. Ten years later, he could sample all persons in their thirties, and so forth. This would constitute a cohort study of a given age group. Also, this could be accomplished through a secondary analysis of previously collected data. At a given point in time, the researcher could analyze the 20-year-old respondents in a 1940 study, the 30-year-old respondents in a 1950 study, the 40-year-old respondents in a 1960 study, and so forth.

Panel Studies: Both trend and cohort studies permit the analysis of process and change over time, which is not easily possible in a cross-sectional survey. There are severe shortcomings, however. While the researcher may determine through a trend study that voters—as a group—are switching from Candidate A to Candidate B, he cannot tell *which* people are switching, thereby hampering his attempts to explain why switching is occurring.

Panel studies involve the collection of data over time from the same *sample* of respondents. The sample for such a study is called the *panel.* In a political study, the researcher might reinterview all the members of his panel at one-month intervals throughout the campaign. Each time he would ask them who they planned to vote for; then, when switching occurred, he would know which persons were switching in which direction. By analyzing other characteristics of the "switchers" and "nonswitchers," he might be able to explain the reasons for switching. (Of course, he could also ask them why they had switched their voting intentions.)

Except for certain limiting cases, panel studies would have to be conducted as part of a particular research program. While trend studies and cohort studies might be carried out through a secondary analysis of previously collected data, panel studies could not. As a result, panel studies tend to be expensive and time-consuming. Panel studies suffer from two additonal problems.

Panel *attrition* refers to the extent of nonresponse that occurs in later waves of the study interviewing. Some persons, interviewed in the first survey, may be unwilling or unable to be interviewed later on. Since the strength of panel studies hinges on the ability to examine the same respondents at different points in time, this advantage is lost among those who do not participate in the several surveys.

Second, the analysis of panel data can be rather complicated. The chief analytical device is the *turnover table,* which cross-tabulates a given characteristic at more than one point in time. For example, those preferring Candidate A in the first survey are divided into those who still prefer him and those who prefer Candidate B in the second survey. Those who prefer Candidate B the first time are similarly divided. As the number of surveys, the number of variables, and the complexity of those variables increase, the analysis and presentation of the data can become unmanageable (see Chapter 14 on the difficulties of typological analysis).

For all these several reasons, panel studies are less frequently conducted in survey research. Yet, the reader should note that this is the most sophisticated survey design for most explanatory purposes. (It most closely approximates the classic laboratory experiment.)

Approximating Longitudinal Surveys

The cross-sectional survey is clearly the most frequently used study design. Yet, many if not most of the questions that a researcher wishes to answer involve some notion of change over time. There are a number of devices that may be employed in a cross-sectional survey for approximating the study of process or change.

First, the respondents to a given survey may be able to provide data relevant to such questions. They might be asked to report their family incomes for the current year and for the previous year as well. The researcher might then use these data as though they had been collected in a panel study with two waves of interviewing set a year apart. Two dangers appear here, however. First, there is the danger that respondents may not be able to report such information accurately. The farther back they are forced to reach into their memories, the less accurate the information is likely to be. Second, the researcher should not be misled into interpreting the earlier-year data as a cross section of the population at that time, since his sample is limited to the present population.

Second, age or cohort comparisons within a cross-sectional survey may be used to approximate a study over time. Young people in a given study may be less religious than old people, and the researcher might interpret this as a decline in religiosity in the population. (He should be strongly warned, however, that people become more religious as they grow older, and this may completely account for the observed differences.) Or the researcher may find freshmen less intellectually sophisticated than seniors and conclude that college education increases sophistication. (He should be warned, however, that

the population from which new freshmen are drawn might be less sophisticated, pointing to a trend rather than a process. Or it might be the case that
less sophisticated students who entered with the senior class dropped out of
school before the survey.)

Finally, cross-sectional data may sometimes be interpreted in *logical*
terms to indicate a process over time. A student drug study, for example,
indicated that all students who reported they had ever used marijuana also
report past experience with alcohol. Moreover, all those who reported they
had ever used LSD also reported they had also used marijuana (and alcohol).
It is reasonable to conclude from these data that the progression of drug use
over time is from alcohol to marijuana to LSD. If, for example, some students
used marijuana before using alcohol, then the cross-sectional survey should
have uncovered some who had used marijuana but not alcohol; by the same
token, some should have been found who had used LSD but not the other
drugs if LSD was used prior to the others. Since no such students were found
at the given point in time, while many students were found to have used
alcohol only and others had used all but LSD, the researchers concluded on
logical grounds that the process over time was from alcohol to marijuana to
LSD. (*Note:* This conclusion does not warrant the assumption that one drug
leads to another physiologically.)

4.4   Variations on Basic Designs

The preceding discussions outlined the basic survey de-
signs available to the researcher. All surveys could be characterized in the
terms discussed. At the same time, these basic designs can be modified in a
variety of ways to meet the particular requirements of a given study. This
section will discuss briefly some of the more typical modifications.

Parallel Samples

Sometimes a research problem may be particularly rele-
vant to more than one population. For example, an educational researcher
might wish to sample student attitudes toward a proposed student conduct
code. At the same time, he might be interested in knowing how faculty
members, and perhaps administrators, felt about the code. In such an instance, he could separately sample each population and administer the same
(or slightly modified) questionnaire to each sample. The results produced
could then be compared.

As another example, he might wish to examine the religious beliefs of
Methodist church members and compare them with the beliefs held by
Methodist clergymen. Again, each population would be sampled and studied.

In some instances, the sample from one population could be used to generate the sample from the other. University students might be sampled and questionnaires could be sent to both the students and their parents. The responses given by students as a whole could be compared with the responses given by their parents as a whole.

Contextual Studies

As noted in the earlier discussion of units of analysis, persons may be described in terms of groups to which they belong. While a family can be described as being large, members of that family can be described as belonging to a large family. When data are collected about some portions of a person's environment or milieu and used to describe the individual, this is called a *contextual* study: an examination of his context.

In the last example under parallel samples, data collected from parents could be used to describe their particular children. A student in the study could then be described as having a politically liberal father, an elderly mother, and so forth. These data could then be used in the analysis of the student's own attitudes.

In studying church members, the researcher could collect data about the church each belonged to and, perhaps, about its minister. A given church member, then, could be described as belonging to a rich, large church in the center city that had a minister less than 40 years of age.

To permit such analyses, however, the data collected about the respondent's context would have to be identified with him so as to include them in his data file. It would not be possible to mail anonymous questionnaires to the sample of students and parents and accomplish this. Students would have to be identified on the questionnaire (by name or number) and parents would have to be identified in some fashion that would link them to their particular children.

Sociometric Studies

Typically, surveys study a sample of a given population, collecting data about the individuals in the sample for purposes of describing and explaining the population that they represent. The basic survey format, however, may be used for a more comprehensive examination of a given group, noting the interrelationships among the members of that group. A sociometric design would be a good example of this.

Suppose that the researcher wants to learn something about the selection of close friends among school children. He might conduct a conventional survey among a sample of students and ask them to provide a variety of information about their closest friends. In a sociometric design, he would study *all* students in a given class and ask each to identify his friends by name. In this fashion, he could determine that Jack chose Bill as his best friend, but Bill, in turn, chose Frank. Or he might determine that five members of the class chose Mary as their best friend, and nobody chose Ruth. These sorts of analyses could be extended in complexity to provide a comprehensive examination of a whole friendship network. In seeking to explain why certain students were chosen more often than others, he would have a whole body of data about the chosen students—from their self-reporting of characteristics—including whom they chose.

In this fashion, the researcher could examine the possible factors governing friendship formation, such variables as sex, race, economic status, intelligence, and so forth. By collecting data from all the members of the group, the researcher would be spared the considerable task of asking respondents to describe their selections in detail; in addition, he would have access to the friendship network. Variants on this technique could be used with any intact group, and the study could be conducted over time as well as cross-sectionally.

4.5   Choosing the Appropriate Design

Realizing the several options available to the survey researcher, the question becomes "Which design should I select?" Clearly this question cannot be answered in the abstract, since different research problems call for different designs. Nevertheless, it is possible to provide some general guidelines.

First, if the researcher's aim is single-time description, then a cross-sectional survey is probably the most appropriate. He would identify the population relevant to his interests, select a sample of respondents from that population, and conduct his survey. The same would hold for a research interest involving subset description. The researcher interested in documenting the differences in political attitudes of men and women could deal with this interest through a cross-sectional survey.

More typically, however, the researcher is interested in examining some type of dynamic process—involving change over time. When the researcher addresses himself to the sources and/or consequences of religiosity, for example, the issue of change over time is implicit if not explicit. Implicitly, it is assumed that some people become religious and that being religious has subsequent effects on other attitudes and/or behavior. Ideally, the researcher should select a sample of respondents—taken at a point in life prior to the development of a religious orientation—and study them over time, covering the period during which some of those respondents become religious and following them through the period during which religiosity has effects on other aspects of life.

Clearly, a study such as the one described above would take years to complete. The researcher would probably begin with a sample of preadolescents and follow them through middle age and into their later life. The time required by such a study—and the attendant costs—would in all likelihood preclude it. Because of this fact, such issues are more frequently dealt with in cross-sectional surveys. Rather than noting the effects of various social conditions and experiences as they occur, the researcher examines their possible effects by comparing respondents who have or have not experienced them in the past.

For example, married people are generally less religious than the unmarried. The panel study would permit the researcher to note the decline in religiosity following the marriage for given respondents. Using a cross-sectional survey, instead, the researcher would compare the levels of religiosity among married and unmarried respondents—at one point in time—noting that married respondents were less religious on the whole. While he could not observe the effects of marriage on religiosity at the time of marriage, he might be willing to infer such an effect on the basis of the single-time difference.[3] (The logic of such inferences is discussed in Part Three.)

Panel surveys are most feasible when the phenomenon under study is relatively short in duration. An election campaign might be an example of this. Whereas a given campaign should take less than a year, it might be feasible to conduct several waves of interviews with the survey panel over the course of the campaign, monitoring changes in voting intentions over the period and collecting data relevant to explaining such changes. With a duration this short, the difficulties of panel attrition should be reduced, and the researcher should be able to locate respondents over time. (For a longer period of time, many willing respondents may simply move out of town and thereby be difficult to reach.)

In summary, whenever the research problem involves an examination of individual change over time, a panel survey would be the most appropriate design in theory. If the process of change occurs during a relatively short period of time a panel survey might be feasible. More typically, however, the researcher will be forced to rely on cross-sectional data to make inferences about the process of change in individuals over time.

If, on the other hand, the research problem merely deals with broad trends over time—from a descriptive standpoint—the researcher will have less trouble in most cases. In many instances, he will find that other researchers have already collected and reported all the data he requires. If he is interested in overall changes of attitudes toward the war in Indochina, he will find that academic and commercial researchers have been collecting relevant information for years. His job, then, may consist only of locating such studies,

---

[3]Recognize, of course, that such an inference from cross-sectional data will always be subject to challenge. In this case, it might be argued that religious people are less likely to get married, that the causal direction is the opposite of that inferred.

comparing the nature of the questionnaire items involved and the sample designs, and then providing a discussion of the observed changes.

In other situations, the researcher may find that only one prior survey has collected data relevant to his research interest—or that the latest such study is rather dated. In such a case, he may wish to conduct a new cross-sectional survey—comparable in sample design and questionnaire items—to provide a new measure for purposes of examining trends.

Summary

These, then, are the basic designs and common variations available to the survey researcher. The preceding discussions by no means exhaust the design possibilities, but they should provide the reader with sufficient stimulus and guidance for constructing the study design most appropriate to his own research needs.

The best studies are often those that combine more than one design, since each provides a different perspective on the subject under study. At the same time, the researcher should guard against designing a survey so complex that he will have neither the time nor the money to execute it. As stressed in Chapter 3, all survey designs represent compromises. The good researcher reaches the best compromise possible.

Additional Readings

Campbell, Donald T., and Julian C. Stanley, *Experimental and Quasi-Experimental Designs for Research.* (Chicago: Rand McNally & Co., 1963).

Glock, Charles Y., "Survey Design and Analysis in Sociology," in Charles Y. Glock (ed.), *Survey Research in the Social Sciences* (New York: Russell Sage Foundation, 1967), pp. 1–62.

Hyman, Herbert H., *Survey Design and Analysis* (New York: The Free Press, 1955), chap. 2.

Lazarsfeld, Paul F., and Morris Rosenburg (eds.), *The Language of Social Research* (New York: The Free Press, 1955), sec. III.

Chapter Five   The Logic of Survey Sampling

5.1   Introduction

In this book, as in many others, the term "survey" has been used to mean implicitly "sample survey," as opposed to a study of all members of a given population or group. Typically, survey methods are used in the study of a segment or portion—a sample—of a population for purposes of making estimated assertions about the nature of the total population from which the sample has been selected. While the practice of using samples in this connection is more or less tacitly accepted, the reasons for sampling are not generally known. It is appropriate to consider those reasons briefly before turning to the logic and skills of sampling.

Why Sample?

Most readers can no doubt give two reasons for sampling: time and cost. The interviewing alone for a comprehensive interview survey may require one to three hours and $20 to $30 per interview. The savings in studying 2,000 people rather than, say, 500,000 are apparent. A survey project requiring a two-month interviewing period at a cost of $40,000 might very well be judged feasible, while a 10-year interviewing project costing $10 million very probably would not. Thus sampling often makes a project possible, whereas a refusal to sample would rule out the study altogether.

Sampling should not be regarded as a necessary evil, however. It is not generally recognized, perhaps, but sample surveys are often *more accurate* than would be the case for a total census—interviewing every member of a given population. There are several reasons for this seemingly bizarre fact, growing out of the logistics of survey interviewing.

First, an enormous interviewing project would require a very large staff of interviewers. Where researchers typically attempt to limit their staffs to the best available interviewers, such a project would probably require them to employ everyone in sight, with the result that the overall quality of interviewers would be lower than usually achieved. The quality of data collected would be reduced by the decreased quality of interviewers. Also, a smaller-scale study would permit more diligent follow-up procedures, thereby increasing the rates of interview completion.

Second, interviewing all members of a given, large population would require a lengthy interviewing period. As a result, it would be difficult if not impossible to specify the *time* to which the data refer. If the study were aimed at measuring the level of unemployment in a given large city, the unemployment rate produced by the survey data would not refer to the city as of the beginning of interviewing or as of the end. Rather, the researcher would be forced to attribute the unemployment rate to some hypothetical date—representing perhaps the midpoint of the interviewing period. (Asking respondents to answer in terms of a uniform date introduces the problem of inaccurate recall.) While this problem is inherent in any interviewing project that is not executed all in one moment, the seriousness of the problem grows with the duration of interviewing. If the interviewing took 10 years to complete—with the unemployment rate presumably changing during that period —the resultant rate would be meaningless.

Finally, the managerial requirements of a very large survey would be far greater than normally faced by survey researchers. Supervision, record keeping, training, and so forth would all be more difficult in a very large survey. Once again, the quality of data collected in a very large survey might be lower than that obtained in a smaller, more manageable one. (It is worth noting that the Bureau of the Census follows its decennial census with a sample survey for purposes of evaluating the data collected in the total enumeration.)

Are Sample Data Really Accurate?

Despite the foregoing, many readers no doubt still feel somewhat uneasy about sampling. Since it is clearly possible for a sample to misrepresent the population from which it is drawn, there is an inevitable danger to the researcher who utilizes sampling methods. Nevertheless, as will be shown in this chapter, established sampling procedures can reduce this danger to an acceptable minimum. Ultimately, sample surveys can provide very accurate estimates about the populations that they portray. However, the sample survey researcher must be prepared to tolerate a certain ambiguity: we are seldom able to determine exactly how accurate our sample findings are.

Political pollsters are one group of survey researchers who are given an opportunity to check the accuracy of their sample findings. Election day is the final judgment for political pollsters, and their mixed experiences are instructive in the more general question of sample survey accuracy.

Most critics of sample survey methods are familiar with the 1936 *Literary Digest* poll that predicted Alfred M. Landon to win over Franklin D. Roosevelt by a landslide. Polling a sample of more than 2 million voters by mail, the *Digest* predicted that Landon would beat Roosevelt by nearly 15 percentage points. The primary reason for this failure lay in the *sampling frame* (see below) used by the pollsters. The *Digest* sample was drawn from telephone directories and automobile registration lists. This sampling procedure had seemed sufficient in the 1920, 1924, 1928, and 1932 elections, but by 1936 it did not provide a representative cross section of American voters. In the wake of the Depression, and in the midst of the New Deal, unprecedented numbers of poor Americans came to the polls. These people, however, were not adequately represented by telephone directories and automobile registration lists.

In 1936, George Gallup correctly predicted that Roosevelt would win a second term. Gallup's sampling procedures differed from those of the *Literary Digest,* however. Gallup's American Institute of Public Opinion had pioneered in the use of *quota sampling* (see below), which better insured that all types of American voters—rich and poor—would be adequately represented in the survey sample. Where the *Digest* poll failed to reach and question the poor—and predominantly Democratic—voters, Gallup's quota sampling did.

Twelve years later Gallup, and most political pollsters, suffered the embarrassment of predicting victory for Thomas Dewey over Harry Truman. As Goodman Ace acidly noted, "Everyone believes in public opinion polls. Everyone from the man in the street . . . up to President Thomas E. Dewey."[1] A number of factors conspired to bring about the 1948 polling debacle. For one thing, most pollsters finished their polling too soon despite a steady trend toward Truman over the course of the campaign. The large numbers of voters who said they did not know whom they would vote for went predominantly to Truman. Most important, however, the failure in 1948 pointed to serious shortcomings inherent in quota sampling—the method that was such an improvement over the *Literary Digest* sampling methods. In 1948 a number of academic survey researchers had been experimenting with *probability sampling* methods. By and large, they were far more successful than the quota samplers, and probability sampling remains the most respected method used by survey researchers today.

The brief discussion above has presented a partial history of early survey sampling in America but has perhaps done so at the expense of the reader's modicum of faith in sample survey methods. To counterbalance this possible effect, it will be useful to consider the more recent score sheet of political polling accuracy. In November 1968, Richard Nixon received 42.9 percent of the popular vote for President. In their latest preelection polls, George Gallup and Louis Harris respectively predicted Nixon would receive 43 and 41 percent. This accuracy was accomplished, moreover, in the face of the uncertain effect of George Wallace's third-party candidacy. And, in place of the 2

---

[1]Requoted in *Newsweek*, July 8, 1968, p. 24.

million voters polled by the *Literary Digest* in 1936, approximately 2,000 voters were sufficient to predict the voting of some 73 million who went to the polls in 1968.

Sample surveys can be extremely accurate. At the same time, we should concede that they often are not, even today. The remainder of this chapter is devoted to presenting the reasons and rules for accuracy in sampling.

Two Types of Sampling Methods

It is useful to distinguish two major types of sampling methods: *probability* sampling and *nonprobability* sampling. The bulk of this chapter will be devoted to probability sampling, as it is currently the most respected and useful method. A smaller portion of this chapter will consider the various methods of nonprobability sampling methods.

We shall begin with a discussion of the logic of probability sampling, followed by a brief taxonomy of sampling concepts and terminology. Then we shall turn to the concept of sampling distribution: the basis of estimating the accuracy of sample survey findings. Following these theoretical discussions, we shall turn to a consideration of populations and sampling frames —focusing on practical problems of determining the target group of the study and how to begin selecting a sample. Next, we shall examine the basic types of survey designs: simple random samples, systematic samples, stratified samples, and cluster samples. Then, a short discussion and description of nonprobability sampling is presented.

Finally, the chapter closes with a brief consideration of some nonsurvey uses of sampling methods in such fields as content analysis, participant observation, and historical analyses. Hopefully, the reader will have become so familiar with the *logic* of survey sampling that he will be able to profit from that knowledge in a broader variety of situations.

5.2   The Logic of Probability Sampling

It should be apparent from the history of political polling that sample surveys can be very accurate. At the same time it should be equally apparent that samples must be selected in a careful fashion. We might consider briefly why this is the case.

The Implications of Homogeneity and Heterogeneity

If all members of a population were identical to one another in all respects, there would be no need for careful sampling procedures. In such a case, any sample would indeed be sufficient. In this extreme case of homogeneity, in fact, *one* case would be sufficient as a sample to study characteristics of the whole population.

Before this idea is dismissed as impossible, recall that much scientific sampling is carried out on this basis. In the physical sciences, it is sometimes safe to make this assumption and proceed on the basis of it in research. The chemist who wishes to test certain properties of carbon, for example, need not undertake a painstaking enumeration of all the carbon in the world and then carefully select a probability sample of carbon molecules for study.

By the same token, the medical scientist—or the practicing physician— who wishes to examine a person's blood need not draw out all of the person's blood and select a probability sample of blood cells. Again, for most purposes, any sample of blood from the person may suffice.

Faced with variation or heterogeneity in the population under study, however, more controlled sampling procedures are required. The broader applicability of this principle—beyond social research—is worth noting. The origins of modern sampling theory are to be found in agricultural research, especially in the work of R. A. Fisher whose name is still attached to some commonly used survey statistics.

For our purposes, it is more important to note the heterogeneity of social groups. People differ in many ways. A given human population, then, is comprised of varied individuals. A sample of individuals from that population, if it is to provide useful descriptions of the total population, must contain essentially the same variation as exists in the population. Probability sampling provides an efficient method for selecting a sample that should adequately reflect the variation that exists in the population.

Conscious and Unconscious Sampling Bias

Of course anyone could select a survey sample, even without any special training or care. To select a sample of 100 university students, a person might go to the university campus and begin interviewing students found walking around campus. This kind of sampling method is often used by untrained researchers, but it has very serious problems.

To begin, there is a danger that the researcher's own personal biases may affect the sample selected in this manner—hence the sample would not truly represent the student population. Let's assume that the researcher is personally somewhat intimidated by "hippy-looking" students, feeling that they would ridicule his research effort. As a result, he might consciously or semi-consciously avoid interviewing such people. Or, he might feel that the attitudes of "straight-looking" students would not be relevant to his research purposes and would avoid interviewing such students. Even if he sought to interview a "balanced" group of students, he probably would not know the proper proportions of different types of students making up such a balance, or he might be unable to identify the different types just by watching them walk by.

Even if the researcher made a conscientious effort to interview every tenth student entering the university library, this would not insure him of a representative sample, since different types of students visit the library with different frequencies. Thus, the sample would overrepresent students frequenting the library more often.

Representativeness and Probability of Selection

Survey samples must represent the populations from which they are drawn if they are to provide useful estimates about the characteristics of that population. Realize that they need not be representative in all respects; representativeness, as it has any meaning in regard to sampling, is limited to those characteristics that are relevant to the substantive interests of the study. (This will become more evident in the discussion of stratification below.)

A basic principle of probability sampling is the following. *A sample will be representative of the population from which it is selected, if all members of the population have an equal chance of being selected in the sample.*[2] Samples that have this quality are often labeled EPSEM samples (equal probability of selection method). While we shall discuss variations of this principle later, it is the primary one providing the basis of probability sampling.

Moving beyond this basic principle, we must realize that samples—even carefully selected EPSEM samples—are seldom if ever *perfectly* representative of the populations from which they are drawn. Nevertheless, probability sampling offers two special advantages for researchers.

First, probability samples, while never perfectly representative, are typically *more representative* than other types of samples because the biases discussed in the preceding section are avoided. In practice, there is a greater likelihood that a probability sample will be representative of the population from which it is drawn than that a nonprobability sample would be.

Second, and more important, probability theory permits the researcher to estimate the accuracy or representativeness of his sample. Conceivably, an uninformed researcher might, through wholly haphazard means, select a sample that nearly perfectly represents the larger population. The odds are against his doing so, however, and he would be unable to estimate the likelihood that he has achieved representativeness. The probability sampler, on the other hand, can provide an accurate estimate of his success or failure.

Following a brief taxonomy of sampling terminology, we shall examine the means whereby the probability sampler estimates the representativeness of his sample.

---

[2]We shall see shortly that the size of the sample selected as well as the actual characteristics of the larger population affect the *degree* of representativeness.

5.3   Sampling Concepts and Terminology

The following discussions of sampling theory and practice utilize a number of technical terms. To facilitate the reader's understanding of those discussions, it is important to quickly define those terms. For the most part, I will employ terms commonly used in other sampling and statistical textbooks so that readers may better understand those other sources.

In presenting this taxonomy of sampling concepts and terminology, I would like to acknowledge a debt to Leslie Kish and his excellent textbook on survey sampling.[3] While I have modified some of the conventions used by Kish, his presentation is easily the most important source of our discussion.

Element

An *element* is that unit about which information is collected and which provides the basis of analysis. Typically, in survey research, elements are people or certain types of people. It should be recognized, however, that other kinds of units might constitute the elements for a survey; families, social clubs, corporations, and so forth, might be the elements of a survey.

Universe

A *universe* is the theoretical and hypothetical aggregation of all elements, as defined for a given survey. If the individual American is the element for a survey, then "Americans" would be the universe. A survey universe is wholly unspecified as to time and place, however, and is essentially a useless term.

Population

A *population* is the theoretically specified aggregation of survey elements. While the vague term "Americans" might be the universe for a survey, the delineation of the population would include a definition of the element Americans (for example, citizenship, residence) and the time referent for the study (Americans as of when?). Translating the universe "adult New Yorkers" into a workable population would require a specification of the age defining "adult," the boundaries of New York, and so forth. Specifying the term "college student" would include a consideration of full-

---

[3]Leslie Kish, *Survey Sampling* (New York: John Wiley & Sons, Inc., 1965).

time and part-time students, degree candidates and nondegree candidates, undergraduate and graduate students, and similar issues.

While the researcher must begin with a careful specification of his population, poetic license usually permits him to phrase his report in terms of the hypothetical universe. For ease of presentation, even the most conscientious researcher normally speaks of "Americans" rather than "resident citizens of the United States of America as of November 12, 1971." The primary guide in this matter, as in most others, is that the researcher should not mislead or deceive his readers.

Survey Population

A *survey population* is that aggregation of elements from which the survey sample is actually selected. Recall that a population is a theoretical specification of the universe. As a practical matter, the researcher is seldom in a position to guarantee that every element that meets the theoretical definitions laid down actually has a chance of being selected in the sample. Even where lists of elements exist for sampling purposes, the lists are usually somewhat incomplete. Some students are always omitted, inadvertently, from student rosters. Some telephone subscribers request that their names and numbers be unlisted. The survey population, then, is the aggregation of elements from which the sample is selected.

Often researchers may decide to limit their survey populations more severely than indicated in the above examples. National polling firms may limit their "national samples" to the 48 adjacent states, omitting Alaska and Hawaii for practical reasons. A researcher wishing to sample psychology professors may limit the survey population to psychology professors who are serving in psychology departments, omitting those serving in other departments. (In a sense, we might say that these researchers have redefined their universes and populations, providing that they have made the revisions clear to their readers.)

Sampling Unit

A *sampling unit* is that element or set of elements considered for selection in some stage of sampling. In a simple, single-stage sample, the sampling units are the same as the elements. In more complex samples, however, different levels of sampling units may be employed. For example, a researcher may select a sample of census blocks in a city, then select a sample of households on the selected blocks, and finally select a sample of adults from the selected households. The sampling units for these three stages of sampling are, respectively, census blocks, households, and adults, of which only the last of these are the elements. More specifically, the terms "primary sampling units," "secondary sampling units," and "final sampling units" would be used to designate the successive stages.

Sampling Frame

A *sampling frame* is the actual list of sampling units from which the sample, or some stage of the sample, is selected. If a simple sample of students is selected from a student roster, the roster would be the sampling frame. If the primary sampling unit for a complex population sample is the census block, the list of census blocks would comprise the sampling frame—either in the form of a printed booklet, an IBM card file, or a magnetic tape file.

In a single-stage sample design, the sampling frame is a list of the elements comprising the survey population. In practice, the existing sampling frames often define the survey population rather than the other way around. The researcher often begins with a universe or perhaps a population in mind for his study; then he searches for possible sampling frames. The frames available for his use are examined and evaluated, and the researcher decides which frame represents a survey population most appropriate to his needs.

The relationship between populations and sampling frames is critical and one that has not been given sufficient attention. A later section of the present chapter will pursue this issue in greater detail.

Observation Unit

An *observation unit*, or unit of data collection, is an element or aggregation of elements from which information is collected. Again, often the unit of analysis and unit of observation are the same—the individual person—but this need not be the case. Thus the researcher may interview heads of households (the observational units) to collect information about every member of the household (the units of analysis).

The researcher's task is simplified when the unit of analysis and observational unit are the same. Often this is not possible or feasible, however, and in such situations the researcher should be capable of exercising some ingenuity in collecting data relevant to his units of analysis without actually observing those units.

Variable

A *variable* is a set of mutually exclusive characteristics such as sex, age, employment status, and so forth. The elements of a given population may be described in terms of their individual characteristics on a given variable. Typically, surveys aim at describing the distribution of characteristics comprising a variable in a population. Thus a researcher may describe the age distribution of a population by examining the relative frequency of different ages among members of the population.

It should be noted that a variable, by definition, must possess *variation;* if all elements in the population have the same characteristics, that characteristic is a *constant* in the population, rather than part of a variable.

Parameter

A *parameter* is the summary description of a given variable in a *population.* The mean income of all families in a city and the age distribution of the city's population are parameters. An important portion of survey research involves the estimation of population parameters on the basis of sample observations.

Statistic

A *statistic* is the summary description of a given variable in a survey sample. Thus the mean income computed from a survey sample and the age distribution of that sample are statistics. Sample statistics are used to make estimates of population parameters.

Sampling Error

This term will be discussed in more detail below. Probability sampling methods seldom, if ever, provide statistics exactly equal to the parameters that they are used to estimate. Probability theory, however, permits us to estimate the degree of error to be expected for a given sample design.

Confidence Levels and Confidence Intervals

These terms will also be discussed more fully below. The computation of sampling error permits the researcher to express the accuracy of his sample statistics in terms of his level of confidence that the statistics fall within a specified interval from the parameter. For example, he may say he is "95 percent confident" that his sample statistics (for example, 50 percent favor Candidate X) is within plus or minus ($\pm$) 5 percentage points of the population parameter. As the confidence interval is expanded for a given statistic, his "confidence" increases and he may say that he is 99.9 percent confident that his statistic falls within $\pm$7.5 percentage points of the parameter.

5.4   Probability Sampling Theory and Sampling Distribution

This section will examine the basic theory of probability sampling as it applies to survey sampling, and we shall consider the logic of sampling distribution and sampling error with regard to a *binomial* variable —a variable comprised of two characteristics.

Probability Sampling Theory

The ultimate purpose of survey sampling is to select a set of elements from a population in such a way that descriptions of those elements (statistics) accurately describe the total population from which they are selected. Probability sampling provides a method for enhancing the likelihood of accomplishing this aim, and it also provides methods for estimating the degree of probable success.

Random selection is the key to this process. A random selection process is one in which each element has an equal chance of selection that is independent of any other events in the selection process. Flipping a perfect coin is the most frequently cited example, whereby the "selection" of a head or a tail is independent of previous selections of heads or tails. Rolling a perfect set of dice is another example.

Such images of random selection seldom apply directly to survey sampling methods, however. The survey sampler more typically utilizes tables of random numbers or computer programs that provide a random selection of sampling units. The wide availability of such research aids makes this an adequate beginning point for our discussion of random sampling.

The reasons for using random selection methods—using random-number tables or computer programs—are twofold. First, this procedure serves as a check on conscious or unconscious bias on the part of the researcher. The researcher who undertakes the selection of cases on an intuitive basis might very well select cases that would support his research expectations or hypotheses. Random selection, then, erases this danger.

More important, random selection offers the researcher access to the body of probability theory, which provides the basis for his estimates of population parameters and estimates of error. We shall turn now to an examination of this latter aspect.

Binomial Sampling Distribution

To discuss the concept of sampling distribution, it will be clearest to utilize a simple survey example. Let us assume for the moment that we wish to study the student population of State University to determine approval or disapproval of a student conduct code proposed by the administration. The survey population will be that aggregation of students contained in a student roster: the sampling frame. The elements will be the individual students at SU. The variable under consideration will be attitudes toward the code, a binomial variable: approve and disapprove. We shall select a random sample of students for purposes of estimating the entire student body.

Figure 5-1 presents an x axis that represents all possible values of this parameter in the population—from 0 percent approval to 100 percent approval. The midpoint of the axis—50 percent—represents the situation in which half the students approve of the code while the other half disapprove.

Figure 5-1

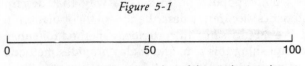

Percent of students approving of the student code

Let us assume for the moment that we have given each student on the student roster a number and have selected 100 random numbers from a table of random numbers. The 100 students having the numbers selected are then interviewed and asked for their attitudes toward the student code: whether they approve or disapprove. Let us further assume that this operation provides us with 48 students who approve of the code and 52 who disapprove. We may represent this statistic by placing a dot on the x axis at the point representing 48 percent.

Now let us suppose that we select another sample of 100 students in exactly the same fashion and measure their approval/disapproval of the student code. Perhaps 51 students in the second sample approve of the code, and this might be represented by another dot in the appropriate place on the x axis. Repeating this process once more, we may discover that 52 students in the third sample approve of the code.

Figure 5-2

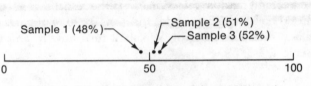

Percent of students approving of the student code

Figure 5-2 presents the three different sample statistics, representing the percentages of students in each of the three random samples who approved of the student code. The basic rule of random sampling is that such samples drawn from a population provide estimates of the parameter that pertains in the total population. Each of the random samples, then, gives us an estimate of the percentage of students in the total student body who approve of the student code. Unhappily, however, we have selected three samples and now have three separate estimates.

To retrieve ourselves from this dilemma, let's go on to draw more and more samples of 100 students each, question each of the samples as to their approval/disapproval of the code, and plot the new sample statistics on our summary graph. In drawing many such samples, we will begin to discover that some of the new samples provide the same estimates given by earlier samples. To take account of this situation, we shall add a *y* axis to the figure, representing the number of samples providing a given estimate. Figure 5-3 is the product of our new sampling efforts.

Figure 5-3

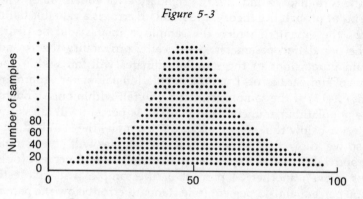

Percent of students approving of the student code

The distribution of sample statistics provided in Figure 5-3 is called the *sampling distribution.* We note that by increasing the number of samples selected and interviewed, we have also increased the range of estimates provided by the sampling operation. In one sense we have increased our dilemma in attempting to guess the parameter in the population. Probability theory, however, provides certain important rules regarding the sampling distribution presented in Figure 5-3.

First, if many independent random samples are selected from a population, the sample statistics provided by those samples will be *distributed around the population parameter* in a known way. While we see that there is a wide range of estimates, more of them are in the vicinity of 50 percent than elsewhere in the graph. Probability theory tells us, then, that the true value is in the vicinity of 50 percent.

Second, probability theory provides us with a formula for estimating *how closely* the sample statistics are clustered around the true value. This formula contains three factors: the parameter, the sample size, and the *standard error* (a measure of sampling error).

Formula: $S = \sqrt{\dfrac{PQ}{n}}$

Symbols: P, Q: the population parameters for the binomial; if 60 percent of
the student body approves the code and 40 percent disapproves,
P and Q are 60 percent and 40 percent, or .6 and .4. Note that
$Q = 1 - P$ and $P = 1 - Q$.

n: the number of cases in each sample.

s: the standard error.

Let us assume that the population parameter in the study survey example
is 50 percent approving of the code and 50 percent disapproving. Recall that
we have been selecting samples of 100 cases each. When these numbers are
put into the formula, we find that the standard error equals .05 or 5 percent.

In terms of probability theory, the standard error is a valuable datum, for
it indicates the extent to which the sample estimates will be distributed
around the population parameter. Specifically, probability theory indicates
that certain proportions of the sample estimates will fall within specified
increments of standard errors from the population parameter. Approximately
34 percent (.3413) of the sample estimates will fall within one standard error
above the population parameter, and another 34 percent will fall within one
standard error below the parameter. In our example, the standard error is 5
percent, so we know that 34 percent of our samples will give estimates of
student approval between 50 percent (parameter) and 55 percent (one standard error above); another 34 percent of the samples will give estimates
between 50 percent and 45 percent (one standard error below the parameter).
Taken together, then, we know that roughly two-thirds (68 percent) of the
samples will give estimates within (plus or minus) 5 percent of the parameter.

Moreover, probability theory dictates that roughly 95 percent of the
samples will fall within plus or minus two standard errors of the true value,
and 99.9 percent of the samples will fall within plus or minus three standard
errors. In our present example, then, we know that only one sample out of
a thousand would give an estimate lower than 35 percent approval or higher
than 65 percent.

The proportion of samples falling within one, two, or three standard
errors of the parameter are constants for any random sampling procedure
such as the one just described, providing that a large number of samples are
selected. The size of the standard error in any given case, however, is a
function of the population parameter and the sample size. If we return to the
formula for a moment, we note that the standard error will increase as a
function of an increase in the quantity: P times Q. Note further that this
quantity reaches its maximum in the situation of an even split in the population. If $P = .5$, $PQ = .25$; if $P = .6$, $PQ = .24$; if $P = .8$, $PQ = .16$; if $P =
.99$, $PQ = .0099$. By extention, if P is either 0.0 or 1.0 (either 0 percent or 100

percent approve of the student code), the standard error will be 0. If everyone in the population has the same attitude (no variation), then every sample will give exactly that estimate.

The standard error is also a function of the sample size—an *inverse* function. As the sample size increases, the standard error decreases. As the sample size increases, the several samples will be clustered nearer to the true value. Another rule of thumb is evident in the formula: because of the square root in the formula, the standard error is reduced by half if the sample size is *quadrupled*. In our present example, samples of 100 produce a standard error of 5 percent; to reduce the standard error to 2.5 percent, it would be necessary to increase the sample size to 400.

All the foregoing is provided by established probability theory in reference to the selection of large numbers of random samples. If the population parameter is known, and very many random samples are selected, we are able to predict how many of the samples will fall within specified intervals from the parameter. These conditions do not typically pertain in survey sampling, however.

Typically, the survey researcher does not know the parameter, but he conducts a sample survey in order to estimate that value. Moreover, he does not typically select large numbers of samples, but he selects only one sample. Nevertheless, the preceding discussion of probability theory provides the basis for inferences about the typical survey situation.

Whereas probability theory specifies that 68 percent of the samples will fall within one standard error of the parameter, the survey sampler infers that a given random sample has a likelihood of 68 percent of falling within that range. In this regard we speak of *confidence levels:* the researcher is "68 percent confident" that his sample estimate is within one standard error of the parameter. Or he may say he is "95 percent confident" that the sample statistic is within two standard errors of the parameter, and so forth. Quite reasonably, his confidence increases as the margin for error is extended. He is virtually positive (99.9 percent confident) that he is within three standard errors of the true value.

While he may be confident (at some level) of being within a certain range of the parameter, we have already noted that he seldom knows what the parameter is. To resolve this dilemma, the survey sampler substitutes his sample estimate for the parameter in the formula; lacking the true value, he substitutes the best available guess.

The result of these inferences and estimations is that the survey researcher is able to estimate a population parameter and also the expected degree of error on the basis of one sample drawn from a population. Beginning with the question "What percentage of the student body approve of the student code?" the researcher could select a random sample of 100 students and interview them. He might then report his best estimate is that 50 percent of the student body approves of the code, and that he is 95 percent confident that between 40 and 60 percent (plus or minus two standard errors) approve. The range from 40 to 60 percent is called the *confidence interval*.

This then is the basic logic of probability sampling. Random selection permits the researcher to link his sample survey findings to the body of probability theory for purposes of estimating the accuracy of those findings. All statements of accuracy in sampling must specify both a confidence level and a confidence interval. The researcher may report that he is x percent confident that the population parameter is between two specified values. It does not make sense, however, for a researcher to report that his findings are "x percent accurate."

The foregoing discussion has considered only one type of statistic: the percentages produced by a *binomial* or dichotomous variable. The same logic, however, would apply to the examination of other statistics, such as mean income for example. Whereas the computations are somewhat more complicated in such a case, I have chosen to consider only binomials in this introduction.

The reader should be cautioned that the survey uses of probability theory as discussed above are not wholly justified technically. The theory of sampling distribution, for example, makes assumptions that almost never apply in survey conditions. The number of samples contained within specified increments of standard errors, for example, assumes an infinitely large population, an infinite number of samples, and sampling with replacement. Moreover, the inferential jump from the distribution of several samples to the probable characteristics of one sample has been grossly oversimplified in the above discussion.

The above cautions are offered for reasons of perspective. Researchers often appear to overestimate the precision of estimates produced by the use of probability theory in connection with survey research. As will be mentioned elsewhere in this chapter and throughout the book, variations in sampling techniques and nonsampling factors may further reduce the legitimacy of such estimates. Nevertheless, the calculations discussed in this section can be extremely valuable to the researcher in understanding and evaluating his data. Although the calculations do not provide as precise estimates as some researchers might assume, they can be quite valid for practical purposes; they are unquestionably more valid than less rigorously derived estimates based on less rigorous sampling methods.

Most important, the reader should be familiar with the basic *logic* underlying the calculations. If he is so informed, he will be able to react sensibly to his own data and to those reported by others.

5.5   Populations and Sampling Frames

The immediately preceding section has dealt with a theoretical model for survey sampling. While it is necessary for the survey consumer, student, or researcher to understand that theory, it is no less important that he appreciate the less-than-perfect conditions that exist in the field. The present section is devoted to a discussion of one aspect of field conditions that requires a compromise with regard to theoretical conditions and assumptions. We shall consider the congruence of, or disparity between, populations and sampling frames.

Simply put, a sampling frame is the list, or reasonable facsimile, of elements from which a probability sample is selected. The following section will deal with the methods for selected samples, but we must first consider the sampling frame itself. Properly drawn samples will provide information appropriate for describing the population of elements comprising the sampling frame—nothing more. It is necessary to make this point in view of the all-too-common tendency for researchers to select samples from a given sampling frame and then make assertions about a population similar to, but not identical to, the survey population defined by the sampling frame. The problem involved here is the broader social scientific one of generalization and is akin to studying a small Lutheran church in North Dakota for purposes of describing religion in America.

In the remainder of this section, we shall examine different survey purposes and discuss the good and bad sampling frames that might be used to satisfy those purposes.

Surveys of organizations are often the simplest from a sampling standpoint because organizations typically have membership lists. In such cases, the list of members constitutes an excellent sampling frame. If a random sample is selected from a membership list, the data collected from that sample may be taken as representative of all members—*if all members are included in the list.* If some members are omitted from the membership list, an effort must be made to sample those nonlisted members, or else the sample survey findings can be taken as representative only of those members on the list.

Populations that often can be sampled from good organizational lists include elementary school, high school, and university students and faculty; church members; factory workers; fraternity or sorority members; members of social, service, or political clubs; members of professional associations.

The above comments apply primarily to local organizations. Often statewide or national organizations do not have a single membership list easily available. There is, for example, no single list of Episcopalian church members. However, a slightly more complex sample design could take advantage of local church membership lists: by first sampling churches, and then subsampling the membership lists of those churches selected. (More about this below.)

Other lists of individuals may be especially relevant to the research needs of a particular survey. Government agencies maintain lists of registered voters, for example, if the researcher wishes to conduct a preelection poll or a more detailed examination of voting behavior—but the researcher must insure that the list is up-to-date. Similar lists contain the names of automobile

owners, welfare recipients, taxpayers, business permit holders, licensed professionals, and so forth. While it may be difficult to gain access to some of
these lists, they may provide excellent sampling frames for specialized research purposes.

Realizing that the sampling elements in a survey need not be individual
persons, it may be noted that lists of other types of elements also exist:
universities, businesses of various types, cities, academic journals, newspapers, unions, political clubs, professional associations, and so forth.

Telephone directories are frequently used for "quick and dirty" public
opinion polls. Undeniably they are easy and inexpensive to use, and this is
no doubt the reason for their popularity. And, if one wishes to make assertions about telephone subscribers, the directory is a *fairly good* sampling
frame.[4] Unfortunately, telephone directories are all too often taken to be a
listing of a city's population or of its voters. There are many defects in this
reasoning, but the chief one involves a social-class bias. Poor people are less
likely to have telephones; a telephone directory sample, therefore, is likely
to have a middle- or upper-class bias.

The class bias inherent in telephone directory samples is often hidden.
Preelection polls conducted in this fashion are sometimes quite accurate. The
reason for this would seem to be in the class bias evident in voting itself: poor
people are less likely to vote. Frequently, then, these two biases nearly coin-
cide and the results of a telephone poll may come very close to the final
election outcome. Unhappily, the pollster never knows for sure until after the
election. And often, as in the case of the 1936 *Literary Digest* poll, he may
discover that the voters were unaware of the expected class biases. The
ultimate disadvantage of this method, then, is the researcher's inability to
estimate the degree of error to be expected in his sample findings.

Street directories and tax maps are often used for easy samples of
households, but they may suffer from many of the same disadvantages as the
telephone directory: incompleteness and possible bias. For example, in strictly
zoned urban regions, "illegal" housing units are unlikely to appear on official
records. As a result, such units would have no chance of selection, and sample
findings could not be representative of those units, which are often typically
poorer and more overcrowded.

Review of Populations and Sampling Frames

Surprisingly little attention has been given to the issues
of populations and sampling frames in survey research literature. With this
in mind, I have devoted special attention to the topic here. To further emphasize the point, it seems appropriate to list, in review, the main guidelines to
be borne in mind.

---

[4]Realize, of course, that a given directory will not include new subscribers or those who have requested
unlisted numbers. Sampling is further complicated by the inclusion in directories of nonresidential listings.

1. Sample survey findings can be taken only as representative of the aggregation of elements that comprise the sampling frame.

2. Often, sampling frames do not truly include all the elements that their names might imply. (Student directories do not include all students; telephone directories do not include all telephone subscribers.) Omissions are almost inevitable. Thus a first concern of the researcher must be to assess the extent of omissions and to correct them if possible. (Realize, of course, that he may feel he can safely ignore a small number of omissions that cannot easily be corrected.)

3. Even to generalize to the population comprising the sampling frame, it is necessary for all elements to have equal representation to the frame: typically, each element should appear only once. Otherwise, elements that appear more than once will have a greater probability of selection, and the sample will, overall, overrepresent these elements.

Other, more practical, matters relating to populations and sampling frames will be treated elsewhere in this book. For example, the form of the sampling frame is very important: a list in a publication, a 3x5 card file, addressograph plates, IBM cards, or magnetic tapes. It should be noted here that such considerations may often take priority over scientific considerations: an "easier" list may be chosen over a "harder" one, even though the latter is more appropriate to the target population. We should not take a dogmatic position in this regard, but all researchers should carefully weigh the relative advantages and disadvantages of such alternatives. Most important of all, he must be aware—and must so inform his reader—of the shortcomings of whatever sampling frame is chosen.

5.6   Types of Sampling Designs

Introduction

Perhaps the reader will have reached this point in his reading somewhat aghast at the importance and difficulties of organizing his sampling frame; such a feeling would be altogether appropriate and healthy. Once it has been established, the researcher must then actually select a sample of elements for study.

Up to this point, we have focused on *simple random sampling.* And, indeed, the body of statistics typically used by survey researchers assumes such a sample. As we shall see shortly, however, the researcher has a number of options in choosing his sampling, and he seldom if ever chooses simple random sampling. There are two reasons for this. First, with all but the simplest sampling frame, simple random sampling is not possible. Second, and probably surprising, simple random sampling may not be the best (not the most accurate) method available. We shall turn now to a discussion of simple random sampling and the other options available.

Simple Random Sampling

As noted above, simple random sampling (SRS) is the basic sampling method assumed in survey statistical computations. The mathematics of random sampling are especially complex, and we shall detour around them in favor of describing the field methods of employing this method.

Once a sampling frame has been established in accord with the discussion above, the researcher may then assign numbers to each of the elements in the list—assigning one and only one number to each and not skipping any number in the process. A table of random numbers could then be used in the selection of elements for the sample.

If the researcher's sampling frame is in a machine-readable form—IBM cards or magnetic tape—a simple random sample could be selected automatically through the use of a computer. (In effect, the computer program would number the elements in the sampling frame, generate its own series of random numbers, and print out the list of elements selected.)

Systematic Sampling

Simple random sampling is seldom used in practice. As we shall see in later sections, it is not usually the most efficient sampling method and, as we have already seen, it can be rather laborious if done manually. SRS typically requires a list of elements; when such a list is available, researchers usually employ a *systematic* sampling method rather than simple random sampling.

In systematic sampling, every *k*th element in the total list is chosen (systematically) for inclusion in the sample. If the list contains 10,000 elements and the researcher desires a sample of 1,000, he will select every tenth element for his sample. To insure against any possible human bias in using this method, the researcher selects the first element at random. Thus, in the above example he would begin by selecting a random number between 1 and 10; the element having that number would be included in the sample, plus every tenth element following it. This is technically referred to as a "systematic sample with a random start."

Two terms are frequently used in connection with systematic sampling. The *sampling interval* is the standard distance between elements selected in the sample: 10 in the example above. The *sampling ratio* is the proportion of elements in the population which are selected: one-tenth in the example above.

In practice, systematic sampling is virtually identical to simple random sampling. If, indeed, the list of elements is "randomized" in advance of sampling, one might argue that a systematic sample drawn from that list is in fact a simple random sample. By now, debates over the relative merits of simple random sampling and systematic sampling have been resolved largely in favor of the simpler method: systematic sampling. Empirically, the results are virtually identical. And, as we shall see in a later section, systematic sampling, in some instances, is slightly more accurate than simple random sampling.

There is one danger involved in systematic sampling. The arrangement of elements in the list can make a systematic sample unwise. This danger is usually referred to by the term *periodicity*. If the list of elements is arranged in a cyclical pattern that coincides with the sampling interval, it is possible that a grossly biased sample may be drawn. Two examples should suffice.

In one study of soldiers during World War II, the researchers selected a systematic sample from unit rosters. Every tenth soldier on the rosters was selected for the study. The rosters, however, were arranged in a table of organization: sergeants first, then corporals and privates—squad by squad and each squad had 10 members. As a result, every tenth person on the roster was a squad sergeant. The systematic sample selected contained only sergeants. It could, of course, have been the case that no sergeants were selected for the same reason.

As another example suppose we wish to select a sample of apartments in an apartment building. If the sample were drawn from a list of apartments arranged in numerical order (for example, 101, 102, 103, 104, 201, 202, and so on), there would be a danger of the sampling interval coinciding with the number of apartments on a floor or some multiple thereof. In such a case, the samples might include only northwest-corner apartments or only apartments near the elevator. If these types of apartments had some other particular characteristic in common (for example, higher rent), the sample would be biased. The same danger would appear in a systematic sample of houses in a subdivision arranged with the same number of houses on a block.

In considering a systematic sample from a list, then, the researcher should carefully examine the nature of that list. If the elements are arranged in any particular order, he should ascertain whether that order will bias the sample to be selected and should take steps to counteract any possible bias, (for example, take a simple random sample from cyclical portions).

In summary, however, systematic sampling is usually superior to simple random sampling, in convenience if nothing else. Where problems exist in the ordering of elements in the sampling frame, these can usually be remedied quite easily.

Stratified Sampling

In the two preceding sections we have discussed two alternative methods of sample selection from a list. Stratified sampling is not an alternative to these methods, but it represents a possible modification in their use.

Simple random and systematic sampling are important in that they insure a degree of representativeness and permit an estimate of the error present. Stratified sampling is a method for obtaining a greater degree of representativeness—decreasing the probable sampling error. To understand why this is the case, we must return briefly to the basic theory of sampling distribution.

We recall that sampling error is reduced by two factors in the sample design. First, a large sample produces a smaller sampling error than does a small sample. Second, a homogeneous population produces samples with smaller sampling errors than does a heterogeneous population. If 99 percent of the population agree with a certain statement, it is extremely unlikely that any probability sample will greatly misrepresent the extent of agreement. If, on the other hand, the population is split fifty-fifty on the statement, then the sampling error will be much greater.

Stratified sampling is based on this second factor in sampling theory. Rather than selecting his sample from the total population at large, the researcher insures that appropriate numbers of elements are drawn from homogeneous subsets of that population. In a study of university students, for example, the researcher may first organize his population by college class and draw appropriate numbers of freshmen, sophomores, juniors, and seniors. In a nonstratified sample, representation by class would be subjected to the same sampling error as other variables. In a sample stratified by class, the sampling error on this variable is reduced to zero.

The researcher might wish to utilize an even more complex stratification method. In addition to stratifying by class, he might also stratify by sex, by grade point average, and so forth. In this fashion he might be able to insure that his sample would contain the proper numbers of freshman men with a 4.0 average, of freshman women with a 4.0 average, and so forth.

The ultimate function of stratification, then, is to organize the population into homogeneous subsets (with heterogeneity, between subsets) and to select the appropriate number of elements from each. To the extent that the subsets are homogeneous on the stratification variables, they may also be homogeneous on other variables as well. Since age is related to college class, a sample stratified by class will be more representative in terms of age as well. Since occupational aspirations are related to sex, a sample stratified by sex will be more representative in terms of occupational aspirations.

The choice of stratification variables typically depends on what variables are available. Sex can often be determined in a list of names. University lists are typically arranged by class. Lists of faculty members may indicate their departmental affiliation. Governmental agency files may be arranged by geographical region. Voter registration lists are arranged according to precinct.

In selecting stratification variables from among those available, however, the researcher should be concerned primarily with those that are presumably related to variables that he wishes to represent accurately. Since sex is related to many variables and is often available for stratification, it is often used. Education is related to many variables, but it is often not available for stratification. Geographical location within a city, state, or nation is related to many things. Within a city, stratification by geographical location usually increases representativeness in social class, ethnic group, and so forth. Within a nation, it increases representativeness in a broad range of attitudes as well as in social class and ethnicity.

Methods of stratification in sampling vary. Working with a simple list of all elements in the population, two are predominant. First, the researcher may group the population elements into discrete groups based on whatever stratification variables are being used. On the basis of the relative proportion of the population represented by a given group, he selects—randomly or systematically—a number of elements from that group constituting the same proportion of his desired sample size. For example, if freshman men with a 4.0 average comprise 1 percent of the student population and the researcher desires a sample of 1,000 students, he would select 10 students from the group of freshman men with a 4.0 average.

As an alternative method, he may group students as described above and then put those several groups together in a continuous list: beginning with all the freshman men with 4.0 average and ending with all the senior women with a 1.0 or below. He would then select a systematic sample, with a random start, from the entire list. Given the arrangement of the list, a systematic sample would select proper numbers (within an error range of 1 or 2) from each of the subgroups. (*Note:* A simple random sample drawn from such a composite list would cancel out the stratification.)

The effect of stratification is to insure the proper representation of the stratification variables to enhance representation of other variables related to them. Taken as a whole, then, a stratified sample is likely to be more representative on a number of variables than would be the case for a simple random sample. Although simple random sample is still regarded as somewhat sacred, it should now be clear that a researcher can often do better.

Implicit Stratification in Systematic Sampling

It was mentioned above that systematic sampling can, under certain conditions, be more accurate than simple random sampling. This is the case whenever the arrangement of the list is such as to create an implicit stratification. As already noted, if a list of university students is already arranged by class, then a systematic sample will provide a stratification by class where a simple random sample would not. Other typical arrangements of elements in lists can provide the same feature.

If a list of names comprising the sampling frame for a study is arranged alphabetically, then the list is somewhat stratified by ethnic origins. All the McTavishes are collected together, for example, as are the Lees, Wongs, Yamamuras, Schmidts, Whitehalls, Weinsteins, Gonzaleses, and so forth. To the extent that any of these groups comprise a substantial subset of the total population, that group will be properly represented in a systematic sample drawn from an alphabetical list.

In a study of students at the University of Hawaii, after stratification by school class, the students were arranged by their student identification numbers. These numbers, however, were their social security numbers. The first three digits of the social security number indicate the state in which the number was issued. As a result, within a class, students were arranged by the state in which they were issued a social security number, providing a rough stratification by geographical origins.

The researcher should be aware, therefore, that an ordered list of elements may be more useful to him than an unordered, randomized list. This point has been stressed here in view of an unfortunate belief that lists should be randomized before systematic sampling. Only if the arrangement presents the problems discussed earlier should the list be rearranged.

Multistage Cluster Sampling, General

The four preceding sections have dealt with reasonably simple procedures for sampling from lists of elements. Such a situation is ideal. Unfortunately, however, much interesting social research requires the selection of samples from populations that cannot be easily listed for sampling purposes. Examples would be the population of a city, of a state, or of a nation, all university students in the United States, and so forth. In such cases, it is necessary to create and execute a more complex sample design. Such a design typically involves the initial sampling of *groups* of elements—clusters—followed by the selection of elements within each of the selected clusters.

The varieties and procedures of multistage cluster sampling will be spelled out in some detail in the sampling examples of Chapter 6. Nevertheless, it is appropriate here to outline the method.

Cluster sampling may be used when it is either impossible or impractical to compile an exhaustive list of the elements comprising the target population. All church members in the United States would be an example of such a population. It is often the case, however, that the population elements are already grouped into subpopulations, and a list of those subpopulations either exists or can be created practically. Thus, church members in the United States belong to discrete churches, and it would be possible to discover or create a list of those churches. Following a cluster sample format, then, the list of churches would be sampled in some manner as discussed above (for example, a stratified, systematic sample). Next, the researcher would obtain lists of members from each of the selected churches. Each of the lists obtained would then be sampled, to provide samples of church members for study.[5]

Another typical situation concerns sampling among population areas such as a city. While there is no single list of a city's population, citizens reside on discrete city blocks or census blocks. It is possible, therefore, to select a sample of blocks initially, create a list of persons living on each of the selected blocks, and subsample persons on each block.

In a more complex design, the researcher might sample blocks, list the households on each selected block, sample the households, list the persons residing in each household, and, finally, sample persons within each selected household. This multistage sample design would lead to the ultimate selection of a sample of individuals but would not require the initial listing of all individuals comprising the city's population.

Multistage cluster sampling, then, involves the repetition of two basic steps: listing and sampling. The list of primary sampling units (churches, blocks) is compiled and, perhaps, stratified for sampling. Then a sample of those units is selected. The selected primary sampling units are then listed and perhaps stratified. The list of secondary sampling units is then sampled, and so forth. The actual methods of listing and sampling will be spelled out in considerable detail in the examples in Chapter 6.

Cluster sampling is highly recommended by its efficiency, but that efficiency comes at a price in terms of accuracy. Whereas a simple random sample drawn from a population list is subject to a single sampling error, a two-stage cluster sample is subject to two sampling errors. First, the initial sample of clusters will represent the population of clusters only within a range of sampling error. Second, the sample of elements selected within a given cluster will represent all the elements in that cluster only within a range of sampling error. Thus, for example, the researcher runs a certain risk of selecting a sample of disproportionately wealthy city blocks, plus a sample of disproportionately wealthy households within those blocks. The best solution to this problem lies in the number of clusters selected initially and the number of elements selected within each.

Typically, the researcher is restricted to a total sample size; for example, he may be limited to conducting 2,000 interviews in a city. Given this broad limitation, however, the researcher has several options in designing his cluster sample. At the extremes he might choose one cluster and select 2,000 elements within that cluster. Or he might select 2,000 clusters with one element selected within each. Of course, neither of these extremes is advisable, but the researcher is faced with a broad range of choices between them. Fortu-

---

[5]For an example, see Charles Y. Glock, Benjamin B. Ringer, and Earl R. Babbie, *To Comfort and to Challenge* (Berkeley: University of California Press, 1967), app. A.

nately, the logic of sampling distributions provides a general guideline to be followed.

Recall that sampling error is reduced by two factors: an increase in the sample size and an increased homogeneity of the elements being sampled. These factors operate at each level of a multistage sample design. A sample of clusters will best represent all clusters if a large number are selected and if all clusters are very much alike. A sample of elements will best represent all elements in a given cluster if a large number are selected from the cluster and if all the elements in the cluster are very much alike.

With a given total sample size, however, if the number of clusters is increased, the number of elements within a cluster must be decreased. In this respect, the representativeness of the clusters is increased at the expense of more poorly representing the elements comprising each of those clusters, or vice versa. Fortunately, the factor of homogeneity can be used to ease this dilemma.

Typically, the elements comprising a given natural cluster within a population are more homogeneous than are all elements comprising the total population. The members of a given church are more alike than are all church members; the residents of a given city block are more alike than are all the residents of a whole city. As a result, relatively fewer elements may be needed to adequately represent a given natural cluster, while a larger number of clusters may be needed to adequately represent the diversity found among the clusters. This fact is most clearly seen in the extreme case of very different clusters that are comprised of exactly identical elements within each. In such a situation, a large number of clusters would adequately represent the variety among clusters, while only one element within each cluster would adequately represent all its members. Although this extreme situation never exists in reality, it is closer to the truth in most cases than its opposite: identical clusters comprised of grossly divergent elements.

The general guideline for cluster design, then, is to maximize the number of clusters selected while decreasing the number of elements within each cluster. It must be noted, however, that this scientific guideline must be balanced against an administrative constraint. The efficiency of cluster sampling is based on the ability to minimize the listing of population elements. By initially selecting clusters, the researcher must list only the elements comprising the selected clusters, not all elements in the entire population. Increasing the number of clusters, however, goes directly against this efficiency factor in cluster sampling. A small number of clusters may be listed more quickly and more cheaply than a large number. (Remember that all the elements in a selected cluster must be listed even if only a few are to be chosen in the sample.)

The final sample design will reflect these two constraints. In effect, the researcher probably will select as many clusters as he can afford. Lest this issue be left too open-ended at this point, one rule of thumb may be presented. Population researchers conventionally aim for the selection of five households per census block. If a total of 2,000 households are to be interviewed, the researcher would aim at 400 blocks with five household interviews on each. We shall return to this rule of thumb in the later examples of sample designs, but it is mentioned at this point to buoy up the spirits of the reader.

Before turning to more detailed procedures available to cluster sampling, it bears repeating that this method almost inevitably involves a loss of accuracy. The manner in which this appears, however, is somewhat complex. First, as noted earlier, a multistage sample design is subject to a sampling error at each of its stages. Since the sample size is necessarily smaller at each stage than the total sample size, the sampling error at each stage will be greater than would be the case for a single-stage random sample of elements. Second, sampling error is estimated on the basis of observed variance among the sample elements. When those elements are drawn from among relatively homogeneous clusters, the estimates of sampling error will be too optimistic and must be corrected in the light of the cluster sample design. (This will be discussed in detail in the later consideration of univariate analysis.)

Multistage Cluster Sampling, Stratification

Thus far, we have discussed cluster sampling as though a simple random sample were selected at each stage of the design. In fact, it is possible to employ stratification techniques as discussed earlier to refine and improve the sample being selected.

Later examples will detail possible methods of stratification, but for the present we should note that the basic options available are essentially the same as those possible in single-stage sampling from a list. In selecting a national sample of churches, for example, the researcher might initially stratify his list of churches by denomination, geographical region, size, rural-urban location, and perhaps by some measure of social class. United States census information may be used by population researchers to stratify census blocks in terms of ethnic composition, social class, property values, quality of structures, nature of property ownership, and size.

Once the primary sampling units (churches, blocks) have been grouped according to the relevant, available stratification variables, either simple random or systematic sampling techniques could be used to select the sample. The researcher might select a specified number of units from each group or *stratum*, or he might arrange the stratified clusters in a continuous list and systematically sample that list.

To the extent that clusters are combined into homogeneous strata, the sampling error at this stage will be reduced. The primary goal of stratification, as before, is homogeneity.

There is no reason why stratification could not take place at each level of sampling. The elements listed within a selected cluster might be stratified prior to the next stage of sampling. Typically, however, this is not done. (Recall the assumption of relative homogeneity within clusters.)

Probability Proportionate to Size (PPS) Sampling

Thus far we have spoken in a general way about the assignment of sample elements to selected clusters: how many clusters should be selected, how many elements within each cluster. This section discusses in greater detail two options available to the researcher.

To insure the overall selection of a representative sample of elements, the researcher should give each element in the total population an equal chance of selection. The simplest way to accomplish this in a cluster sample would be to give each cluster the same chance of selection and to select a given *proportion* of elements from each selected cluster. Thus with a population of 100,000 elements grouped in 1,000 clusters (of varying sizes) and a total sample target of 1,000 elements, the researcher might select one-tenth of the clusters (100) with equal probability and subselect one-tenth of the elements in each of the clusters initially chosen. In this fashion approximately 1,000 elements would be selected and each element in the population would have had the same $(1/10 \times 1/10 = 1/100)$ probability of selection. While this type of sample selection technique is the clearest and simplest, it is not the most efficient.

Most cluster sampling involves clusters of grossly different sizes (in numbers of elements). The religion researcher finds very large churches and very small ones. The population researcher finds city blocks containing many people and blocks containing very few. Moreover, it is often the case that the small clusters outnumber the large ones, although the large ones may account for a large proportion of the total population. Thus a few, very large, city blocks may contain a large proportion of a city's population, while the large number of small blocks actually contain only a small proportion of the population.

The selection of clusters with equal probability, with a fixed proportion of elements being taken from the selected clusters, will result in the following situation. (1) A relatively small number of large clusters would be selected in the first stage of sampling. (2) The elements selected to represent all elements in large clusters would be drawn from very few such clusters. In the extreme, then, all of a city's population residing on 10 large city blocks might be represented by a people living in only one of those blocks.

An earlier section on cluster sampling discussed the greater efficiency inherent in the selection of many clusters with few elements being drawn from each of those clusters. This principle is put into practice through the method of *probability proportionate to size* (PPS) sampling. This method provides for the selection of more clusters, insures the representation of elements contained in large clusters, and also gives each element in the population an equal chance of selection.

In the first stage of sampling, each cluster is given a chance of selection proportionate to its size (in number of elements). Large clusters have a better chance of selection than small ones. In the second stage of sampling, however, the same *number* of elements are chosen from each selected cluster. The effect of these two procedures is to equalize the ultimate probabilities of selection of all elements, since elements in large clusters stand a poorer chance of selection *within* their cluster than those in small clusters. For example, a city block containing 100 households will have 10 times the chance of selection as a block containing only 10 households. However, if both blocks are selected, and the same number of households is selected from each, households on the large block will have only 1/10 the chance of selection of those on the small one. The following formula indicates a given element's probability of selection in a PPS sample design.

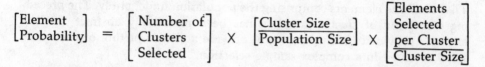

$$\begin{bmatrix} \text{Element} \\ \text{Probability} \end{bmatrix} = \begin{bmatrix} \text{Number of} \\ \text{Clusters} \\ \text{Selected} \end{bmatrix} \times \begin{bmatrix} \dfrac{\text{Cluster Size}}{\text{Population Size}} \end{bmatrix} \times \begin{bmatrix} \dfrac{\text{Elements} \\ \text{Selected} \\ \text{per Cluster}}{\text{Cluster Size}} \end{bmatrix}$$

If 100 clusters are selected and 10 elements are selected from each of those out of a total population of 100,000, the overall probability of selection for each element will be 1,000/100,000 or 1/100. In a cluster containing 100 elements, that cluster has a probability of selection equal to 100 (clusters to be selected) times 100/100,000 (cluster size/population size) or 1/10; each element has a chance of 10/100 (elements per cluster/cluster size) or 1/10 of being selected *within* that cluster; the element's overall chance of selection in this case is 1/10 times 1/10 or 1/100. For a cluster containing only 10 elements, that cluster's probability of selection is 100 times 10/100,000 or 1/100, but each element's chance of selection within the cluster is 10/10 or 1, making the overall chance of selection equal to 1/100.

Regardless of the number of elements in a cluster, then, each element has the same probability of selection ultimately. This may be seen more clearly in the formula when we note that cluster size appears in both the numerator and the denominator and may be cancelled out: the probability of selection then becomes the number of clusters to be chosen times the number of elements to be chosen from each selected cluster, divided by the population size. This is, of course, the sample size divided by the population size.

Two modifications are typically made in this PPS sample design. First, the researcher may feel it is imperative that *very* large clusters be represented in the sample; he may wish to insure that all city blocks (or churches) with more than, say, 1,000 elements be included in the sample. In such a case, he may select all those clusters in the beginning (with a probability of 1.0) and the elements in those clusters should be given a probability equal to the overall sampling ratio. In the previous example, 1/100 of the elements on each of the large blocks might be selected.

The second modification concerns small clusters. If a standard number of elements is to be selected from each of the clusters chosen, clusters containing fewer elements than that standard number present a problem. If the target is 10 households from each selected city block, what will he do with blocks containing five households? The usual solution to this problem is to combine small clusters so that each combination contains at least the standard number to be selected. (If the clusters are stratified, combinations should be accomplished within strata. Similarly, small clusters may be attached to larger ones if this procedure will insure a greater homogeneity within the combined cluster.) The example of an area cluster sample in Chapter 6 indicates the necessity of taking this step to insure the consideration of blocks believed to have no households on them.

By way of summary, cluster sampling is a difficult though important sampling method—it may be required whenever it is impossible to compile a list of all the elements comprising the population under study. The preceding discussion of cluster sampling has been regrettably abstract, but the example provided in Chapter 6 will provide a clearer picture of the actual steps involved in a complex sample selection.

5.7   Disproportionate Sampling and Weighting

Ultimately, a probability sample is representative of a population if all elements in the population have an equal chance of selection in that sample. Thus, in each of the preceding discussions we have noted that the various sampling procedures result in an equal chance of selection—even though the ultimate selection probability is the product of several partial probabilities.

More generally, however, a probability sample is one in which each population element has a *known nonzero* probability of selection—even though different elements may have different probabilities. If controlled, probability sampling procedures have been used, any such sample may be representative of the population from which it is drawn if each sample element is assigned a weight equal to the inverse of its probability of selection. Thus, where all sample elements have had the same chance of selection, each is given the same weight: 1. (This is called a "self-weighting" sample.)

Disproportionate sampling and weighting come into play in two basic ways. First, the researcher may sample subpopulations disproportionately to insure sufficient numbers of cases from each for analysis. For example, a given city may have a suburban area containing one-fourth of its total population. Yet the researcher may be especially interested in a detailed analysis of households in that area and may feel that one-fourth of this total sample size would be too few. As a result, he may decide to select the same number of households from the suburban area as from the remainder of the city. Households in the suburban area, then, are given a disproportionately better chance of selection than those located elsewhere in the city.

As long as the researcher analyzes the two area samples separately or comparatively, he need not worry about the differential sampling. If he wishes to combine the two samples to create a composite picture of the entire city, however, he must take the disproportionate sampling into account. If n is the number of households selected from each area, then the households in the suburban area had a chance of selection equal to n divided by one-fourth of the total city population. Since the total city population and the sample size are the same for both areas, the suburban-area households should be given a weight of $1/4n$ while the remaining households should be given a weight of $3/4n$. This weighting procedure could be simplified by merely giving a weight of 3 to each of the households selected outside the suburban area. (This procedure would give a *proportionate* representation to each sample element. The population figure would have to be included in the weighting if population estimates were desired.)

Disproportionate sampling and weighting procedures are sometimes used in situations involving the errors and approximation that are often inherent in complex, multistage sampling. This will be discussed in some detail in the example of an area cluster sample in Chapter 6, but it is appropriate to list here the basic conditions under which weighting is often required.

1. In stratified *cluster sampling, a given number of clusters may be selected from each stratum, although the sizes of the different strata will vary. Differential weighting may be used to adjust for these variations.*

2. A given cluster may be selected in a PPS sample design on the basis of its expected or estimated size, but a field investigation may later indicate the initial estimate was in error. Thus the cluster was given a disproportionately high or low chance of selection, and weighting may be used to adjust for that error.

3. A sample design may call for the selection of one-tenth of the elements in a cluster, but the cluster might contain 52 elements, only five of which are selected for study. Weighting can be used to adjust for the .2 element which logically could not be selected.

4. Ten elements might have been selected for study within a cluster, but two of these could not be studied (for example, refused to be interviewed). Assuming homogeneity within the cluster, the researcher might assign a weight of 1.25 to each of the studied elements to make up for the two that were not studied.

All of these uses of weighting will be illustrated in the final sampling example of Chapter 6. With the exception of case 4 above, however, the researcher can derive his own weighting procedure by carefully determining the probability of selection—step-by-step—for each sample element and assigning a weight equal to the inverse of that probability. Three further comments should be made before moving on from the topic of weighting.

Degrees of Precision in Weighting

In any complex sample design, the researcher faces a number of options with regard to weighting in connection with purposively and/or inadvertently disproportionate sampling. He may compute weights for each element to several decimal places, or he may assign rough weights to account for only the grossest instances of disproportionate sampling. In the previous case of the city in which the suburban area was oversampled, it is unlikely that the population of that area comprised exactly one-fourth of the city's population: suppose it actually comprised .25001, .2600, or .2816 of the total population. In the first instance, it seems quite likely that the researcher would choose to apply the rough overall weighting of cases described if no other disproportionate sampling were involved at other stages in the sample design. Perhaps he would do the same in the second and third instances as well. The precision he will seek in weighting should be commensurate with the precision he desires in his findings. If his research purposes can tolerate errors of a few percentage points, he will probably not waste his time and effort in weighting exactly. In deciding the degree of precision required, moreover, he should take into account the degree of error to be expected from normal sampling distribution, plus all the various types of nonsampling error.

Ultimately, there is no firm guideline for the researcher to follow in determining the precision to be sought in weighting. As in so many other aspects of survey design, he is afforded considerable latitude. At the same time, however, he should bear his decision in mind when reporting his findings. He should not employ only a rough weighting procedure and then suggest that his findings are accurate within a minuscule range of error.

Methods for Weighting

Having outlined the scientific concerns for determining the degree of precision desired in weighting, it should be noted that the choice will often be made on the basis of available methods for weighting. There are three basic methods for weighting.

1. *For the rough weighting of samples drawn from subpopulations, weighted tables can be constructed from the unweighted tables for each of the subsamples. In   the*

earlier example, the researcher could create a raw table of distributions for the suburban sample and for the nonsuburban sample separately, triple the number of cases in each cell of the nonsuburban table, add the cases across the two tables, and compute percentages for the composite table.

2. For more extensive and faster, though still rough, weighting, IBM cards can be mechanically reproduced for those cases requiring weights. In the previous example two additional copies of each card relating to a nonsuburban household could be made (for a total of three each), the enlarged nonsuburban file could then be combined with the suburban file, and the entire card file could be analyzed as though three times as many nonsuburban households had been studied.

3. If the data are to be analyzed by computer, a special program may be designed to assign a precise weight to each case in the original data file. Only this latter method is appropriate to refined weighting, since it is impossible to reproduce fractions of IBM cards with any meaning.

As mentioned at the outset of this section, scientific concerns in weighting are usually subjugated to practical concerns in this instance as in others. If the analysis is to be conducted through IBM cards only, weighting must of necessity be approximate rather than precise.

Weighting and Statistical Inference

The reader should be advised that the weighting procedures described in this section have serious effects on most computations related to statistical inference. Researchers whose research purposes require precise statistical inferences (for example, population estimates) on the basis of carefully weighted data should consult a special source[6] on this matter or, better yet, should consult a sampling statistician *before the sample is designed.*

Probability Sampling in Overview

The preceding, lengthy and detailed, discussion has been devoted to the key sampling method utilized in controlled survey research: probability sampling. In each of the variations examined, we have seen that elements are chosen for study from a population on a basis of random selection with known nonzero probabilities.

Depending on the field situation, probability sampling can be very simple, or it can be extremely difficult, time-consuming, and expensive. Whatever the situation, however, it remains the most effective method for the selection of study elements. There are two reasons for this.

---

[6]For example, Kish, op. cit.

First, probability sampling avoids conscious or unconscious biases in element selection on the part of the researcher. If all elements in the population have an equal (or unequal and subsequently weighted) chance of selection, there is an excellent chance that the sample so selected will closely represent the population of all elements.

Second, probability sampling permits estimates of sampling error. While no probability sample will be perfectly representative in all respects, controlled selection methods permit the researcher to estimate the degree of expected error in that regard.

Having discussed probability sampling at some length, we shall turn now to a briefer examination of some popular methods of nonprobability sampling.

5.8   Nonprobability Sampling

Despite the accepted superiority of probability sampling methods in survey research, nonprobability methods are sometimes used instead—usually for situations in which probability sampling would be prohibitively expensive and/or when precise representativeness is not necessary. The primary methods of nonprobability sampling are described briefly below.

Purposive or Judgmental Sampling

Occasionally it may be appropriate for the researcher to select his sample on the basis of his own knowledge of the population, its elements, and the nature of his research aims. Especially in the initial design of his questionnaire, he might wish to select the widest variety of respondents to test the broad applicability of questions. While the survey findings would not represent any meaningful population, the test run might effectively uncover any peculiar defects in his research instrument. This situation would be referred to as a pre-test, however, rather than a survey proper.

In some instances, the researcher may wish to study a small subset of a larger population in which many members of the subset are easily identified but the enumeration of all would be nearly impossible. For example, he might want to study the leadership of a student protest movement; many of the leaders are easily visible, but it would not be feasible to define and sample all leaders. In studying all or a sample of the most visible leaders, he may collect data sufficient for his purposes.

In a multistage sample design, the researcher may want to compare left-wing and right-wing students. As he may not be able to enumerate and sample from all such students, he might decide to sample the memberships of Students for a Democratic Society and Young Americans for Freedom.

While such a sample design would not provide a good description of either left-wing or right-wing students as a whole, it might suffice for general comparative purposes.

Selected Precinct Sampling. Sampling of selected precincts for political polls is a somewhat refined judgmental process. On the basis of previous voting results in a given area (city, state, nation), the researcher purposively selects a group of voting precincts that, in combination, produces results similar to those of the entire area. Then, in subsequent polls, he selects his samples solely from those precincts. The theory is, of course, that the selected precincts provide a cross section of the entire electorate.

Each time there is an election that permits the researcher to evaluate the adequacy of his group of precincts, he considers revisions, additions, or deletions. His goal is to update his group of precincts to insure that it will provide a good representation of all precincts.

To be done effectively, selected precinct sampling requires considerable political expertise. The researcher should be well versed in the political and social history of the area under consideration so that the selection of precincts is based on an *educated* guess as to its persistent representativeness. In addition, this system of sampling requires continuing feedback to be effective. The researcher must be in a position to conduct frequent polls and must have periodic electoral validations.

Quota Sampling

As mentioned in an earlier section, quota sampling begins with a matrix describing the characteristics of the target population. The researcher must know what proportion of the population is male and what proportion female, for example; and for each sex, what proportion falls into various age categories, and so forth. In establishing a national quota sample, he must know what proportion of the national population is say, urban, Eastern, male, under 25, white, working class, and the like, and all the other permutations of such a matrix.

Once such a matrix has been created and a relative proportion assigned to each cell in the matrix, the researcher collects data from persons having all the characteristics of a given cell. All the persons in the given cell are then assigned a weight appropriate to their portion of the total population. When all the sample elements are so weighted, the overall data should provide a reasonable representation of the total population.

There are a number of inherent problems in quota sampling. First, the quota frame (the proportions that different cells represent) must be accurate, and it is often difficult to get up-to-date information for this purpose. The

Gallup failure to predict Truman as the presidential victor in 1948 was due partly to this problem.

Second, biases may exist in the selection of sample elements within a given cell—even though its proportion of the population is accurately estimated. An interviewer, instructed to interview five persons meeting a given, complex set of characteristics, may still avoid persons living at the top of seven-story walk-ups, persons having particularly run-down homes and/or vicious dogs.

In recent years, attempts have been made to combine probability and quota sampling methods, but the effectiveness of this effort remains to be seen. At present, the researcher would be advised to treat quota sampling warily.

Reliance on Available Subjects

Stopping people at a street corner or some other location is almost never an adequate sampling method, although it is employed all too frequently. It would be justified only if the researcher wanted to study the characteristics of people passing the sampling point at specified times.

University researchers frequently conduct surveys among the students enrolled in large lecture classes. The ease and inexpense of such a method explains its popularity, but it seldom produces data of any general value. It may serve the purpose of a pre-test of a questionnaire, but such a sampling method should not be used for a study purportedly describing students as a whole.

5.9   Nonsurvey Uses of Sampling Methods

In the preceding discusssions of sampling logic and methods, we have focused, appropriately, on survey research: selecting elements from a population for interviewing or self-administered questionnaires. The basic logic of sampling, however, gives the preceding discussions a more generalized value for the social researcher using other data collection methods. It might be useful to close this chapter with some brief comments on the nonsurvey uses of sampling methods.

Content Analysis

A content analyst codifies and analyzes documents for the purpose of making descriptive or explanatory assertions about the literature comprised of the documents, the author(s) of the documents, and/or the social milieu of which the documents are a part. He may analyze a nation's newspapers, a novelist's works of fiction, the language of legislative bills, and so forth.

Often the volume of documents to be analyzed is too great for complete coverage. In such a case, the sampling techniques discussed in this chapter could easily be adapted to the situation. The sampling units might be individual words, sentences, paragraphs, articles, books, and so forth. The sampling units could be stratified in any appropriate manner, and random, systematic, or even cluster samples could be selected.

Laboratory Experiments

Subjects for laboratory experiments are often selected from among volunteers responding to an advertisement. Sometimes the experimental design will call for matching of subjects in the experimental and control groups. In some cases, quotas will be set for different types of subjects.

Whenever the number of potential subjects greatly exceeds the number required for the experiment, standard sampling techniques might be used. Stratification methods could be used as an aid in filling quota requirements.

Participant Observation

Unlike survey researchers, participant observers typically attempt to immerse themselves in the totality of the phenomenon under study. They may attempt to observe all major events taking place, speak to as many participants as possible, and so forth. It should be obvious, however, that no one can observe everything; some selectivity is inevitable. To the extent that such selectivity is uncontrolled, the researcher runs the risk of amassing a biased set of observations, just as the inept survey researcher may select a bias sample of respondents.

While it is not suggested that all participant observers everywhere in every research setting should attempt to establish rigorous sampling methods, I am convinced that a participant observer well versed in the logic, and perhaps some of the methods, of survey sampling will be more likely to obtain a representative set of observations. In assessing the mood of students assembled for a protest demonstration, he will caution himself against speaking only with the demonstration leaders, he will consider the possible difference between students seemingly attending alone and those attending with friends, he will perhaps speak with students at different locations in the gathering, and he might be careful to speak with early arrivers and late comers. While he will probably not be able to stratify his sample of respondents in a rigorous fashion, I suspect he might be more sensitive to noting any differences related to such variables and would refine his observations accordingly.

Summary

This rather lengthy chapter has attempted to familiarize the reader with the major considerations in the logic of survey sampling and with the most common sampling techniques. Clearly, this discussion will not be sufficient to equip the researcher for every field condition that he will face, but I hope that an understanding of the logic of sampling will make it possible for him to make reasonable and sound judgments on his own.

The following chapter describes four survey samples with which I am intimately familiar. By presenting the specific details of these rather different sample designs and the several decisions that went into their execution, I hope to give the reader some concrete experiences in sampling. Again, these examples cannot exhaust the field situations that readers may later face, but the particular sample designs have been chosen to represent the most common sampling situations found in survey research.

Additional Readings

Cochran, William G., *Sampling Techniques* (New York: John Wiley & Sons, Inc., 1963).

Hansen, M. H., W. N. Hurwitz, and W. G. Madow, *Sample Survey Methods and Theory, 2 Vols.* (New York: John Wiley & Sons, Inc., 1953).

Kish, Leslie, *Survey Sampling* (New York: John Wiley & Sons, Inc., 1965).

Chapter Six

Examples of Sample Designs

Chapter 5 presented the basic logic of survey sampling and outlined some of the procedural options available to the researcher. This chapter will present four case studies of sample designs, representing different sampling situations and designs.

The first example is a stratified systematic sample of students attending the University of Hawaii during the fall 1968 semester. The second example is a cluster sample of medical school faculty members, with the primary sampling units selected with equal probability. The third concerns a cluster sample of Episcopal women in northern California, using a PPS (probability proportionate to size) design for primary sampling unit selection. The final example is a complex area sample designed for a household survey in Oakland, California, in 1966.

6.1 Sampling University Students

The purpose of this study was to survey, with a self-administered instrument, a representative cross section of students attending the main campus of the University of Hawaii in 1968. The following sections will describe the steps and decisions involved in selecting that sample.

Survey Population and Sampling Frame

The obvious sampling frame available for use in this sample selection was the magnetic registration tape maintained by the university administration. The tape contained students' names, local and permanent addresses, social security numbers, and a variety of other information such as field of study, class, age, sex, and so forth.

The registration tape, however, contains files on all persons who could, by any conceivable definition, be called students, many of whom seemed inappropriate to the purposes of the study. As a result, it was necessary to define the *survey population* in a somewhat more restricted fashion. The final definition included those 15,225 day program degree candidates registered for the fall 1968 semester on the Manoa campus of the university, including all colleges and departments, both undergraduate and graduate students, and both American and foreign students. The computer program used for sampling, therefore, limited consideration to students fitting this definition.

Stratification

The sampling program also permitted the stratification of students prior to sample selection. In this instance, it was decided that stratification by college class would be sufficient, although the students might have been further stratified within class if desired, by sex, college, major, and so forth.

Sample Selection

Once the students had been arranged by class (by the sampling program), a systematic sample was selected across the entire rearranged list. The sample size for the study was initially set at 1,100. To achieve this sample, the sampling program was set to employ a 1/14 sampling fraction. The program, therefore, generated a random number between 1 and 14; the student having that number, plus every fourteenth student thereafter were selected in the sample.

Once the sample had been selected in this fashion, the computer was instructed to print each student's name and mailing address on six self-adhesive mailing labels. These labels were then simply transferred to envelopes for mailing the questionnaires.

Sample Modification

The preceding describes the initial design of the sample for the study of university students. Prior to the mailing of questionnaires, it was discovered that unexpected expenses in the production of the questionnaires made it impossible to cover the costs of mailing to some 1,100 students. As a result, one-third of the mailing labels were systematically selected (with a random start) for exclusion from the sample. The final sample for the study was thereby reduced to about 770.

This modification to the sample is mentioned here to illustrate the frequent necessity to change aspects of the study plan in midstream. Since a systematic sample of students was omitted from the initial systematic sample, the resulting 770 students could still be taken as reasonably representing the survey population. The reduction in sample size did, of course, increase the range of sampling error.

6.2   Sampling Medical School Faculty

This section reports the sample design employed to select a sample of medical school faculty members for a national survey on the effects of scientific orientations on humane patient care. The study design called for a national sample of medical school faculty members in the departments of medicine and pediatrics.

Under ideal conditions, the researcher would have obtained or constructed a single list of all faculty members in the two departments and would have selected his sample from that list. Unfortunately, no such list appeared to exist, so the decision was made to select a two-stage cluster sample. In the first stage, a sample of medical schools would be selected; then faculty members would be selected from each of those schools.

The sample design was hampered by unavailable data from the very beginning. The study design called for an examination of both full-time and part-time faculty members. While there were approximately 3,700 full-time faculty in the two departments nationally at the time of the study, there were no good data concerning the numbers of part-time faculty. An analysis of existing data, however, suggested that the total number of both full-time and part-time faculty was around 12,000. For the purposes of the study, it was decided that a sample of 2,000 would be sufficient (an overall sampling fraction of 1/6).

The Selection of Medical Schools

At the time of the study, there were 84 four-year medical schools belonging to the Association of American Medical Colleges. These schools comprised the survey population of schools. The schools were arranged into geographical strata, and they were then arranged by size (number of students) within strata.

The stratified list of schools was numbered from 1 to 84, and a random number was selected between 1 and 6 (the sampling interval). The school having the number so selected, and every sixth school thereafter was selected at the first stage of sampling. Letters were then sent to the deans of the selected schools, explaining the purpose of the survey and asking their assistance in getting a list of the faculty members in their departments of medicine and pediatrics.

Fourteen medical schools were initially selected. Not all deans were willing to cooperate with the study, however. As refusals were received, an alternative school for each was selected from the list: a school adjacent to the refusal was chosen through the toss of a coin.

Faculty Member Selection

As soon as medical school deans agreed to cooperate with the survey, lists were compiled of all the faculty members in the departments of medicine and pediatrics at each school. All such faculty were included in the final sample and were mailed survey questionnaires.

It should be noted that this sample design was not the best one which might have been employed. The entire sample of faculty members was selected from relatively few schools. A better design would have selected more schools, with fewer faculty selected from each. For example, one-third of the schools might have been selected with half the faculty at each studied.

The actual sample design was prompted by administrative rather than scientific concerns. A pilot study in the project had shown the difficulty of gaining approval and cooperation from deans. Even when a dean agreed to cooperate with the study, he might be rather slow in providing a list of faculty members. The main bottleneck in sampling came at this point. Increasing the number of schools would directly increase the time and problems involved in the overall sample selection. For this reason alone, the decision was made to take one-sixth of the schools and all the appropriate faculty at each.

6.3   Sampling Episcopal Churchwomen

The purpose of this study was to examine the attitudes of women members of churches in a diocese of the Episcopal Church. A representative sample of all churchwomen in the diocese was desired. As the reader will by now expect, there was no single list of such women, so a multistage sample design was created. In the initial stage of sampling, churches would be selected, and then women would be selected from each. Unlike the medical school sample, the church sample was selected with *probability proportionate to size* (PPS).

Selecting the Churches

The diocese in question publishes an annual report that contains a listing of the 100 or so churches comprising it with their respective sizes, in terms of membership. This listing constituted the sampling frame for the first stage of sampling.

A total of approximately 500 respondents were desired for the study, so the decision was made to select 25 churches with probability proportionate to size and take 20 women from each of those selected. To accomplish this, the list of churches was arranged geographically, and then a table was created similar to the partial listing shown in Table 6-1.

Table 6-1. Form Used in Listing of Churches

Church	Membership	Cumulative Membership
Church A	3,000	3,000
Church B	5,000	8,000
Church C	1,000	9,000

Beside each church in the table, its membership was entered and that figure was used to compute a cumulative total running through the list. The final total came to approximately 200,000. The object at this point was to select a sample of 25 churches in such a way that each would have a chance of selection proportionate to the number of members in it. To accomplish this, the cumulative totals were used to create ranges of numbers for each church equaling the number of members in that church. Church A in the table above was assigned the numbers 1 through 3,000; Church B was assigned 3,001 through 8,000; Church C was assigned 8,001 through 9,000; and so forth.

By selecting 25 numbers ranging between 1 and 200,000, it would be possible to select 25 churches for the study. The 25 numbers were selected in a systematic sample as follows. The sampling interval was set at 8,000 (200,000/25) and a random start was selected between 1 and 8,000. Let us say the random number was 4,538. Since that number fell within the range of numbers assigned to Church B (3,001–8,000), Church B was selected.

Increments of 8,000 (the sampling interval) were then added to the random start, and every church within whose range one of the resultant numbers appeared was selected into the sample of churches. It should be apparent that in this fashion, each church in the diocese had a chance of selection directly proportionate to its membership size. A church with 4,000 members had twice the chance of selection as a church of 2,000 and 10 times the chance of selection as one with only 400 members.

Selecting the Churchwomen

Once the sample of churches was selected, arrangements were made to get lists of the women members of each. It is worth noting here that in practice the lists varied greatly in their form and content. In a number of cases, lists of all members (men and women) were provided, and it was necessary to sort out the women before sampling the lists. The form of the lists varied from typed lists to 3 x 5 cards printed from addressograph plates.

As the list arrived from a selected church, a sampling interval for that church was computed on the basis of the number of women members and the number desired (20). If a church contained 2,000 women, the sample interval, therefore, was set at 100. A random number was selected and incremented by the sampling interval to select the sample of women from that church. This procedure was repeated for each church.

Note that this sample design ultimately gives every woman in the diocese an equal chance of selection *only* if the assumption that half the members of each church are women (or if a constant proportion of them are). This is due to the fact that churches were given a chance of selection based on their *total* membership (numbers of women were not available). Given the aims of this particular study, the slight inequities of selection were considered insignificant.

A more sophisticated sample design for the second stage would have resolved this possible problem. Since each church was given a chance of selection based on an assumed number of women (assuming 1,000 women in a church of 2,000), the sampling interval could have been computed on the basis of that assumption rather than on the actual number of women listed. If it was assumed in the first stage of sampling that a church had 1,000 women (assuming 1,000 women in a church of 2,000), the sampling interval could have been computed on the basis of that assumption rather than on the actual number of women listed. If it was assumed in the first stage of sampling that a church had 1,000 women (out of a membership of 2,000), the sampling interval could have been set at 50 (1,000/20). Then this interval could have been used in the selection of respondents regardless of the actual number of women listed for that church. If 1,000 women were in fact listed, then their church had the proper chance of selection and 20 women would be selected from it. If 1,200 women were listed, this would mean that the church had too small a chance of selection, but this would have been remedied through the selection of 24 women using the preestablished sampling interval. If only 800 women were listed, on the other hand, only 16 would have been selected.

6.4   Sampling Oakland Households

This final example represents one of the most complex sample designs typical of survey research: an *area cluster sample.* The purpose of this study, conducted in 1966, was to collect data relevant to the study of poverty in the poorer areas of Oakland, California, using the remainder of the city for purposes of comparison. Since the findings of the survey were to be used, in part, to support requests for federal funding for Oakland, it was essential that the data collected provided an accurate description of the city.

For purposes of the study, the city was divided into seven areas; four were officially designated poverty areas, while the remaining three were tradition-

ally viewed as distinct sections of the city. The total sample size for the city
was set at 3,500 households on the basis of computations whose complexity
exceeds the scope of this book. It is worth noting, however, that the determination of the sample size began with policy discussion concerning the
"chance" city officials were willing to take that the survey would—through
normal sampling error—underestimate poverty and unemployment levels
sufficiently to disqualify the city in its request for funding. If these levels
were, in fact, high enough to warrant the award of funds, then a perfectly
accurate sample would demonstrate this fact. With a small sample, however,
the range of sampling error opened the possibility of underestimation. As the
sample size was increased, of course, the chance of this underestimation was
reduced. It was in this manner, then, that the ultimate sample size of 3,500
was established. (*Note:* This is the way sample sizes *should* be established.)

Since the study called for the comparison of all seven areas of the city
with one another, it was important that all areas be described with equal
degrees of accuracy. Therefore the sample was designed so as to select 500
households from each area even though they differed greatly in their total
numbers of households. The remainder of this discussion will be devoted to
the sample selection procedures used in only one of the seven areas, since the
procedures were essentially replicated for each.

General Considerations

As noted above, an area cluster sample was designed for
the study. At the first stage of sampling, a stratified sample of census blocks
was to be selected with probability proportionate to size. Blocks selected in
this manner were to be listed: enumerators would visit each selected block
physically and prepare lists of all the households found there. Then a systematic sample of five households was to be selected from each of those blocks.

As noted in the preceding chapter, five households per block is a common
convention in area cluster sampling. Both sampling theory and survey experience suggest that five households represents the point of diminishing returns
in the description of blocks. Five households will provide a reasonably accurate description of a given block, due to the homogeneity typically found
among households on a single block. While six households, of course, provide
a more accurate description of that block, this advantage would be more than
offset by the corresponding decrease in the accuracy of the sample of blocks
selected in describing the population of all blocks. (This assumes that the total
survey sample size is fixed.) To illustrate this point in the extreme, the
researcher could limit his sample to all those households found on a single
block; this would provide a perfectly accurate description of that block, but
the block in itself would not provide a very accurate description of all blocks
and, by extension, of all households in the city.

Since 500 households were to be selected from each area of the city, this meant that 100 blocks would be selected, with five households taken from each. Moreover, to permit rigorous analyses of the variance in descriptions of households, it was decided to organize the blocks into relatively homogeneous strata and to select two blocks from each stratum. Thus, the initial task in each area was to create 50 strata, then two blocks would be selected from each and, finally, five households would be selected from each block—making the total of 500 households in the area.

The First-Stage Sampling Frame

Two kinds of data were required for describing census blocks. Most importantly, it was necessary to know approximately how many households there were on each of the blocks so that a PPS block sample could be selected. For purposes of stratification, however, it was also necessary to know certain relevant characteristics about the blocks, such as their racial composition and socioeconomic levels.

Both kinds of data were available to the research team in the form of the 1960 United States census block statistics. This file indicated the 1960 size of all blocks (in numbers of housing units) and also provided such variable descriptions as (1) percent nonwhite, (2) percent renter-occupied, (3) percent deteriorating, and (4) value of the structures (either rent or valuation). Unfortunately, however, the study was being conducted six years after the census data had been collected, so it was anticipated that many of the housing counts would be out of date.

Before the sampling began, two months were spent examining city planning maps of each area. Housing units constructed or demolished since the 1960 census were noted, and these data were used to correct the estimated number of households per block. At the conclusion of this process, an IBM card was prepared for each census block in the city—showing its current expected size (in households) and the several characteristics compiled in the 1960 census (there was no way of updating these).

The following comments describe the sample selection procedures used in Poverty Area D, which had an estimated 9,938 households at the time of sampling. Since the sample target for the area was 500 households, the overall sampling fraction was 1/20.

Large Block Selection

Each of the areas of the city had some census blocks that contained very large numbers of households. Some of these were large blocks in geographical size, others contained several large apartment houses. Whereas the presence of these blocks might hinder the stratification techniques planned for the study, and since they were considered very important blocks for purposes of the study, an initial decision was made that every block containing 200 or more households would be automatically included in the sample. Each such block would be listed, and 1/20th (overall sampling ratio for the area) of the households listed would be selected for interviewing.

In Poverty Area D, the large blocks contained a total of 702 households. Therefore 35 households were to be selected from those blocks, leaving 465 to be selected from the remainder of the area.

Handling Small Blocks and Zero Blocks

Several blocks in Poverty Area D (and elsewhere) contained very few households, and some were estimated to contain none. These blocks presented a special problem. First, a block having an expected size of zero would have no chance of selection. If the estimates were incorrect and the block did in fact have households on it, then those households would have no chance of selection.

Second, since the basic sample design called for the selection of five households from each selected block, those having fewer than five would present a problem. Moreover, if the size estimates were incorrect, some blocks believed to contain more than five households might in fact have fewer.

To resolve these problems, each zero block and each block with an expected size of fewer than 10 was "attached" to an adjacent block. The number of households expected on the small block—if any—was added to the number for the adjacent block and the pair of blocks was treated as a single block for purposes of sampling. The pair had a chance of selection proportionate to their combined size, and if the pair was selected in the sample of blocks, both were listed and sampled as though they were a single block.

Stratification

Since 35 households were to be taken from the very large blocks, 465 were to be selected from the remainder of the area with its total of 9,236 estimated households. With five households to be taken from each sample block, 93 blocks would be required. And, since two blocks would be taken from each stratum, the task at this point was to create 47 (rounded from 46.5) strata.

Each of these strata—or groups of blocks—had to have two characteristics. First, the blocks in the stratum should be as similar to one another as possible, in terms of racial composition, SES (socioeconomic status), and so forth. This would insure that all types of blocks would be selected in their proper proportion for the total sample. Second, each of the strata should contain a total of approximately 200 households. Since 10 households were to be selected from each stratum (two blocks, five households from each), a stratum size of 200 would produce an ultimate sampling fraction of 1/20: the fraction established for the whole area. Of course, all the blocks contained specified numbers of households, so it was not possible to create strata containing *exactly* 200 households. (A later discussion will deal with the statistical correction for such variations.)

In creating homogeneity among the blocks grouped in a given stratum, it was possible to employ the block characteristics provided by the 1960 census. To avoid confusion in the following empirical descriptions, it should be noted that the creation of homogeneity was undertaken on a largely ad hoc and arbitrary basis. While one might be tempted to create a stratification format on theoretical grounds at the outset (for example, all blocks with more than 75 percent nonwhite residents, more than 50 percent renter-occupied, and with average monthly rent less than $150 would be combined into a stratum), such an approach would not necessarily be appropriate to the nature of the blocks being stratified. Instead, each group of blocks (comprising an area of the city or a subset thereof) was examined to determine the variations of their characteristics, and a stratification system was developed to suit those particular characteristics. This meant that different areas of the city were stratified differently; moreover, it should be recognized that the particular stratification format for a given area was only one of several, perhaps equally appropriate, possibilities.

As a general rule, however, the available stratification variables were considered in a set order for each area of the city: racial composition, percent renter/owner occupied, property value, and deterioration. To begin, then, an attempt was made to create relatively homogeneous groups of blocks in terms of racial composition. Each of those groups would then be subdivided into relatively homogeneous subgroups in terms of percentages occupied by renters or by owners, and so forth. Whenever this ordering of stratification variables was inappropriate to a given area, the inappropriate variables were simply ignored or considered at a different point in the stratification. For example, one area of the city of Oakland was, at the time of study, virtually all white. As a result, it made little sense to try stratifying the blocks in that area in terms of racial composition, even though it would have been possible to group together those blocks with *any* nonwhite residents. If, on the other hand, one small group of blocks in the area had, say, 20 percent or more nonwhite residents, these might have been put in a separate stratum.

As a general rule, however, the stratification variables were considered, and typically employed, in the order described above. Prior to the consideration of those variables, however, a somewhat different variable was used to divide each of the seven areas of the city for the first step of stratification.

When the updated IBM cards were created for each census block, a notation was made as to the number of housing units constructed subsequent to the 1960 census. Since it was felt that blocks containing new construction would differ from others, this datum was used as the first stratification variable. All those blocks in Poverty Area D containing any new units, then, were pulled out for separate stratification. Altogether these blocks contained an estimated 1,254 households. At 200 households per stratum, the "growth" blocks were to be grouped into six strata.

The second stratification variable used was racial composition. All the growth blocks were arranged in terms of the percentage nonwhite living in each. Some of the blocks were found to have 80 percent or more nonwhite residents. Taken together, these blocks contained 247 households. As this was relatively close to the target of 200 households per stratum, these blocks were designated as the first stratum.

The blocks containing between 30 and 79 percent nonwhite residents had a total of 385 households, so it was decided to create two strata from these. The second stratification variable was the percentage of households occupied by renters (as opposed to owners). In the present case, those blocks with 36 percent or more of the households occupied by renters had a total of 214 households; the remaining 171 households were on blocks with less than 36 percent renters. These two groups of blocks were designated as the second and third strata. (*Note:* There is nothing intrinsically meaningful about the cutting point of 36 percent renters. The goal here was to create strata of equal size so the cutting point that accomplished the goal was used.)

Blocks having less than 30 percent nonwhite residents contained 622 households, calling for three strata. In examining these blocks in terms of all the stratification variables, it was discovered that one group of blocks had more than 10 percent of their households designated as "deteriorating" by the census. These blocks contained a total of 214 households. Whereas 10 percent deterioration is quite high in the context of all blocks, this group was designated as the fourth stratum.

The remaining blocks contained 408 households, calling for two strata. When renter-occupation was examined, it was discovered that those blocks with 86 percent or more renters contained 201 households, and these were designated as the fifth stratum. The blocks containing the remaining 207 households were designated the sixth stratum.

In view of the complexity of this procedure, Table 6-2 presents a schematic summary of the stratification of the growth blocks in Poverty Area D. The groups of blocks designated as strata are indicated by the notation S1, S2, and so forth.

Recall that the goal of stratification was to create relatively homogeneous groups of blocks. We might pause for a moment to note the characteristics that all the blocks in Stratum 5 have in common: (1) all are located in Poverty Area D of Oakland; (2) all have fewer than 200 households; (3) all have experienced a growth in households since 1960; (4) all have less than 36 percent nonwhite residents; (5) all have less than 10 percent of their structures deteriorating; and (6) all have more than 85 percent renters. The extreme homogeneity of this group of blocks should be apparent.

Table 6-2. Stratification of Growth Blocks in Poverty Area D

All Growth Blocks (1254hh*)	
80% or more nonwhite (247 hh)	S1
30–79% nonwhite (385hh)	
36% or more renters (214 hh)	S2
35% or less renters (171 hh)	S3
29% or less nonwhite (622 hh)	
10% or more deteriorating (214 hh)	S4
9% or less deteriorating (408 hh)	
86% or more renters (201 hh)	S5
85% or less renters (207 hh)	S6

Note: hh = household. This term has been used rather than the technically more correct term--dwelling unit--to assist the reader who is having his first contact with survey sampling. A dwelling unit is a room or set of rooms intended for the residential use of a person or a family; a household is the person or group of people residing in a dwelling unit.

The reader will do well to recognize that the above discussion is limited to the creation of six strata in Poverty Area D. Forty-one more strata were created in this fashion in the same area, and the whole process was replicated six more times for the other areas of the city. Using a desk calculator and a counter-sorter-puncher, the actual stratification required about 30 man hours of intensive work.

Block Selection within Strata

Two blocks were to be selected from each stratum with probabilities proportionate to their sizes. Stratum 1 in the previous example, containing 247 households, will be used to illustrate the procedure used in block selection.

Table 6-3. Block Selection Procedure

Census Tract	Census Block	Number of Households	Cumulative Total	Cumulative Range
27	18	12	12	1-12
27	5	30	42	13-42 (selected)
27	23	26	79	43-68
28	4	80	148	69-148
27	14	48	196	149-196 (selected)
28	2	51	247	197-247

Total hh/2 = 123.5; random number between 1 and 123.5 = 35; random number + total hh/2 = 158.5.

To begin, all the blocks (IBM cards) in Stratum 1 were shuffled to approximately "randomize" their order. Then, Table 6-3 was created from the household estimates for each block.

The first two columns in the table simply identify the blocks by census tract number and census block number (within the tract). The third column presents the estimated block sizes, followed by the cumulative total across the six blocks. The final column in the table presents the range of numbers assigned to each block on the basis of its size.

Since two blocks were to be selected, the cumulative total for the stratum (247) was divided by 2 (123.5). A random number (35) was then selected between 1 and 123.5. Block 27/5, with a range of 13–42, contained this random number, so it was selected into the sample of blocks. The random number was then added to 123.5. Block 27/14, with a range of 149–196, contained this new number (158.5), so it was the second block selected into the sample.

For this particular study, a computer program was prepared to carry out most of the steps described above. The IBM cards representing the blocks were grouped by strata. The computer read the cards in a given stratum, computed and printed the cumulative totals for that stratum, divided the total by 2 and printed that number, and finally generated and printed a random number between 1 and the half-total. The researcher then determined which blocks were to be included in the sample.

Household Selection within Blocks

The procedure described above resulted in the selection of approximately 700 census blocks throughout the city of Oakland. Five households (usually) were to be interviewed on each block. To accomplish this, maps were prepared to clearly identify each of the selected blocks, and enumerators were sent to prepare a list of all the households on each block. The lists were prepared through the use of standard forms and looked something like the example presented as Table 6-4.

To prepare the listing, the enumerator went to a designated corner of the block and proceeded to walk around it in a circle until returning to the starting point, entering on the form each household as it appeared. Each household, whether it was a single-family house, half a duplex, or an apartment, was entered separately. As it was entered on the list, each household was assigned a number in continuous serial order.

The listing process provided a new estimate of the number of households on each block. (Since enumerators could make mistakes in listing, this should still be regarded as an *estimate.*) However, we should recall that each block was selected on the basis of an earlier estimate of its size. To take account of discrepancies between these two estimates, the researchers employed a technique mentioned in the earlier discussion of sampling Episcopal churchwomen.

Table 6-4. Sample List Sheet

Hh Number	Street Name	Street Number	Apartment Number or Other Identification
01	Walnut St.	2301	
02	Walnut St.	2303A	Duplex
03	Walnut St.	2303B	
04	Tenth Ave.	(102?)	No number; brown house with hedge
05	Tenth Ave.	104	Apt. 101
06	Tenth Ave.	104	Apt. 102
07	Tenth Ave.	104	Apt. 201
⋮			
47	Ninth Ave.	103	
48	Ninth Ave.	101	

The sampling interval to be used in selecting households from a given block was computed on the basis of the earlier estimate of its size and the five households intended to be selected. If the block size had been estimated at 50 households, then the sampling interval was set at 10. This interval was used in household selection, even if the listed size of the block was larger or smaller. If the block contained 60 households instead of the estimated 50, 6 households were selected in the sample; if it contained only 40, then 4 were selected. (A more precise correction was also employed and this will be discussed shortly.)

The selection of households was accomplished by selecting a random number between 1 and the sampling interval. That random number was then incremented by the sampling interval, and the households listed beside those numbers in the list sheet were designated for interviewing.

When the initial estimates of block size were greatly inaccurate and when the procedures just outlined would produce only 1 or 2 sample households (or would produce more than 10), a different procedure was used. In such cases, an arbitrary number of households (no more than 10) was selected, and a note was made for separately weighting those interviews during the analysis. (See below.)

This completes the set of procedures used in the selection of some 3,500 households throughout the city of Oakland, California, in 1966. Including the updating of census block sizes and the listing of sample blocks, the whole process took about five months and a staff of approximately 20 people at its peak.

"Weighting" the Sample Households

In the simple sample design, each element in the population has the same probability of selection. As a result, the aggregated sample can be taken as representative of the population from which it was selected. If 2,000 respondents were selected from a population of 2,000,000, then each respondent would be taken to "represent" an additional 999 people who were not selected. To estimate the *number* of people in the population who have a given characteristic, we would multiply the number having that characteristic in our sample times 1,000. This *weight* is the inverse of respondents' probabilities of being selected into the sample. When all respondents have the same probability of selection, weighting is irrelevant except for estimating *numbers* in the population.

When respondents have different probabilities of selection, weighting becomes more important—relevant even in the computation of percentages. The Oakland study provides an example of the need for, and methods of, weighting sample elements in a complex sample design. No matter how complex the sample design, however, the basic principle still holds: a respondent's weight is the inverse of his probability of selection into the sample.

In computing a given respondent's overall probability of selection, we must recall that if several stages of sampling are employed with separate probabilities of selection at each stage, these probabilities must be multiplied by each other to determine the overall probability. If the respondent belongs to a group (church, block) that has a 1/10 chance of selection and he has a 1/10 chance of selection *within* that group, his overall probability of selection is 1/100.

In the computation of household weights for the Oakland sample, we must take into account two separate probabilities of selection: the probability of a block being selected and the probability of a household being selected within that block. These two probabilities would be computed as follows.

Block Probability: Each block had a probability of selection equal to its estimated size (EBS) divided by the size of the stratum (SS) times 2 (two blocks selected per stratum). We will write this as 2EBS/SS. Note that this formula takes account of the PPS sampling plus the variation in strata sizes. Block 27/5 in our earlier example had an estimated size of 30 households in a stratum containing 247; its probability of selection therefore was .2429.

Household Probability: Within a given block, each selected household had a probability of selection equal to the number selected on the block (n) divided by the actual number (ABS) listed for the whole block: n/ABS. If Block 27/5 was found in listing to have 34 households (instead of 30) and 5 of those were selected, each would have a probability of selection equal to .1471.

Overall Probability: Putting together the separate for-
mulas, we have the following: (2EBS)(n)/(SS)(ABS). For the example used
above, the overall probability of selection is .0357 or about 1/28. Note that
this probability is less than the target sampling fraction of 1/20 for Poverty
Area D. This is due to the fact that Stratum 1 had 247 households instead of
the target of 200, and Block 27/5 had 34 households instead of the 30 estimated. As a result, each of the five households selected on Block 27/5 had
a lesser probability of selection than had been intended intially.

Note, however, that if the estimated and actual block size were identical,
the probability formula would be reduced from (2EBS)(n)/(SS)(ABS) to
2n/SS, or twice the number of households selected divided by the number
of households in the stratum. And if the SS = 200, the target sampling
fraction of 1/20 would be achieved, since five households would have been
selected on the block.

Weighting the Households: All the differences in
probabilities of selection were taken care of in the assignment of weights
equal to the inverse of a household's overall probability of selection. In the
first example above, each of the households interviewed on Block 27/5 would
have been assigned a weight of 28. Each of those households would be
assumed to represent itself plus another 27 households in the city of Oakland.

Additional Weighting for Nonresponse: One final comment should be made. Surveys of this sort never succeed in interviewing *all*
the households initially selected in the sample. Some persons in the sample
will refuse to be interviewed, others will be unavailable.

In this particular study, an additional weight was assigned to households
to take account of such nonresponse. It was assumed that households that
could not be interviewed were more like those that had been interviewed on
the same block than any other possible estimate. As a result, each completed
interview was assigned a weight equal to the number of households selected
on that block divided by the number actually completed. If four out of five
were completed, each of the completed interviews received an additional
weight of 1.25. If all selected households were successfully interviewed, of
course, the additional weight was 1.

Summary and Conclusions

The preceding four examples of sample designs have
been presented to give the reader a more realistic picture of the sampling

situations that he is likely to face in practice. While these examples do not exhaust the range of variation in field conditions, study objectives, and sampling techniques, they illustrate the most typical ones. Hopefully, these examples will have illustrated the basic logic behind survey sampling and will better equip the reader to improvise wisely when faced with a novel problem.

Additional Readings

The following research reports provide reasonably detailed discussions of the sampling methods employed.

Almond, Gabriel, and Sidney Verba, *The Civic Culture* (Princeton, N.J.: Princeton University Press, 1963).

Babbie, Earl R., *Science and Morality in Medicine* (Berkeley: University of California Press, 1970).

Glock, Charles Y., and Rodney Stark, *Christian Beliefs and Anti-Semitism* (New York: Harper & Row, Publishers, 1966).

————, Benjamin B. Ringer, and Earl B. Babbie, *To Comfort and to Challenge* (Berkeley: University of California Press, 1967).

Stouffer, Samuel A., *Communism, Conformity, and Civil Liberties* (New York: John Wiley & Sons, Inc., 1966).

Chapter Seven

Conceptualization and Instrument Design

Scientific research aims at two primary goals: description and explanation. The researcher measures the empirical distribution of values on variables (description) and measures the associations between variables for purposes of explaining the distribution of values. Chapter 12 discusses the logical interconnections between description and explanation. The purpose of the present chapter is to lay the necessary prior groundwork by examining the logic and skills of descriptive measurement.

Whether working from a rigorously deduced theory or from a set of tentative suspicions or curiosities, the researcher at some point is faced with a set of unspecified, abstract concepts that he believes will assist his understanding of the world around him. In survey research, these concepts must be converted into questions in a questionnaire, thus permitting the collection of empirical data relevant to analysis.

This chapter begins with a few general notes regarding the logic of conceptualization and operationalization. Next, we shall consider the different types of data that may be collected by a survey. Finally, we shall turn to some of the techniques available for constructing good questions.

7.1 Logic of Conceptualization

Frequently the researcher is interested in studying such concepts as social class, alienation, prejudice, intellectual sophistication, and so forth. He may suspect that alienation decreases with rising social class. He may feel that intellectual sophistication reduces prejudice. Before he engages in his empirical research, however, these concepts may be only general ideas held by the researcher. He would undoubtedly be hard pressed to define precisely what any of these concepts means to him.

"Social status" is a frequently used concept in social research, yet its ultimate meaning is by no means clear. Different definitions of social class include the following elements: income, occupational prestige, education, wealth, power, traditional family status, moral valuation, and so forth. Probably no specific combination of these elements would produce a definition of social status that would fully satisfy any researcher, let alone all researchers.

Such unspecified concepts are often said to have a "richness of meaning," in that they contain a variety of elements, thereby summarizing a complex phenomenon. Although the term "social status" evokes different images in different researchers, those images are likely to seem important and meaningful. To permit rigorous, empirical research, however, such general concepts must be specified; they must be reduced to specific, empirical indicators. Inevitably, the *operationalization* of concepts is unsatisfying to researchers and to their audiences. Ultimately, concepts rich in meaning must be reduced to oversimplified, inevitably superficial, empirical indicators. Given the significance of this problem, a few additional comments are in order.

It is the position of this book that most concepts of interest to social researchers have *no* real meanings, no ultimate definitions. Social status is a good example for illustrating this point.

The general concept of social status is surely an old one. While the idea may not have been verbalized in abstract terms, the earliest organized men recognized that some of their numbers had greater social status than others. Some were more powerful, some were held in greater respect, some were granted greater authority over their fellows. The recognition of such differences has persisted throughout man's history. Max Weber drew out many of the implications of such differences. Karl Marx derived a theory of society based on such differences. W. Lloyd Warner and other American sociologists of the 1930s and 1940s noted the same differences among the residents of small towns, and they discovered that members of a community could identify those neighbors with greater or lesser social status.

The existence of status differences among members of a society is clear. Moreover, such differences seem important to an understanding of other aspects of society. In view of this, the term "social status" has been accepted as a summary notation for the phenomenon. But what does the term "social status" *really* mean? Since it is merely a summary term for denoting a general concept, it has no *ultimate meaning*. Social status, per se, does not exist except as a convenient notation for a variety of empirical observations. From this standpoint, then, no researcher can measure social status correctly or incorrectly, he can only make more or less useful measurements.

In this sense, then, scientists never collect data, *they create data*. This is essentially the same sentiment expressed by Whitehead when he wrote:

Nature gets credit which should in turn be reserved for ourselves; the rose for its scent; the nightingale for his song; and the sun for its radiance. The poets are entirely mistaken. They should address their lyrics to themselves, and should turn them into odes of self-congratulation on the excellency of the human mind. Nature is a dull affair, soundless, scentless, colourless; merely the hurrying of material, endlessly, meaninglessly.[1]

---

[1] Alfred North Whitehead, *Science in the Modern World* (New York: The Macmillan Company, 1925), p. 56.

When a survey researcher asks several questions and combines the answers to those questions into an index that he calls social class, he has *created* a measure of social class; in a real sense, he has *created* a social class ranking and grouping among his respondents. He has not simply tapped a grouping and ranking that already existed in a real sense.

Perhaps the measurement he has created will be useful. It may assist him in understanding the data at hand; it may be useful in the development of social theories involving social class. It is senseless to ask whether he has *really* measured social class in any ultimately valid sense, however, since the concept exists only in our minds.

The notion that researchers create data rather than collecting it is even more basic than the social status illustration suggests. In the earlier days of World War II, Hadley Cantril conducted two national surveys of the American people.[2] The design of the samples and the cross-checking of their characteristics indicated that both provided good estimates of the United States population. In one of the surveys, respondents were asked: "Do you think that the United States will succeed in staying out of the war?" Most (55 percent of those with an opinion) said "yes." In the other survey, respondents were asked: "Do you think the United States will go into the war before it is over?" Most (59 percent of those with an opinion) said "yes."

These items are often cited as an example of the effects of "biased" questions. Whenever the example is presented to students, however, they typically ask, "Which question provided the correct answer regarding American expectations about our getting into the war?" There is no answer to this question; the question cannot be answered. We can only conclude that in 1939, there was no such thing as "the American attitude on the likelihood of our getting into the war." There was no percentage representing the proportion who *really* thought we would enter the war. Thus, the researcher could not *collect* such data, he could only create it by asking questions, and those questions largely determined the answers received.

In a very real sense, then, the researcher can never make *accurate* measurements, only *useful* ones. This should not be taken as a justification for scientific anarchy, however. Rigorous research is still possible; it is simply more difficult than might have been imagined. The remainder of this chapter is devoted to the logic and skills of making useful measurements.

7.2   An Operationalization Framework

As the preceding discussion has indicated, concepts are general codifications of experience and observations. We observe people living in different types of residential structures and develop the concept of

---

[2]Reported in Claire Selltiz, *et al.*, *Research Methods in Social Relations* (New York: Rinehart & Winston, Inc., 1959), p. 564.

dwelling unit. We note differences in social standing and develop the concept of social status. We note differences in the degree of religious commitment among people and develop the concept of religiosity. It is imperative to recognize, however, that all such concepts are summary notations for experience and observations.

Often in science, such concepts take the form of *variables:* bringing together a collection of related attributes. Thus, the concept "sex" summarizes two distinct attributes: male and female. College class is a variable made up of the attributes freshman, sophomore, junior, senior, graduate student. Religious affiliation might include such attributes as Protestant, Catholic, Jew, Buddhist, and so forth.

Most of the more interesting concepts in science represent *ordinal variables* made up of values arranged along a *dimension.* Thus, the concept of social status implies a ranking of values such as "high status," "moderate status," "low status," and so forth. Religiosity, prejudice, alienation, intellectual sophistication, liberalism, and other such concepts imply similarly ranked sets of values.

Operationalization is the process whereby the researcher specifies empirical observations that may be taken as indicators of the attributes contained within a given concept. If the concept is religiosity, operationalization is the process for specifying empirical measurements that will indicate whether respondents are highly religious, moderately religious, unreligious, and so forth. Typically, the researcher will specify several such indicators and combine those during the analysis of data to provide a composite measure (index or scale) representing the concept.

Since virtually all concepts are ad hoc summaries of experience and observations, they do not have real, ultimate meanings. Thus the researcher cannot make correct or incorrect measurements, only more or less useful ones: how well do those contribute to our understanding of the empirical data at hand and to the development of theories of social behavior? From this perspective, it is possible to provide a set of guidelines to the operationalization process that may enhance the utility of the process in given research activities.

Let's assume for the moment that the researcher is interested in studying religiosity. Perhaps he wishes to learn why some people are more religious than others; perhaps he wants to know the consequences of being more or less religious. Although he no doubt begins with a general notion of what he means by religiosity, it is equally likely that he has no specific indicator in mind. As a beginning of the operationalization process, he should begin by enumerating all the different subdimensions of this variable. In doing this, he should pay attention to previous research on the topic, as well as on the commonsensible conceptions of it.

Charles Y. Glock has devoted considerable theoretical and empirical attention to the different subdimensions of religiosity, and these may provide an excellent starting point for our considerations.[3] Glock discusses *ritual involvement* as participation in such activities as weekly church services, communion (for Christians), prayers before meals, and so forth. *Ideological involvement* concerns the acceptance of traditional religious beliefs. *Intellectual involvement* refers to the extent of a person's knowledge about his religion. *Experiential involvement* refers to the extent of religious experiences that the person has: hearing God speak to him, having a religious seizure, and so forth. Finally, Glock examined *consequential involvement* as the extent to which social behavior is motivated by religious concerns and in accord with religious teachings.

While these five subdimensions of religiosity help to organize many possible indicators, there are others that might not easily fit into them. Giving money to the church or to church-related activities might be considered an indication of religiosity. So might participation in church social activities. The list could go on and on. The researcher's first task, then, is to compile as exhaustive a list as possible of all the different things that might be included within his general concept of religiosity.

At the same time that he is deciding all the things that religiosity possibly *is,* the researcher must also consider what it is *not.* He must take special care not to design questionnaire items that tap not only religiosity but also the variables that he will relate to it in the analysis. If, for example, he wishes to determine the relationship between religiosity and attitudes toward war, items measuring commitment to the Christian doctrine of "peace on Earth" would not be good measures of religiosity for this purpose. Since the responses will reflect respondents' attitudes toward war—aside from religious concerns—such measures would be called "contaminated." Responses to the items would surely relate to attitudes regarding participation in war, but this finding might contribute nothing useful to understanding the general relationship between religiosity and war attitudes.

Moving beyond this point, the researcher should pay special attention to the opposite of the variable he is attempting to measure. If his goal is to measure religiosity, he should be sensitive to the variable of antireligiosity. While some people may be very religious, and others not religious, still others are antireligious. And antireligiosity can vary in intensity. The researcher, then, must determine the conceptual range of variation on his variable. Perhaps he will wish to settle for a measure of religiosity from low to high, with the antireligious respondents grouped with those who are simply not positively religious. Or perhaps he will wish to extend the variable from very religious to very antireligious. In either event, the items constructed for measurement should be based on this decision. Consider the following example of a questionnaire item:

---

[3]Charles Y. Glock and Rodney Stark, *Religion and Society in Tension* (Chicago: Rand McNally & Co., 1965), pp. 18–38.

Please indicate whether you agree or disagree with following statement. "Organized religion does more harm than good."

Agreement with the item would indicate an antireligious orientation. Disagreement with the statement, on the other hand, would not necessarily indicate religiosity. While the responses to this item would surely intercorrelate strongly with measures of religiosity, the item itself does not measure religiosity, only antireligiosity.

This example illustrates a common problem in the measurement of dimensions. Rather than measuring a variable from low to high, the researcher often makes measurements between two polar opposites. For example, we seldom measure degrees of political conservatism, but measure variations between liberalism and conservatism. A recent study of science and medicine attempted to measure differing commitments to scientific perspectives among physicians, but the researcher found himself continually involved in considerations of antiscientific perspectives as well.

This problem has no clear-cut solution. Research interests vary too greatly to permit the elucidation of adequate rules of procedure. The only advice that can be given at this point is for the researcher to undertake the time-consuming exercise of listing all the possible subdimensions of the variable, noting the dimensions to be excluded from the concept, and specifying the conceptual end points of the dimension describing the concept. Each questionnaire item considered should then be evaluated against those decisions. The researcher should ask himself the implications of a respondent giving *each* of the possible responses. How does that particular response reflect on the basic concept? Only through this process can the researcher generate data relevant to a meaningful later analysis.

7.3   Types of Data

The survey research format permits the generation of many types of data useful to social research. This section provides a suggestive overview of the different types.

Although this chapter began with the assertion that data do not exist except through the scientific process of generating them, it makes sense, nonetheless, to regard some kinds of data as "facts." In this regard, we mean items of information that the respondent believes to represent *truth* and which the researcher generally accepts as such. Respondents' demographic characteristics fit into this category. When the researcher asks the respondent to indicate his or her sex as male or female, the respondent believes the answer to represent an indisputable fact and the researcher accepts it as such. The same might be said for reports of age, race, region of origin, and so forth.

Sometimes the respondent is asked to report information which he accepts as a statement of truth, but which the researcher does not necessarily accept as such. For example, the respondent might be asked whether or not God exists. In answering "yes" or "no," the respondent indicates what he believes to be the truth of the matter. The researcher, on the other hand, regards the response only as a description of the respondent, not an answer to the question of whether God exists. Asked to agree or disagree with the statement "Negroes are naturally lazy," the respondent reports what he considers to be the truth, but again the researcher takes the answer only as a description of the respondent.

In other cases, the researcher asks the respondent to provide information that both recognize as subjective attitudes. The researcher may ask, "Do you personally think that the President is doing a good job or a bad job?" Both the respondent and the researcher understand that the respondent is giving an opinion and not a fact.

Often, the distinction between beliefs and attitudes in this sense is not clear. Nevertheless, in certain research problems, it can be an important distinction.

Much interesting social research involves measuring orientations that are often not even recognized by the respondents. Prejudice is a good example. In a survey, the researcher may ask several questions that, in combination, permit him to describe respondents as being more or less prejudiced. In many cases, the respondent does not understand the latent purpose of the questions, and he might very well dispute the characterization of himself in the analysis.

Survey research does not permit the direct measurement of behavior, although social behavior is frequently the ultimate referent of social research. Survey research does permit the *indirect* measurement of behavior, however, and often in useful ways.

Respondents can be asked to report on their past behavior. Did they go to church last week? Whom did they vote for in the last election? Such questions are subject to problems of recall and honesty, of course. The respondent may not remember for whom he voted—say, in the 1940 presidential election. And he may let his memory play tricks on his candor, especially if the behavior in question is currently regarded as either good or bad. (Post-election political polls often show a higher percentage of the electorate voting for the winner than was the case in the actual voting.) Despite these shortcomings, reports of past behavior can often be very useful.

Survey research can also examine prospective behavior, either real or hypothetical. Thus, political polls ask, "Who will you vote for?" And sometimes it is useful to create hypothetical situations and ask the respondent how he would behave. "If your political party nominated a Jew for President, do you think you would vote for him?"

Measures of prospective behavior are less reliable than measures of past behavior in most instances. In any event, the researcher should bear their shortcomings in mind when generating such data. In asking whether respondents would vote for a Jew nominated for President by their party, the researcher will probably learn little of value to a prospective Jewish candidate. The descriptive data produced by responses to such a question would probably be quite unreliable. At the same time, however, the item might be very useful in describing respondents as more or less anti-Semitic.

7.4   Levels of Measurement

We have seen in the preceding section that the survey researcher is able to measure a variety of social variables. In this section, we shall look at such variables from a different perspective, considering four levels of measurement: nominal, ordinal, interval, and ratio.[4]

Nominal Measurements

Nominal measurements merely distinguish the categories that comprise a given variable. Sex, for example, is a nominal variable comprised of the categories male and female. Other examples would be religious or political affiliation, region of the country, college major, and so forth.

The categories comprising a nominal variable are mutually exclusive, but they bear no other relationship to one another. The remaining levels of measurement discussed below reflect additional relationships among the categories.

Ordinal Measurements

Ordinal measurements reflect a rank-order among the categories comprising a variable. Social class would be an example of an ordinal variable, comprised perhaps of the categories lower class, middle class, and upper class. Other examples would be religiosity, alienation, anti-Semitism, and so forth.

Ordinal measurements are used very often in social scientific research. Although such measurements are often represented by numbers on an index or scale, these numbers have no meaning other than the indication of rank order. Thus, a person scored 5 on an index of alienation would be assumed

---

[4]An excellent treatment of this topic is to be found in James A. Davis, *Elementary Survey Analysis* (Englewood Cliffs, N.J.: Prentice-Hall, 1971), pp. 9ff. Most treatments of these levels of measurements use the term "scale" (e.g., *nominal scale*), following the example of S. S. Stevens, "On the Theory of Scales of Measurement," *Science*, Vol. 103 (1946), pp. 677–680. Since this book uses the term "scale" in a different sense (see Chapter 14), I have avoided its use in this context.

to be *more* alienated than a person scored 4 on that index, but this ordinal measurement would give us no indication of *how much more* alienated the first was.

Interval Measurements

Interval measurements also utilize numbers to describe conditions, but these numbers have more meaning than is the case for ordinal measurements: the distances between points have a real meaning. The most common example of an interval measurement is the Fahrenheit temperature scale. The difference between 80 degrees and 90 degrees is the same as the difference between 60 degrees and 70 degrees. (Note that the difference between scores of 4 and 5 on an index of alienation is not necessarily the same as the difference between scores of 3 and 4.)

Ratio Measurements

Ratio measurements have all the same characteristics of interval measurements, but they have the additional characteristic of a *true zero.* In comparison with the Fahrenheit temperature scale (an interval measurement), the Kelvin temperature scale (based on absolute zero degrees temperature) is a ratio measurement. Thus, while 40 degrees Fahrenheit is *not* twice as warm as 20 degrees Fahrenheit, 200 degrees Kelvin *is* twice as warm as 100 degrees Kelvin.

In the context of social scientific research, age would be an example of a ratio measurement. A 20-year-old person is twice as old as one 10 years of age. Height, weight, and length of residence in a given city would be other examples.

Implications of Levels of Measurement

In the discussion of survey analysis in Part Three of this book, we shall see that different analytical techniques may require specific levels of measurement. If the researcher is analyzing the relationship between two nominal variables, some analytical techniques would be inappropriate for use.

At the same time, it is important to realize that a given variable may be treated differently in terms of the levels of measurements discussed above. Recall, for example, that age is a ratio measurement. Thus, the researcher would be justified in computing a regression equation linking age with height (another ratio measurement). Let's assume, however, that the researcher is studying a sample of high school students, ranging in age from, say, 14 to 20. Within this limited range, the researcher would probably take advantage of the equal intervals between ages but not the ratio character of the variable. In another type of study, the researcher might choose to group ages into ordinal categories: Under 40 years = *Young,* 40 to 60 years = *Middle Aged,* and Over 60 = *Old.* Finally, age might be converted to a nominal measurement for certain purposes. Survey respondents might be categorized as members of the post-World War II "baby boom" or not; they might be categorized as being born during the Depression of the 1930s or not. (Another nominal measurement—based on birthdate rather than age—would be assignments in terms of astrological signs.)

In designing his questionnaire, the researcher must consider the type of analysis he will conduct after the collection of his data. He must determine whether and how he can measure a given variable in such a way as to permit the analysis required. If the analysis requires data in the form of ratio measurements, the researcher must not construct his questionnaire items so as to create nominal variables only.

7.5   Guides to Question Construction

In the construction of questionnaire items, the researcher has several options at his disposal. At the same time, the past experience of survey researchers provides a wealth of guidelines that may assist in the generation of data useful to analysis. This section will deal with both topics.

Questions and Statements

Survey research is commonly viewed as involving the asking of questions, yet an examination of a typical survey will probably uncover as many statements as questions. This is not without reason. Often, the researcher is interested in determining the extent to which respondents hold a particular attitude or perspective. If he is able to summarize the attitude in a fairly brief statement, he will often present that statement and ask respondents whether they agree or disagree with it. Rensis Likert has greatly formalized this procedure through the creation of the "Likert scale," a format in which respondents are asked to "strongly agree," "agree," "disagree," "strongly disagree," or perhaps "strongly approve," "approve," and so forth.

Both questions and statements may be used profitably in survey research. Using both in a given questionnaire gives the researcher more flexibility in the design of items and can make the questionnaire more interesting as well.

Open- and Closed-Ended Questions

In the realm of questions, the researcher has two options. He may ask *open-ended* questions in which case the respondent is asked to provide his own answer to the question. For example, the respondent might be asked "What do you feel is the most important issue facing the United States today?" and be provided with a space to write in his answer (or be asked to report it verbally to an interviewer).

In the case of *closed-ended* questions, the respondent is asked to select his answer from among a list provided by the researcher. Closed-ended questions are very popular in survey research since they provide a greater uniformity of responses and because they are more easily processed. Open-ended responses must be coded prior to keypunching and there is a danger that some respondents will give answers that are essentially irrelevant to the researcher's intent. Closed-ended responses, on the other hand, can often be keypunched directly from the questionnaire and in some cases can be marked directly on optical-sensing sheets by respondents for automatic punching.

The chief shortcoming of closed-ended questions lies in the researcher's structuring of responses. Where the relevant answers to a given question are relatively clear, this may present no problem. In other cases, however, the researcher's structuring of responses may overlook some important responses. In asking about "the most important issues facing the United States," for example, the researcher might provide a checklist of issues, but in doing so he might overlook certain issues that respondents would have said were important. (Recall the earlier assertion that data are created rather than collected.)

Two guidelines should always be followed in the construction of closed-ended questions. The response categories provided should be *exhaustive;* they should include all the possible responses that might be expected. Often, researchers support this effort by adding a category labeled "Other (please specify)." In doing this, however, the researcher should realize that respondents will attempt to fit their personal answer into one of the provided categories, even though the fit may not be perfect.

Second, the answer categories must be *mutually exclusive,* the respondent should not feel compelled to select more than one. (In some cases, the researcher may wish to solicit multiple answers, but these will create difficulties in processing.) This may be insured by carefully considering each combination of responses and asking whether a person could reasonably give both. Often, the researcher asks the respondent to "select the one *best* answer," but this should not be used to make up for a poorly thought out set of responses.

Make Items Clear

It should go without saying that questionnaire items should be clear and unambiguous, but the broad proliferation of unclear and ambiguous questions in surveys makes the point worth stressing here. Often the researcher becomes so deeply involved in the topic under examination that opinions and perspectives are clear to him but will not be clear to his respondents—many of whom have given little or no attention to the topic.

Or, on the other hand, the researcher may have only a superficial understanding of the topic and fail to specify the intent of his question sufficiently. The question "What do you think about the proposed antiballistic missile system?" may evoke in the respondent a counterquestion: "*Which* proposed antiballistic missile system?" Questionnaire items should be precise so that the respondent knows exactly what the researcher wants an answer to.

Avoid Double-Barreled Questions

Very frequently, researchers ask respondents for a single answer to a combination of questions. This seems to happen most often when the researcher has personally identified with a complex position. For example, he might ask respondents to agree or disagree with the statement "The United States should abandon its space program and spend the money on domestic programs." While many people would unequivocally agree with the statement and others would unequivocally disagree, still others would be unable to answer. Some would want to abandon the space program and give the money back to taxpayers. Others would want to continue the space program, but also put more money into domestic programs. These latter respondents could neither agree nor disagree without misleading the researcher.

As a general rule, whenever the word "and" appears in a question or questionnaire statement, the researcher should check whether he is asking a double-barreled question.

Respondent Must Be Competent to Answer

In asking respondents to provide information, the researcher should continually ask himself whether they are able to do so reliably. In a study of child rearing, he may ask respondents to report the age at which they first "talked back" to their parents. Quite aside from the problem of defining "talking back to parents," it is doubtful if most respondents would remember with any degree of accuracy.

As another example, student government leaders occasionally ask their constituents to indicate the manner in which students' fees ought to be spent. Typically, respondents are asked to indicate the percentage of available funds that should be devoted to a long list of activities. Without a fairly good knowledge of the nature of those activities and the costs involved in them, the respondents cannot provide meaningful answers. ("Administrative costs" will receive little support although they may be essential to the program as a whole.)

One group of researchers examining the driving experience of teen-agers insisted on asking an open-ended question concerning the number of miles driven since receiving a license. While consultants argued that few drivers would be able to estimate such information with any accuracy, the question was asked nonetheless. In response, some teen-agers reported driving hundreds of thousands of miles.

Questions Should Be Relevant

Similarly, questions asked in a survey should be relevant to most respondents. When attitudes are requested on a topic that few respondents have thought about or really care about, the results are not likely to be very useful. Of course, the respondents may express attitudes even though they have never given any thought to the issue, and the researcher runs the risk of being misled.

This point is illustrated occasionally when researchers ask for responses relating to fictitious persons and issues. In one study of political images, respondents were asked whether they were familiar with each of 15 political figures in the community. In regard to one purely fictitious figure, 9 percent of the respondents said they were familiar with him. Of those respondents, about half reported seeing him on television and reading about him in the newspapers.

When responses are obtained with regard to fictitious issues, the researcher can disregard those responses. But when the issue is real, he may have no way of telling which responses genuinely reflect attitudes while others reflect meaningless answers to an irrelevant question.

Short Items Are Best

In the interest of being unambiguous and precise and pointing to the relevance of an issue, the researcher is often led into long and complicated items. This should be avoided. That the intent of an item is clear when studied carefully is irrelevant for respondents who do not give it the necessary study. The respondent should be able to read an item quickly, understand its intent, and select or provide an answer without difficulty. In general, the researcher should assume that respondents *will* read items quickly and provide quick answers; therefore, he should provide clear, short items that will not be misinterpreted under those conditions.

Avoid Negative Items

The appearance of a negation in a questionnaire item paves the way for easy misinterpretation. Asked to agree or disagree with the statement "The United States should not recognize mainland China," a sizable portion of the respondents will read over the word "not" and answer on that basis. Thus, some will agree with the statement when they are in favor of recognition, while others will agree when they oppose it. And the researcher may never know which is which.

In a study of civil liberties support, respondents were asked whether they felt "the following kinds of people should be prohibited from teaching in public schools," and were presented with a list including such items as a Communist, a Ku Klux Klansman, and so forth. The response categories "yes" and "no" were given beside each entry. A comparison of the responses to this item with other items reflecting support for civil liberties strongly suggested that many respondents gave the answer "yes" to indicate willingness for such a person to teach, rather than to indicate that such a person should be "prohibited." (A subsequent study in the series gave as answer categories "permit" and "prohibit" and produced much clearer results.)

Avoid "Biased" Items and Terms

I have frequently repeated the contention of this book that survey data are created rather than simply collected. The manner in which data are sought, therefore, determines the nature of the data received. The researcher, then, must be continually sensitive to the effect of question wording on the results that he will obtain.

Most researchers would recognize the likely effect of a question that began "Don't you agree with the President of the United States in the belief that . . ." and no reputable researcher would use such an item. Unhappily, the biasing effect of items and terms is far subtler than this example suggests.

The mere identification of an attitude or position with a prestigious person or agency can bias responses. The item "Do you agree or disagree with the President's proposal to . . ." would have this effect. "Do you agree or disagree with the recent Supreme Court decision that . . ." would have a similar effect. I should make it clear that I am not suggesting that such wording will necessarily produce consensus or even a majority in support of the position identified with the prestigious person or agency, only that support would likely be increased over what would have been obtained without such identification.

Questionnaire items can be biased negatively as well as positively. "Do you agree or disagree with the position of Adolph Hitler when he stated that . . ." would be an example. In recent years in the United States, it has been very difficult to ask questions relating to China. Identifying the country only as "China" would result in confusion between mainland China and Taiwan. Referring to "Red China" or "Communist China" would evoke a more negative response from many respondents. At the same time, of course, the researcher's purpose must be taken into account. Referring to "mainland China" might produce less hostile responses when anticommunist feelings were an important aspect of the research.

As in all other examples, the researcher must carefully examine the purpose of his inquiry and construct items that will be most useful to it. He should never be misled into thinking there are ultimately "right" and "wrong" ways of asking the questions.

7.6   General Questionnaire Format

The format of a questionnaire can be just as important as the nature and wording of the questions asked. An improperly laid out questionnaire can lead respondents to miss questions, can confuse them as to the nature of the data desired, and, in the extreme, can lead to respondents throwing the questionnaire away. Both general and specific guidelines can be suggested.

As a general rule, the questionnaire should be spread out and uncluttered. The researcher should maximize the "white space" in his instrument. Inexperienced researchers tend to fear their questionnaires will look too long, and as a result, they squeeze several questions on a single line, abbreviate questions, and try to use as few pages as possible. All these efforts are ill-advised and even dangerous. Putting more than one question on a line will result in some respondents skipping the second question. Abbreviating questions will result in misinterpretations. And more generally, the respondent who finds he has spent considerable time on the first page of what seemed a short questionnaire will be more demoralized than the respondent who quickly completed the first several pages of what initially seemed rather long. Moreover, the second respondent will have made fewer errors and will not have been forced to reread confusing, abbreviated questions. Nor will he have been forced to write a long answer in a tiny space.

The desirability of spreading questions out in the questionnaire cannot be overemphasized. Squeezed-together questionnaires are disastrous whether used in mail surveys or in interviews.

Formats for Responses

A variety of methods are available for presenting a series of response categories for the respondent to check in answering a given question. It has been my experience that *boxes* adequately spaced apart are the best. If the questionnaire is to be set in type, this can be accomplished easily and neatly. It is also possible to do this with a typewriter, however.

If the questionnaire is typed on a typewriter with brackets, excellent boxes can be produced by a left-bracket, a space, and a right-bracket: [ ]. If brackets are not available, parentheses work reasonably well in the same fashion: ( ). The researcher should be discouraged from utilizing slashes and underscores, however. First, this technique will require considerably more

typing effort; and, second, the result is not very neat, especially if the response categories must be single-spaced. Figure 7-1 provides a comparison of
the different methods.

Figure 7-1

```
[ ] Yes          ( ) Yes          /7 Yes
[ ] No           ( ) No           /7 No
[ ] Don't Know   ( ) Don't Know   /7 Don't Know
```

The worst method of all is to provide open blanks for check marks, since
respondents will often enter rather large check marks and it will not be
possible to determine which response was intended. As a general rule, moreover, it is always best to double-space between response categories to avoid
ambiguous check marks.

A very different method might also be considered. Rather than providing
boxes to be checked, the researcher might consider entering code numbers
beside each response and ask the respondent to *circle* the appropriate number.
This has the added advantage of specifying the number to be punched later
in the processing stage. I have had little experience with this method, but my
initial experimentation has been favorable. If this method is used, however,
the researcher should provide clear and prominent instructions to the respondent, as many will be tempted to cross out the appropriate number, thereby
making punching even more difficult. (*Note:* The technique can be used more
safely in interview surveys, as interviewers can be instructed and tested.)

Contingency Questions

Often in survey research, certain questions will clearly
be relevant only to a subset of the respondents. The researcher may ask
respondents if they are familiar with a certain issue and then ask those who
are what they think about it. He may be interested in the draft status of young
people—realizing that only men will have a draft status. Or he may ask if
respondents belong to a certain organization and, if so, whether they have
ever held an office in that organization.

The second question in each of the above examples is called a *contingency
question.* By this is meant that the second question is *contingent* upon the
responses to the first. Thus, whether the researcher asks for attitudes toward
the issue is contingent upon whether the respondent is familiar with it.

The proper use of contingency questions can facilitate the respondent's
task in answering the questionnaire and can also improve the quality of the
data produced. The alternative to contingency questions should be avoided
for the same reasons: Do not ask the question "If you have ever belonged to

the PTA did you ever hold an office in it?" This latter format will force all respondents to read the question—even though it is irrelevant to many—and those for whom it is irrelevant may be forced to decide whether to skip the question, write in "not applicable," answer "no," or throw the questionnaire away.

There are a number of contingency question formats. I feel the best is one in which the contingency questions are indented on the questionnaire, set off in boxes, and connected with the base question by arrows from appropriate responses. Figure 7-2 illustrates such a question.

Figure 7-2

23.   Have you ever belonged to the local PTA?

       [ ] Yes
       [ ] No

```
┌─────────────────────────────────────────┐
│ If yes:  Have you ever held an office    │
│          in the local PTA?               │
│                                          │
│          [ ] Yes                         │
│          [ ] No                          │
└─────────────────────────────────────────┘
```

Used properly, complex sets of contingency questions can be constructed without confusing the respondent, as Figure 7-3 illustrates.

While the above examples have referred primarily to self-administered questionnaires, the proper presentation of contingency questions is even more important in interview questionnaires. (The mail questionnaire respondent can reread a question with some dissatisfaction, but if the interviewer becomes confused and asks improper questions, the whole interview is jeopardized.)

Figure 7-4 shows a portion of an interview questionnaire aimed—in this question—at determining the person's occupational status. By reading through the question, giving different answers and following the appropriate arrows to the next question, the reader will gain a sense of the researcher's intent as well as seeing how easily the interviewer was able to collect the relevant information from all respondents.

7.7   Ordering Questions in a Questionnaire

The order in which questions are asked can affect the responses as well as the overall data collection activity. First, the appearance of one question can affect the answers given to subsequent ones. For example,

if a number of questions have been asked about the dangers of communism
to the United States and a subsequent question asks respondents to volunteer
(open-ended) what they believe to represent dangers to the United States,
"communism" will receive more citations than would otherwise be the case.

If respondents are asked to assess their overall religiosity ("How important is your religion to you in general?"), their responses to later questions
concerning specific aspects of religiosity will be aimed at consistency with the
prior assessment. The converse would be true as well. If respondents are first
asked specific questions about different aspects of their religiosity, their subsequent overall assessment will reflect the earlier answers.

Some researchers attempt to overcome this effect by "randomizing" the
order of questions. This is usually a futile effort. To begin, a "randomized"
set of questions will probably strike the respondent as chaotic and worthless.
It will be difficult for him to answer, moreover, since he must continually
switch his attention from one topic to another. And, finally, even a randomized ordering of questions will have the effect discussed above—except that
the researcher will have no control over the effect.

Figure 7-3

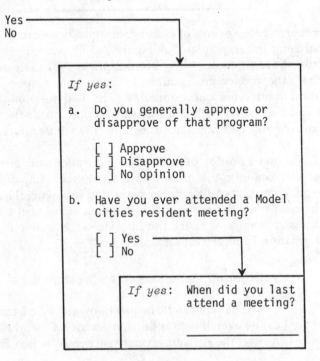

Figure 7-4

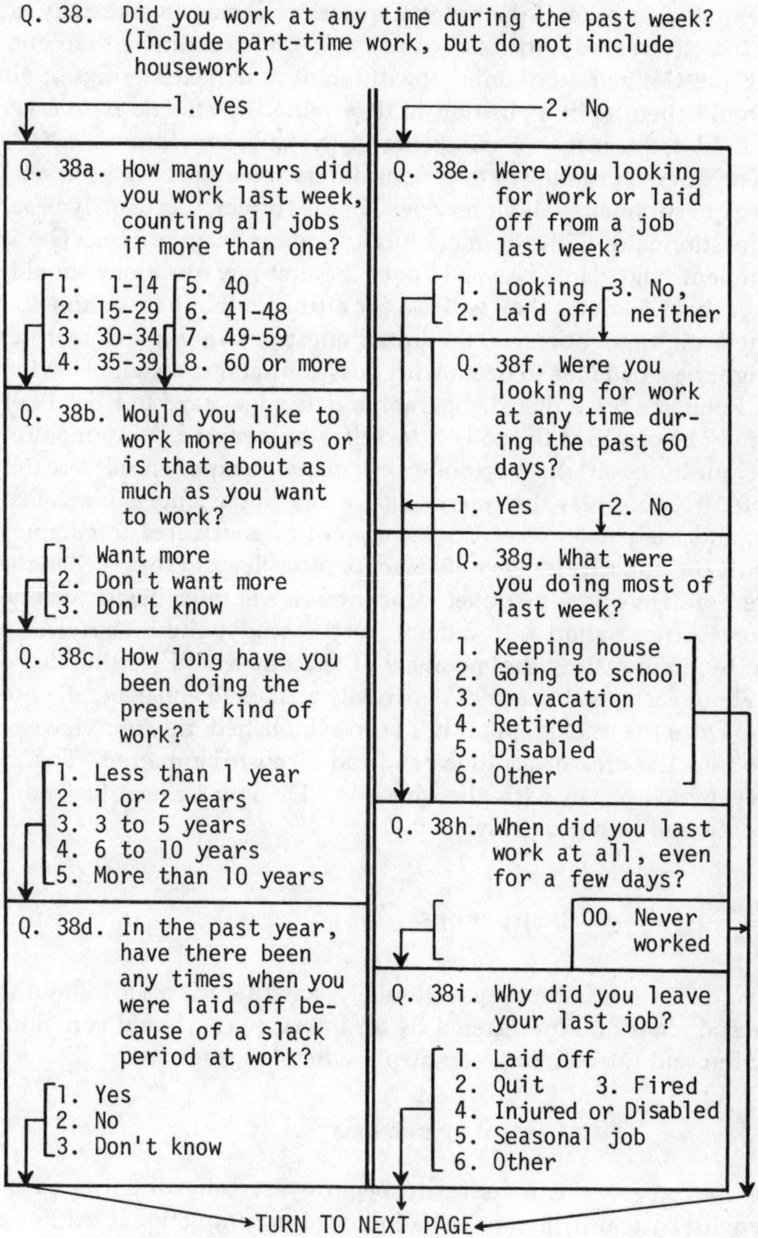

Q. 38. Did you work at any time during the past week?
(Include part-time work, but do not include housework.)

─────1. Yes   ─────2. No

Q. 38a. How many hours did you work last week, counting all jobs if more than one?

1.   1-14   5. 40
2. 15-29   6. 41-48
3. 30-34   7. 49-59
4. 35-39   8. 60 or more

Q. 38b. Would you like to work more hours or is that about as much as you want to work?

1. Want more
2. Don't want more
3. Don't know

Q. 38c. How long have you been doing the present kind of work?

1. Less than 1 year
2. 1 or 2 years
3. 3 to 5 years
4. 6 to 10 years
5. More than 10 years

Q. 38d. In the past year, have there been any times when you were laid off because of a slack period at work?

1. Yes
2. No
3. Don't know

Q. 38e. Were you looking for work or laid off from a job last week?

1. Looking   3. No,
2. Laid off   neither

Q. 38f. Were you looking for work at any time during the past 60 days?

1. Yes   2. No

Q. 38g. What were you doing most of last week?

1. Keeping house
2. Going to school
3. On vacation
4. Retired
5. Disabled
6. Other

Q. 38h. When did you last work at all, even for a few days?

00. Never worked

Q. 38i. Why did you leave your last job?

1. Laid off
2. Quit   3. Fired
4. Injured or Disabled
5. Seasonal job
6. Other

TURN TO NEXT PAGE

The safest solution is sensitivity to the problem. While the researcher cannot avoid the effect of question order, he should be in a position to estimate what that effect will be. Thus, he will be able to interpret results in a meaningful fashion. If the order of questions seems an especially important issue in a given study, the researcher might construct more than one version of the questionnaire containing the different possible orderings of questions. He would then be in a position to determine the effects. At the very least, he should pre-test his questionnaire in the different forms.

The desired ordering of questions differs somewhat between self-administered questionnaires and interviews. In the former, it is usually best to begin the questionnaire with the most interesting set of questions. The potential respondent who glances casually over the first few questions should *want* to answer them. Perhaps they will ask for attitudes that he is aching to express. At the same time, however, the initial questions should not be threatening. (It might be a bad idea to begin with questions about sexual behavior or drug use.) Requests for duller demographic data (age, sex, and the like) should generally be placed at the end of the self-administered questionnaire. Placing these questions at the beginning, as many inexperienced researchers are tempted to do, gives the questionnaire the initial appearance of a routine form, and the person receiving it may not be motivated to complete it.

Just the opposite is generally true for interview surveys. When the potential respondent's door first opens, the interviewer must begin quickly gaining rapport. After a short introduction to the study, the interviewer can best begin by enumerating the members of the household, getting demographic data about each. Such questions are easily answered and generally nonthreatening. Once the initial rapport has been established, the interviewer can then move into the area of attitudes and more sensitive matters. The interview survey which began with the question "Do you believe in God?" would probably end rather quickly.

7.8   Instructions

Every questionnaire, whether to be self-administered by the respondent or administered by an interviewer, should contain clear instruction and introductory comments where appropriate.

General Instructions

It is useful to begin every self-administered questionnaire with basic instructions to be followed in completing it. Although many respondents these days are familiar with normal survey techniques, it is useful to begin by telling the respondent that he is to indicate his answers to certain questions by placing a check mark or an X in the box beside the appropriate answer or by writing in his answer when called for. If many open-ended questions are used, he should be given some guide as to whether brief or lengthy answers are expected. If the researcher encourages written-in answers to elaborate on responses given to closed-ended questions, this should be noted.

Introductions

If a questionnaire is arranged into content subsections—political attitudes, religious attitudes, background data—it is useful to introduce each section with a short statement concerning its content and purpose. For example, "In this section, we would like to know what people around here consider the most important community problems." Demographic items at the end of a self-administered questionnaire might be introduced thusly: "Finally, we would like to know just a little about you so we can see how different types of people feel about the issues we have been examining."

Short introductions such as these help make sense out of the questionnaire for the respondent. They make the questionnaire seem less chaotic, especially when it taps a variety of data. And they help put the respondent in the proper frame of mind for answering the questions.

Specific Instructions

Some questions may require special instructions to facilitate proper answering. This is especially true if a given question varies from the general instructions pertaining to the whole questionnaire. Some specific situations will illustrate this.

Despite the desirability for mutually exclusive answer categories in closed-ended questions, it is often the case that more than one answer will apply for respondents. If the researcher wants a single answer, he should make this perfectly clear in the question. An example would be "From the list below, please check the *primary* reason for your decision to attend college." Often the main question can be followed by a parenthetical note: "Please check the *one* best answer." If, on the other hand, the researcher wishes the respondent to check as many answers as apply, this should be made clear as well.

When a set of answer categories are to be rank-ordered by the respondent, the instructions should indicate as much and a different type of answer format should be used (for example, blanks instead of boxes). These instructions should indicate how many answers are to be ranked (for example, all, first and second, first and last, most important and least important) and the order of ranking (for example, "place a 1 beside the most important, a 2 beside the next most important, and so forth"). (*Note:* Rank-ordering of responses is often difficult for respondents, since they may have to read and reread the list several times.)

In multiple-part "matrix" questions, it is useful to give special instructions unless the same format is used throughout the questionnaire. Sometimes the respondent will be expected to check one answer in each column of the matrix, while in others he will be expected to check one answer in each row. Whenever the questionnaire contains both types, it will be useful to add an instruction clarifying which is expected in each case.

Interviewer Instruction

Whereas a confusing self-administered questionnaire can lower the morale of the respondent, a confusing interview questionnaire can lower the morale of both the respondent and the interviewer and will endanger the efficiency of the latter. It is particularly important, then, to provide clear supplementary instructions where appropriate to interviewers.

It is essential in an interview questionnaire that different formats be used for those instructions that the interviewer is to read to the respondents and those that are not to be read. For example, the latter might always be typed in parentheses or in capital letters. An interview could be destroyed by an interviewer reading aloud something on the order of "If the respondent is nearly illiterate, then . . ."

It is equally important that an interview questionnaire contain a *verbatim script* for the interviewer to read in interviewing.[5] Under ideal circumstances, an interviewer should be able to conduct an entire interview from initial introduction ("Hello, my name is . . .") to final remarks ("That completes the interview. We would like to thank you for . . .") without ad libbing a single word. All transitional statements throughout the questionnaire should be included ("Now we would like to turn from community problems to national problems . . .") so that the verbatim script sounds natural and conversational. The same is true for the demographic enumeration of household members. Rather than instructing the interviewer to obtain the age of each family member, the researcher should provide a standardized question for each ("How old was [he/she] on January 1, 1971?"). Chapter 9 will stress the importance of the interviewer following the questionnaire wording exactly, but it should be recognized in advance that this will not be possible unless the questionnaire is properly constructed.

7.9   Precoding and Punch-Direct

In laying out the format for a questionnaire, the researcher should give special attention to the method of data processing that will be used. This is essential, especially if the questionnaire is to be key-

---

[5]Of course, this would not be appropriate for an unstructured interview in an exploratory study. In that case, the interviewer should be given an outline of topics to cover and perhaps a set of possible questions.

punched directly. The following suggestions will facilitate punching directly from the questionnaire.

The questionnaire should be precoded to facilitate punching (or coding for that matter). Items of data should be assigned to IBM cards and columns in advance and notations in the questionnaire should indicate those assignments. There are two types of precoding. First, card and column assignments should be indicated, although it is normally not necessary to enter separate notations for each column. Since experienced keypunchers will not check each column number as it is punched, it is normally sufficient to enter the range of column numbers assigned to a questionnaire page or section of a page. Then, the keypuncher can check to insure she is punching the correct column once or twice per page.

The second type of precoding concerns punch assignments with a given column. Wherever a given column contains three or fewer response categories, precoding can normally be omitted, as the keypuncher can easily determine the appropriate punch if logical assignments are made. Whenever there are more than three response categories, it is normally safest to enter the punch assignments. Figure 7-5 presents examples of precoding appropriate for punching direct.

Several things should be noted in Figure 7-5. First, note that the column assignments are presented in parentheses; columns 23 to 29 are assigned to approval/disapproval of the political figures, while column 30 is assigned to political party identification. The punch assignments for question 14 are presented above the response category columns. In question 15, with only one set of responses, the punch assignments are presented beside the spaces for checking answers.

Finally, note that all responses in the two questions are located on the same side of the page. This is important as it facilitates punching. The keypuncher is able to punch both questions without moving his eyes back and forth across the page. If the location of responses moves around on the page, the keypuncher will work more slowly and will be more likely to miss items.

Whenever precoding is used on a self-administered questionnaire, it is normally a good idea to mention the precoding in an introductory note to the questionnaire. ("The numbers shown in parentheses and beside answer categories should be ignored; they are included only to assist the processing of your answers.") In any event, precoding should be kept as inconspicuous as possible, since it may confuse the respondent. If the questionnaire is set in type, the precoding should be entered in a smaller type face.

Even if the questionnaire is not to be punched directly, the format should take intended processing methods into account. Most of the suggestions made above will facilitate hand coding. If the questionnaire is to be read by an optical-sensing machine, then the researcher must check his format against the requirements of that machine.

One further technique facilitates both coding and keypunching whenever more than one IBM card is required for recording the questionnaire

Figure 7-5

14. Beside each of the political figures listed below,
please indicate whether you strongly approve (SA),
approve (A), disapprove (D), or strongly disapprove
(SD) of that person's political philosophy as you
understand it.

	(23-29)	SA 1	A 2	D 3	SD 4
a. Richard Nixon................		[ ]	[ ]	[ ]	[ ]
b. Eugene McCarthy..............		[ ]	[ ]	[ ]	[ ]
c. Edmund Muskie................		[ ]	[ ]	[ ]	[ ]
d. George Wallace...............		[ ]	[ ]	[ ]	[ ]
e. Spiro Agnew..................		[ ]	[ ]	[ ]	[ ]
f. George McGovern..............		[ ]	[ ]	[ ]	[ ]
g. Eldridge Cleaver.............		[ ]	[ ]	[ ]	[ ]

15. What is your political party affiliation, if any?

                  (30)

Democratic Party............................ 1 [ ]

Republican Party............................ 2 [ ]

American Independent Party.................. 3 [ ]

Peace and Freedom Party..................... 4 [ ]

Other, please specify:_____ 5 [ ]

None, no party identification............... 6 [ ]

responses. Experience has shown that both coders and keypunchers work
more efficiently if they are able to code or punch a given set of responses (a
single card) for several questionnaires in a series rather than coding or punching all cards for a given questionnaire before moving on to the next questionnaire. This is especially true for keypunching, since the keypunch machine
can be set to make automatic skips. Thus it is more efficient for the keypuncher, for example, to punch all of the "card 1's" before moving on to the
"card 2's" and so forth.

    To facilitate this, card and column assignments should be made so as to
begin each new card at the top of a questionnaire page. If necessary, the last
few columns of the previous card can be left blank. Doing this will make it
easier for keypunchers and/or coders to work on one card at a time. Going
one step further, moreover, all the questionnaire pages assigned to a particular
IBM card can be pulled out of the questionnaire and stapled into a "packet."

If this is done for each card, then different keypunchers and/or coders can be working on different cards simultaneously, thus speeding the processing. (*Note:* It is essential in such a case that the same identification number be placed on the first page of each packet prepared for a given questionnaire.)

7.10   Reproducing the Questionnaire

Having constructed a questionnaire that will collect data relevant to the researcher's aims and one that will be efficiently processed, it is necessary to produce enough copies for the actual data collection. The method of reproducing the questionnaires is important to the overall success of the study, as a neatly reproduced instrument will encourage a higher response rate, thereby providing better data.

There are several alternative methods for reproducing questionnaires, and the researcher's decision will depend on funds available, local facilities, and timing. Ditto or mimeograph reproductions are generally cheaper and more readily available, but they are the least professional looking in quality. Photo-offsetting a typed copy of the questionnaire provides better quality and, beyond a certain number of copies, it may even be cheaper. (A single photo-offset master will make countless copies, while a ditto or mimeograph master must be recut after a few hundred copies have been run off.)

The best method of reproduction from the standpoint of professional quality is type-set. This is also the most expensive, however, and it may not be feasible for some projects. Also, type-setting generally takes longer than other methods. In any event, the researcher should explore the local possibilities, balancing the relative values of time, money, and quality.

The questionnaire can be constructed in several different ways, also. In some cases, it may be appropriate to print the questionnaire on an oversized single sheet of paper to be folded into a quasi-booklet of unfolding panels. If several pages are required for the questionnaire, it may be appropriate to connect them with a corner staple. The most professional looking long questionnaire is the printed booklet held together with a saddle stitch. Again, this is the most expensive as well.

One final concern in the reproduction of the questionnaire is how many to order. In arriving at this decision, the researcher must consider his sample size, the number of follow-up mailings, if any, in a mail survey, and the possible need for discussion copies, samples for other researchers, copies for inclusion as appendixes in research reports, code books, and so forth. As a rough rule of thumb, the researcher should estimate the number required for data collection and multiply that figure by a factor of 1.5 to 2.0 in determining the number to be ordered. Bear in mind that additional copies produced in the initial run of the questionnaires will be far cheaper than a second run.

Summary and Conclusions

This chapter has covered a variety of subjects ranging from the theoretical and philosophical to the technical and even mundane. It began with the general issues of conceptualization and operationalization in the design of questionnaire items appropriate to the creation of data appropriate to the researcher's aims. Some general and specific guidelines were provided with regard to the writing of questions and the presentation of those questions in the research instrument. The chapter has concluded with a brief discussion of the technical side of questionnaire production.

The combination of such topics in a single chapter may seem bizarre. There has been a purpose in this, however. The ultimate *scientific* value of a survey can depend as much on the manner in which the questionnaire is reproduced as on the imagination which went into the operationalization of concepts. The results of survey research are a product of many steps, ranging from the theoretical to the mundane, and a weakness in any step threatens the whole.

Additional Readings

Kaplan, Abraham, *The Conduct of Inquiry* (San Francisco: Chandler Publishing Co., 1964).

Lazarsfeld, Paul F., and Morris Rosenberg (eds.), *The Language of Social Research* (New York: The Free Press, 1955), pp. 15–108.

Oppenheim, A. N., *Questionnaire Design and Attitude Measurement* (New York: Basic Books, Inc., Publishers, 1966).

Payne, Stanley L., *The Art of Asking Questions* (Princeton, N. J.: Princeton University Press, 1965).

Selltiz, Clair, *et al.*, *Research Methods in Social Relations* (New York: Holt, Rinehart & Winston, Inc., 1959), pp. 235–278.

Chapter Eight

Data Collection I: Self-Administered Questionnaires

This chapter and Chapter 9 discuss the manner in which the survey researcher actually collects his data for analysis. Having constructed a questionnaire which is appropriate to his research aims, the researcher must now go about distributing copies of it to his sample of respondents. The present chapter considers the techniques for accomplishing this through the use of self-administered questionnaires, while Chapter 9 deals with interview surveys.

While the mail survey is the typical form of self-administered study, there are several additional methods in this regard. In some cases, it may be appropriate to administer the questionnaire to a group of respondents gathered at the same place at the same time. A survey of students taking Introductory Psychology might be conducted in this manner during class. High school students might be surveyed during homeroom period.

Some recent experimentation has been conducted with regard to the home delivery of questionnaires. Research workers deliver the questionnaires to the homes of sample respondents and explain the study. Then, the questionnaire is left for the respondent to complete, and it is picked up subsequently by the researcher.

Home delivery and the mail can be used in combination as well. In many parts of the country, the 1970 United States census was conducted in this fashion. Questionnaires were mailed to families, and then a census enumerator visited the home to pick up the questionnaire and check it for completeness. In just the opposite method, questionnaires have been hand delivered by research workers with a request that the respondent mail the completed questionnaire to the research office.

On the whole, the appearance of a research worker, either delivering the questionnaire, picking it up, or both, seems to produce a higher completion rate than is normally true for straightforward mail surveys. Additional experimentation with this method is likely to point to additional techniques for improving completion while reducing costs.

Mail surveys are the typical form of self-administered survey, however, and the remainder of this chapter is devoted specifically to that type of study.

8.1   Mail Distribution and Return

Basic Method

The basic method for data collection through the mail has been the transmission of a questionnaire, accompanied by a letter of explanation and a return envelope. The respondent then completes the questionnaire and returns it to the research office through the mail, using the envelope provided for that purpose.

Alternative Method

In some cases, it is possible to further facilitate this process through the use of a *self-mailing* questionnaire. The questionnaire is constructed in such a manner that the research office's return address and postage are printed on the questionnaire itself. Upon completion, then, it can be dropped in the mail without requiring an envelope.

The researcher should plan this method with caution, however, as the post office has special requirements regarding the form of materials that can be mailed. In particular, questionnaires must be sealed in some manner. This can be accomplished in a number of ways.

If the questionnaire is printed in the form of a booklet, it may be possible to obtain a three-panel rather than two-panel cover. In this form, the back cover has a fold-out panel with an adhesive strip on it. When questionnaires are mailed out, the fold-out panel is tucked inside the back of the questionnaire. Upon completion of the questionnaire, the respondent may unfold the extra panel, lick the adhesive, and fold the panel around the questionnaire booklet. If the research office return address and postage is already printed on the extra panel, it can be placed directly in the mail for return.

This method simplifies the assembly of mailing pieces since it is unnecessary to include a return envelope. And the respondent cannot lose the return envelope without losing the questionnaire itself. Finally, there is an added appeal to the respondent in this form of questionnaire. It has a certain "toy value." To some extent, the respondent may want to complete the questionnaire so that he can then play with the cover.

If it is not possible to produce a three-panel cover, the researcher may be able to have adhesive tabs affixed to the booklet. Rather than folding the entire panel around the completed questionnaire, a smaller tab may be used to seal it.

Finally, the researcher may ask the respondent to close and seal the booklet himself—perhaps with a staple or scotch tape. This is a little risky, however, for several reasons. First, forcing the respondent to go to extra effort is likely to reduce the response rate. Perhaps he will not have anything readily available for sealing it at the time of completion, put it off, and eventually forget to return the questionnaire. Second, the variety of sealing methods that respondents will devise will probably hinder the processing of returned questionnaires. (I have received questionnaires sealed with glue, trading stamps, paper clips, string, and so forth.) Finally, many respondents will neglect to seal the questionnaires at all, and the researcher may have difficulty getting them delivered by the post office.

Ultimately, self-mailing questionnaires have many advantages in terms of ease, economy, and response rate, but they should be planned and pretested with care. It is vital, moreover, for all experimental models to be cleared with the post office.

8.2   Postal Options and Relative Costs

In a mail survey, the researcher has a number of options available for the transmission of questionnaires—both outgoing and incoming. Postal rates change frequently; and the researcher should, of course, check current postal rates in planning his study, and he should allow some extra funds for this purpose if the study will be delayed in getting into the field.

Postal Class Options

First class and bulk rate are the primary postal-class options available to the researcher. First class is more expensive, but it is also more flexible and better. Nevertheless, bulk-rate postage can often be used effectively.

In bulk-rate mailing, each mailing piece must be printed with a bulk-rate permit. This permit may be set in type for printing on the envelope, it may be mimeographed, or a rubber stamp may be created and used. The researcher must obtain a permit number from the post office, however. (*Note:* Universities or other agencies may already have a number, which the researcher could use.) This bulk-rate mailing permit on the envelope takes the place of a stamp.

To take advantage of bulk-rate mailing, the researcher must send a minimum of 250 pieces, and these must be arranged in bundles according to zip codes. (Check with the post office for specific details.) Thus the post office is able to transmit bundles of questionnaires to a given zip code without separating and sorting them.

Both first-class and bulk-rate mail seem to move at the same speed through the mails, so this presents no disadvantage for bulk-rate mailing. Changes of addresses can present a problem, however. Technically, bulk-rate pieces will be forwarded only within a given city, but in practice there are variations in both directions. Some bulk-rate pieces are not forwarded even within a city, and others are forwarded between cities. First-class mail is clearly safer in this regard.

The primary advantage of bulk rate is cost. Currently, a single mailing piece costs around 1.5 cents. When hundreds or thousands of pieces are involved, the savings are considerable.

Finally, bulk-rate mailing can be accomplished only for outgoing questionnaires. They must be returned by first class mail.

Stamps and Business Reply

Two basic options are available with regard to return postage for questionnaires. The researcher may affix stamps to the envelope or self-mailing questionnaire to cover postage, or he may have them imprinted with a business-reply mailing permit. Researchers differ in their assessments of the relative merits of these two methods.

The business-reply permit is similar to the bulk-rate permit in that it is printed on the mailing piece in place of postage stamps. (Check with the post office for additional format requirements.) Business-reply rates are those of first-class mail, however, plus a surcharge of around 5 cents per piece returned through the mail. As a result, the researcher pays postage only on those returned, but he pays more per questionnaire than if stamps were used. If stamps are affixed to the envelopes, however, the researcher is paying postage whether the questionnaire is returned or not.

As a general rule, then, the researcher will save money using stamps if he achieves a very high return rate, and he will save money with business-reply postage if the rate is low. Other factors are involved in the decision, however.

Business-reply postage is easier for the researcher in that permits can be printed quickly and inexpensively, and he avoids the time and cost of licking and sticking hundreds or thousands of stamps. On the other hand, some researchers feel that the presence of postage stamps on the envelopes will be regarded as a sign of sincerity, and respondents will be more likely to return them. (Others fear that respondents will steam the stamps off for use on other mail.)

The methodological studies of this issue do not appear to have resolved the matter. My personal preference is to use business reply permits for reasons of ease and efficiency.

8.3   Monitoring Returns

The mailing of questionnaires sets the stage for an anal compulsive activity that may prove very valuable to the study. As questionnaires are returned to the researcher, he should not sit back idly, but should undertake a careful recording of methodological data.

An invaluable tool in this activity will be a return rate graph. The day on which questionnaires were mailed should be labeled Day 1 on the graph; and, every day thereafter, the number of returned questionnaires should be logged on the graph. Since this is a rather minor activity, it is usually best to compile two graphs. One should show the number returned each day—rising then dropping. Another should report the *cumulative* number or percentage. In part, this activity provides the researcher with gratification as he gets to draw a picture of his successful data collection. More important, however, it is his guide to how the data collection is going. If he plans follow-up mailings, the graph provides a clue as to when such mailings should be launched. (The dates of subsequent mailings should be noted on the graph.)

As completed questionnaires are returned, each should be opened, perused, and assigned an identification number. These numbers should be assigned serially as the questionnaires are returned—even if other identification (ID) numbers have already been assigned. This can have important advantages. Two examples should illustrate these.

Let's assume that the researcher is studying attitudes toward a political figure. In the middle of the data collection, let's further assume that the figure in question is discovered to be supporting a mistress. By knowing the date of that disclosure and the dates when questionnaires were received, the researcher would be in a position to determine the effects of the disclosure.

As a less sensational example, serialized ID numbers can be valuable in estimating nonresponse biases in the survey. Barring more direct tests of bias, the researcher may wish to assume that those respondents who failed to answer the questionnaire will be more like those who delayed answering than like those who answered right away. An analysis of questionnaires received at different points in the data collection might then be used for estimates of sampling bias. For example, if grade-point averages (GPA) reported by students decrease steadily through the data collection, with those replying right away having higher GPAs and those replying later having lower GPAs, then the researcher might tentatively conclude that those who failed to answer at all have lower GPAs yet. While it would not be advisable to make statistical estimates of bias in this fashion, the researcher could take advantage of approximate estimates.

If respondents have been identified for purposes of follow-up mailing, then, preparations for those mailings should be made as the questionnaires are returned. The case study that follows in this chapter will discuss this in greater detail.

8.4   Follow-up Mailings

The methodological literature on follow-up mailings strongly suggests this is an effective method for increasing return rates in mail surveys. In general, the longer a potential respondent delays replying, the less likely he is to do so at all. Properly timed follow-up mailings, then, provide additional stimuli for responding.

The effects of follow-up mailings will be seen in the response rate curves recorded during data collection. The initial mailing will be followed by a rise and subsequent subsiding of returns; the follow-up mailing will spur a resurgence of returns; and more follow-ups will do the same. In practice, three mailings (an original and two follow-ups) seems the most efficient.

The timing of follow-up mailings is also important. Here the methodological literature offers less precise guides, but it has been my experience that two or three weeks is a reasonable space between mailings. (This period might be increased by a few days if the mailing time—out and in—is more than two or three days.)

When the researcher conducts several surveys over time to the same population, such experience should help him to develop more specific guidelines in this regard. The Survey Research Office at the University of Hawaii conducts frequent student surveys and has been able to refine the mailing /remailing procedure considerably. Indeed, a consistent pattern of returns has been found, which appears to transcend difference of survey content, quality of instrument, and so forth. Within two weeks after the first mailing, approximately 40 percent of the questionnaires are returned; within two weeks after the first follow-up, an additional 20 percent are received, and within two weeks after the final follow-up an additional 10 percent are received. There are no grounds for assuming that a similar pattern would appear in surveys of different populations, but this illustration should indicate the value of carefully tabulating return rates for every survey conducted.

Follow-up mailings may be administered in a number of ways. In the simplest, nonrespondents are simply sent a letter of additional encouragement to participate. A better method, however, is to send a new copy of the survey questionnaire with the follow-up letter. If potential respondents have not returned their questionnaires after two or three weeks, there is a good likelihood that the questionnaires will have been lost or misplaced. Receiving a follow-up letter might encourage them to look for the original questionnaire, but if it is not easily found, the letter may go for naught. (The response rates reported in the above paragraph all involved the sending of additional questionnaires.)

If the individuals in the survey sample are not identified on the questionnaires, it may not be possible to remail only to nonrespondents. In such a case, the researcher should send his follow-up mailing to all initial members of the sample, thanking those who may have already participated and encouraging those who have not to do so. (The case study reported in a later section of this chapter describes another method that may be used in an anonymous mail survey.)

8.5 Acceptable Response Rates

A question that new survey researchers frequently ask concerns the percentage return rate that should be achieved in a mail survey. It bears repeating here that the body of inferential statistics used in connection with survey analysis assumed that *all* members of the initial sample complete and return their questionnaires. Since this almost never happens, response bias becomes a concern, with the researcher testing (and hoping for) the possibility that the respondents are essentially a random sample of the initial sample, and thus a somewhat smaller random sample of the total population.[1]

Nevertheless, overall response rate is one guide to the representativeness of the sample respondents. If a high response rate is achieved, there is less chance of significant response bias than if a low rate is achieved. But what is a *high* response rate?

A quick review of the survey literature will uncover a wide range of response rates. Each of these may be accompanied by a statement something like "This is regarded as a relatively high response rate for a survey of this type." (A United States senator made this statement regarding a poll of constituents that achieved a 4 percent return rate.) Despite the great variety of actual return rates and reactions to those rates, there are some rules of thumb that might be followed.

I feel that a response rate of at least 50 percent is *adequate* for analysis and reporting. A response rate of at least 60 percent is *good.* And a response rate of 70 percent or more is *very good.* The reader should bear in mind, however, that these are only rough guides, they have no statistical basis, and a demonstrated lack of response bias is far more important than a high response rate.

In computing response rates, the accepted practice is to omit all those questionnaires that could not be delivered. In his methodological report, the researcher should indicate the initial sample size, then subtract the number that could not be delivered due to bad addresses, death, and the like. Then the number of completed questionnaires is divided by the *net* sample size to produce the response rate. As a result, the response rate is really a measure of the researcher's success in persuading sample members to participate, and he does not count against himself those whom he could not even contact.

While this is the accepted practice, the reader should be aware of the logical assumption upon which it is based: that nondeliverable questionnaires represent a random sample of the initial sample. Of course, this may not be the case at all. Persons whose questionnaires cannot be delivered are, at the

---

[1]For more detailed examinations of nonresponse biases, see Marjorie N. Donald, "Implications of Nonresponse for the Interpretation of Mail Questionnaire Data," *Public Opinion Quarterly,* vol. 24, no. 1 (1960), pp. 99–114, and K. A. Brownlee, "A Note on the Effects of Nonresponse on Surveys," *Journal of the American Statistical Association,* vol. 52, no. 277 (1957), pp. 29–32.

very least, probably more mobile than others in the sample, and mobility may be related to a variety of other variables. Here again, tests for nonresponse bias are the best guide.

8.6   A Case Study

The steps involved in the administration of a mail survey are many and can best be appreciated in a walkthrough of an actual study. We shall conclude this chapter, then, with a detailed description of a survey conducted among University of Hawaii students in the spring of 1969. As the reader will note shortly, the study did not represent the theoretical ideal for such studies, but in that regard it serves present purposes all the better.

Sample Selection

The sample design and selection for this study have been reported as a case study in Chapter 6. By way of general overview, it will be recalled that approximately 1,100 students were selected from the university registration tape through a stratified, systematic sampling procedure. For each student so selected, six self-adhesive mailing labels were printed by the computer.

By the time the research team was prepared to distribute the questionnaires, it became apparent that their research funds were inadequate to cover several mailings to the entire sample of 1,100 students. (Questionnaire printing costs were higher than anticipated.) As a result, a systematic ⅔ sample of the mailing labels was chosen, yielding a subsample of 770 students.

Postcards

An earlier decision had been made to keep the survey anonymous in the hope of encouraging more candid responses to some sensitive questions. (Subsequent surveys of the same issues among the same population indicate this was unnecessary.) Thus, the questionnaires would carry no identification of students on them. At the same time, it was hoped that follow-up mailing costs could be reduced by remailing only to nonrespondents.

To achieve both of these aims, a special postcard method was devised. Each student was mailed a questionnaire that carried no identifying marks, plus a postcard addressed to the research office—with one of his mailing labels affixed to the reverse side of the card. The introductory letter asked him to complete and return the questionnaire—assuring him anonymity—and to return the postcard simultaneously. Receipt of the postcard would tell the researchers that he had returned his questionnaire—without indicating *which* questionnaire was his. This procedure would then facilitate follow-up mailings. (See below.)

Questionnaire

The 32-page questionnaire was printed in the form of a booklet (photo-offset and saddle-stitched). A three-panel cover—described elsewhere in this chapter—permitted the questionnaire to be returned without an additional envelope.

Introductory Letter

A letter introducing the study and its purposes was printed on the front cover of the booklet. It explained why the study was being conducted (to learn how students feel about a variety of issues), how they had been selected for the study, the importance of each student responding, and the mechanics of returning the questionnaire.

Students were assured that the study was anonymous, and the postcard method and rationale were explained. This was followed by a statement of the auspices under which the study was being conducted, and a telephone number was provided for those who might want more information about the study. (About five students called for information.)

By printing the introductory letter on the questionnaire, it was not necessary to enclose a separate letter in the outgoing envelope, thereby simplifying the task of assembling mailing pieces.

Mailing-Piece Assembly

The assembly of materials for the initial mailing involved the following steps. (1) One mailing label for each student was stuck on a postcard. (2) Another label was stuck on an outgoing manila envelope. (3) One postcard and one questionnaire were placed in each envelope—with a check to insure that the name on the postcard and on the envelope were the same in each case.

This was accomplished through an assembly-line procedure involving the several members of the research team. Although the procedure was somewhat organized in advance, it should be noted that a certain amount of actual practice was required before the best allocation of tasks and persons was discovered.

It is also worth noting that the entire process was delayed several days while the initial batch of manila envelopes were exchanged for larger ones.

This could have been avoided if a walkthrough of the assembly process had been carried out in advance.

Mailing

The distribution of the survey questionnaires had been set up for a bulk-rate mailing. Once the questionnaires had been stuffed into the envelopes, they were grouped by zip codes, tied in bundles, and delivered to the post office.

Receiving Returned Questionnaires

Shortly after the initial mailing, questionnaires and post-cards began arriving at the research office. Questionnaires were opened, perused, and assigned identification numbers as described earlier in the chapter.

The processing of postcards, however, pointed to an oversight in sample design. Recall from the earlier discussion of the sample design (Chapter 6) that the final arrangement of students in the sampling frame had been by social security number, thereby providing a quasi-stratification by region of origin. As a result, the mailing labels were printed in that order (within class strata). Social security numbers had not been printed on the mailing labels, however, as this was not relevant to the study.

Given a postcard bearing a particular name and address, then, it was very difficult to locate the corresponding labels among those remaining in the several sheets of computer printout. Thus it was necessary to cut apart all the labels from the printout sheets and alphabetize them. Then it was possible to locate a given student's label with a minimum of effort. (*Note:* The labels could have been printed in alphabetical order initially, if this problem had been anticipated.) For every postcard received, then, a search was made for that student's labels, and they were destroyed.

Follow-Up Mailings

After a period of two or three weeks, all the mailing labels remaining were used to organize a follow-up mailing. The assembly procedures described above were repeated with one exception. A special, separate letter of appeal was prepared and included in the mailing piece. The new letter indicated that many students had returned their questionnaires already, but that it was very important for all others to do so as well. The letter also indicated that the research office records might be in error, and if the student had already returned his questionnaire, he should ignore the second appeal and accept our thanks for his assistance. If he had not already participated, he was encouraged to do so.

The follow-up mailing stimulated a resurgence of returns as expected, and the same logging procedures were continued. Postcards were used as a basis for destroying the additional mailing labels. Unfortunately, time and financial pressures made it impossible to undertake a third mailing as had been initially planned, but the two mailings resulted in an overall return rate of 62 percent.

Summary and Conclusions

This chapter has been addressed to the nuts and bolts of collecting data through the medium of the self-administered questionnaire. Two summary observations are in order in this regard.

First, it is my contention that such mundane matters are vital to high-quality scientific research. The researcher who believes the quality of his research is solely a function of his analytical and theoretical abilities is sorely misled. A brilliant research design that is improperly executed will result in failure. No detail is too small or too mundane to be safely ignored.

Second, the detailed chronicle of one mail survey—with all its problems —should bring home the importance of pre-tests and pilot studies relating to *all* aspects of a study design. Only such advanced testing can uncover problems that might eventually scuttle an entire study.

Additional Readings

Moser, C. A., *Survey Methods in Social Investigation* (London: William Heinemann, 1958), pp. 175–184.

Chapter Nine

Data Collection II: Interviewing

This chapter essentially parallels Chapter 8 in that it represents an alternative method of data collection. Rather than asking respondents to read questionnaires and enter their own answers, members of the research team ask the questions verbally and record the respondents' answers. Interviewing is typically done in a face-to-face encounter, and this chapter will focus on such interviewing situations. However, telephone interviewing should follow most of the same guidelines.

9.1 Importance of Interviewer

There are a number of advantages in having a questionnaire administered by an interviewer rather than by the respondent himself.[1] To begin, interview surveys typically attain higher response rates than mail surveys. A properly designed and executed interview survey ought to achieve a completion rate of at least 80 to 85 percent. (Federally funded surveys often require this.) It would seem that respondents are more reluctant to turn down an interviewer standing on their doorstep than they are to throw away a mail questionnaire.

Within the context of the questionnaire, the presence of an interviewer generally decreases the number of "don't knows" and "no answers." If minimizing such responses is important to the study, the interviewer can be

---

[1] In drafting this chapter, I found myself confronted with a stylistic and moral dilemma: the choice of *gender* in referring to interviewers and other members of the research team. Conventional English usage calls for the masculine pronoun in referring to a person of indeterminate sex. Thus, since either men or women can serve as interviewers, it would seem appropriate to refer to an interviewer in the text as "he" or "him," just as the project director has been referred to as "he." An early draft of this chapter followed that convention. Unfortunately, it sounded artificial and far removed from actual survey experience.

In fact, most survey interviewers are women. Most project directors, on the other hand, are men. I have decided, therefore, to use pronouns that correspond to the typical gender of the persons being referred to: project directors are "he" and interviewers are "she." It has not been my intention to engage in sex-role discrimination, only to present a realistic picture of survey research in practice. (*Note:* There are good reasons for the predominance of women among interviewers. For example, male interviewers may appear somewhat threatening to the female respondent, especially if she is at home alone. On the other hand, I can think of no good reasons for the predominance of men among project directors.)

instructed to probe for answers. ("If you had to pick one of the answers, which do you think would come closest to your feelings?")

Interviewers can also provide a guard against confusing questionnaire items. If the respondent clearly misunderstands the intent of a question or indicates that he does not understand, the interviewer can clarify matters, thereby obtaining relevant responses. (Such clarifications must be strictly controlled, however, through formal *specifications*. See below.)

Finally, the interviewer can observe as well as ask questions. For example, the interviewer can note the respondent's race if this is considered too delicate a question to ask. Similar observations can be made regarding the quality of the dwelling, the presence of various possessions, the respondent's ability to speak English, the respondent's general reactions to the study and so forth. In one survey of students, respondents were given a short self-administered questionnaire to complete—concerning sexual attitudes and behavior—during the course of the interview. While the student completed the questionnaire, the interviewer made detailed notes regarding the dress and grooming of the respondent.

Neutral Role of Interviewer

Survey research is of necessity based on an unrealistic *stimulus–response* theory of cognition and behavior. It must be assumed that a questionnaire item will mean exactly the same thing to every respondent, and every given response must mean the same when given by different respondents. Although this is an impossible goal, survey questions are drafted in such a way as to closely approximate the ideal.

The interviewer must also fit into this ideal situation. The interviewer's presence should not affect a respondent's perception of a question nor the answer given. The interviewer, then, should be a *neutral* medium through which questions and answers are transmitted.

If this is successfully accomplished, different interviewers would obtain exactly the same responses from a given respondent. This has a special importance in area samples. To save time and money, a given interviewer is typically assigned to complete all the interviews in a particular geographical area —a city block or group of nearby blocks. If the interviewer does anything to affect the responses obtained, then the bias thus interjected might be interpreted as a characteristic of the area under study.

Let's suppose that a survey is being done to determine attitudes toward low-cost housing, to help in the selection of a site for a new government-sponsored development. An interviewer assigned to a given neighborhood might—through word or gesture—communicate her own distaste for low-cost housing developments. Her respondents might thereby tend to give responses generally in agreement with her own position. The results of the survey would indicate that the neighborhood in question would strongly resist construction of the development in their area.

9.2 General Rules for Interviewing

The manner in which interviews ought to be conducted will vary somewhat by survey population and will be affected somewhat by the nature of the survey content as well. Nevertheless, it is possible to provide some general guidelines that would apply to most if not all interviewing situations.

Appearance and Demeanor

As a general rule, the interviewer should dress in a fashion fairly similar to that of the people she will be interviewing. A richly dressed interviewer will probably have difficulty getting good cooperation and responses from poorer respondents. And a poorly dressed interviewer will have similar difficulties with richer respondents.

To the extent that the interviewer's dress and grooming differ from those of her respondents, it should be in the direction of cleanliness and neatness in modest apparel. If cleanliness is not next to godliness, it appears to be next to neutrality. Whereas middle-class neatness and cleanliness may not be accepted by all sectors of American society, it remains the primary norm and is more likely to be acceptable to the largest number of respondents.

Dress and grooming are typically regarded as signals to a person's attitudes and orientations. At the time this is being written, a man wearing colorful clothes, beads and sandals and sporting long hair, sideburns, and a beard communicates—correctly or incorrectly—that he is politically on the left, sexually permissive, antiwar, favorable to drug use, and so forth. His appearance will communicate these orientations to a respondent as much as if he began the interview by saying "Hi there, I'm a hippy!"

In demeanor, the interviewer should be pleasant if nothing else. Since she will be prying into the respondent's personal life and attitudes, she must communicate a genuine interest in getting to know the respondent without appearing to be a spy. She must be relaxed and friendly without being too casual or clinging. One of the most important natural abilities that interviewers must have is the ability to determine very quickly the kind of person the respondent will feel most comfortable with; the kind of person the respondent would most enjoy talking to. There are two aspects to this. Clearly, the interview will be more successful if the interviewer can become the kind of person the respondent is comfortable with. At the same time, however, there seems to be an ethical issue here. Since the respondent is asked to volunteer a portion of his time and to divulge personal information about himself, he deserves the most enjoyable experience that the researcher and the interviewer can provide.

Familiarity with Questionnaire

If the interviewer is unfamiliar with the questionnaire, the study suffers and an unfair burden is placed on the respondent. In the latter respect, the interview is likely to take more time than necessary and be generally unpleasant. Moreover, this cannot be accomplished by having the interviewer skim through the questionnaire two or three times. It must be studied carefully, question by question, and the interviewer must practice reading it aloud. (See "interviewer training" section later in this chapter.)

Ultimately, the interviewer must be able to read the questionnaire items to respondents without error, without stumbling over words and phrases. A good guide for interviewers is the actor reading lines in a play or motion picture. The lines must be read as naturally as though they constituted a natural conversation, but that conversation must follow exactly the language set down in the questionnaire. Of course, the interviewer should not attempt to memorize the questionnaire.

By the same token, the interviewer must be familiar with the specifications prepared in conjunction with the questionnaire. Inevitably some questions will not exactly fit a given respondent's situation, and a question will arise as to how the question should be interpreted in that situation. The specifications provided to the interviewer should provide adequate guidance in such cases, but the interviewer must know the organization and contents of the specifications sufficiently to permit efficient reference to them. It would be better for the interviewer to leave a given question unanswered than to spend five minutes searching through the specifications for clarification and/or trying to interpret the relevant instructions.

Follow Question Wording Exactly

An earlier chapter discussing conceptualization and instrument construction pointed to the significance of question wording for the responses obtained. Thus, a slight change in the wording of a given question may lead a respondent to answer "yes" rather than "no."

While the researcher will very carefully phrase his questionnaire items in such a way as to obtain the information he needs and to insure that respondents will interpret items in a manner appropriate to those needs, all this effort will be wasted if interviewers rephrase questions in their own words.

Record Responses Exactly

Whenever the questionnaire contains open-ended questions, those soliciting the respondent's own answer, it is very important that the interviewer record those answers exactly as given. No attempt should be made to summarize, paraphrase, or correct bad grammar. The response should be written down exactly as given.

This is especially important since the interviewer will not know how the responses are to be coded prior to processing—indeed, the research director may not know this until he has had an opportunity to read a hundred or so such responses. For example, the questionnaire might ask respondents how they feel about the traffic situation in their community. One respondent might answer that there were too many cars on the roads and that something should be done to limit their numbers. Another might say there was a need for more roads. If the interviewer recorded these two responses with the same summary—"congested traffic"—the researcher would not be able to take advantage of the important differences in the original responses.

Sometimes, the respondent may be so inarticulate that the verbal response is too ambiguous to permit interpretation. However, the interviewer may be able to understand the intent of the response through the respondent's gestures or tone. In such a situation, the exact verbal response should still be recorded, but the interviewer should add marginal comments giving her interpretation and her reasons for arriving at it.

More generally, it will be useful to the researcher to have any marginal comments explaining aspects of the response not conveyed in the verbal record, such as the respondent's apparent uncertainty in answering, anger, embarrassment, and so forth. In each case, however, the exact verbal response should also be recorded.

Probing for Responses

Sometimes respondents will respond to a question with an inappropriate answer. For example, the question may present an attitudinal statement and ask the respondent to "strongly agree, agree somewhat, disagree somewhat, or strongly disagree." The respondent, however, may reply: "I think that's true." The interviewer should follow this reply with: "Would you say you strongly agree or agree somewhat?" If necessary, the interviewer might explain that she must check one or the other of the categories provided. If the respondent adamantly refuses to choose, the interviewer should write in the exact response given by the respondent.

Probes are more frequently required in eliciting responses to open-ended questions. For example, in response to the previous question about traffic conditions, the respondent might simply reply, "Pretty bad." The interviewer could obtain an elaboration on this response through a variety of probes. Sometimes the best probe is silence; if the interviewer sits quietly with pencil poised, the respondent will probably fill the pause with additional comments. (This is a technique used effectively by newspaper reporters.) Appropriate verbal probes might be "How is that? In what ways?" Perhaps the most generally useful probe is "Anything else?"

It is frequently necessary to probe for answers that will be sufficiently informative for analytical purposes. In every case, however, it is imperative that such probes be completely *neutral.* The probe must not in any way affect the nature of the subsequent response. Whenever the researcher anticipates that a given question may require probing for appropriate responses, he should present one or more useful probes next to the question in the questionnaire. This practice has two important advantages. First, he will have more time to devise the best, most neutral probes. Second, all interviewers will use the same probes whenever they are needed. Thus, even if the probe is not perfectly neutral, all respondents will be presented with the same stimulus. This is the same logical guideline discussed for question wording. While a question should not be loaded or biased, it is essential that every respondent be presented with the same question, even a biased one.

9.3   Interviewer Training

Even if the researcher is fortunate enough to organize an interviewing team comprised wholly of intelligent, experienced interviewers, a careful interviewer training course will be absolutely essential. Every survey and every questionnaire differs from every other one, and interviewers must be retrained for each new survey. The amount of time required for such training will depend on the scope and nature of the survey and the relative experience of the interviewers. For the typical household survey, using a combination of experienced and inexperienced interviewers, however, it may normally require about two weeks, one week of classroom instruction and practice, and another week of practice in the field. The following comments will touch on the various aspects of interviewer training.

General Instruction

The interviewer training should begin with some general comments about the nature of the survey and its ultimate purpose. It is a bad idea to regard and treat interviewers as unthinking automatons or as technicians who can be instructed to perform their duties by rote. Generally speaking, if interviewers understand why the survey is being conducted and can see that it is an important undertaking, they will be more diligent and careful in their work.

The general description of the study should include the sponsor of the survey, the primary purpose of the study, how the sample of respondents was selected, and so forth. It is also a good idea to give interviewers a general picture of the other steps involved in the survey: how the questionnaire was designed, how the data will be processed, and how they will be analyzed. If they can understand how they fit into the overall process, they will probably feel more a part of the research team and will respond accordingly.

Administrative details should be covered early in the training. How long will the interviewing last? How many hours per week are interviewers expected to work? How often will they get paid? The interviewer who is personally worried about such details will be unable to concentrate on the intricacies of questionnaire items.

Even if all the interviewers are experienced, the training sessions should cover the general guidelines and rules for interviewing. It will be most useful if the researcher can prepare a set of general guidelines to pass out and discuss with the interviewers. Often the most experienced interviewers will be able to elaborate on some of the rules through examples from their past encounters, and the newer interviewers will get a better idea of what to expect in the field.

Studying the Questionnaire and Specifications

Interviewers and the supervisor and/or project director should then go through the entire questionnaire step by step. The purpose of items should be explained, and all possible ambiguities should be discussed. It is essential that this portion of the training be conducted informally, as a discussion rather than a lecture. Interviewers who do not understand a particular point should be encouraged to ask for clarification immediately. The instructor's response should in no way reflect dissatisfaction, or else interviewers may sit quietly and not fully understand what is expected of them.

The examination of the questionnaire should simultaneously involve an examination of the specifications. Thus, the instructor should read the question and the answer categories, explain what is intended by the question, describe some simple situations and the appropriate action by the interviewer, then describe some more complicated questions, turn to the appropriate section of the specifications, and show how those specifications would resolve such a situation.

Much of the discussion during this activity will take the form of "What do I do if the respondent says . . .?" Where appropriate, the instructor should turn to the specifications and show how the situation would be resolved. Ultimately, however, the desired handling of the situation presented should be described clearly. The interviewers should know exactly how the instructor would have handled the situation in question.

There is another side to this issue, however. Quite often, a situation will be suggested that the instructor cannot easily resolve. The possibility of such a situation might not have occurred to the researcher, and it will not have been covered in the specifications. The instructor should not make snap decisions in such cases. Rather, he should say he does not know, and that the issue will be resolved before the next meeting. The researcher should then carefully work out the appropriate solution, determine and explain how it fits into the overall logic of the question's intent. The resolution should be explained to the interviewers at the next meeting, and the specifications should be updated to take it into account. The worst procedure is for the instructor to provide off-the-cuff, arbitrary answers without taking care to integrate such answers into the overall logic of the question and the specifications. Such responses will add up until interviewers will have too many specific instructions to keep track of, and they will no longer have a general logical understanding to guide them in their own interpretations.

It should be apparent from the foregoing that interviewer training cannot be conducted effectively without an active role being played by the project director. Unhappily, as survey research has become more organized and specialized, technical staffs have been created, there has developed a tendency for the project director to turn over such aspects of the study to the "experts." Quite clearly, the most qualified interviewing supervisor cannot always fully understand what the researcher wishes to get out of a given questionnaire or a given item. If he forces the supervisor to resolve difficult situations, he will have no assurance that the decisions will be appropriate to his data needs. Moreover, the supervisor's morale is likely to decline under such conditions, and this will quickly become apparent to the interviewers. Ultimately, the field staff decide that if precision is not important to the researcher, there is no reason for them to work hard to achieve it.

Preferably, the project director should participate in the entire training session. He should not direct the instruction unless he is the best qualified person to do so; the interviewer supervisor probably knows more about interviewing per se than he does. His continuing presence in the training session, however, demonstrates his personal concern for and commitment to professional data collection, and he will facilitate the training by being able to clarify confusion.

Practice Interviews in Class

Once the questionnaire and specifications have been studied in detail, the session should be organized around a series of practice interviews. To begin, two or three interviews should be conducted in front of the whole class. The best beginning would be for the project director to interview the supervisor and vice versa. Since these interviews should serve as models for the interviewers, they should be conducted in precise accord with the previous general and specific instructions. The person being interviewed should either report his own condition and attitudes or take on a fictional, but consistent, identity. The person doing the interviewing should act just as though it were a real interview.

Sometimes a specific development in the practice interview will warrant an explanatory comment to the class, but this should not be allowed to break the general frame of a real interview being conducted. At the completion of each interview, the class should be encouraged to discuss it, ask questions, and so forth.

After the series of practice interviews in front of the class, the interviewers should be paired up to practice interviewing each other. This practice need not be done in front of the class, but the several practice interviews should go on simultaneously. The interviewing supervisor should walk around the classroom, stopping to listen to the practice interviews; but for the most part, it would be better to make notes and then discuss them with the entire class after a round of practice interviews has been completed.

The interviewers should be re-paired and more practice interviews conducted. This portion of the training, then, should be an alternation of practice and discussion.

Practice Interviews in the Field

Once the classroom instruction has been completed, interviewers should be assigned practice interviews in the field. This portion of the training should be exactly like the real thing. Assignments of respondents and/or addresses should be made just as will be done in the final survey. Normally, the person responsible for selecting the survey sample will provide a list of respondents who were not selected in the main sample.

The interviewers should be given exactly the materials they will use in the final survey. They will make their contacts with respondents and conduct their interviews. (Respondents should not be told that they have been selected for a practice interview as this will destroy the realism of the practice.) Moreover, interviewers should practice all administrative procedures at this point as well; they should fill out time sheets, logs and so forth. In effect, the practice interviews in the field provide a pilot study of the entire interviewing operation.

Normally, it will be sufficient for interviewers to complete about five practice interviews in the field, although this can vary in accord with the nature of the survey. One aspect of the interviewing operation may be modified for practice, however. In the final survey, interviewers may be asked to make a specified minimum number of calls to a given respondent before judging that person "unavailable." To facilitate practice interviewing, this aspect can be omitted. To take account of such a modification, however, each interviewer should be given enough assignments to insure that the specified number of interviews can be conducted. If they are not able to contact enough of these assignments, they should be given instructions for obtaining more assignments from the research office.

As each interviewer completes her practice interviews, she should bring them back to the interviewing supervisor. The supervisor would then go through the completed questionnaires with the interviewer to locate and discuss any problems and to answer any new questions the interviewer may have. As a variation on this, it might be a good idea to have interviewers report back with their first two or three interviews, then return to the field to complete the rest.

Although it is normally a good idea to establish a specific number of practice interviews to be completed, the more general rule is that every interviewer must complete enough practice interviews to demonstrate that she fully understands the task or that she will probably not be able to understand it. Thus some interviewers may have to conduct more practice interviews than others. This is quite appropriate even if the subsequent practice interviews overlap in time with the beginning of actual interviewing. It is far preferable for some interviewers to begin late than to have them make mistakes in interviewing the final sample. Otherwise, it might be necessary to omit the incorrectly interviewed respondents, reinterview them, or play games with the sample design: all are bad ideas.

After the completion of all or most of the practice interviews in the field, the interviewers should be brought together for a final session in the classroom to discuss their experiences and to receive last-minute changes in interview procedures. This also provides an excellent opportunity for a final pep talk from the project director.

9.4   The Interviewing Operation

The ongoing interviewing operation must be organized and controlled as carefully as the training session. While the details of this will vary from survey to survey, some general points can be made.

Staff

The number of interviewers required is determined on the basis of (1) the number of interviews to be conducted, (2) the average time required for each, (3) the period of time allotted to the entire interviewing operation, and, importantly, (4) the number of qualified interviewers available.

A good rule of thumb is to determine the number required on the basis of points 1, 2, and 3 above, then recruit and train twice that number. During

the course of training, many prospective interviewers will drop out volun-
tarily, others should be asked to drop out. It is generally better to begin
interviewing with a few good interviewers than with a lot of bad ones, as the
latter usually cost more money, take up more of the supervisory time, and
ultimately produce a lower quality of data. After weeding out bad interviewers, it would be best to begin the actual interviewing with somewhat more
than it is anticipated will be needed throughout. Interviewers will continue
to drop out during the study, and it will become apparent that others should
be asked to drop out. Typically, the interviewing staff is terminated in a
staggered fashion near the end of the operation, and the best interviewers can
be asked to stay on longer for the wrap-up.

Often, the scope of a survey will require more than a single supervisor.
While one person should be responsible for supervising the entire operation,
he might be assisted by a staff of supervisors. As a general rule of thumb, 1
supervisor for every 10 interviewers should suffice. In a very large interview
survey, with several interviewing supervisors, the person in overall charge
should not be assigned interviewers to supervise. He will have enough work
handling the logistics of the operation, coordinating with the project director,
possibly recruiting and training additional interviewers, and, of course, supervising the supervisors.

Interview Assignment and Record Keeping

The survey sample design will specify that a certain list
of persons (or addresses) be interviewed. Several copies of this list should be
maintained. A household survey might be handled in the following manner.
First, there should be a master list kept someplace safe. It might be a printed
list or could be stored on magnetic tape in the event that it was prepared in
that manner. This is the back-up reference in the event that portions of the
list are lost or destroyed during the interviewing operation.

Second, it might be useful to print the sample on separate self-sticking
labels. If the sample has been selected by computer, this can be done quite
simply. These labels, in turn, can be attached to individual questionnaires.

Third, each supervisor should have a copy of the list, or the portion he
is responsible for. If a cluster sample of households has been selected, it could
be printed on standard forms with all the households on a given block put
on one sheet. The standard form should permit the recording of the following
kinds of information: (1) the name or code of the interviewer assigned to the
respondent, (2) any reassignment to another interviewer, (3) the final disposition of the interview: completed, refused, and so forth, (4) the date of completion or refusal, and (5) any identification number assigned to it for subsequent
data processing.

The supervisor would then assign a group of interviews to a given interviewer, giving her the appropriate questionnaires, and recording the assign-

ment. In this fashion, the location and status of all interviews prescribed by the sample design will be known. Moreover, such records will permit a continuous monitoring of the operation.

As a rule of thumb, the supervisor may assign 20 to 30 interviews to an interviewer at a time. Of course, good interviewers may be assigned more than that, while poorer ones should be assigned fewer. Also, interviewers who are at remote locations or are given interview assignments in such locations may be given more as appropriate. The more general guideline, however, is that the supervisor should make assignments on the assumption that the interviewer will drop dead, lose the questionnaires in a fire, or run away to Mexico with them. In any of these contingencies, it must be possible to reassign the interviews with a minimum of delay and confusion.

Wherever possible, interview assignments should be made efficiently. If five interviews are to be conducted in a given remote city block, they should normally all be assigned to a single interviewer at one time. In this fashion, the time and cost involved in going to the block will be minimized. If five separate interviewers were forced to make the identical trip, the time and cost would both be increased. At the same time, it would be a bad idea to have a single interviewer conduct all the interviews in a larger geographical area, especially if that area had a distinctive class, race, or other characteristic. The interviews in such an area should be split among several interviewers. Otherwise, what might appear a special characteristic of the respondents in that area might in fact reflect only the peculiar biases or practices of the single interviewer. Thus, it might appear that most of the poor black respondents in the survey were opposed to Medicare, when in fact this merely reflected the manner in which the interviewer assigned to that area asked the question and recorded the responses.

Clearly, this is another example of the compromises that make up survey research in practice. Scientific and administrative concerns must be balanced against one another. While it is impossible to prescribe the best compromise for every field condition, an understanding of the issues involved should assist the researcher in making such a decision.

Supervision and Editing

Procedures should be established concerning the regular reporting of interviewers to their supervisor. Perhaps the best procedure is to establish a regular, weekly appointment for each interviewer. At the appointed time, she would check in with all her completed interviews, go over them with the supervisor, and get a new set of assignments.

The supervisor might begin by asking for and discussing any problems that arose in the interviews at hand. Then, he should read through each of the completed questionnaires, looking for missing answers, apparent errors, illegible entries, and anything else that makes the questionnaire difficult to use and interpret and/or suggests the interviewer does not understand the task or some part of it. Each error should be pointed out and discussed. The interviewer should end up knowing precisely how the situation should have been handled, so that the same error will not recur.

It is quite reasonable for the supervisor to vary both assignments and editing for given interviewers on the basis of their initial performances. The interviewer who is doing a good job, then, may be assigned more interviews at a time, and the supervisor may not have to be quite as careful in reading through completed questionnaires in the interviewer's presence. At the same time, the supervisor cannot afford to develop a "halo effect" with regard to interviewers. Even if a given interviewer has been doing a perfect job in the beginning, it is essential for the supervisor to continue monitoring her later work.

Ultimately, every completed questionnaire must be edited in its entirety. In some cases, this task may be assigned to special editors, but it is normally a good idea for the interviewer supervisors to do much if not all of it.

Reassigning Interviews

Interviewers should be trained in the importance of completing the interviews assigned to them. They should be prepared, in some instances, to persuade uncertain respondents to participate. At the same time, they should be warned against being too forceful in that attempt.

Frequently, an interviewer will arrive at a bad time and be turned down by the respondent. Or perhaps something about the interviewer's appearance or demeanor led to an initial refusal. The interviewer should not force the respondent into adamant rejection, since it may be possible for the supervisor to telephone the respondent to discuss the survey and arrange for a different interviewer to return to the household.

Some interviewers are simply more successful in gaining cooperation than others. They are able to establish better and faster rapport with respondents. These people will become identifiable over the course of the survey, and it may be advisable to have them specialize on difficult interviews. (If this is done, their efficiency should not be judged on the same basis as other interviewers, since it typically takes more time to complete the difficult interviews. Also, it might be appropriate to pay them more, on the basis of the difficulty of the task and their special importance to the survey.)

Verification of Interviews

All or a portion of the interviews should be verified by the supervisor. This may take several forms. As a minimum, the supervisor should call the respondent by telephone, identify himself, and verify that the interview was in fact conducted. In a more rigorous verification procedure, he might re-ask certain key questions and check the responses against those reported in the questionnaire. Requestioning should not be too extensive, however, as it takes up the supervisor's time, takes up the respondent's time (he has already volunteered time and information), and it may make the respondent worry about the confidentiality of the survey.

There are two reasons for verifying interviews. Some interviewers may make honest mistakes in contacting assigned respondents. This is especially possible with a complex household sample design. Others will simply cheat. The researcher should not let himself assume that all his interviewers will faithfully attempt to contact and interview those people assigned to them. In fact, it is probably a rare survey in which no cheating occurs. Some interviewers will conduct only cursory interviews, and fill in the questionnaire on that basis. Others will interview more convenient respondents. Still others will complete their questionnaires over a beer in the comfort of their own homes.

Whenever the researcher discovers cheating, he should, of course, put an end to it. But at the same time, he should try to find out why it occurred in the first place. He may conclude, if he is honest with himself, that it is attributable in part to his own handling of the interviewing operation. He may have asked too much of the interviewers, may have provided them with ambiguous instructions, or may simply have conveyed the impression that he regarded the field work as below his status. While such discoveries may not save the survey under way, they might guide his subsequent behavior.

Firing Interviewers

In practice, it seems very difficult to fire interviewers. No one wants to do it, especially after working closely with the interviewer during training and if the interviewer seems to be trying very hard. Nevertheless, some interviewers will inevitably turn out unequal to the task. Keeping them at work, however, hurts the financing, timing, and quality of the study.

In every large interviewing operation, one supervisor usually appears better at firing people than the others. He probably does not enjoy it any more than the others, but he gets the job done. There will be a great temptation to let such a person do all the firing, but this should normally be avoided, since it will give him a bad reputation among the interviewers. Instead, a policy should be established whereby the person in overall charge does all the firing, or else each supervisor is responsible for those under him.

Whenever a person is not working out as an interviewer, you should bear in mind that interviewing requires very special skills. The lack of those, largely interpersonal, skills does not mean the person is unqualified for other jobs. It may be the case that a person who is a total failure as an interviewer will turn out to be the best of all coders. Both the interviewer and the project might profit from a reassignment rather than a simple termination.

Summary

This chapter has only touched on some of the important elements of an effective interviewing operation. It has not been my intention to train interviewing supervisors through these comments, but to inform the prospective project director about what is involved. A good interviewing operation requires supervisors and interviewers whose own training and experience will provide a far greater elaboration on each of the points covered so briefly here.

At the same time, the project director must play an active role in the interviewing process. He must know what is involved so as to adjust his demands to the realities of field interviewing and to be in a better position to evaluate the meaning of the data he will receive. And, as noted frequently in this chapter, his very presence in the interviewing process can have an important effect on morale and on the quality of work accomplished.

Additional Readings

Gorden, Raymond L., *Interviewing: Strategy, Techniques, and Tactics* (Homewood, Ill.: Dorsey Press, 1969).

Kahn, Robert L., and Charles F. Cannell, *The Dynamics of Interviewing* (New York: John Wiley & Sons, Inc., 1967).

Richardson, Stephen A., *et al., Interviewing: Its Forms and Functions* (New York: Basic Books, Inc., Publishers, 1965).

Chapter Ten   Data Processing

The immediately preceding chapters have dealt with methods for collecting (or generating) survey data. At this point in the study, the researcher would have in his possession a large (if he is fortunate) collection of completed questionnaires or interview schedules. The purpose of the present chapter is to discuss the methods by which those questionnaires are converted into a *machine-readable* form: a form which can be analyzed through the use of a computer or other such equipment.

To insure that the reader understands what machine-readable data look like, the first section of this chapter will present a brief overview of the data-processing and analysis hardware. Then we shall discuss the coding of questionnaires and, finally, the several options available for processing.

10.1   A Quick Look at Hardware

People often object to social research for attempting to reduce living, breathing human beings to holes punched in IBM cards. Part One of this book dealt with this as a philosophical issue; this section and the rest of this chapter will deal with the mechanics of accomplishing it.

An IBM card (figure 10-1) is divided into 80 vertical columns which are usually numbered, running from left to right. All of the mechanized data-processing equipment is designed to locate (and read) any specified columns. Data are stored on cards by punching holes within the columns. Each vertical column is further divided into 12 spaces. Ten of those spaces are numbered: 0, 1, 2, 3, 4, 5, 6, 7, 8, 9, from top to bottom. Above the 0 space, two unnumbered spaces are provided: moving up from 0, they are designated minus (–) and plus (+) or sometimes called 11 and 12, or X and Y, respectively.

A keypunch machine punches holes in the spaces in columns of IBM cards. Using a keyboard similar to that of a typewriter, the keypunch operator can punch specified holes (0, 1, 2, . . .) into specified columns of a given card. Alphabetical letters and special characters may also be punched, in the form of multiple-punches in a column; but for our purposes, we shall consider only single-punch, numerical data.

Figure 10-1

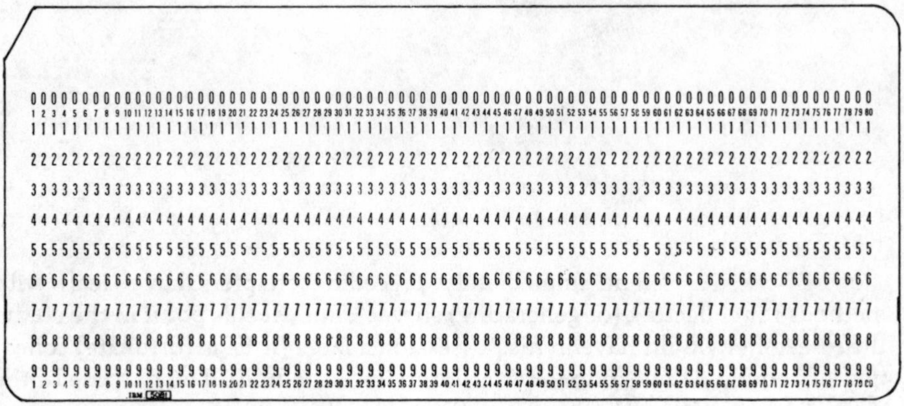

The keypunch machine also has the capacity to read the punches in a given column of one card and transfer those punches to the same column of the card following it in the deck (duplicate option). Finally, the keypunch machine may be programmed to carry out certain operations automatically, which will be mentioned in a later section of this chapter.

Questionnaire data are put in machine-readable format by assigning one or more specific columns of an IBM card to a variable and assigning punches within that column to the various responses or attributes within the variable. For example, the respondent's sex might be recorded in column 5 of the card. If the respondent is a male, a 1 might be punched in that column; if a female, a 2. The respondent's age might be assigned to columns 6 and 7 (a two-column code): if the person was 35 years of age, 3 and 5 would be punched in those columns. Or, ages could be recorded in categories and stored in a single column: for example, 1-punch for under 20, 2-punch for 20 to 29, and so forth.

A given IBM card, then, represents the data provided by or about a given respondent—the unit of analysis, in the terms of Chapter 4. (As we shall see in a moment, two or more cards can be and often are used for each respondent.)

Several other pieces of equipment are capable of reading IBM cards. The basic machine among these is the counter-sorter. This machine may be set to read a given column. Then when the cards are fed into it, they are sorted into pockets corresponding to the punches found in the column, and a counter indicates the number having each of the punches. If sex is recorded in column 5, the sorter would be set on that column and men and women would be sorted into the 1 and 2 pockets respectively.

The counter-sorter can be used for tabulating the distributions of responses given to questions in a survey simply by counting the punches to be found in the columns assigned to the questions. The counter-sorter can also be used to examine the relationships between variables.

Suppose the researcher wished to determine whether men or women attend church more often. Having separated the respondents by sex as described above, the counter-sorter should then be set to read the column containing responses to the question: "On the average, how often do you attend church services?" All the men would then be rerun through the counter-sorter to determine the frequency of church attendance as indicated by the punches contained in that column. The same procedure would be repeated for the women, and the distributions of responses would then be compared.

The counter-sorter has three basic limitations for the analysis of data. First, it is limited to counting and sorting cards. While the researcher may use these capabilities for extremely sophisticated analyses, the machine itself cannot perform sophisticated manipulations of data. Second, the counter-sorter is rather slow in comparison with other available machines. Third, it is limited to the examination of one IBM card per respondent in the analysis of relationships among variables. In effect, the researcher is thereby limited to 80 columns of data per respondent. (*Note:* Other machines provide for the construction of "work-decks" containing all the data required for a particular phase of the analysis. Data contained on several different cards can be transferred to a single deck, thereby permitting the use of the counter-sorter.)

Most sophisticated analysis today is conducted by the use of computers. The computer—through manipulation programs—can solve all the limitations of the counter-sorter. First, it can go beyond simple counting and sorting to perform intricate computations and provide sophisticated presentations of the results. The computer can be programmed to examine several variables simultaneously and to compute a variety of statistics. Second, if the data are stored on magnetic tape or magnetic disc rather than on cards, those data can be passed through the machine much faster than is possible by the use of cards and the counter-sorter. Moreover, the capability for simultaneous extensive manipulations and computations further speeds the overall analysis. Finally, the computer can analyze data contained on several IBM cards per respondent.

This chapter will discuss the steps (and options) involved in converting the responses contained in survey questionnaires into forms amenable to the use of counter-sorters and computers. Following a brief presentation of selected data-processing terminology, we shall discuss the coding process and then turn to an enumeration of the several methods of keypunching the data.

10.2   Selected Data-Processing Terminology

The following discussion identifies some of the terms commonly used in connection with survey data processing. The later discussions of this chapter will utilize those terms that are most likely to be familiar to inexperienced researchers. Nevertheless, the reader should become familiar with the other terms frequently used.

Case.   The term *case* in survey research is related to the unit of analysis. Where the unit of analysis is the person responding to a survey questionnaire, a case is a specific respondent. Thus, respondent John Smith may become case No. 1234. The *number of cases* would be the number of respondents in such a situation.

File.   A *file* is the collection of data pertaining to a given case. Thus, all the information obtained from or about John Smith (his questionnaire responses, interviewer observations, and so forth) would constitute his data file.

Record.   A file is comprised of one or more *records.* Typically, a record is an IBM card, and the data pertaining to a given respondent may be recorded on one or more IBM cards. In this instance, *records per case* would refer to the number of cards per respondent. (*Note:* Most general-purpose computer programs require that each case be assigned the same number of records.) When survey data are stored on magnetic tapes or discs, the term "card" becomes somewhat artificial and records may have different configurations (see *record length* below). Even when tapes and discs are used, however, the card format is often maintained.

Deck.   Whenever a file contains more than one record, the location of a specific data item (for example, questionnaire response) must include an indication of the appropriate record. Let's imagine a study in which each respondent is assigned three IBM cards for the storage of his information. These cards would be identified as card 1, card 2, and card 3 with each such card containing a specified set of information. A given question in the questionnaire might be assigned to card 2, column 35 and the responses given to this question would be punched in this location for all the respondents. A *deck* refers to the set of IBM cards of a given record identification for all respondents. *Deck 1,* then, consists of all the card 1's punched for all respondents. In the coding and keypunching of survey data consisting of more than one record per case, it is essential that each card contain, in a specified location, a *deck identification,* indicating whether it is a card 1, card 2, and so forth.

Byte.   *Byte* is a technical computer term that generally corresponds to the notion of an IBM card column in survey analysis. It
specifies a location within a record. Whenever survey data are stored on
magnetic tapes or discs, and the IBM card format is abandoned, the term
"column" becomes somewhat anachronistic and "byte" would be more appropriate.

Code.   *Code* is also a technical term that generally corresponds to the notion of a punch in the language surrounding IBM cards.
Since magnetic tapes and discs do not have holes punched in them, the term
"punch" may seem as inappropriate as "card" and "column." (*Note:* The
coding process to be discussed shortly refers to the assignment of codes to
represent questionnaire responses—typically in the form of punches in columns of cards.)

Record length.   When a survey record is an IBM card,
the *record length* is 80 columns or 80 bytes, regardless of whether all 80 are
actually used. Using tapes and discs, however, the researcher need not be
constrained by the conventional 80-column format. With his data initially
punched on, say, three cards per respondent, the researcher might create, on
tape or disc, files each comprised of one record, 240 bytes in length. It would
be as though he had manufactured a long IBM card with 240 columns. A
given data item, then, might be located at byte 200 rather than at column 40
of card 3. (*Note:* Most general-purpose computer programs require that every
record of every case have the same record length.)

10.3   Coding

Ultimately, all survey data must be transformed into
machine-readable punches in cards. Many variables are easily suited to this
form of presentation. Sex, for example, can be coded as a 1-punch for men
and a 2-punch for women. Similarly, religious affiliation could be coded:
Protestant, 1; Catholic, 2; Jew, 3; none, 4; other, 5. If respondents were asked
to agree or disagree with a given statement in the questionnaire, these responses could be coded as 1 and 2 respectively.

Most closed-ended questions can be coded very easily. The responses
provided to respondents for answering questions can simply be assigned
numbers within a column and punched accordingly. Moreover, this process
can be speeded up if the punches to be assigned are printed beside the
responses in the questionnaire (precoding).

Open-ended questions present a greater problem for coding. Suppose a
question in the survey asked: "What is your occupation?" The responses

produced by such a question would vary considerably. Moreover, such written-in answers cannot be manipulated by a sorter or computer. It would be necessary, therefore, to translate the several answers into categories.

In the case of occupation, there are a number of preestablished coding schemes (none of them very good, however). One such scheme would distinguish "professional and managerial occupations," "clerical occupations," "semiskilled occupations," and so forth. Another scheme distinguishes among different sectors of the economy: manufacturing, health, education, commerce, and so forth. Still others combine both.

The occupational coding scheme used should be appropriate to the analyses intended in the study. From one perspective, it might be sufficient to code all occupations as either "white-collar" or "blue-collar." From another perspective, "self-employed" and "not self-employed" might be sufficient. Or a peace researcher might only wish to know whether the occupation was dependent on the defense establishment or not.

While the coding scheme ought to be tailored to meet the particular requirements of the analysis, one general rule of thumb should be kept in mind. If the data are coded so as to maintain a great deal of detail, code categories can always be combined during an analysis that does not require such detail. If the data are coded into relatively few, gross categories, however, there is no way during analysis for recreating the original detail. Thus, the researcher would be well advised to code his data in somewhat more detail than he plans to use in the analysis.

There are two basic approaches to the coding process. First, the researcher may begin with a relatively well developed coding scheme. His task, then, is to train coders so that they will be able to assign given responses to the proper categories. He must be able to explain the meaning of the several code categories and give many examples for each. This training is best accomplished through the actual coding of several questionnaires. The researcher should begin by coding several questionnaires with the coders, explaining the reasons for each code assignment. Then he should code several more questionnaires by himself and ask each coder to code those same questionnaires independently. Once they have finished, the coder's work should be compared with the researcher's. Once he is convinced that the coders understand the coding scheme, they should be set to work. However, the researcher should be continually available to resolve problem cases, and he should "check code" a portion of each coder's work throughout the coding process to insure that each is performing correctly.

The second approach to coding is appropriate whenever the researcher is not sure initially how the data should be coded. Suppose he has asked the question: "What do you think about the John Birch Society?" It is unlikely that he will be able to predict in advance the variety of responses that such a question will produce. In such a situation, he should have one of the coders prepare a list of perhaps the first 100 responses. He would then review the list and decide the kinds of categories of responses are appropriate to both his analytical aims and the nature of the responses themselves. On this basis he would draw up a coding scheme and begin training his coders as described above.

Like closed-ended responses in a questionnaire, code categories should be both exhaustive and mutually exclusive (see Chapter 7). Every response should fit into *one and only one* code category. Problems arise whenever a given response appears to fit equally well into more than one of the code categories or when it fits into none.

The researcher should *never* permit more than one code to be entered in a single IBM card column—that is, do not permit *multiple-punching*. Whenever respondents give (and are sometimes requested to give) more than one answer to a given question, the inexperienced researcher may be tempted to record both answers in the column assigned to that question. Do not do this. Since most computer programs used in survey analysis will not accept multiple punches, you will not be able to analyze data recorded in this fashion. (*Note:* Using alphabetical codes to gain 26 code possibilities instead of the 12 numerical ones causes the same problem, since alpha codes are in fact multiple punches.)

Whenever the researcher neither requires nor desires multiple answers to a given question, he should bend every effort to draft a question that respondents will be able to answer with a single answer. If multiple answers are given in such cases, the researcher has several options. He may select a single answer on some established priority basis (for example, select the most "extreme" response if the set of responses can be ranked ordinally). As an alternative procedure, special single-punch codes might be assigned to the several possible combinations of responses (for example, a 5-punch might represent those who checked both responses 1 and 2, a 9-punch might represent those who checked all responses). If the list of responses provided is too long to permit this latter procedure, the researcher might simply assign a single code to all respondents who gave multiple answers, without differentiating which answers were given. None of these procedures is likely to be wholly satisfactory, however, so the best procedure is to write questionnaire items that respondents will be able to answer with a single response.

When the researcher desires more than one answer (for example, "In the list below, please check all those organizations to which you currently belong."), two procedures are usually most appropriate. First, each of the answer possibilities might be treated as a separate question, with a separate IBM card column assigned to each. (In the example immediately above, the researcher might provide a "yes/no" option for membership in each of the organizations listed. Each response would be treated as a separate question.) Second, whenever a specified number of responses (more than one) is desired, the researcher might assign a separate column for each of the number of responses desired. For example, the researcher might provide a sample of college students with a list of nine possible reasons for attending college and say "In the list below, please check the three reasons which *best* describe your reasons for attending college." Each of the reasons in the list could then be assigned a code, from 1 to 9. The codes assigned to the reasons checked by a given respondent would be single-punched in the three columns assigned to the question. The respondent who checked reasons 1, 3, and 9 would have these three codes punched in the three columns assigned—one punch per column. At the very least, the researcher will then be able to examine the distribution of punches found in each of the three columns, combining those distributions to determine how many times each of the reasons for attending college was checked. (Many computer programs will permit the researcher to combine the three columns as though they were a single, multiple-punched column.)

The researcher should also be warned against the use of blanks to achieve an additional code category in a given column. Leaving a column blank (unless it is assigned as a blank column for all respondents) is inadvisable for two reasons. First, this procedure creates a problem from the standpoint of quality control in data processing. Discovering that a respondent has no punch in a given column, the researcher will not know for sure whether this represents the assigned code or indicates that the key puncher simply failed to enter the appropriate punch in the column. Even "no answer" should be assigned a numerical punch.

The second difficulty created by the use of a blank to represent a response code is more technical. Some computers assign a special value to blanks as part of their internal operations. Depending on the type of analysis being employed by the researcher, this may confuse or abort the desired computations.

Multiple punching and the use of blanks are both part of the legacy of an earlier era in survey analysis—when researchers were limited to a single IBM card (80 columns) per respondent. Today, most researchers have access to computer programs that permit the use of many cards per case. In this circumstance, IBM card columns become the cheapest ingredient in the survey process, so these older techniques are unnecessary.

As noted earlier, it is essential for the researcher to keep track of the coding process as it progresses. In part, this has the function of checking on the continued quality of coding. At the same time, it will serve to warn the researcher of basic inadequacies in the initial coding scheme. It is conceivable that midway in the coding process he will discover a number of special responses that are being coded in an "other" category. If he decides that the response is sufficiently frequent and important for the analysis, he may wish to revise the coding scheme to provide a separate coding for that response. If he feels it necessary to revise the coding scheme in this fashion, it would be necessary for the coders to review all the previously coded questionnaires to insure that the given response is recoded every time it appears.

In a major research project, it is likely that the researcher will have the benefit of an organized research facility that is experienced in coding and other aspects of data processing. He may be able to use trained coders and coding supervisors. Despite the obvious advantage of such a situation, there is a hidden danger. In using the services of experienced specialists, the researcher may be tempted to remove himself from the coding process altogether. After discussing his general coding desires, he may then return to his office and hope that the coding team will perform according to his wishes. Unhappily, the most experienced coder and coding supervisor are unlikely to understand fully the theoretical significance of a particular coding scheme; only the researcher who will analyze the data has such knowledge. Unless he continues to involve himself in the coding process, the researcher has no assurance that the coding will be appropriate to his analytical requirements. (It should be noted that coders are seldom guilty of "cooling out" the researcher in this regard. Rather, they more frequently complain that the researcher is never available for consultation. This demoralizing factor almost inevitably results in poorer quality work.)

10.4 Codebook Construction

A *codebook* is the document that describes the location of variables in the survey data file and the keypunch assignments given to specific attributes making up those variables. The codebook serves two essential functions. First, it is the primary guide to coders as they prepare questionnaire responses for keypunching. Second, it is the researcher's guide to locating variables in his data file during analysis. When he decides to examine the correlation between sex and religiosity, the researcher consults the codebook to discover the card columns containing those variables and the meaning of the punches found in them.

In the simplest of surveys, it may be sufficient to indicate column and punch assignments on a blank copy of the questionnaire itself. This will be facilitated, of course, by any precoding that has been done in advance. It is always safest, however, to prepare a separate codebook; in a complex survey, it is essential.

Figure 10-2 illustrates portions of a survey codebook, requiring more than one card per case. We note that columns 1 through 4 have been assigned to the respondent's identification number. With more than one IBM card prepared for each respondent, this number will be punched into each card in columns 1 through 4, thereby permitting the researcher to match data stored in different cards for a given respondent. Column 5 in the example has been assigned to the card or deck identification. This tells the researcher which of the several cards prepared for a given respondent is involved. Note that the card containing the first set of information has a 1 punched in column 5, while the second card has a 2 punched in column 5.

Figure 10-2. Codebook Illustration

DECK 1 CODEBOOK

COLUMN   DESCRIPTION

1-4   Respondent identification number

5   Deck identification number: 1

6   Sex:
            1. Male
            2. Female
            0. No answer

7-8   Age: (Actual age coded in two columns)

9   Marital Status:
            1. Single, never married
            2. Married
            3. Widowed, divorced, or separated
            0. No answer

DECK 2 CODEBOOK

COLUMN   DESCRIPTION

1-4   Respondent identification number

5   Deck identification number: 2

6   "What this country needs is more law and order."
            1. Strongly agree
            2. Agree somewhat
            3. Disagree somewhat
            4. Strongly disagree
            5. Don't know
            0. No answer

7   "The police should be disarmed."
            1. Strongly agree
            2. Agree somewhat
            3. Disagree somewhat
            4. Strongly disagree
            5. Don't know
            0. No answer

In reality, of course, a given card would contain up to about 80 columns of information. The illustration has been truncated for purposes of presentation.

In the illustration, if a researcher wished to discover whether men and women differ on the issue of "law and order," he would be able to examine this question through a reference to the codebook. He would note that card 1, column 6 tells him the respondents' sexes (1 for male, 2 for female), and that responses to the "law and order" item are contained in card 2, column 6 (the codebook indicates the meaning of the several punches he will find in that column). With this information, he could proceed to conduct a computer analysis of his data file and determine whether men and women differ on the issue.

Now we shall turn to the several data-processing options available to the researcher in converting his data from questionnaires to IBM cards of the form discussed above.

10.5   Track One Processing

The traditional method of data processing involves the coding of questionnaires and the transfer of code assignments to a "transfer sheet" or "code sheet." Such sheets are ruled off in 80 columns corresponding to the IBM card columns and in rows representing individual cards. Coders write numbers corresponding to the desired punches in the appropriate columns of the sheets.

The code sheets are then given to the keypunchers who punch IBM cards corresponding to the sheets. Once they are punched, the IBM cards are then *verified*. A *verifier* looks very much like a keypunch machine, but instead of punching holes in cards, it reads the punches that have already been punched. The verifier operator loads the deck of punched cards (instead of blank cards) and then simulates the repunching of the code sheets. Whenever the "punch" attempted for a given column by the verifier operator is the same as the punch already in that column of the card, the card advances to the next column. If the "punch" attempted by the verifier operator differs from that found in the column, a red light goes on and the machine stops. The verifier operator has two more chances to "punch" the correct number. If an incorrect punch was entered initially, the card is "notched" over the erroneous column for later correction. After verification and correction, the researcher is provided with a deck of IBM cards that accurately represent the data contained in the questionnaire.

10.6   Track Two Processing

Edge coding provides a data-processing method that does away with the need for code sheets. The outside margin of each page of the

questionnaire is left blank and/or is marked with spaces corresponding to
IBM card columns. Rather than transferring code assignments to a separate
sheet, the coder writes in the appropriate spaces in the margin.

The edge-coded questionnaires are then given to keypunchers. The questionnaires are used for the punching and verifying of IBM cards.

10.7   Track Three Processing

If the questionnaires have been adequately designed and
precoded, it may be possible to simplify the process even further. In such
cases, the keypunchers may *punch direct* from the questionnaires. The precoded questionnaire would contain indications of the columns and the punches assigned to questions and responses, and the keypunchers and verifier
operators could directly transfer responses to IBM cards..

When a *punch-direct* method is to be used, it is essential that questionnaires be *edited* prior to punching. An editor should read through each questionnaire to insure that every question has been answered (enter a 0 or some
other standard code when no answer is given), to insure there are no multiple
answers (change to a single code according to a uniform procedure), and to
clarify any unclear responses.

If most of the questionnaire is amenable to direct punching (that is,
closed-ended questions presented in a clear format), it is also possible to code
a few open-ended questions on the questionnaire and still punch directly. In
such a situation, the editor should enter the code for a given question in a
specified location near the question to ease the keypuncher's job.

The layout of the questionnaire is extremely important for effective direct
punching. The several question and response categories must be arranged in
a logical "flow." If most response categories are presented on the right-hand
side of the page but one set is presented on the left-hand side, keypunchers
frequently miss the deviant set. (*Note:* Many respondents will make the same
mistake, so a questionnaire carefully designed for keypunching will be more
effective for data collection as well.)

Direct punching can be made more effective by careful questionnaire
design. Since the keypunch machine can be programmed to perform certain
operations automatically, the keypuncher can speed up her work by using
that feature. If a blank column is assigned to the bottom of each questionnaire
page and/or at the end of a section of the questionnaire page, the keypunch
machine can be programmed to skip those columns automatically. This practice reduces the need for the keypuncher to continually compare the IBM card
column being punched with the column that is supposed to be punched. The
keypuncher simply punches a whole page (or designated section) without
checking columns. If the keypunch machine automatically skips a column at

the appropriate point in the questionnaire, the keypuncher knows she is on the right column.

To use this feature of the keypunch machine it is necessary for multicard files to be punched one card at a time. If each respondent is to have two IBM cards, for example, the keypuncher must punch card 1 for all respondents since the location of blank columns will differ on the two cards and then punch card 2 for all respondents. This in itself has an advantage, however. If the keypuncher is able to punch the same set of questions over and over on several questionnaires, her growing familiarity with the questionnaire format will speed up the punching and will increase accuracy.

Ideally, the questionnaire should be designed to permit its separation into "packets" corresponding to the different IBM cards. (An identification number must be used to insure that the several portions of a given questionnaire can be related to one another later.) This facilitates the keypunching described above and also makes it possible for several keypunchers to be working on the questionnaire at the same time.

Once the IBM cards are keypunched, the punched decks and questionnaires (or packets) are given to a verifier operator as discussed in the earlier sections.

10.8   Track Four Processing

Manual keypunching can be avoided through the use of an *optical scanner.* This machine reads black pencil marks on a special code sheet and punches IBM cards to correspond with those marks. (These sheets are frequently called *mark-sense* sheets.)

It is possible for coders to transfer questionnaire data to such special sheets in the form of black marks rather than in the form of numbers on a code sheet. The sheets are then fed into an optical scanner and IBM cards are automatically punched. In some instances, it may be necessary to "translate" the initial punches through the use of a special computer program. In any event, the researcher is ultimately provided with a deck of IBM cards without the necessity of manual punching. Moreover, it is unnecessary to verify the punching separately.

This use of the optical scanner provides greater accuracy and speed of keypunching. There are several disadvantages, however, which should be mentioned. First, coders find it very difficult to transfer data to the special sheets. Using a conventional code sheet, the coder simply writes the appropriate code number in the next blank space on the sheet. The configuration of op-sense sheets, however, hampers this. Often, it is more difficult to locate the appropriate column and once the appropriate column is found, the coder must search for the appropriate space to blacken. (The severity of this problem can only be appreciated by attempting to code in both manners.) Past experience suggests that these difficulties result in a greater expenditure of time and greater inaccuracy, which offset the gains.

Second, the optical scanner has relatively rigid tolerances. Unless the black marks are sufficiently black, the scanner may fail to read and punch. (The researcher will have no way of knowing when this has happened until he begins his analysis.) Moreover, if the op-sense sheets are folded or mutilated, the scanner may refuse to read them at all.

10.9   Track Five Processing

The coding difficulties inherent in the use of op-sense sheets can be resolved in some cases by asking respondents (or interviewers) to record the original responses on such sheets. Either standard op-sense sheets can be provided with instructions on their use, or special sheets can be prepared for the particular study. Questions can be presented with the several answer categories, and the respondent could be asked to black-in the space provided beside the answer he chooses. If such sheets were properly laid out, the optical scanner could then read and punch the answers directly.

This procedure would avoid the necessities of both coding and key-punching (although the sheets should be edited). It might be rather effective when used with respondents who have had previous experience with such sheets (for example, students). There are limitations inherent in this method, however.

The researcher would be limited to asking closed-ended questions. Only those that could be answered through the selection of a previously coded response could be handled. If the respondent was unwilling to select any of the answers provided, he would be unable to communicate his answer to the researcher. Furthermore, the dangers of insufficiently blackened spaces and mutilated sheets are present here as in the previous example. (This would hamper the administration of mail surveys, although it might be possible with proper planning and testing.)

10.10   Comparison and Evaluations of
Options

Although data-processing methods depend importantly on the nature and aims of the study, it is possible to make some general comments about the several tracks outlined above.

Track Three Processing (punching directly from questionnaires) is usually best. It permits a flexibility of format (open-ended and closed-ended), accuracy, and speed. While it requires a carefully laid out questionnaire, this should be done anyway.

At the other extreme, Track Four Processing (coding to op-sense sheets) seems the least desirable method for all the reasons discussed. I can think of no study design that could not be better satisfied by another method.

Track Five Processing (original responses recorded on op-sense sheets) is an effective method when a very large number of respondents drawn from a literate population are being studied. The researcher must limit his data collection to relatively simple closed-ended questions. (This is the price he will pay for an economical study of many respondents.)

Track One Processing (coding to transfer sheets) is most appropriate for a complicated questionnaire. Often, the nature of the data collected prevents a simplified format suitable to direct punching. While it is a relatively expensive and time-consuming method, it may be necessary for accuracy.

I am not especially enamored with Track Two Processing (edge coding), although I recognize that this method is very popular among some researchers. My feeling is that a well laid out questionnaire can be more efficiently processed through direct punching, and a complicated questionnaire should be coded on transfer sheets for more certain accuracy of coding and later punching.

10.11   Data Cleaning

Whichever data processing method has been used, the researcher now has a set of IBM cards in hand that purport to represent the answers originally provided by respondents in the survey. The next, important, step is the *cleaning* of these data.

No matter how, or how carefully, the data have been transferred to IBM cards, some errors are inevitable. Depending on the data-processing method, these errors may result from incorrect coding, incorrect reading of written codes, incorrect sensing of blackened marks, and so forth. Even keypunch verification is not perfect.

Two types of cleaning should be done: *possible-punch* cleaning and *contingency* cleaning. First, for any given questionnaire item, there is a specifiable set of legitimate responses, translated into a set of possible punches. In the case of sex there will be perhaps three possible punches: 1 for male, 2 for female, and some other punch (for example, 0) for those respondents who neglected to give an answer. If a respondent has, say, a 7-punch in the column assigned to sex, it is clear that an error has been made.

Possible-punch cleaning can be accomplished in two different ways. First, the researcher may have access to computer programs designed for this purpose. He may be able to specify the possible punches associated with each IBM card column, and the computer will then read all the data cards and indicate those cards that have one or more errors. Alternatively, the researcher can examine the distribution of responses punched for each column (using either the computer or the sorter) and determine whether there are any inappropriate punches. If the column assigned to sex has a 7-punch reported, the researcher might use the sorter to locate the card having this punch. Then he could locate the questionnaire corresponding to that card (using the ID number), determine what the punch should have been, and make the necessary correction.

Contingency cleaning is more complicated. The logical structure of the questionnaire may place special limits on the responses of certain respondents. For example, the questionnaire may ask for the military draft status of *male respondents only*. All male respondents, then, should have a response punched (or a special code for failure to answer), while no female respondent should have a punch (or should have a special punch indicating the question is inappropriate). If a given female respondent is punched as having a 1-A draft status, an error has been made and should be corrected.

Contingency cleaning may be accomplished through computer programs, if available, or through the use of the counter-sorter. In either event, however, the process is more complicated than is true of possible-punch cleaning. Computer programs will require a rather complicated set of "if–then" statements. Manual cleaning will require two or more passes through the counter-sorter to clean each set of items.

Although data cleaning is an essential step in data processing, it should be acknowledged that it may be safely avoided in certain cases. Perhaps the researcher will feel he can safely exclude the very few illegal punches that appear in a given column—if the exclusion of those cases will not significantly affect his results. Or, some illegal contingency responses may be safely ignored. If some women respondents have been given a draft status, he can limit his analysis of this variable to male respondents. These comments notwithstanding, however, the researcher should not use them as rationalizations for sloppy research. "Dirty" data will almost always produce misleading research findings.

Summary

The preceding discussions of data-processing options and requirements should emphasize the absolute necessity for proper survey planning. The researcher cannot reasonably collect his data and then begin considerations of how they will be processed. The data-processing method should be selected before the questionnaire is designed.

There is a common tendency among researchers to breathe a sigh of relief once the questionnaires have been completed and are safely stored in the research office. The danger of not getting the data has been avoided; now all the researcher has to do is put them in order for analysis. In fact, this sense of well-being may be unfounded. If the data have been collected in an appropriate format, it may still be impossible to put them in a meaningful order. Only if he has carefully thought out his data processing in advance and designed a data-collection technique appropriate to those plans may he safely be relieved.

Chapter Eleven   Pre-tests and Pilot Studies

By now, probably every research textbook admonishes researchers to conduct some form of testing of their research design prior to their major research effort. The arguments for this are compelling. No researcher wishes to invest large sums of money and considerable effort in a faulty research design. No one wishes to expend all his allotted resources only to discover that he has failed to achieve his objectives due to some unforeseen error.

In this chapter I shall distinguish two types of testing: *pre-tests* and *pilot studies*. Pre-tests will refer to initial testing of one or more aspects of the study design: the questionnaire, the sample design, a computer program for analysis, and so forth. Pilot studies will refer to miniaturized walkthroughs of the entire study design.

11.1   Conducting Pre-tests

As noted above, pre-tests represent initial tests of one or more aspects of the research design. Most commonly, this has meant the administration of a draft questionnaire to a group of subjects, but the concept of pre-testing is more broadly applicable.

Pre-testing the Sample Design

Often a sample design may seem reasonable on paper, only to prove unmanageable in practice. If the design calls for the creation of a sampling frame, a portion of that frame might be created in a pre-test. For example, in an area cluster sample design the researcher might attempt to update block-size estimates within one or more census tracts before setting his staff to work updating all block sizes. If the design calls for the listing of households, he might send listers into the field to list selected blocks to determine any unexpected difficulties.

If the researcher will be selecting his sample from an existing list, he should carefully scrutinize the list of problems. If stratification is intended, he should make a trial run of the stratification procedure. Can stratification be done manually? Try it. Or will a computer program be required? Test it.

The same steps are in order with regard to sample selection. If a computer program is to be used, it should be tested with partial or even hypothetical data. If manual selection is intended, a pre-test on partial or even hypothetical data will point to problems and may even suggest that the task is impossible or extremely difficult: perhaps computer selection is more feasible.

The pre-test of a sample design, then, can indicate whether that design is possible, provide an assessment of its difficulty, and give a rough estimate of the time and cost that will be involved. Pre-tests serve another function also. Inevitably the researcher fails to recognize in advance all the decisions he must make. Although he may have been explicit in defining his survey population, the *act* of sampling uncovers hidden problems of definition. In an area sample will he interview transients (for example, tourists) as well as residents? Will foster children be considered family members? In a university study, he will soon discover that "students" and/or "faculty" are extremely difficult creatures to define. Hopefully, a pre-test will turn up such problems (some of them at least), and he will be able to make his decisions at the outset. In such a situation, his decisions can be more carefully considered, and he will be able to insure that those decisions are acted upon consistently throughout the final study.

Pre-testing the Research Instrument

The purpose of pre-testing the instrument should be obvious, but the methodological options may not be as clear. The following points are offered by way of clarification.

1. Either the entire instrument or a portion thereof may be pre-tested. Perhaps the researcher will be primarily concerned about the utility of a particular set of questions. If so, he may devote most of his attention to several pre-tests of that portion of the questionnaire, and modifications of it. While this is a legitimate endeavor, he should be aware that the context in which the questions appear will affect their reception. Thus, while initial testing of portions of the questionnaire is undoubtedly worth while, it would be better to wrap up the activity with one or more pre-tests of the whole instrument.

2. Preferably, the instrument should be pre-tested in the manner intended for the final study: self-administered questionnaires and interview schedules should be pre-tested in the appropriate manners. Nevertheless, this in no way prohibits the initial testing of the instrument through a different method. It is especially worth while to pre-test an early draft of what ultimately will be a self-administered questionnaire by interviewing. This procedure will permit a greater determination of problems in that an interviewer can detect confusion and probe into the nature of that confusion on the spot. Ultimately, however, the instrument should be pre-tested in the form which will be used.

3. An open-ended format may be used profitably in the pre-test to determine appropriate response categories for what will become a closed-end question ultimately. Respondents may be used to give their own answers to a question; those answers would then be coded by the researcher, and standardized response categories would be thereby created. However, it is important that the eventual closed-ended questions be tested also. Thus a new pre-test should be conducted to uncover any bugs in the standardized categories.

4. The selection of subjects for instrument pre-tests can profitably be kept flexible and varied. For the most part, controlled sampling should be ignored altogether at this point. (Pilot studies are quite a different matter.) I make this point in recognition of the fact that researchers often cut short their pre-testing due to the difficulties of sampling. The single guideline I would recommend for selection of subjects is that they should be reasonably appropriate respondents for the questions under consideration. Ideally, every individual item should be initially pre-tested among the members of the research staff, although this is not a sufficient test. If the study is aimed at a particular population, then any members of that population or any persons similar to that population may serve as pre-test subjects. However, it should be understood that this point is aimed, not only to make pre-testing easier, but also to make it easily more extensive.

In more rigorous pre-testing of the research instrument, little concern should be given to strict representativeness; rather the attempt should be made to achieve the broadest range of respondent types—including those who may represent a small minority of the population. In a study of political attitudes, for example, the researcher should pre-test the instrument on subjects drawn from the entire political spectrum of his population. This means that the extremes—right and left—will be overrepresented in the test. This is fine, for he must insure that the instrument will make sense to, and be useful in understanding, all types of respondents in the population. (Of course, the instrument should be tested among "moderates" as well.) The goal of pre-testing is to refine the research instrument rather than to provide descriptions of the population.

5. Pre-testing lends itself to comparative testing of different methods for obtaining desired data. Different drafts of the questionnaire may be tested simultaneously, and successive revisions and retesting over time should have the same effect.

6. It may be useful to utilize the same subjects more than once in pre-testing the instrument. This is of special value in that the overall subject profile thus derived

*offers a general basis for evaluating responses to specific items. On the other hand,
the final draft should be pre-tested among new subjects to take account of the
inevitable learning process that will take place among the earlier subjects.*

These, then, are some of the options and guidelines relevant to the execution of pre-tests. I would emphasize that pre-testing should be a multistage,
cumulative process, and the researcher should not think in terms of *the*
pre-test. A later section will consider the evaluation of questionnaire pre-
tests.

Pre-testing Data Collection

By now, much has been written about techniques of data
collection, and experienced researchers have probably regularized their own
basic methods. Nevertheless, every study is different in the particulars of data
collection.

If a mail-out questionnaire is to be used, the researcher should physically
try out the procedures for assembling and mailing the questionnaires. Only
in this manner can the several steps be properly organized. Rubber stamping,
label sticking, letter folding, envelope stuffing, and so forth, can be more
difficult in practice than in theory.

An experienced researcher can probably organize such work, lay out his
work space, and assign tasks to his staff in a mental runthrough. Nevertheless,
only a physical test can indicate that questionnaires do not really fit into
envelopes, that return envelopes do not fit into outgoing envelopes, and so
forth. If a questionnaire indentification number must be matched with the
mailing label on the envelope, only a physical practice will point to the
dangers (and, one hopes, preventions) of mixing.

Since the nature of problems to be uncovered varies so much with the
nature of the study design, it is perhaps pointless to continue the listing of
examples. Suffice it to say that the researcher who does not pre-test the
execution of a questionnaire mailing runs a considerable risk.

The necessity for pre-testing data-collection methods in an interview
survey is even greater. Since this falls in the area of interviewer training,
testing, and supervision, that discussion has been presented elsewhere in this
book.

Pre-testing Data Processing

There is a tendency for researchers to be very tense about
the data-collection phase of a survey (Will the data come in?) and to be
relatively more sanguine about the later stages. There is a feeling that once

the questionnaire or interview schedules are in hand, the pressure is off, and the researcher can cope with problems in a more leisurely manner. In large part, this is true, but it can be seriously dysfunctional if it prevents the researcher from pre-testing his data-processing procedures.

The nature of the data-processing pre-test depends, of course, on the nature of the data processing itself. Following one track, the researcher will wish to pre-test his coding and keypunching operations. The results of such a pre-test have important implications for the format of the research instrument. Often a few minor modifications in the layout of the questionnaire will vastly improve the efficiency of coding (or keypunching if the questionnaires are punched directly). It will point to the needs for pre-coding—either calling for more, or indicating that less would suffice. The only way to make such determinations, however, is to have coders practice coding. This may be done with hypothetical data or with completed pre-test questionnaires. If this is delayed until the final questionnaires are coming in, however, the whole point is lost.

If the questionnaires are to be keypunched directly from the completed questionnaires, the above comments apply. In addition, such a test will point to the needs for editing of questionnaires prior to punching. If keypunching is to be done from coded transfer sheets, the test will point to any requirements keypunchers may make on coders.

If the data are to be keypunched through the use of optical scanning equipment, I cannot overemphasize the need for a pre-test of this. A pre-test should point to machine tolerances with regard to mutilated score sheets and lightly marked spaces. (One major survey transferred questionnaire data to op-sense sheets, and did not learn until the completion of coding that the coders used pencils with the wrong degree of softness. The entire project staff spent two weeks of full-time drudgery "blacking over" the initial markings.)

If open-ended questions are used in the questionnaire, some early attention should be given to the organization of their coding. A pre-test will suggest the most efficient *order* for coding the open-ended and close-ended questions.

A pre-test of the coding and keypunching will also offer an opportunity to consider additional time-saving procedures. As noted in Chapter 10, it is often more efficient to have keypunchers separate questionnaire booklets into sections to be punched on particular cards (if more than one IBM card of data will be generated for each respondent). Keypunch program cards can be used in such a case, and the keypuncher becomes more efficient when she is punching the same kind of information over a period of time. For this to be possible, the questionnaire pages must be laid out in such a way as to permit easy separation into pages relating to a given card, and a pre-test of this stage will enhance success.

Postkeypunching processing, such as data transfer to tape and data cleaning—should also be pre-tested. General-purpose computer programs may be available for accomplishing these steps, but only an actual test will insure that the particular survey data will be appropriately organized for the utilization of such programs. If the study calls for the construction of multilevel data files (for example, household file, family file, person file), rather complex manipulation of data may be required and this manipulation must be pre-tested.

Finally, pre-tests of the data-processing stage(s) should show the way to an efficient interrelation of the separate elements. The logging of completed questionnaires, initial editing, coding, keypunching, transfer to tape, cleaning or whatever elements are involved in the processing of a given study must be coordinated. In one sense, this means that the outputs of one stage must be appropriate inputs to the next. In another, more mundane, sense it means such decisions as who will carry the questionnaires from one room to another, where they will be stored at any given point, and so on.

Pre-testing the Analysis

Some readers may consider it bizarre to talk about pre-testing the analysis, all the more so for this book's insistence that analysis is an open-ended and often serendipitous activity. Nevertheless, I am quite serious in suggesting this step. While the survey analyst inevitably does things with his data that he did not initially intend to do, he must insure that he will be able to do those things he *does* intend to do.

While I shall devote more space to analysis with regard to pilot studies, it is useful to mention two kinds of analytical pre-testing. First, the researcher should walk through all the steps from raw data to finished product with regard to table construction, index building, scale construction, regressions, factor analysis, or whatever analytical mode(s) he has in mind. He should go through each step from the IBM card punches to the written presentation. The purpose of this step is to insure that he *can* get there from here. Often the form in which information is to be collected does not lend itself to the analysis intended. Here are some examples.

A population survey may collect data on each member of the household. The data are standardized with a separate IBM card for each household member. In such a format, however, the researcher may not be able easily to determine the *number* of persons in each household. Or while it may be possible to count the number of person-cards for each household, it may not be possible to utilize that information as an analytical variable. (*Solution*: Have coders count persons and code the person count on a separate household file.) By the same token, it may be difficult to relate household data (for example, age of household head) to the individual person files unless steps are taken in advance to permit this.

Sometimes the form in which the data are to be collected is not appropriate to the desired analysis. In pre-testing his analysis, the researcher may discover that he wishes to present age as a *mean* to permit comparisons with other data; if he has asked for age in gross categories rather than asking for exact age, he may be in trouble. On the other hand, asking for precise information (requiring a multiple-column code) may hamper simplified analyses.

The second type of analytical pre-testing concerns the intended use of mechanized data manipulation: either through the use of unit-record equipment (for example, counter-sorters) or computers and computer programs. Walking through these steps will indicate what is feasible/possible and what is not. The difficulties of counter-sorter analysis or the bugs in computer programs should become evident. Either they can be corrected in advance, or else the analysis should be redesigned. If the latter is the case, then it may be necessary and/or advisable to redesign other aspects of the study (for example, the questionnaire format).

11.2 Conducting Pilot Studies

Conducting pre-tests of the various individual aspects of the study design and analysis is extremely important, as I have tried to indicate. Ideally, extensive pre-tests of each aspect are in order. Moreover, the researcher should continually be on the alert for the implications of the pre-testing on one aspect for other aspects and work to interrelate all. Nevertheless, the best method of insuring such interrelations is to conduct a pilot-study—a miniaturized walkthrough of the entire study from sampling to reporting. The pilot study should differ from the final survey only in scale: fewer cases studied (and less time used). The following comments are elaborations on this basic principle.

Pilot-Study Sampling

Unlike a pre-test, a pilot study should be directed at a representative sample of the target population. The pilot-study sample, then, should be selected in exactly the same fashion as is intended for the final survey. One exception may be entered in this regard, however.

Since the researcher may wish to avoid studying the same respondents in both the pilot study and the final survey, he may wish to select both samples at the same time as an insurance against that possibility. This may be accomplished in one of two ways. First, the researcher may select his final sample or his primary sampling units (for example, census blocks) and then select a pilot-study sample from the remainder of the population. Or he might select an initial sample containing enough elements for both and subsample from that list for his pilot study.

If overlap is not considered a problem, then the pilot-study sample should be selected in exactly the same manner as is intended for the final survey. In either event, the researcher will have tested his sample design (or actually drawn his final sample).

Pilot-Study Research Instrument

As nearly as possible the pilot study should involve the administration of a research instrument identical to the one intended for the final survey. If a rather elaborate mailing piece is to be used, however, it should be recognized that it may not be feasible to produce the numbers required for the pilot study and then produce a revised batch for the final survey. If the researcher must choose between committing himself to the final instrument (by producing enough for both the pilot study and final survey) or using a more modest form for the pilot survey (for example, dittoed or mimeographed), the latter course is probably preferable.

The pilot-study questionnaire should contain all the intended questions presented in the wording, format, and sequence that pre-testing has indicated are the best for the final survey. The pilot study should not be a vehicle for trying out new items that have not been pre-tested.

Having said this, one exception is in order. It is quite reasonable for the pilot-study instrument to contain somewhat more questions than are intended to be included in the final survey. Often uncontrolled pre-testing is not sufficient for determining which of several methods of obtaining certain data will be the most useful for the study. In some instances, then, the researcher might include both in the same questionnaire (provided they do not present a gross repetition to the respondent), with the intention of evaluating them through the pilot study.

A better (though more complex) way of handling this situation would be to use different versions of the questionnaire among subsamples of the pilot study. In this fashion, pilot-study respondents will be reacting to what might become the final survey instrument, providing for a better test.

If a single pilot-survey instrument is used to evaluate alternative methods of asking for given data, the researcher must be careful not to create a significantly larger instrument. The lessons he learns from the administration of a long (and somewhat repetitious) pilot-study instrument may be inappropriate to the final, shorter instrument.

Pilot-Study Data Collection and Data Processing

As in other phases of the pilot study, data collection and data processing should represent a miniaturized walkthrough of the final survey design. To the extent that the research instruments are comparable, they should be administered exactly as the researcher intends for the final survey. Where they differ, the researcher must be especially conscious of the implications of those differences—attempting to learn from inference rather than experience. The completed questionnaires should be coded, key-punched, transferred, cleaned, and, and we shall see next, analyzed exactly as planned for the final research.

Pilot-Study Analysis

Bizarre as it may seem, *organized* research should begin with a drafting of the written report. That draft report should contain the logical arguments of the study, blank or hypothetical tables, and all the verbal glue that holds them together. In this fashion, the organized researcher insures that he knows what information he will need, whom he needs it from, and the form in which he needs it. The pilot-study analysis, like the final analysis, should consist of filling in the empirical blanks, noting unexpected developments, and elaborating on them.

The pilot-study analysis should be carried out with all the vigor and imagination intended for the final analysis. Since the pilot-study sample is drawn to represent the target population, the results of the pilot-study analysis should be essentially the same as those of the final survey. The latter should be a more substantial replication of the former.

In reality, however, study designs are never perfect nor is the logical reasoning upon which they are based. As a result, the pilot-study analysis never quite turns out as we had expected. More often it points to errors in reasoning and/or design. The methods for determining those errors are discussed in the following section. At this point, I would emphasize the importance of pushing the pilot survey as far as possible so as to uncover as many errors as possible before committing the major resources to the final survey.

If needed data are missing in the pilot study, they should be approximated if possible to permit the greatest possible elaboration on the intended analysis. If the analysis suggests that income levels should be taken into account and you have not collected income data, use education or occupation as a rough approximation. If you have no approximate data, then construct hypothetical tables, presenting all the possible outcomes due to income. For each possible outcome, how would it be explained, what other data ought to be considered in that explanation? If further analyses are suggested by this approach, follow up on them through the pilot-study data; approximate if necessary, or create new hypothetical tables and try to explain them.

It is altogether too easy to note a problem and its immediate implications and resolve to correct the problem in the final survey. This is a dangerous procedure. To profit from doing a pilot study, the researcher must consider the second-order, third-order, and fourth-order implications of the problem and its possible solutions.

11.3   Evaluating Pre-tests and Pilot Studies

This section offers some guidelines and criteria for the evaluation of pre-tests and pilot studies. While I shall offer no laws for resolving this issue, I shall attempt to link research objectives to evaluation criteria. In doing this, moreover, I shall limit our discussion to the uses of analysis in evaluating the research instrument.

The guts of survey research are the collection, manipulation, and understanding of data. Above all else, pre-tests and pilot studies are aimed at insuring the creation of useful data. We shall now consider the ways of recognizing useful data.

Question Clarity

To be useful, questions should make sense to respondents, even though the most important implications of those questions may not be evident to them. By the same token, the answer categories (if provided) should make sense, both in themselves and in their relation to the question and to each other. The danger signs that may be apparent in pre-test or pilot-study results are the following.

Failure to answer.   Typically, every respondent skips some questions, and every question is skipped by someone, but when a given question produces a number of "no answers," this is a clue to problems in it.

Multiple answers.   Even when respondents are asked to select only one answer from a list of alternatives, some will persist in selecting more than one. Again, if one question produces a number of multiple answers, the researcher should suspect that either his answer categories are not mutually exclusive or else the question is being misunderstood. The solution to this problem varies with the type of multiple responses. If the same two categories are frequently chosen together, perhaps they can be better distinguished or, alternatively, combined. If several combinations of answers are being selected, then something more basic is wrong and the whole question should be examined.

"Other" answers.   It is often appropriate in closed-ended questions to offer the respondent the alternative of volunteering his

own answer. Whether or not this option is offered, a large number of responses that are written-in (or volunteered to an interviewer) indicates that the categories provided are not sufficiently exhaustive. If the other answers fit conceptually into one or more logical categories that do not overlap with the existing ones, perhaps they should be added to the list of alternatives.

This should not be done, of course, if it conflicts with the objectives of the study or of the particular question. For example, communications researchers in the United States sometimes ask respondents to indicate their primary source of political information: choosing from a list including newspapers, friends, radio, magazines, and political circulars. Television is purposely omitted from the list on the assumption that most respondents would choose it if it were included. If respondents volunteer this response, the researcher still would not want to include it in his list. If a large number of respondents do so, however, he might decide it was necessary for him to specifically exclude it in the basic question (for example, "Aside from television, which of the following ... ?").

Qualified answers. Respondents often qualify their answers, both in selecting a provided category and in answering an open-ended question. Asked to report his "annual income," the respondent may note he is reporting last year's income or his estimate of this year's. Asked to report his father's age, he may note he is reporting his *step*father's age, or his father's age at death. Asked for his political party affiliation, he may note he has checked his party registration but that he generally votes independently of that registration, or just the opposite: that he is not registered in a party, but that he generally votes for the party indicated.

Qualified answers such as these point to a lack of clarity in the questions and/or answers. One such response may be sufficient to warrant a revision of the question if the lack of clarity may result in different understanding of the question. Several such responses demand revision.

Direct comments. Often respondents point directly to problems in question wording or format (for example, "This is a lousy question"). While the researcher must be relatively thick-skinned in reviewing such comments, he should be on the alert for particular questions that generate more than their share.

Questionnaire Format

All the above danger signs may point to errors in format as well as errors in wording. Missing answers, for example, may indicate that the "flow" of the questionnaire is not proper. This is especially the case for contingency questions, which often are (and *should be*) set off to the side of the questionnaire page. Better instruction, boxes, arrows, and similar devices should resolve this problem.

Sometimes respondents will answer a series of "yes/no" questions simply by checking some "yeses." The researcher may ask them what kinds of organizations they belong to and provide a list of different types with a "yes/no" beside each. If the respondent checks only "yes" in some cases, the problem is one of not knowing if the organizations he did not check are ones he does not belong to or if he skipped over them inadvertently in going through the list. Perhaps more explicit instruction (for example, "Please an- swer for *each.*") will alleviate this problem. If the researcher is especially concerned for the accuracy of responses in such a situation, asking about membership in each organization as a separate question, rather than as a list, should solve the problem, although it will lengthen the questionnaire.

Variance in Responses

A primary concern in evaluating tests of a research in- strument should be the distribution of answers that each question evokes. Are the responses about evenly distributed among the several answer catego- ries provided, or did most respondents select the same answers? While the consideration of this aspect of pre-test and pilot-study results is essential, the evaluation of the situation depends on the objectives of the study and of the particular questions.

If the question is designed to measure factual information that permits an independent evaluation (for example, students are asked to report their grade point averages, and the researcher knows the distribution of the popu- lation), then the pilot-test responses provide a clue as to the clarity of the question and/or the reliability of the respondents (assuming of course that the test data are taken from a representative sample).

If the particular question—as worded—is intrinsically interesting, the researcher may be satisfied with whatever distribution of responses are ob- tained. It may be interesting and valuable to know, for example, that every- one in the population says he is in favor of a proposed law before the legislature, and the researcher may wish to replicate this finding in his more substantial final survey.

More frequently in social research, however, the researcher is interested in the *relationships among variables.* He wants to know why some people favor a proposed law while others do not. He wants to know why some people are religious while others are not. If there is no variation in the responses elicited by a given question, the researcher cannot explain the answers given. He cannot explain differences that do not appear through his data collection.

In such cases—which involve the most interesting part of social research —variance in responses must be obtained. The reader would do well to recall earlier discussions in this book which declared that social data are *created* rather than neutrally collected and the discussions which declared that social concepts and variables do not exist in any absolute sense. It is in these senses that the researcher must *create* variance in the responses provided by his research instrument. If his questions tapping religiosity suggest that everyone is religious, he must tighten his criteria for religiosity, rewording the questions in such a way as to push more respondents into apostasy. This point is made bluntly here because it is a difficult one for new researchers to accept. Unfortunately, the traditional literature of the scientific method has created an unfounded belief that researchers must conceptualize variables and positions on those variables to closely reflect *reality*. Thus many new researchers spend considerable time attempting to define precisely such concepts as "religiosity" and to define what constitutes "the religious man."

The epistemological base of this book is the conviction that such concepts as "religiosity" and "religious" cannot be defined in any ultimate sense. The best we can hope for in the present era is the generation of perhaps several useful conceptualizations of religiosity, thus permitting us to speak roughly of *more* and *less* religious men. (The same is true of such concepts as social status, liberalism, alienation, knowledgeability, and so forth.) Conceptualizations are "useful" to the extent that they help the researcher understand his empirical data and facilitate the construction of coherent theories.

If the researcher wishes to explain why some people are more religious than others, then he must define and measure religiosity in such a way as to permit him to score some of his respondents as more religious and others as less—even if this scoring method does not completely jibe with his personal belief about what the "religious man" is ultimately.

If the researcher is ultimately interested in explaining variance, then he should try to maximize that variance among his respondents. In a question offering dichotomous answers he should seek to obtain a 50-50 distribution of responses. For more answer possibilities, he should aim for an even distribution. Doing this will provide him with a greater potential for analysis later on. In evaluating his pre-test or pilot-study results, then, he may wish to manipulate the variance produced by given questions. The following are some guidelines for accomplishing this.

1. Variance may be manipulated by changing the emphasis of the question. Suppose for example that we wish to examine students' commitments to the vocational training aspect of a liberal arts college education. We might ask them to agree or disagree with the statement: "Learning a vocational skill is an important part of my college education." If nearly all students in a pilot study agreed with the statement, it would not be possible for us to analyse those responses, due to a lack of variance. The variance might be manipulated by "toughening" the statement: "Learning a vocational skill is the most important part of my college education." We should expect that fewer students would agree with the second statement than agreed with the first.

By the same token if the modified statement had been asked in a pilot study and very few students agreed with it, we might consider changing it to the easier form: "an important part."

2. Changing the emphasis of answer categories can have the same effect. Suppose respondents in a public health survey were asked: "How often do you wash your hands before eating?" and were given the following answers: always, sometimes, never. If few or no respondents in a pilot study said "always," this answer might be profitably changed to "almost always."

3. Expanding the list of answer categories will almost inevitably increase variance in responses. Increasing the answer possibilities from "agree/disagree" to "strongly agree, agree, disagree, strongly disagree" will almost always spread out the responses. (The researcher should realize, however, that he may end up explaining the difference between "strongly agree," on the one hand, and "agree" to "strongly disagree" on the other.)

Similarly, respondents are sometimes reluctant to select an "extreme" answer, especially in attitudinal or orientational items. Asked to characterize their political orientations as either "very liberal," "moderately liberal," "moderately conservative," or "very conservative," perhaps relatively few respondents will select either of the two extreme characterizations. If the terms "radical left" and "radical right" were added to the extremes of the list, we should expect more people to select the "very liberal" and "very conservative" categories; at the very least, more respondents should be found selecting either "radical left" or "very liberal" than would have selected "very liberal" in the first list.

The above examples involve the expansion of the answer categories toward both extremes of the variable. Sometimes it is useful to skew the answers in only one direction: expanding only one extreme of the variable. Thus in the example given above, campus researchers often add only "New Left" or "Socialist" to the initial list of answer categories.

Variance in responses is a very important criterion for evaluating the worth of questions. The manner in which variance is evaluated, however, still depends on the purpose of the study or of the question. If the researcher's purpose is description, he may consider little variance interesting and important when the form of the given question is clearly appropriate; or he may take the lack of variance as an indication that the question is poorly worded, that the description produced is misleading. If his purpose is explanation, however, he must have variance. His respondents must appear different if he is to explain their differences.

Internal Validation of Items

Thus far we have discussed only the independent evaluation of individual items. Items can also be evaluated through the examination of their relationships with other items. Suppose the researcher has included in his pilot-study questionnaire several items that he believes measure "alienation." One function of the pilot-study evaluation would be to determine whether each item serves that purpose. If all items do indeed measure the same disposition among respondents, then the answers to one item should be correlated with the answers given to others.

Typically, all or most of the items designed to measure a single variable will be empirically related to one another, but the strengths of the relationships will vary among the pairs of items. If one of the items is very weakly related to the others, the researcher may conclude that it does not really measure the variables and may decide to drop it from the questionnaire. (The possibility that it is the *only* item measuring the variable is one of those problems that researchers must learn to live with.) The reader should not resolve now to drop all such items automatically, however. Quite possibly he will decide on substantive grounds that the item in question represents a somewhat different dimension of the variable, empirically unrelated but conceptually important nonetheless. Or he may decide that the lack of a relationship is descriptively interesting and wish to replicate the findings in his more substantial, final survey.

At the opposite extreme, a very high correlation between two items might suggest that it is unnecessary to include both in the final questionnaire. Deleting one or more redundant items would save space to be used for the items that were overlooked in the pilot study questionnaire.

Evaluating the Analysis and Reporting

The evaluation of a pilot study ultimately rests on the same criteria as the eventual evaluation of a finished research project: its ability to tell an interesting and useful story. While the preceding comments point to some specific evaluative criteria, each of the specific points is contained within the success of the pilot-study analysis and reporting. As noted earlier, the researcher should analyze and write up his pilot-study data as though they represented the final survey. Basically, where the pilot-study design permits the construction of an interesting and useful story, it should be retained; where the design prevents such construction, it should be modified.

Problems of question wording, format, variance, validity, and relationships among items are ultimately evaluated in terms of their dysfunctions for the story line. Only a full analysis and reporting can permit the determination of this. The researcher, then, should go through all the intended steps in the analysis: constructing tables, indexes, scales, factors, correlations, regressions, and so forth, presenting explanations for the findings. I repeat: this is the *only* adequate method for evaluating pilot-study results.

By seriously analyzing the pilot-study data, the researcher will recognize that certain data have been overlooked—at a time when it is still possible to modify the design. Equally important, he will learn the analytical surprises that are in store for him in the final survey analysis. If his primary research hypothesis is simply not supported by the pilot-study data, he should analyze those data to the fullest extent in the attempt to discover why the hypothesis was not supported. Has the measurement of variables been adequate? Do other factors interfere with the expected relationship among variables? Was the hypothesis simply unfounded? While he may not be able to answer all these questions satisfactorily, the pilot-study analysis should at least provide him with some clues as to what else ought to be examined in the final survey. At the very least, the pilot study findings should give the researcher time in which to tone down his declarations of the hypothesis around lunch at the faculty club. (He might also withdraw his offer of a paper for the annual professional meetings.)

Summary and Conclusions

It is appropriate to end this chapter on a realistic note. While the pre-testing and pilot studies described above would surely lead to more professional and more valuable survey research, there are few if any past research examples that could be held up as exemplifying the rules and guidelines discussed. The reader should be aware of the reasons why past researchers typically have not made, and probably future researchers typically will not make, adequate use of pre-tests and pilot studies.

Good survey research is almost always time-consuming and expensive; pre-testing and pilot studies seem to add to both time and costs. This is especially the case for good pilot studies. Since survey research (especially interview surveys) is labor-intensive, the survey researcher must always cope with the problem of personnel management. It may be impossible for him to conduct a good pilot study and keep his interviewers, coders, keypunchers, and so forth waiting several months or years while he carries out an extensive pilot-study analysis. More basically, the overall study budget and time period may not permit a great deal of pre-testing and a good pilot study. Or issues, attitudes, sampling frames, and so forth may change significantly between the pilot study and a delayed final survey. These are but a few of the reasons why pre-testing and pilot studies are not presently used properly and will probably not be used to their fullest in the future.

At the same time, the above constraints do allow for a better use of these methods than is typically the case, and the following suggestions ought to be considered. First, pre-testing should be a multistage, continuing process throughout the study design, as noted earlier. Researchers should not think in terms of conducting *the* pre-test as a research ritual, but should take every opportunity to pre-test each aspect of the study design under whatever testing conditions may be available.

Second, if there is insufficient time for a detailed analysis of the pilot-study results prior to the revision and printing of the final questionnaire, the following steps should be considered. As soon as pilot-study questionnaires begin arriving, they should be coded and keypunched. Do not wait until all are returned. Beginning immediately may point to some processing difficulties, and these can be modified promptly. Once a substantial batch of questionnaires—say a hundred or so—have been processed, an initial analysis should begin. The marginal distributions should be run immediately to permit an initial evaluation of the individual items. These tentative conclusions can be verified more substantially as new batches of pilot-study questionnaires are available.

As soon as sufficient numbers of questionnaires have been processed, the more detailed explanatory analysis should begin—again, this should be done even on a partial data file. If it is not possible to conduct an exhaustive analysis prior to the deadlines for revising and printing the final survey questionnaire, the pilot-study analysis should not end when the revised questionnaire is sent to the printer. If the sample design and data-collection method have been sufficiently organized in advance, the printing of the final questionnaire typically provides the researcher with one of the few "dead spots" in the project schedule. This period may very profitably be spent in a more detailed analysis of the pilot study even though he has committed himself to the final questionnaire form. Sometimes missing or faulty data can be corrected through modifications in the data-collection procedures without changing the questionnaire itself. Moreover, this detailed analysis will serve to give the researcher a head start in his final analysis.

Having noted that the ideal procedures outlined in this chapter cannot be followed religiously, it is important to stress the value of adhering to them as much as possible. This chapter has attempted to suggest some guidelines and procedures for conducting and evaluating pre-tests and pilot studies in survey research. As this topic has received little or no attention in the previous research literature, the present offering must be viewed as fragmentary and tentative. I hope that future writers will round out the picture with reports of their own experiences. Until such time, this initial effort will hopefully be of use.

Part Three

Survey Research Analysis

The following portion of the book is devoted to a number of topics involved in the analysis of survey data. In the chapters to follow we shall pick up the study at the point where the researcher finds himself surrounded by boxes and boxes of IBM cards or magnetic tapes and shall discuss some of the steps along the way to the publication of his findings.

Chapter 12 discusses the logic of measurement and association. This chapter is, in a sense, a continuation of the discussion contained in Chapter 7 on conceptualization and instrument design. We shall again find ourselves concerned with the meaning of responses to survey questionnaire items. How can questionnaire responses be taken as indications of variables such as religiosity, prejudice, alienation, and so forth? In Chapter 12, however, we shall examine this issue from an empirical standpoint, whereas the earlier discussion was limited to conceptual manipulations.

Chapter 13 is addressed to the logic of contingency tables. Many researchers may regard this analytical format as rather rudimentary, but we shall give special attention to it as a basis for understanding the logic of all survey analysis. The discussion will begin at the very beginning: with univariate analysis. Then we shall proceed to bivariate analysis and more elaborate multivariate analyses. In the process, we shall move from the logic of description to the logic of explanation. The reader should emerge from this chapter with two important abilities: he should be able to construct contingency tables from his own survey data and he should be able to understand the tables constructed and published by other researchers.

Chapter 14 returns to the persistent topic of measurement, this time focusing on index and scale construction. As in Chapters 7 and 12, our concern will still be the measurement of meaningful variables through the manipulation of survey responses. Having learned the logic of table construction, however, the reader will be properly equipped to learn the logic and skills of creating composite measures of variables. Again, we shall focus on the most rudimentary methods. Most of the chapter is devoted to index construction. While a good deal of the existing methodological literature discusses scale construction, relatively little attention has been given to indexes, even though they are more frequently used in social research.

The key to Part Three of this book is Chapter 15, dealing with the *elaboration model.* Here we shall examine the basic logic of scientific explanation in the survey context. Basically, we shall seek an understanding of the empirical relationship between two variables through the controlled introduction of additional variables. Having noted that lower-class women are more religious than upper-class women, for example, we shall see how the manipulation of additional variables can shed some light on why this is the case.

For the most part, this book deals with the *logic* of research rather than the statistics involved. I believe that if the reader fully understands the logic of research, he will be in an excellent position to marshal whatever statistical manipulations are relevant to his needs. From this perspective, Chapter 16 provides an overview of some common statistics employed in survey analysis. The chapter does not give a full explanation of the computations of such statistics—several excellent statistics texts serve this function—but attempts to place them within the logic of analysis as discussed throughout this book. In this regard, special attention is given to tests of statistical significance—those seemingly convenient shortcuts to understanding.

As noted above, this text primarily examines survey analysis through the medium of contingency tables, as I feel the logic of analysis is more clearly seen in this way. At the same time, other, more complex, modes of analysis provide the analyst with greater explanatory potential and such modes are more appropriate in many situations. Several such additional methods of analysis are discussed in overview in Chapter 17. I have not attempted to provide a cookbook in this instance, but have hoped, rather, to place such methods within the same logic as informs the discussion of contingency tables. Hopefully, the reader will come away from the presentation with a general understanding of the constraints and potentials of such methods and will take advantage of other relevant texts in actually employing them where appropriate.

Chapter 18 is devoted to a topic that has received relatively little attention previously: the reporting of survey findings. Here I have discussed some general guidelines in the communication of research, considering the different types of presentations which may be made.

Chapter Twelve
The Logic of Measurement and Association

The heart of survey analysis lies in the twin goals of description and explanation. The survey analyst makes measurements of variables and then examines the associations among them. As noted in Chapter 1 of this book, however, there is considerable confusion as to the nature of activities involved in this process.

Now that the reader has received some exposure to the various aspects of survey design—especially conceptualization and instrument design—it will be useful to return to the traditional image of the scientific method. Having reviewed that image, utilizing a survey example, we shall depict the traditional image schematically. Then we shall examine some alternative, more appropriate, images of science in practice. In this latter regard, we shall consider the notions of "interchangeability of indexes" and "fixed-point analysis."

12.1 The Traditional Image

The traditional perspective on the scientific method is based on a set of serial steps, which scientists are believed to follow in their work. These steps may be summarized as follows:

1. *Theory construction*
2. *Derivation of theoretical hypotheses*
3. *Operationalization of concepts*
4. *Collection of empirical data*
5. *Empirical testing of hypotheses*

Before refuting this traditional perspective, we should examine it in somewhat more detail.

Theory Construction.   Faced with an aspect of the natural or social world that interests him, the scientist is believed to create an abstract, deductive theory to describe it. This is presumably a purely logical exercise. Let us assume for the moment that a social scientist is interested in deviant behavior. He presumably constructs—on the basis of existing sociological theory—a theory of deviant behavior. Among other things, this theory includes a variety of concepts relevant to the causes of deviant behavior.

Derivation of Theoretical Hypotheses.   On the basis of his total theory of deviant behavior, the scientist presumably derives hypotheses relating the various concepts comprising his theory. This, too, is a purely logical procedure. Following the above example, let us suppose that the scientist logically derives the hypothesis that juvenile delinquency is a function of supervision. As supervision increases, juvenile delinquency decreases.

Operationalization of Concepts.   The next step in the traditional view of the scientific method involves the specification of empirical indicators to represent the theoretical concepts. Whereas theoretical concepts must be somewhat abstract and perhaps vague, the empirical indicators must be precise and specific. Thus, in our example, the scientist might operationalize the concept "juvenile" as anyone under 18 years of age; "delinquency" might be operationalized as being arrested for a criminal act; and "supervision" might be operationalized as the presence of a nonworking adult in the home.

The effect of operationalization is to convert the theoretical hypothesis into an empirical one. In the present case, the empirical hypothesis would be: Among persons under 18 years of age, those living in homes with a nonworking adult will be less likely to be arrested for a criminal act than will be true of those without a nonworking adult in the home.

Collection of Empirical Data.   Based on the operationalization of theoretical concepts, the scientist then presumably collects data relating to the empirical indicators. In the present example, he might conduct a survey of persons under 18 years of age. Among other things, the survey questionnaire would ask of each whether the person lived in a home with a nonworking adult and whether the person had ever been arrested for a criminal act.

Empirical Testing of Hypotheses.   Once the data have been collected, the final step involves the statistical testing of the hypothesis. The scientist determines, empirically, whether those juveniles with nonworking adults in the home are less likely to have been arrested for criminal acts than is the case for those lacking nonworking adults. The confirmation or disconfirmation of the empirical hypothesis is then used for purposes of accepting or rejecting the theoretical hypothesis.

12.2   A Schematic Presentation

Figure 12–1 depicts the traditional image of science in schematic form. We note that the scientist begins with a particular interest about the world, creates a general theory about it, and that deductive theory is used to generate a hypothesis regarding the association between two variables. This hypothesis is represented in the form: $Y = f(X)$. This expression would be read "Y is a function of X", meaning that values of Y are determined or caused by values of X. In our example, delinquency (Y) is a function of supervision (X).

Next the scientist operationalizes the two variables by specifying empirical measurements to represent them in the real world. He collects data relevant to such measurements and, finally, tests the expected relationship empirically.

Figure 12–1. The Traditional Image of Science

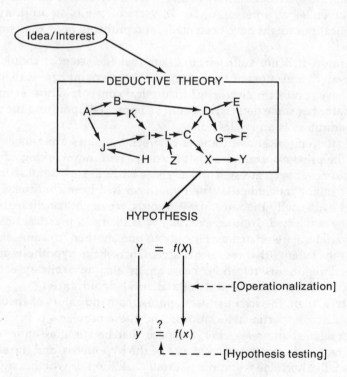

Two Basic Problems

The preceding description of the traditional view of the scientific method may persuade most readers that scientific research is a relatively routine activity. All the scientist must do is move faithfully through steps 1 to 5 and he will have discovered truth.

Unhappily, scientific research is not that neat. The empirical world that the scientist studies is not that neat. The traditional view of the scientific method simply does not represent what goes on in scientific research—social or otherwise. There are two basic problems that prevent the dream from coming true.

First, theoretical concepts seldom if ever permit unambiguous operationalization. Whereas concepts are abstract and general, every specification of empirical indicators must represent an approximation. In the previous example, it is unlikely that the general concept of "supervision" is adequately represented by the presence of a nonworking adult in the home. The presence of such an adult does not assure supervision of the juvenile. And in some homes lacking such an adult, other arrangements may be made for the juvenile's supervision.

Being arrested for a criminal act cannot be equated with the abstract concept "delinquency." Some juveniles may engage in delinquent behavior without being arrested. Others may be arrested falsely. Moreover, the specification of "juvenile" as a person under 18 years of age is an arbitrary one. Other specifications might have been made, and probably none is unambiguously correct.

Furthermore, it is not sufficient to argue that the scientist should have specified "better" indicators of his concepts. The key point here is that there are almost never perfect indicators of theoretical concepts. Thus, every empirical indicator has some defects; all could be improved upon, and the search for better indicators is an endless one.

Second, the empirical associations between variables are almost never perfect. In the previous example, if all juveniles with nonworking adults in the home had never been arrested and all those without such adults had been arrested, we might conclude that the hypothesis had been confirmed. Or if both groups had exactly the same arrest records, we might conclude that the hypothesis was rejected. Neither eventuality is likely in practice, however. Nearly all variables are related empirically to one another "to some extent." Specifying the "extent" that represents acceptance of the hypothesis and the "extent" that represents rejection, however, is also an arbitrary act. (See Chapter 16 for a discussion of tests of statistical significance.)

Ultimately, then, the scientist uses approximate indicators of theoretical concepts to discover partial associations. And these problems conspire with one another against the researcher. Suppose that he specifies an extent of association that will constitute acceptance of the hypothesis, and the empirical analysis falls short. He will quite naturally ask himself whether different indicators of the concepts might have produced the specified extent of association.

The purpose of the preceding comments has been to indicate that the traditional view of the routine scientific method is inappropriate to research in practice. Research does not simply happen through the dogged traverse through steps 1 to 5. This realization should not be the source of dismay, however, but should serve as a challenge to the researcher. It should not be taken as a denial of the possibility of scientific research, but it should lay the basis for an enlightened, truly scientific, research.

Measurement and association are interrelated concepts. The scientist must handle both simultaneously and logically. Rather than moving through a fixed set of steps, the scientist moves back and forth through them endlessly. Often his theoretical constructions are built around the previously observed associations between empirical indicators. Partial theoretical constructions may suggest new empirical data to be examined, and so forth. It is hoped that, after each activity, the scientist understands his subject matter a little better. The "critical experiment" that ultimately determines the fate of an entire theory is a rare thing indeed.

Scientific research, then, is a never-ending enterprise aimed at the understanding of some phenomenon. To that end, the scientist continually measures and examines associations. And he must be constantly aware of the nature of their interrelations. The following sections should clarify the nature of the interrelations.

12.3   The Interchangeability of Indexes

Paul Lazarsfeld, in his discussions of the "interchangeability of indexes" has provided an important conceptual tool for our understanding of the relationship between measurement and association and as a partial resolution to the two problems discussed in the previous section.[1] His comments grow out of the recognition that there are several possible indicators for any concept.

Let us return for the moment to the notion of a theoretical hypothesis: $Y = f(X)$. Lazarsfeld recognizes that there are several possible indicators of supervision; we might write these as x_1, x_2, x_3, and so forth. While there may be reasons for believing that some of the possible indicators are better than others, they are essentially interchangeable. Thus, the scientist faces the dilemma of which to use in the testing of the hypothesis: $Y = f(X)$.

The solution to the dilemma lies in the use of *all* indicators. Thus the scientist tests the following empirical hypotheses: $y = f(x_1)$, $y = f(x_2)$, $y = f(x_3)$, and so forth. Rather than having one test of the hypothesis, he has several, as indicated schematically in Figure 12–2.

---

[1]Paul F. Lazarsfeld, "Problems in Methodology," in Robert K. Merton (ed.), *Sociology Today* (New York: Basic Books, Inc., Publishers, 1959), pp. 39–78.

Figure 12–2. The Interchangeability of Indexes

$$Y = f(X)$$

$$y \overset{?}{=} f(x_1)$$
$$y \overset{?}{=} f(x_2)$$
$$y \overset{?}{=} f(x_3)$$
$$y \overset{?}{=} f(x_4)$$
$$y \overset{?}{=} f(x_5)$$

The reader may have already anticipated a new dilemma. If the scientist following the traditional view of the scientific method faced the problem that the single empirical association might not be perfect, the present scientist will be faced with several empirical associations, none of which will be perfect and some of which may conflict with one another. Thus, even if he has specified a particular extent of association that will be sufficient to confirm the hypothesis, he may discover that the tests involving x_1, x_3, and x_5 meet that specified criterion, but the tests involving x_2 and x_4 do not. His dilemma is seemingly compounded. In fact, however, the real situation may be clarified.

In terms of the notion of "the interchangeability of indexes," the theoretical hypothesis is accepted as a *general* proposition if it is confirmed by all the specific empirical tests. If, for example, juvenile delinquency is a function of supervision in a broadly generalized sense, then juvenile delinquency should be empirically related to every empirical indicator of supervision.

If, however, the scientist discovers that only certain indicators of supervision have this property, then he has specified the kinds of supervision for which the proposition holds. In practice, this may help him to reconceptualize "supervision" in more general terms. Perhaps, for example, juvenile delinquency is a function of structural constraints, and some kinds of supervision are indicators of constraints, while others really are not.

It is very important to realize what the scientist will have accomplished through this process. Rather than routinely testing a fixed hypothesis relating to supervision and delinquency, he will have gained a more comprehensive understanding of the nature of that association. This will make sense, however, only if we view the goal of science as understanding rather than simply theory construction and hypothesis testing.

There is one additional step required, however, before our understanding of the scientific process is clear. The notion of interchangeable indexes discussed above focused on the variability of one of the concepts, when in fact all concepts have this property. This will be the topic of the next section.

12.4   Fixed-Point Analysis

In the preceding section, we noted that given the theoretical hypothesis $Y = f(X)$, there were several possible indicators of X: written as x_1, x_2, x_3 and so forth. It should also be evident that Y may be specified in several ways: y_1, y_2, y_3, and so forth. In short, none of the theoretical concepts have unambiguous empirical indicators. Thus, in a two-variable hypothesis, the number of possible tests is manifold. And the interpretation of so many tests—given many indicators—will be severely taxing.

The dilemma facing the scientist at this point may be represented in a paraphrase of William James as "a buzzing, whirling mess of variables" wherein no indicator can be accepted as a true measure of a given concept, illustrated schematically in Part I of Figure 12–3. There is no safe anchoring point upon which the scientist can begin to build his analysis. Given such total uncertainty, the inexperienced researcher may give up in despair or retreat into the comfort of the traditional view of the scientific method as a serial set of routine steps.

The experienced scientist extricates himself from this morass through careful pragmatism and a healthy tolerance of ambiguity. One way he might deal with the situation is the following.

He begins by recognizing that he has, say, five possible indicators of delinquency and five indicators of supervision. Realizing that there are no natural fixed points from which to proceed, he arbitrarily fixes one. For example, he may specify, based on his best judgment, that y_1 will be fixed as the indicator of Y (arrest as an indicator of delinquency). He does this knowing full well that it may not be the best possible indicator.

Having fixed Y as y_1, he then permits himself to vary the possible measures of X, following the general format described in the interchangeability of indexes. (Part II of Figure 12–3). He does this as though there were no ambiguity as to the measurement of delinquency. The result of this activity is a better understanding of the nature of his possible indicators of X. As suggested above, he will discover that some indicators of X (supervision) are associated with y_1 (being arrested) while others are not. This should lead to a reconceptualization of the types and nature of supervision. In the present illustration, he has decided the best index of supervision is a combination of x_1, x_3, and x_4.

Once he has achieved a better understanding of X in this fashion, he then turns the process around: he "fixes" X and allows Y to vary (Part III of Figure 12–3). If x_1, x_2, x_3 now seems closest to his general concept of supervision —on the basis of the initial analyses—he uses that combination of items as *the* measure of supervision. His subsequent analyses ask *which* indicators of

Figure 12–3. Fixed-Point Analysis

I

$$y_3$$
$$x_1 \qquad\qquad x_3$$
$$y_5 \qquad x_4$$
$$\qquad\qquad y_1 \qquad x_2$$
$$y_2 \qquad y_4$$
$$\qquad\qquad x_5$$

II

$$y_1 \overset{?}{=} f(x_1)$$
$$y_1 \overset{?}{=} f(x_2)$$
$$y_1 \overset{?}{=} f(x_3)$$
$$y_1 \overset{?}{=} f(x_4)$$
$$y_1 \overset{?}{=} f(x_5)$$

III

$$y_1 \overset{?}{=} f(x_1 x_3 x_4)$$
$$y_2 \overset{?}{=} f(x_1 x_3 x_4)$$
$$y_3 \overset{?}{=} f(x_1 x_3 x_4)$$
$$y_4 \overset{?}{=} f(x_1 x_3 x_4)$$
$$y_5 \overset{?}{=} f(x_1 x_3 x_4)$$

IV

$$y_2 y_3 \overset{?}{=} f(x_1 x_3 x_4)$$
$$y_2 y_3 \overset{?}{=} f(x_2 x_3 x_5)$$
$$y_2 y_3 \overset{?}{=} f(x_1 x_2)$$
$$y_2 y_3 \overset{?}{=} f(x_1 x_3)$$
etc.

V

$$y_1 y_4 y_5 \overset{?}{=} f(x_1 x_3)$$
$$y_2 y_3 y_4 \overset{?}{=} f(x_1 x_3)$$
etc.

VI

$$y_i = f(x_i)$$

Y (delinquency) are indeed functions of the newly fixed indicator of X (supervision). The result of these analyses will be a better understanding of the types and nature of his indicators of delinquency. Thus the fixed indicator of supervision may be importantly associated with whether or not a juvenile is arrested for a delinquent act, but not associated with whether or not he commits one. Thus the two indicators of delinquency are not interchangeable indexes of the same general concept in the context of the analysis.

Once the scientist has gained a better conceptualization of delinquency, he may then turn the process around again—using his new conceptualization to refine his understanding of the different indicators of supervision (Part IV of Figure 12–3). This procedure can, of course, go on endlessly (Part V). Thinking about a line of scientific inquiry rather than a specific research project, the procedure does indeed go on endlessly.

The ultimate result of this procedure should be carefully examined as it is quite different from what is suggested in the traditional view of the scientific method. The scientist neither asks nor answers the question "*Is* Y a function of X?" Rather, he asks: "*How* is Y a function of X?" (Under what operationalizations is Y a function of X?) He does not address himself to the straightforward question of whether delinquency is decreased by increasing supervision. Rather, he asks: "What kinds of delinquency are affected by what kinds of supervision in what kinds of ways?" The answer to this question is presented in Part VI of Figure 12–3 with the subscript i used to indicate the most useful indexes of X and Y. In practice, of course, the researcher might arrive at several such answers. This latter line of inquiry is more appropriate to the kinds of phenomena that scientists typically study, and the understanding generated by it will be more sophisticated and more useful as well.

12.5   Implications

The implication of the preceding comments is that measurement and association are importantly intertwined. The measurement of a variable makes little sense outside the empirical and theoretical contexts of the associations to be tested. Asked "How should I measure social class?" the experienced scientist will reply, "What is your purpose for measuring it?" The "proper" way of measuring a given variable depends very heavily on the variables to be associated with it. One further example should make this point clearer.

A controversy has raged recently in the sociology of religion concerning the relationship between religiosity and prejudice. A book by Charles Y. Glock and Rodney Stark entitled *Christian Beliefs and Anti-Semitism*[2] reported empirical data indicating that Christian church members holding orthodox beliefs were more likely to be anti-Semitic than were less orthodox members. The book's findings stirred considerable discussion within the churches, and it resulted in follow-up research on the same topic by other researchers.

One subsequent research project arrived at the directly opposite conclusion from that of Glock and Stark. The researchers reported that as orthodoxy increased, prejudice decreased. Upon closer examination, however, it was noted that the measures of orthodoxy were based on acceptance of questionnaire statements reflecting the traditional Christian doctrines of "All men are brothers" and "Love thy neighbor." Not surprisingly, survey respondents who accepted the statements based on these doctrines appeared less prejudiced than those who rejected them. Normally, these research findings would be (and were) challenged on the grounds of "contamination." The two variables being examined (religious orthodoxy and prejudice) actually measured

[2](New York: Harper & Row, Publishers, 1967).

the same or similar qualities. Calling one set of indicators "orthodoxy" and the other "prejudice" does not prove that prejudice decreases with increasing orthodoxy in a general sense.

The discussions of this chapter suggest a somewhat different reaction to the research findings. Asking *how* orthodoxy and prejudice are associated with each other rather than asking *whether*, we would conclude that orthodoxy measured in terms of the Glock-Stark indicators (belief in God, Jesus, miracles, and the like) is positively associated with prejudice, while orthodoxy measured as commitment to the norms of brotherly love and equality is negatively associated with prejudice. Both conclusions are empirically correct; neither conclusion answers the more general question of *whether* religion and prejudice are related. The final remaining step, of course, is to evaluate the relative utility of the conclusions. The finding that orthodoxy and prejudice are negatively associated would probably be disregarded as either tautological or trivial. (Of course, the measurement of orthodoxy in terms of brotherly love and equality might be extremely useful in some other context.)

Summary and Conclusions

This rather short chapter has aimed at providing a healthy perspective on the twin goals of measurement and association in science. In this regard, I have sought to give the beginning researcher a better understanding of the scientific enterprise per se. The chapter began with a review of the traditional textbook discourse on the scientific method and indicated that it does not accurately reflect scientific research in practice. In place of the traditional perspective, I have tried to offer alternative models, which I believe will be of more use in actual research activities.

The reader should be warned, if he does not already realize, that the perspective put forward in this chapter is by no means an accepted version in methodology instruction. Rather, it is derived from my own research experiences and from discussions with other researchers in both the social and natural sciences. My motivation in dwelling on this issue stems from the hardships of previous, inexperienced researchers who have accepted the traditional perspective as a true picture of how "real" scientists proceed and who have been severely disappointed in their own research. I do not mean to imply that scientific research is sloppy or "unscientific," only that it is far from routine. The scientist is quite different from the technician.

Chapter Thirteen   Constructing and Understanding Tables

Most survey analysis falls within the general rubric of *multivariate* analysis, and the bulk of Part Three of this book is devoted to the varieties of multivariate analysis. The term simply refers to the examination of several variables simultaneously. The analysis of the simultaneous associations among age, education, and prejudice would be an example of multivariate analysis.

The reader should recognize that multivariate analysis is not a specific form of analysis; specific techniques for conducting a multivariate analysis would be factor analysis, smallest-space analysis, multiple correlation, multiple regression, path analysis, among others. The basic *logic* of multivariate analysis can best be seen through the use of simple tables, called contingency tables or cross-tabulations. Thus the present chapter is devoted to the construction and understanding of such tables.

Furthermore, multivariate analysis cannot be fully understood without a firm understanding of even more fundamental analytic modes: univariate and bivariate analyses. The chapter, therefore, will begin with these.

13.1   Univariate Analysis

Univariate analysis refers to the examination of only one variable at a time. In the present context, a variable will be represented by a single questionnaire item. We shall begin with the logic and formats for the analysis of univariate data.

The most basic format for presenting univariate data would be the reporting of all individual responses. If survey respondents were asked to report their ages, the researcher might report all the answers provided: 18, 35, 26, 45, 35, 53, and so forth. Such a report would provide the reader with the fullest details of the data, but it would be too cumbersome for most purposes.

In the present example, the researcher could report his data in a somewhat more manageable form without losing any of the detail. He might report the *frequency distributions* of the several answers provided by respondents: 12

239

respondents aged 18, 34 aged 19, 54 aged 20, and so forth. Such a format would avoid duplicate entries, but would permit the reader to reconstruct the original data completely.

For a more manageable format—with a certain loss of detail—the researcher could report respondents' ages as a frequency distribution of *grouped data:* 46 respondents under 20 years of age, 639 between 20 and 29, 1,356 between 30 and 39, and so forth. In this case, the reader would have fewer data to examine and interpret, but he would not be able to reproduce fully the original responses. Thus, he would know that 46 respondents were under 20 years of age, but he would have no way of knowing how many were aged 19, 18, 17, and so forth. *(Note:* The "cutting points" for the grouping of data into categories generally represent an arbitrary decision.)

Frequency distributions are often referred to by the term "marginals," and this term will be used in the following discussions. The above examples have presented marginals in terms of raw numbers. An alternative format would be the use of *percentages.* Thus, for example, the researcher could report his grouped data as x percent under 20, y percent between 20 and 29, and so forth.

In computing percentages, the researcher frequently must make a decision regarding the *base* for percentaging: that number that represents 100 percent. In the most straightforward case, the base for percentaging would be the total number of respondents in the study. If some of the respondents failed to give an answer to the question being reported, however, the researcher has two alternatives. First, he might still base his percentages on the total number of respondents, with those failing to give their ages being reported as a percentage of the total. Second, he could use the number of persons giving an answer as the base for percentaging. (He should still report the number who did not answer, but they would not figure in the percentaging.)

The choice of a base for percentaging depends wholly on the purposes of the analysis. If, for example, the researcher wishes to compare the age distribution of his survey sample with comparable data describing the population from which the sample was drawn, he will probably want to omit the "no answers" from the percentaging. His best estimate of the age distribution of all respondents is to be found in the distribution discovered among those answering the question. Since "no answer" is not a meaningful age category, its presence in the percentaging would confuse the comparison of sample and population figures.

Moving beyond the report of marginals, the researcher may choose to present his data in the form of summary *averages.* His options in this regard include the *mode* (the most frequently reported answer, either grouped or ungrouped), the arithmetic *mean,* or the median (the middle response). Thus, he might report that most respondents were between ages 30 and 39 (mode), that the mean age of respondents is 34 years, or that the median age is 35.

Averages have the special advantage to the reader of reducing the raw data to the most manageable form: a single number (or category) can represent all the detailed data collected in response to the question. This advantage comes at a cost, of course, since the reader cannot reconstruct the original data from an average.

This disadvantage of averages can be somewhat alleviated through the reporting of summaries of the *dispersion* of responses. The simplest measure of dispersion is the *range*. Thus, in addition to reporting a mean age of 35, the researcher might also indicate that the ages reported ranged from 18 to 69. A somewhat more sophisticated measure of dispersion is the *standard deviation*. The standard deviation for a distribution of values is the range from the mean within which approximately 34 percent of the cases fall provided the values are distributed in a *normal curve*. Other measures of dispersion would be interquartile range and similar statistics.

Throughout the above discussions, we have explored variations on the reporting of a continuous variable, age. If the survey question being analyzed generated a nominal or limited ordinal variable, then some of the techniques discussed above would not be applicable. If the variable in question were sex, for example, marginals in terms of either raw numbers or percentages would be appropriate and useful. The modal response would be legitimate, but it would convey little useful information to the reader. Reports of mean, median, or dispersion summaries would be inappropriate.

In presenting univariate—and other—data, the researcher will be constrained by two often conflicting goals. On the one hand, he should attempt to provide the reader with the fullest degree of detail regarding those data. On the other hand, the data should be presented in a manageable form. As these two goals often go directly counter to each other, the researcher will find himself continually seeking the best compromise between the two goals. One useful solution, however, is to report a given set of data in more than one form. In the case of age, for example, he might report both the marginals on ungrouped ages plus the mean age and standard deviation.

This concludes the introductory discussion of univariate analysis. The reader should have concluded that this seemingly simple matter can be rather complex. The lessons of this section, in any event, will be important as we move now to a consideration of subgroup descriptions and bivariate analyses.

13.2   Subgroup Descriptions

Univariate analyses serve the purpose of *describing* the survey sample and, by extension, the population from which the sample was selected. Bivariate and multivariate analyses are aimed primarily at explanatory issues. Before turning to explanation, however, we should consider the intervening case of subgroup description.

Often the researcher wishes to describe subsets of his survey sample. In a straightforward univariate analysis, he might wish to present the distribution of responses to a question relating to equal rights for women and men. In exploring the answers in greater detail, it would make good sense to examine the responses of men and women in the sample separately. In examining attitudes toward the Ku Klux Klan, it would make sense to describe black and white respondents separately, as well as respondents from different regions of the country.

In computing and presenting stratified descriptions, the researcher follows the same steps as outlined in the section on univariate analysis, but the steps are followed independently for each of the relevant subgroups. For example, all men in the sample would be treated as a total sample representing 100 percent, and the distributions of responses or summary averages would be computed for the men. The same would be done for women. Then, the researcher could report that 75 percent of the women approved of sexual equality, and that 63 percent of the men approved. Each group would have been subjected to a simple, univariate analysis. Frequency distributions for subgroups are often referred to as *stratified* marginals.

In some situations, the researcher presents stratified marginals or other subgroup descriptions for purely descriptive purposes. The reporting of census data often has this purpose. The average value of dwelling units on different census blocks may be presented for descriptive purposes. The reader may then note the average house value for any given block.

More often, the purpose of subgroup descriptions is comparative. In the case of sexual equality, the researcher would clearly be interested in determining whether women were *more likely* to approve of the proposition than were men. Moreover, this comparison is not motivated by idle curiosity in most cases. Typically, it is based on an expectation that the stratification variable will have some form of causal effect on the description variable. Whether a respondent is a man or a woman should affect the attitude toward equality of the sexes. Similarly, whether a respondent is black or white should affect his attitudes toward the Ku Klux Klan. When the analysis is motivated by such expectations, we move into the realm of explanation rather than description. At this point, it is appropriate to turn to a discussion of bivariate analysis.

13.3   Bivariate Analysis

Explanatory, bivariate analysis is basically the same as subgroup descriptions with certain special constraints. In subgroup descriptions, the researcher is completely free to pick whatever stratification variable he desires and to describe each subgroup in terms of any other variable. In the example of sexual equality, he may separately describe men and women in terms of the percentages approving or disapproving (see Table 13-1).

Table 13-1. *"Do you approve or disapprove of the proposition that men and women should be treated equally in all regards?"*

	Men	Women
Approve	63%	75%
Disapprove	37	25
	100%	100%
	(400)*	(400)

*The figures shown in parentheses represent the *base* for percentaging. In this instance, there are 400 men altogether, 63 percent (252 of the men) of whom "approve." Thirty-seven percent (148 of the men) "disapprove."

Or he might describe those approving and those disapproving in terms of the percentages of men and women (see Table 13-2).

Table 13-2

	Approve	Disapprove
Men	46%	60%
Women	54	40
	100%	100%
100% =	(552)	(248)

Either of these tables would be a legitimate presentation of subgroup descriptions. The data presented in the two tables would be read differently, however. From Table 13-1, we would note that 63 percent of the men in the sample approved of sexual equality, as compared with 75 percent of the women. From Table 13-2, we would note that of those approving 46 percent are men whereas of those disapproving 60 percent are men; or, respectively, that 37 percent of the 400 men disapprove, compared with 25 percent of the 400 women (Table 13-1) and that of those approving 54 percent are women, whereas of those disapproving 40 percent are women (Table 13-2).

In an explanatory, bivariate analysis, however, only Table 13-1 would make sense. The reasoning behind this assertion may best be presented as a series of propositions:

1. *Women generally are accorded an inferior status in American society; thus they should be more supportive of the proposed equality of the sexes.*

2. A respondent's sex should therefore affect (cause) his or her response to the questionnaire item: women should be more likely to approve than men.

3. If the male and female respondents in the survey are described separately in terms of their responses, a higher percentage of the women should approve than of the men.

Following this logic, then, Table 13-1 divides the sample into two groups —men and women—and then describes the attitudes of the two groups separately. The percentages approving in the two groups are then compared, and we see that women are indeed more likely to approve than are men.

If Table 13-2 were presented as an explanatory, bivariate analysis, the logic of that table would be as follows. Attitudes on sexual equality affect the sex of the person holding that attitude. Approving of sexual equality will tend to make the person a woman more than it will make the person a man. This reasoning is, of course, absurd. Respondents' sexes are predetermined long before attitudes regarding sexual equality. Different attitudes on sexual equality can have no effect on whether the person holding a given attitude will be a man or a woman.

Realize, however, that Table 13-2 would be legitimate from the standpoint of subgroup description and even for purposes of *prediction*. If for some reason we knew a given respondent's attitude on sexual equality and wanted to predict whether that person was a man or a woman, Table 13-2 would be the appropriate source for such a prediction. If we knew the respondent approved of sexual equality, we would predict that the respondent was a woman. (*Note:* If we made several independent predictions of this sort, we would be wrong 46 percent of the time.) If we knew the respondent disapproved of sexual equality, we would guess that respondent was a man (and be wrong 40 percent of the time in repeated tests).

For purposes of explanation, however, only Table 13-1 is legitimate. In explanation, the reader must understand the logic of *independent* and *dependent* variables. Basically, the researcher attempts to explain values on the dependent variable on the basis of values on the independent variable. In this sense, he reasons that the independent variable *causes* the dependent variable (typically, in a probabilistic sense). In the above example, attitudes toward sexual equality comprise the dependent variable, while respondents' sexes comprise the independent variable. Thus, sex causes attitudes toward sexual equality.

The determination of which of two variables is the dependent and which is the independent variable is sometimes difficult and even arbitrary, but some guidelines are in order. First, whenever there is a clear time order relating to the two variables, that one whose values are determined earlier in time is always the independent variable; the one whose values are determined later in time is always the dependent variable. The notion of causation backward in time is illogical. Since a respondent's sex is determined prior to his or her attitude regarding sexual equality, sex must be the independent variable.

One implication of this is that two variables occurring simultaneously in time cannot be linked causally. A person's sex and race cannot be analyzed per se in an explanatory fashion. Of course, the parents' race and the child's sex could logically be analyzed in this manner if the researcher believed, for example, that black parents were more likely to have male children than were white parents. In such a case, a time order of variables could be determined.

In many instances, however, there is no clear time order relating the two variables. For example, if the researcher wished to examine the causal relationship between education and prejudice, the time order of these two variables would be somewhat more ambiguous than the example of sex and attitudes. One might argue that increasing education will make a person less prejudiced; education would then be the independent variable and prejudice the dependent variable. On the other hand, however, it could be argued that prejudice could affect the amount of education a person will seek or receive. It could be argued that education would be anathema to the deeply prejudiced person and/or such a person would be more likely to flunk out of school. Thus, a case could be made for prejudice being the independent variable with education the dependent.

In those situations in which the time order of variables is not clear, the designation of independent and dependent variable must be made and presented on a logical basis. Often the case for this cannot be made sufficiently strong to satisfy all readers. In other instances, the researcher himself may believe that the two variables affect each other in a cyclical manner. He may say that for some respondents education affects prejudice, while for others the opposite is true, and for still others an even more complex dynamic is at work: an unprejudiced person may be thereby led to get more education and that education will further reduce his prejudices.

No matter what the situation regarding the inherent time order of the variables and/or a logical positing of time order, every explanatory, bivariate table implicitly designates an independent and a dependent variable. If the researcher believes there is no time order connecting them, he must arbitrarily designate a quasi-time order in constructing a table. The following discussion will assume that one variable has been designated as dependent, regardless of the basis for such designation.

Constructing Tables

In constructing explanatory, bivariate tables, the following steps should be followed:

1. The sample is divided into values or categories of the independent variable.

2. Each of these subgroups is then described in terms of the values or categories of the dependent variable.

3. Finally the table is read by comparing the independent variable subgroups in terms of a given value of the dependent variable.

Let's repeat the analysis of sex and attitudes on sexual equality following these steps. For the reasons outlined above, sex is designated as the independent variable; attitudes toward sexual equality constitute the dependent variable. Thus, we proceed as follows:

1. The sample is divided into men and women.

2. Each sex subgroup is described in terms of approval or disapproval of sexual equality.

3. Men and women are compared in terms of the percentages approving of sexual equality.

In the case of the previous example relating race to attitudes toward the Ku Klux Klan, it was noted that race would be the independent variable and attitudes the dependent. We would proceed as follows:

1. Divide the sample into black and white respondents.

2. Describe each racial group separately in terms of their approval or disapproval of the KKK.

3. Compare blacks and whites in terms of the percentages approving of the KKK.

One problem which often confuses inexperienced researchers should be commented on: Should a table be percentaged "down" or "across"? Should a column of percentages total 100 percent or should a row of percentages? The answer to these questions is altogether arbitrary. In this book, I have tended to standardize the procedure by percentaging down, so that columns of percentage figures equal 100 percent but this is only a matter of personal taste and habit.

A very useful guideline follows from this general issue, however. If a table is percentaged down, it should be read across. If it is percentaged across, it should be read down. Taking Table 13-1 as an example, we find it has been percentaged down in the sense that the percentages in each column total to 100 percent. This table is interpreted by reading across: 63 percent of the men approve as compared with 75 percent of the women.

Dogged adherence to this general rule for table construction and interpretation will avoid a common error. Many inexperienced researchers would read Table 13-2 as follows: "Sixty-three percent of the men approve of sexual equality as compared with 37 percent who disapprove. Therefore, men are more likely to approve." This interpretation is misleading. While it is true that men are more likely to approve of sexual equality *than to disapprove,* this has no significance outside of a simple description of men's attitudes. The more important observation is that men are less likely to approve *than are women.* Since the table is percentaged down, it should be read across.

Bivariate Table Formats

The format for presenting contingency table data has never been standardized, with the result that a variety of formats will be found in research literature. As long as a table is easily read and interpreted, there is probably no reason to strive for standardization. At the same time, however, there are a number of guidelines that should be followed in the presentation of most tabular data.

1. Tables should have headings or titles that succinctly describe what is contained in the table.

2. The original content of the variables should be clearly presented—in the table itself if at all possible—or in the text with a paraphrase in the table. This is especially critical when a variable is derived from responses to an attitudinal question, since the meaning of the responses will depend largely on the wording of the questionnaire item.

3. The values or categories of each variable should be clearly indicated. In the case of complex response categories, these will have to be abbreviated, but the meaning should be clear in the table and, of course, the full response should be reported in the text.

4. When percentages are presented in the table, the base upon which they are computed should be indicated. Note that it is redundant to present all of the raw numbers for each percentaged category since these could be reconstructed from the percentages and the bases. Moreover, the presentation of both numbers and percentages often confuses a table and makes it more difficult to read.

5. If any respondents are omitted from the table due to missing data ("no answer" for example), their numbers should be indicated in the table.

Table 13-3 below is an example of a good table.

Table 13-3. *"Do you approve or disapprove of the
general proposition that men and women should be
treated equally in all regards?"*

	Men	Women
Approve	63%	75%
Disapprove	37	25
	100%	100%
	(400)	(400)
No answer =	(12)	(5)

13.4   Multivariate Analysis

The logic of multivariate analysis is the topic of later
chapters in this book—especially Chapter 15. At this point, however, it will
be useful to discuss briefly the construction of multivariate tables, those
constructed from several variables.

Multivariate tables may be constructed on the basis of a more complicated subgroup description—following essentially the same steps outlined
above for bivariate tables. Instead of one independent variable and one dependent variable, however, we will have more than one independent variable.
Instead of explaining the dependent variable on the basis of a single independent variable, we shall seek an explanation through the use of more than one
independent variable.

Returning to the example of attitudes toward sexual equality, suppose
that the researcher believed that age would also affect such attitudes: that
young people would approve of sexual equality more than would older people. As the first step in table construction, we would divide the total sample
into subgroups based on the various values of *both* independent variables
simultaneously: young men, old men, young women, and old women. Then,
the several subgroups would be described in terms of the dependent variable
and comparisons would be made. Table 13-4 is a hypothetical table that
might result.

Following the convention of this textbook, this table has also been percentaged down, and it should, therefore, be read across. The interpretation
of this table warrants several conclusions:

*1. Among both men and women, younger people are more supportive of sexual
equality than are older people. Among women, 90 percent and 60 percent, respectively, approve.*

Table 13-4. "Do you approve or disapprove of the proposition that men and women should be treated equally in all regards?"

	Women		Men	
	Under 30	30 and Over	Under 30	30 and Over
Approve	90%	60%	78%	48%
Disapprove	10	40	22	52
	100%	100%	100%	100%
	(200)	(200)	(200)	(200)
No answer =	(2)	(3)	(10)	(2)

2. *Within each age group, women are more supportive than are men. Among those respondents under 30 years of age, 90 percent of the women approve, compared with 78 percent of the men. Among those 30 and over, 60 percent of the women and 48 percent of the men approve.*

3. *As measured in the table, age would appear to have a stronger affect on attitudes than sex. For both men and women, the effect of age may be summarized as a 30 percentage point difference. Within each age group, the percentage point difference between men and women is 12.*

4. *Both age and sex have independent effects on attitudes. Within a given value on one independent variable, different values of the second still affect attitudes.*

5. *Similarly, the two independent variables have a cumulative effect on attitudes. Young women are the most supportive, while older men are the least supportive.*

Chapter 15 on the *elaboration model* will examine the logic of multivariate analysis in much greater detail. Before concluding this section, however, it will be useful to note an alternative format for presenting such data.

Each of the tables presented in this chapter is somewhat inefficient. Since the dependent variable—attitudes toward sexual equality—is dichotomous (two values), knowing one value permits the reader to easily reconstruct the other. Thus, if we know that 90 percent of the women under 30 years of age approve of sexual equality, then we know automatically that 10 percent disapprove. Reporting the percentages who disapprove, then, is unnecessary. On the basis of this recognition, Table 13-4 could be presented in the alternative format of Table 13-5.

In Table 13-5, the percentages approving of sexual equality are reported in the cells representing the intersections of the two independent variables. The numbers presented in parentheses below each percentage represent the number of cases upon which the percentages are based. Thus, for example,

Table 13-5. *"Do you approve or disapprove of the proposition that men and women should be treated equally in all regards?"*

Percent Who "Approve"	Women	Men
Under 30	90 (200)	78 (200)
30 and over	60 (200)	48 (200)

the reader knows that there are 200 women under 30 years of age in the sample, and 90 percent of those approved sexual equality. This tells him, moreover, that 180 of those 200 women approved, and that the other 20 (or 10 percent) disapproved. This new table is easier to read than the former one, and it does not sacrifice any detail.

Summary and Conclusions

This chapter has introduced the logic and mechanics of table construction. At first glance, tables seem too simple to warrant extended discussion. In fact, they are rather more complex. As a result, tables are frequently misconstructed and misinterpreted.

I have sought to present the logic of table construction and interpretation —beginning with univariate analysis, moving to subgroup description, and then on to the explanatory, bivariate analysis and multivariate analysis. The following chapters of this book will depend heavily on an understanding of contingency tables, so it is essential that the reader feel comfortable with them.

It is worth repeating at this point the essential steps involved in the construction and interpretation of explanatory tables.

1. Divide the sample into subgroups based on the values of the independent variable(s).

2. Describe each subgroup on the basis of values of the dependent variable.

3. Compare the independent variable subgroups in terms of a given value of the dependent variable.

Finally, the reader should commit to memory the following rule of thumb: Percentage down and read across, or percentage across and read down.

Additional Reading

Zeisel, Hans, *Say It With Figures* (New York: Harper & Row Publishers, 1957).

Chapter Fourteen

Index and Scale Construction

As noted in the preceding chapters, much if not most of social research is aimed at determining the associations between variables. Typically, we wish to state that X is related to (or causes) Y. We have also noted, however, that the measurement of variables is often a difficult undertaking. It is normally impossible to arrive at a wholly unambiguous and completely acceptable measure of any variable. Nevertheless, researchers do not give up the attempt to create ever better and more useful measures.

The present chapter is addressed to the problem of measurement. It discusses the construction of indexes and scales as measures of variables. These cumulative measures are very frequently used in social research for several reasons. First, despite the care taken in constructing questionnaires, the researcher is seldom able to arrive at a single question that adequately represents a complex variable. Any single item is likely to misrepresent some of the respondents in the study. In attempting to measure religiosity, frequency of church attendance is probably not sufficient in and of itself. Some respondents who attend church frequently might nevertheless be judged irreligious on other grounds. And some who never attend church might be judged religious. Indexes and scales combine several questionnaire items, and they can, thereby, avoid the biases inherent in single items.

Second, the researcher may wish to employ a rather refined ordinal measure of his variable: arranging respondents into several ordinal categories from—for example—very low to very high on the variable. A single item might not have sufficient answer categories to provide this range of variation, while an index or scale formed from several items would.

Finally, indexes and scales are *efficient* devices for data analysis. If a single questionnaire item gives us only a crude assessment of respondents on a given variable, considering several items may give us a more comprehensive and more accurate assessment. However, it is normally impractical to consider simultaneously all the particular responses that a given respondent provided. Indexes and scales (especially scales) are *data-reduction* devices; a respondent's several responses may be summarized in a single score, while sometimes very nearly maintaining the specific details of those responses.

14.1   Indexes Versus Scales

The terms "index" and "scale" are typically used impre-
cisely and interchangeably in social research literature. The technical definitions originally associated with these terms have subsequently lost their
meanings. Before considering the distinctions that this book will make between indexes and scales, let's first see what they have in common.

Both scales and indexes are typically *ordinal* measures of variables. Scales
and indexes are constructed in such a way as to rank-order survey respondents (or other units of analysis) in terms of specific variables such as religiosity, alienation, socioeconomic status, prejudice, intellectual sophistication,
and so forth. A respondent's *score* on a scale or index of religiosity, for
example, gives an indication of his relative religiosity vis-à-vis other respondents.

As the terms will be used in this book, both scales and indexes are
composite measures of variables: measurements based on responses to more
than one questionnaire item. Thus, a respondent's score on an index or scale
of religiosity would be determined by the specific responses he gave to several
questionnaire items, each of which provides some indication of his religiosity.

For the purposes of this book, we shall distinguish indexes and scales
through the manner in which scores are assigned to respondents. An index
is constructed through the simple cumulation of scores assigned to specific
responses to the individual items comprising the index. A scale is constructed
through the assignment of scores to *response patterns* among the several items
comprising the scale. A scale differs from an index by taking advantage of any
intensity structure that may exist among the individual items. A simple example should clarify this distinction.

Suppose we wish to measure respondents' support for the civil liberties
of Communists. We might ask in the questionnaire whether a Communist
should be allowed to pursue the following occupations: (1) lawyer, (2) doctor,
(3) minister, (4) engineer, (5) newspaper reporter. Some respondents will be
willing to allow Communists to pursue all of the occupations listed; some will
be unwilling to permit any. Others, however, will feel that some are permissi-
ble while others are not. Each respondent who gives a mixed set of responses
will presumably be indicating that he feels some of the occupations are more
important than others. The relative priorities of the different occupations will
vary from respondent to respondent, however; there is no absolute ranking
inherent in the occupations themselves.

Given the responses provided by a survey sample, the researcher might
construct an *index* of respondents' relative commitments to civil liberties for
Communists on the basis of the *number* of occupations respondents would
hold open to Communists. The respondent who would permit Communists
to hold all the occupations clearly supports a greater degree of civil liberties
than one who would close all the occupations to Communists. Moreover, the
researcher would assume that the respondent who would permit Communists

to hold three of the occupations is more supportive of Communists' civil liberties than the respondent who would hold open only one or two of the occupations, regardless of which one, two, or three occupations are involved. Such an index might provide a useful and accurate ordinal measure of civil libertarianism.

Suppose for a moment, however, that the occupations used in the above example had been: (1) ditch digger, (2) high school teacher, and (3) President of the United States. In this situation, there is every reason to believe that these three items have an *intensity structure*. The respondent who would permit a Communist to be President would surely permit him to be a high school teacher and a ditch digger. On the other hand if he would permit Communists to dig ditches, he might or might not permit them in the other two occupations. In all likelihood, knowing the *number* of occupations approved for Communists by a respondent would tell the researcher *which* occupations were approved. In such a situation, a composite measure comprised of the three items would constitute a *scale* as I have used that term.

It should be apparent that scales are generally superior to indexes, if for no other reason than that scale scores convey more information than do index scores. Still the reader should be wary of the common misuses of the term "scale"; clearly, calling a given measure a scale rather than an index does not make it better. Moreover, the reader should be cautioned against two other misconceptions regarding the nature of scaling. First, whether the combination of several questionnaire items results in a scale almost always depends on the *particular sample* of respondents being studied. Certain items may form a scale among one sample but not among another, and the reader should not assume that a given set of items *are* a scale because they formed a scale among a given sample. Second, the use of certain *scaling techniques* to be discussed does not assure the creation of a scale any more than the use of items that have previously formed scales can offer such assurance.

An examination of the substantive literature based on survey data will show that indexes are used much more frequently than scales. Ironically, however, the methodological literature contains little if any discussion of index construction, while discussions of scale construction abound. There appear to be two reasons for this disparity. First, indexes are more frequently used because scales are often difficult or impossible to construct from the data at hand. Second, methods of index construction are not discussed because they seem obvious and straightforward.

Index construction is not a simple undertaking. Furthermore, I feel that the general failure to develop index-construction techniques has resulted in the creation of many bad indexes in social research. With this in mind, I have devoted most of this chapter to the methods of index-construction. Once the logic of this activity is fully understood, the reader will be better equipped to attempt the construction of scales. Indeed, the carefully constructed index may turn out to be a scale anyway.

14.2   Index Construction

Item Selection

A composite index is created for the purpose of measuring some variable. The first criterion for selecting items to be included in the index is *face validity* (or logical validity). If the researcher wishes to measure political conservatism, for example, each of the items considered should appear on its face to indicate respondents' conservatism (or its opposite: liberalism). Political party affiliation would be one such item. If respondents were asked to approve or disapprove of the views of a well-known conservative public figure, the responses to that item might, logically, provide another indication of the respondents' conservatism. A researcher interested in constructing an index of religiosity might consider items reporting respondents' church attendance, acceptance of certain religious beliefs, frequency of prayer, and so forth. Each of these items would appear to offer some indication of respondents' religiosity.

Typically, the methodological literature on conceptualization and measurement stresses the need for *unidimensionality* in scale and index construction: a composite measure should represent only one dimension. Thus, items reflecting religiosity should not be included in a measure of political conservatism, even though the two variables are empirically related to one another. In this sense, an index or scale should be unidimensional.

At the same time, the researcher should be constantly aware of the subtle nuances that exist within the general dimension he is attempting to measure. Thus in the case of religiosity, the items mentioned above represent different *types* of religiosity. If the researcher wishes to measure ritual participation in religion, he should limit the items included in the measure to those specifically indicating this: church attendance, communion, confession, and the like. If, on the other hand, he wishes to measure religiosity in a more general way, he will want to include a balanced set of items, representing each of the different *types* of religiosity. Ultimately, the nature of the items included will determine how specifically or generally the variable is measured.

In selecting items for inclusion in an index, the researcher must also be concerned with the amount of *variance* provided by those items. If an item provides an indication of political conservatism, for example, the researcher should note how many conservatives are indicated by the item. In the extremes, if a given item indicates that no one is a conservative or that everyone is a conservative, the item will not be very useful in the creation of an index. If only 1 percent of a sample approve of a radical right political figure, this item is not likely to be of much use in the construction of an index.

With regard to variance, the researcher has two options. First, he may select several items that divide respondents about equally in terms of the variable. Thus he might select several items, each of which indicates about half conservatives and half liberals. While none of these items would justify the characterization of a respondent as "very conservative," a person who appeared conservative on all of them might be so characterized. The second option is the selection of items differing in variance. One item might indicate about half as conservative, while still another might indicate few of the respondents as conservative. (*Note:* This latter option is necessary for scaling, but it is also reasonable for the construction of an index as well.)

Bivariate Relationships among Items

The second step in index construction is the examination of the bivariate relationships among the items being considered for inclusion. If each of the items does indeed give an indication of the variable—as suggested on grounds of face validity—then the several items should be related to one another empirically. For example if several items all reflect a respondent's conservatism or liberalism, then those respondents who appear conservative in terms of one item should appear conservative in terms of others. Recognize, however, that such items will seldom if ever be perfectly related to one another; persons who appear conservative on one item will appear liberal on another. (This disparity creates the need for constructing composite measures in the first place.) Nevertheless, persons who appear conservative on item A should be more likely to appear conservative on item B than do persons who appear liberal on item A.

The researcher should examine all the possible bivariate relationships among the several items being considered for inclusion in the index to determine the relative strengths of relationships among the several pairs of items. Either percentage tables or correlation coefficients, or both, may be used for this purpose. The primary criterion for evaluating these several relationships is the strengths of the relationships. The use of this criterion, however, is rather subtle.

Clearly, the researcher should be wary of items that are not related to one another empirically. It is unlikely that they measure the same variable if they are unrelated. More to the point, perhaps, a given item that is unrelated to several of the other items probably should be dropped from consideration.

At the same time a *very* strong relationship between two items is another danger sign. At the extreme, if two items are perfectly related to one another, then only one is necessary for inclusion in the index, since it completely conveys the indications provided by the other. (This problem will become even clearer in the next section.)

To illustrate the steps in index construction, an example from the substantive literature of survey research may be useful.[1] A recent survey of medical school faculty members was concerned with the consequences of the

---

[1] The example, including tables presented, is taken from Earl R. Babbie, *Science and Morality in Medicine* (Berkeley: University of California Press, 1970).

"scientific perspective" on the quality of patient care provided by physicians. The primary intent was to determine whether more scientifically inclined doctors were more impersonal in their treatment of patients than were other doctors.

The survey questionnaire offered several possible indicators of respondents' scientific perspectives. Of those, three items appeared—in terms of face validity— to provide especially clear indications of whether or not the doctors were scientifically oriented. The three items were:

1. "As a medical school faculty member, in what capacity do you feel you can make your greatest teaching contribution: as a practicing physician or as a medical researcher?"

2. "As you continue to advance your own medical knowledge, would you say your ultimate medical interests lie primarily in the direction of total patient management of the understanding of basic mechanisms?"

3. "In the field of therapeutic research, are you generally more interested in articles reporting evaluations of the effectiveness of various treatments or articles exploring the basic rationale underlying the treatments?"

In each of the items above, the second answer would indicate a greater scientific orientation than the first answer. Taking the responses to a single item, we might conclude that those respondents who chose the second answer are more scientifically oriented than those who chose the first answer. This *comparative* conclusion is a reasonable one, but we should not be misled into thinking that respondents who chose the second answer to a given item are "scientists" in any absolute sense. They are simply *more scientific* than those who chose the first answer to the item. This important point will become clearer when we examine the distribution of responses produced by each of the items.

In terms of the first item—best teaching role—only about one-third of the respondents appear scientifically oriented. (Approximately one-third said they could make their greatest teaching contribution as medical researchers.) This does not mean that only one-third of the sample are "scientists," however, for the other two items would suggest quite different conclusions in this regard. In response to the second item—ultimate medical interests—approximately two-thirds chose the scientific answer, saying they were more interested in learning about basic mechanisms than learning about total patient management. In response to the third item—reading preferences—about eighty percent chose the scientific answer.

To repeat, these three questionnaire items cannot tell us how many "scientists" there are in the sample, for none of the items is related to a set of criteria for what constitutes being a scientist in any absolute sense. Using the items for this purpose would present us with the problem of three, quite different, estimates of how many scientists there were in the sample.

Rather, these three questionnaire items provide us with three independent indicators of respondents' relative inclinations toward science in medicine. Each item separates respondents into the *more* scientific and the *less* scientific. In view of the different distribution of responses produced by the three items, it is clear that each of the resulting groupings of more or less scientific respondents will have a somewhat different membership from the others. Respondents who seem scientific in terms of one item will not seem scientific in terms of another. Nevertheless, to the extent that each of the items measures the same general dimension, we should find some correspondence among the several groupings. Respondents who appear scientific in terms of one item should be more likely to appear scientific in their responses to another item than would those who appeared nonscientific in their responses to the first. We should find an association or correlation between the responses given to two items.

Table 14–1 provides an examination of the associations among the responses to the three items. Three bivariate (two-variable) tables are presented, showing the conjoint distribution of responses for each pair of items. While each single item produces a different grouping of "scientific" and "nonscientific" respondents, we see in Table 14–1 that the responses given to each of the items corresponds, to a degree, to the responses given to each of the other items.

An examination of the three bivariate relationships presented in Table 14–1 supports the belief that the three items all measure the same variable: scientific orientations. Let's begin by looking at the first bivariate relationship in the table. Faculty assessments of their best teaching roles and their expressions of their ultimate medical interests both give indications of scientific orientations. Those who answer "researcher" in the first instance would appear more scientifically inclined than those who answered "physician." Those who answered "basic mechanisms" would appear more scientifically inclined than those who answered "total patient management" in reply to the question concerning ultimate interests. If both these items do indeed measure the same thing, those appearing scientific on one ("researchers") should appear more scientific in answering the second ("basic mechanisms") than those who appeared nonscientific on the first ("physicians"). Looking at the data, we see that 87 percent of the "researchers" are scientific on the second item, as opposed to 51 percent of the "physicians." (*Note:* The fact that the "physicians" are about evenly split in their ultimate medical interests is irrelevant. It is only relevant that they are *less* scientific in their medical interests than are the "researchers.") The strength of this relationship may be summarized as a 36 percentage point difference.

The same general conclusion is to be reached in regard to the other bivariate relationships. The strength of the relationship between reading preferences and ultimate medical interests may be summarized as a 38 percentage point difference; the strength of the relationship between reading preferences and the two teaching roles may be summarized as a 21 percentage point difference.

Table 14-1.   Bivariate Relationships of Scientific Orientation Items

		Best Teaching Role	
		Physician	*Researcher*
Ultimate Medical Interest	Total patient management	49%	13%
	Basic mechanisms	51	87
		100%	100%

		Reading Preferences	
		Effectiveness	*Rationale*
Ultimate Medical Interest	Total patient management	68%	30%
	Basic mechanisms	32	70
		100%	100%

		Reading Preferences	
		Effectiveness	*Rationale*
Best Teaching Role	Physician	85%	64%
	Researcher	15	36
		100%	100%

Initially the three items were selected on the basis of face validity—each appeared to give some indication of faculty members' orientations to science. By examining the bivariate relationship between the pairs of items, we have found support for the initial belief that they all measure basically the same thing.

Multivariate Relationships among the Items

The discovery of the expected bivariate relationships between pairs of items further suggests their appropriateness for inclusion in a composite index. This is not a sufficient justification, however. The next step in index construction is the examination of the multivariate relationships among the items. The researcher must examine the simultaneous relationships among the several variables before combining them in a single index.

Recall that the primary purpose of index construction is the development of a method for classifying respondents in terms of some variable such as political conservatism, religiosity, scientific orientations, or whatever. An index of political conservatism should identify respondents who are very conservative, moderately conservative, not very conservative, and not at all conservative (or moderately liberal and very liberal, respectively, in place of the last two categories). The several gradations in terms of the variable are provided by the combination of responses given to the several items included in the index. Thus, the respondent who appeared conservative on all the items would be considered very conservative overall.

For an index to provide meaningful gradations in this sense, it is essential that each item add something to the evaluation of each respondent. Recall from the preceding section that it was suggested that two items perfectly related to one another would not be appropriate for inclusion in the same index. If one item were included, the other would add nothing to our evaluation of respondents. The examination of multivariate relationships among the items is another way of eliminating "deadwood." It also determines the overall power of the particular collection of items in measuring the variable under consideration.

The purposes of this multivariate examination will become clearer if we return to the earlier example of measuring scientific orientations among a sample of medical school faculty members. Table 14–2 presents the trivariate relationship among the three items.

Table 14-2.   Trivariate Relationship Among
Scientific Orientation Items

Percent Interested in Basic Mechanisms		Best Teaching Role	
		Physician	Researcher
Reading Preferences	Effectiveness	27% (66)	58% (12)
	Rationale	58% (219)	89% (130)

Table 14–2 has been presented somewhat differently from Table 14–1. In this instance, the sample respondents have been categorized in four groups according to: (1) their best teaching roles and (2) their reading preferences. The numbers in parentheses indicate the number of respondents in each

group. (Thus 66 faculty members said they could best teach as physicians and also said they preferred articles dealing with the effectiveness of treatments.) For each of the four groups, the percentage saying they are ultimately more interested in basic mechanisms has been presented. (Of the 66 faculty mentioned above, 27 percent are primarily interested in basic mechanisms.)

The arrangement of the four groups is based on a previously drawn conclusion regarding scientific orientations. Those in the upper left corner of the table are presumably the least scientifically oriented of the four groups: in terms of their best teaching roles and their reading preferences. Those in the lower right corner of the table are presumably the most scientifically oriented in terms of those items.

Recall that expressing a primary interest in "basic mechanisms" was also taken as an indication of scientific orientations. As we should expect, then, those in the lower right corner are the most likely to give this response (89 percent) and those in the upper left corner are the least likely (27 percent). The respondents who gave mixed responses in terms of teaching roles and reading preferences have an intermediate rank in their concern for basic mechanisms (58 percent in both cases).

This table tells us many things. First, we may note that the original relationships between pairs of items are not significantly affected by the presence of a third item. Recall, for example, that the relationship between teaching role and ultimate medical interest was summarized as a 36 percentage point difference. Looking at Table 14–2, we see that among only those respondents who are most interested in articles dealing with the effectiveness of treatments, the relationship between teaching role and ultimate medical interest is 31 percentage points (58 percent minus 27 percent: first row), and the same is true among those most interested in articles dealing with the rationale for treatments (89 percent minus 58 percent: second row). The original relationship between teaching role and ultimate medical interest is essentially the same as in Table 14–1, even among those respondents judged as scientific or nonscientific in terms of reading preferences.

The same conclusion may be drawn as we examine the columns in Table 14–2. Recall that the original relationship between reading preferences and ultimate medical interests was summarized as a 38 percentage point difference. Looking only at the "physicians" in Table 14-2, we see the relationship between the other two items is now 31 percentage points. The same relationship is found among the "researchers" in the second column.

The importance of these observations becomes clearer when we consider what might have happened. Table 14–3 presents hypothetical data to illustrate this.

The hypothetical data in Table 14–3 tell a much different story than did the actual data reported in Table 14–2. In this instance, it is evident that the original relationship between teaching role and ultimate medical interest persists, even when reading preferences are introduced into the picture. In

Table 14-3.   *Hypothetical Trivariate Relationship*
Among Scientific Orientation Items

Percent Interested in Basic Mechanisms		Best Teaching Role	
		Physician	Researcher
Reading Preferences	Effectiveness	51%	87%
	Rationale	51%	87%

each row of the table the "researchers" are more likely to express an interest in basic mechanisms than are the "physicians." Looking down the column, however, we note that there is no relationship between reading preferences and ultimate medical interests. If we know whether a respondent feels he can best teach as a physician or as a researcher, knowing his reading preference adds nothing to our evaluation of his scientific orientations. If something like Table 14–3 resulted from the actual data, we would conclude that reading preferences should not be included in the same index as teaching roles, since it will contribute nothing to the composite index.

In the present example, only three questionnaire items were involved. If more were being considered, then more complex multivariate tables would be in order. In this instance, we have limited our attention to the trivariate analysis of the three items. The purpose of this step in index construction, again, is to determine the simultaneous interaction of the items to determine whether they are all appropriate for inclusion in the same index.

Index Scoring

Having arrived at the best items for inclusion in the index, the next step involves the assignment of scores for specific responses, thereby creating a single composite index out of the several items. There are two basic decisions to be made in this regard.

First, the researcher must decide the desirable range of the index scores. Certainly one of the primary advantages of an index over a single item is the range of gradations it offers in the measurement of a variable. As noted earlier, political conservatism might be measured from "very conservative" to "not at all conservative" (or "very liberal"). How far to the extremes, then, should the index extend?

In this decision, the question of variance enters once more. Almost always, as the possible extremes of an index are extended, fewer cases are to be found at each end. The researcher who wishes to measure political conservatism to its greatest extreme may find he has almost no one in that category.

The first decision, then, concerns the conflicting desires for (1) the range of measurement in the index and (2) the adequate number of cases at each point in the index. The researcher will be forced to reach some kind of compromise between these conflicting desires.

The second decision concerns the actual assignment of scores for each specific response. Basically the researcher must decide whether to give each item an equal weight in the index or to give them different weights. As we shall see later, scale construction is quite different in this regard, but this is an open issue in index construction. While there are no firm rules to be followed in this regard, I would suggest—and practice tends to confirm this —that items should be weighted equally unless there are compelling reasons for differential weighting. That is, the burden of proof should be on differential weighting; equal weighting should be the norm.

Of course, this decision must be related to the earlier issue regarding the balance of items chosen. If the index is to represent the composite of slightly different aspects of a given variable, then the researcher should give each of those aspects the same weight. In some instances, however, he may feel that, say, two items reflect essentially the same aspect, while the third reflects a different aspect. If he wished to have both aspects equally represented by the index, he might decide to give the different item a weight equal to the combination of the two similar ones. In such a situation, he might wish to assign a maximum score of 2 to the different item and maximum scores of 1 to each of the similar ones.

While the rationale for scoring responses should take such concerns as these into account, the researcher typically will experiment with different scoring methods, examining the relative weights given to different aspects but at the same time worrying about the range and distribution of cases provided. Ultimately, the scoring method chosen will represent a compromise among these several demands. (*Note:* In this activity, as in most survey activities, the decision is open to revision on the basis of later examinations. Validation of the index, to be discussed shortly, may lead the researcher to recycle his efforts and to construct a completely different index.)

In the example taken from the medical school faculty survey, the decision was made to weight each of the items equally, since they had been chosen, in part, on the basis of their representing slightly different aspects of the overall variable—scientific orientations. On each of the items, the respondents were given a score of 1 for choosing the "scientific" response to the item and a score of 0 for choosing the "nonscientific" response. Each respondent, then, had a chance of receiving a score of 0, 1, 2, or 3, depending on the number of "scientific" responses he chose. This scoring method provided what was considered a useful range of variation—four index categories—and also provided sufficient cases in each category for analysis.

Handling Missing Data

In virtually every survey, some respondents fail to answer some questions (or choose a "don't know" response). While this presents a problem at all stages of analysis, it is especially troublesome in index construction. (Again, scaling is different in this regard.) If some respondents failed to provide answers to items being included in a composite index, the researcher faces a particular problem in assigning scores to those respondents in constructing the index. There are, however, several methods for dealing with this problem.

First, if there are relatively few respondents with missing data, the researcher may decide to exclude them from the construction and analysis of the index. The primary concern in this instance is whether the numbers available for analysis will still be sufficient and whether those excluded will result in a biased sample whenever the index is used in the analysis. The latter possibility can be examined through a comparison—on other relevant variables—of those who would be included in and those excluded from the index. (In the medical school faculty example discussed above, this was the decision made regarding missing data.)

Second, the researcher may have grounds for treating missing data the same as one of the available responses. For example, if the questionnaire asked respondents to indicate their participation in a number of activities by checking "yes" or "no" for each, many respondents may have checked some of the activities "yes" and left the remainder blank. In such a case the researcher might decide that a failure to answer meant "no" and score missing data in this case as though the respondents had checked the "no" space.

Third, a careful analysis of missing data may yield an interpretation of their meaning. In constructing a measure of political conservatism, for example, the researcher may discover that those respondents who failed to answer a given question were generally as conservative—in terms of other items—as those who gave the conservative answer. As another example, a recent survey measuring religious beliefs found that respondents who chose "don't know" for a given belief were almost identical to the "disbelievers" in their answers regarding other beliefs. (*Note:* The reader should not take these examples as empirical guides in his own studies, but only as suggestive of ways for analyzing his own data.) Whenever the analysis of missing data yields such interpretations, then, the researcher may decide to score such cases accordingly.

Fourth, the researcher may decide to assign an *intermediate* score for missing data. For example, if a given item is assigned scores of 0, 1, and 2 for its three possible responses, the researcher may assign the intermediate (1) to those respondents who gave no answer. (This is the same logic whereby the answer "undecided" is often scored as lying between "agree" and "disagree.")

Fifth, the researcher may assign index scores *proportionately* on the basis of the answers that a respondent *does* give. For example, let's assume that six items are being combined in an index, with scores of 0 or 1 being assigned to each item. The maximum score that a respondent may receive then is 6. If a given respondent answers only five of the items but receives a score of 5 on those items, he might be given a proportionate score of $5/5 \times 6 = 6$ on the index. The respondent who received a score of 2 on the four items answered might be given a final score of $2/4 \times 6 = 3$. Where these computations result in fractional results, some method for rounding off should be employed to simplify the final index scores.

Finally, the researcher may be unwilling to utilize any of these methods for handling missing data, but he may require that all respondents in the sample be scored for purposes of later analysis. In such a situation, he may decide to assign scores for missing data on a random basis. For an item assigned the possible scores of 0, 1, and 2, the first respondent failing to answer that item might receive a score of 1, the second a score of 0, the third a score of 2, and so forth. This method is the most conservative from a research analysis standpoint, as the researcher is "stacking the deck" against himself. If the resultant index proves a powerful tool in his analysis, he might conclude that it would have been even more powerful if all respondents had answered all questions. (Of course, if his purpose is to show the index is *unrelated* to other variables, he has stacked the deck in his favor.)

The choice of a particular method to be used depends so much on the research situation as to preclude the suggestion of a single best method or to rank-order the several described. In general, I would suggest an examination of the respondents failing to answer both in terms of possible bias in excluding them and with regard to their answers to other items in the index. Understanding one's data is the final goal of analysis anyway.

Index Validation

Up to this point, we have discussed all the steps involved in the selection and scoring of items that result in a composite index purported to measure some variable. If each of the above discussed steps is carried out carefully, the likelihood of the index actually measuring the variable is enhanced. The success of this activity is not proved, however, *Validation* of the index helps to accomplish this. The basic logic of validation is the following. We assume that the composite index measures a variable; that is, the successive scores on the index group respondents in a rank order in terms of that variable. An index of political conservatism rank-orders groups in terms of their relative conservatism. If the index does this successfully, then persons scored as relatively conservative in terms of the index should appear relatively conservative in terms of all questionnaire items (or other indications) that should also reflect political orientations. There are several methods for validating a composite index.

Item Analysis.   The first step in index validation is an internal validation called *item analysis.* The researcher should examine the extent to which the composite index is related to (or predicts responses to) the questionnaire items included in the index itself. If the index has been carefully constructed through the examination of bivariate and multivariate relationships among several items, this step should confirm the validity of that index. In a complex index containing many items, this step provides a more parsimonious test of the independent contribution of each item to the index. If a given item is found to be poorly related to the index, it may be assumed that other items in the index are washing out the contribution of that item. The item in question, then, contributes nothing to the index's power, and it should be excluded.

While item analysis is an important first test of the index's validity, it is scarcely a sufficient test. If the index adequately measures a given variable, it should successfully predict other indications of that variable. To test this we must turn to items not included in the index.

External Validation. Persons scored as politically conservative on the index should appear conservative in their responses to other items in the questionnaire. It must be realized, of course, that we are talking about *relative* conservatism, as we are unable to make a final absolute definition of what constitutes "conservatism" in any ultimate sense. However, those respondents scored as the most conservative in terms of the index should be the most conservative in answering other questions. Those scored as the least conservative on the index should be the least conservative on other items. Indeed, the ranking of groups of respondents on the index should predict the ranking of those groups in answering other questions dealing with political orientations.

Returning to our example of the scientific orientation index, there were several questions in the questionnaire which offered the possibility of further validation. Table 14–4 presents some of those items.

Table 14-4. *Validation of Scientific Orientations Index*

	Index of Scientific Orientations			
	Low			High
	0	1	2	3
Percent interested in attending scientific lectures at the medical school	34	42	46	65
Percent who say faculty members should have experience as medical researchers	43	60	65	89
Percent who would prefer faculty duties involving research activities only	0	8	32	66
Percent who engaged in research during preceding academic year	61	76	94	99

These items provide several lessons regarding index validation. First, we note that the index strongly predicts the responses to the validating items in the sense that the rank order of scientific responses among the four groups is the same as the rank order provided by the index itself. At the same time, each of the items gives a different *description* of scientific orientations overall. For example, the last validating item indicates that the great majority of *all* faculty were engaged in research during the preceding year. If this were the only indicator of scientific orientation, we would conclude that nearly all faculty were scientific. Nevertheless, those scored as more scientific in terms of the index are more likely to have engaged in research than those who were scored as relatively less scientific. The third validating item provides a different *descriptive* picture: Only a minority of the faculty overall say they would prefer duties limited exclusively to research. Nevertheless, the percentages giving this answer correspond to the scores assigned on the index.

Bad Index versus Bad Validators.   A dilemma that must be faced by nearly every index constructor is the apparent failure of external items to validate the index. If the internal item analysis shows inconsistent relationships between the items included in the index and the index itself, something is wrong with the index. But if the index fails to predict strongly the external validation items, the conclusion to be drawn is more ambiguous. The researcher must choose between two possibilities: (1) the index does not adequately measure the variable in question, or (2) the validation items do not adequately measure the variable and thereby do not provide a sufficient test of the index.

The researcher who has worked long and conscientiously on the construction of the index will find the second conclusion very compelling. Typically, he will feel he has included the best indicators of the variable in the index; the validating items are, therefore, second-rate indicators. Nevertheless, he should recognize that the index is purportedly a very powerful measure of the variable; thus, it should be somewhat related to any item that taps the variable even poorly.

When external validation fails, the researcher should reexamine the index before deciding that the validating items are insufficient. One method of doing this involves the examination of the relationships between the validating items and the individual items included in the index. If he discovers that some of the index items relate to the validators while others do not, this will improve his understanding of the index as it was initially constituted.

There is no cookbook solution to this dilemma; it is an agony the serious researcher must learn to survive. Ultimately, the wisdom of his decision regarding the index will be determined by its utility in his later analyses involving that index. Perhaps he will initially decide that the index is a good one and that the validators are defective and later find that the variable in question (as measured by the index) is not related to other variables in the ways expected. At that point, he may return again to the composition of the index.

Considerable attention has been given in this text to the construction of simple indexes for two reasons. First, a review of the empirical research literature points to the popularity of such measures among survey researchers. Second, there has been little if any discussion of the techniques for index construction in the literature or in methodology textbooks. Probably "simple" index construction has been viewed as too simple to warrant such discussions, and the techniques have remained part of the oral tradition of survey research.

Likert "Scaling"

Earlier in this chapter, I defined a scale as a composite measure constructed on the basis of an *intensity structure* among items comprising the measure. In scale construction, response patterns across several items are scored, whereas in index construction, individual responses are scored and those independent scores are summed. By this definition, the measurement method developed by Rensis Likert, called Likert scaling, represents a more systematic and refined means for constructing indexes. I shall discuss this method here, therefore, rather than in the sections on scaling to follow.

The term "Likert scale" is associated with a question format that is very frequently used in contemporary survey questionnaires. Basically, the respondent is presented with a *statement* in the questionnaire and is asked to indicate whether he "strongly agrees," "agrees," "disagrees," "strongly disagrees," or is "undecided." Modifications of the wording of the response categories (for example, "approve") may be used, of course.

The particular value of this format is the unambiguous *ordinality* of response categories. If respondents were permitted to volunteer or select such answers as "sort of agree," "pretty much agree," "really agree," and so forth, it would be impossible to judge the relative strength of agreement intended by the various respondents. The Likert format easily resolves this dilemma.

The Likert format also lends itself to a rather straightforward method of index construction. Whereas identical response categories will have been used for several items intended to measure a given variable, each such item might be scored in a uniform manner. With five response categories, scores of 0 to 4 or 1 to 5 might be assigned, taking the "direction" of the items into account (for example, assign a score of 5 to "strongly agree" for positive items and to "strongly disagree" for negative items). Each respondent would then be assigned an overall score representing the summation of the scores he received for his several responses to the individual items.

The Likert method is based on the assumption that the overall score based on responses to the many items seeming to reflect the variable under consideration provides a reasonably good measure of the variable. These overall scores are not the final product of index construction; rather, they are used for purposes of an *item analysis* resulting in the selection of the *best* items. Essentially, each of the individual items is correlated with the large, composite measure. Items that correlate highest with the composite measure are assumed to provide the best indicators of the variable, and only those items would be included in the index ultimately used for analyses of the variable.

It should be noted that the uniform scoring of Likert-item response categories assumes that each item has about the *same intensity* as the rest. This is the key respect in which the Likert method differs from scaling as the term is used in this book.

The reader should also realize that Likert-type items can be used in a variety of ways; the researcher is by no means bound to the method described above. Such items can be combined with other types of items in the construction of simple indexes; and, similarly, they can be used in the construction of scales. However, if all the items being considered for inclusion in a composite measure are in the Likert format, then the method described above should be considered.

Now we shall turn our attention from indexing methods to a selection of scaling techniques. While many methods are available to the survey researcher, we shall consider only Bogardus, Thurstone, and Guttman scales.

14.3   Scale Construction

Good indexes provide an ordinal ranking of respondents on a given variable. All indexes are based on the assumption that this is the case: a person with two indications of being scientifically inclined should be more scientific than the person with only one such indication. What an index may fail to take into account, however, is that not all indications of a variable are equally important. (Of course, the researcher may attempt to resolve this by weighting indicators differently.)

Scales offer more assurance of ordinality by tapping *structures* among the indicators. The several items going into a composite measure may have different *intensities* in terms of the variable. The three scaling procedures described below will illustrate the variety of techniques available.

Bogardus Social Distance Scale

A good example of a scale is the *Bogardus Social Distance Scale.* Let us suppose that the researcher is interested in the extent to which respondents are willing to associate with blacks. All respondents in the study might be asked the following questions:

1. *Are you willing to permit blacks to live in your country?*

2. *Are you willing to permit blacks to live in your community?*

3. *Are you willing to permit blacks to live in your neighborhood?*

4. *Would you be willing to let a black live next door to you?*

5. *Would you let your child marry a black?*

Note that the several questions increase in the closeness of contact which the respondent may or may not want with black Americans. Beginning with the original concern to measure willingness to associate with blacks, we have developed several questions indicating differing degrees of intensity on this variable.

The clear differences of intensity suggest a structure among the items. Presumably if a respondent is willing to accept a given kind of association, he would be willing to accept all those preceding it in the list—those with lesser intensities. For example, the respondent who is willing to permit blacks to live in his neighborhood will surely accept them in his community and his nation, but he may or may not be willing to accept them as his next-door neighbors or as relatives. This, then, is the logical structure of intensity inherent among the items.

Empirically, one would expect to find the largest number of respondents accepting co-citizenship and the fewest accepting intermarriage. In this sense, we speak of "easy items" (co-citizenship) and "hard items" (intermarriage). More respondents agree to the easy items than to the hard ones. With some inevitable exceptions, logic demands that once a respondent has refused a relationship presented in the scale, he will also refuse all those harder ones which follow it.

The Bogardus Social Distance Scale illustrates the important economy of scaling as a data-reduction device. By knowing *how many* relationships with blacks a given respondent will accept, we know *which* relationships were accepted. Thus, a single number can accurately summarize five or six survey responses without a loss of information.

Thurstone Scales

Often the inherent structure of the Bogardus Social Distance Scale is not appropriate to the variable being measured. Indeed, such a logical structure among several indicators is seldom apparent. *Thurstone scaling* is an attempt to develop a format for generating groups of indicators of a variable that have at least an *empirical* structure among them. One of the basic formats is that of "equal-appearing intervals."

A group of "judges" is given perhaps a hundred items felt to be indicators of a given variable. Each judge is then asked to estimate how strong an indicator of the variable that item is—by assigning scores of perhaps 1 to 13. If the variable were prejudice, for example, the judges would be asked to assign the score of 1 to the very weakest indicators of prejudice, the score of 13 to the strongest indicators, and intermediate scores to those felt to be somewhere in between.

Once the judges had all completed this task, the researcher examines the scores assigned to each item by all the judges to determine which items produced the greatest agreement among the judges. Those items on which the judges disagreed broadly would be rejected as ambiguous. Among those items producing general agreement in scoring, one or more would be selected to represent each scale score from 1 to 13.

The items selected in this manner would then be included in a survey questionnaire. Respondents who appeared prejudiced on those items representing a strength of 5 would then be expected to appear prejudiced on those having lesser strengths and, if some of those respondents did not appear prejudiced on the item(s) with a strength of 6, it would be expected that they would also not appear prejudiced on those with greater strengths.

If the Thurstone Scale items were adequately developed and scored, the economy and effectiveness of data reduction inherent in the Bogardus Social Distance Scale would appear. A single score might be assigned to each respondent (the strength of the hardest item accepted), and that score would adequately represent the responses to several questionnaire items. And as the case with the Bogardus scale, a respondent scored 6 might be regarded as more prejudiced than one scored 5 or less.

Thurstone scaling is seldom if ever used in survey research today, primarily because of the tremendous expenditure of energies required for the "judging" of items. Several (perhaps 10 or 15) judges would have to spend a considerable amount of time for each of them to score the many initial items. Since the quality of their judgments would depend on their experience with and knowledge of the variable under consideration, the task might require professional researchers. Moreover, the meanings conveyed by the several items indicating a given variable tend to change over time. Thus an item having a given weight at one time might have quite a different weight later on. For a Thurstone scale to be effective, it would have to be periodically updated.

Guttman Scaling

A very popular scaling technique used by survey researchers today is the one developed by Louis Guttman. Like both Bogardus and Thurstone scaling, Guttman scaling is based on the fact that some items under consideration may prove to be "harder" indicators of the variable than others. Respondents who accept a given "hard" item also accept the easier ones. If such a structure appears in the data under examination, we may say that the items form a Guttman scale. One example should suffice to illustrate this.

In the earlier example of measuring scientific orientations among medical school faculty members, we recall that a simple index was constructed. As we shall see shortly, however, the three items included in the index essentially form a Guttman scale. This possibility first appears when we look for relatively "hard" and "easy" indicators of scientific orientations.

The item asking respondents whether they could best serve as practicing physicians or as medical researchers is the hardest of the three: Only about one-third would be judged scientific if this were the single indicator of the variable. If the item concerning ultimate medical interests (total patient management versus basic mechanisms) were used as the only indicator, almost two-thirds would be judged scientific. Reading preferences (effectiveness of treatments versus the underlying rationales) is the easiest of the three items: About 80 percent of the respondents would be judged as scientific in terms of this item.

To determine whether a scalar exists among the responses to all three items, we must examine the several possible response patterns given to all three items simultaneously. In Table 14–5, all the possible patterns have been presented in a schematic form. For each of the three items, pluses and minuses have been used to indicate the scientific and nonscientific responses respectively. (A plus indicates a scientific response, while a minus indicates a nonscientific response.)

Table 14-5. Scaling Scientific Orientations

	Reading Preference	Ultimate Interests	Teaching Role	Number of Cases
	+	+	+	116
Scale Types:	+	+	−	127
Total = 383	+	−	−	92
	−	−	−	48
	−	+	−	18
Mixed Types:	+	−	+	14
Total = 44	−	−	+	5
	−	+	+	7

The first four response patterns in the table comprise what we would call the *scale types:* those patterns that form a scalar structure. Following those respondents who selected all three scientific responses (line 1), we see (line 2) that those with only two scientific responses have chosen the two easier ones; those with only one such response (line 3) chose the easiest of the three. And finally, there are those respondents who selected none of the scientific responses (line 4).

The second part of the table presents those response patterns that violate the scalar structure of the items. The most radical departures from the scalar structure are the last two response patterns: those who accepted only the hardest item, and those who rejected only the easiest one.

The final column in the table indicates the number of survey respondents who gave each of the response patterns. It is immediately apparent that the great majority (90 percent) of the respondents fit into one of the scale types. The presence of mixed types, however, indicates that the items do not form a perfect Guttman scale.

We should recall at this point that one of the chief functions of scaling is efficient data reduction. Scales provide a technique for presenting data in a summary form while maintaining as much of the original information as possible.

When the scientific orientation items were formed into an index in our earlier discussion, respondents were given one point on the index for each scientific response they gave. If these same three items were scored as a Guttman scale, some respondents would receive different scores than were received on the index. Respondents would be assigned those scale scores that would permit the most accurate reproduction of their original responses to all three items.

Respondents fitting into the scale types would receive the same scores as were assigned in the index construction. Persons selecting all three scientific responses would still be scored 3. Note that if we were told a given respondent in this group received a score of 3, we could accurately predict that he selected all three scientific responses. For persons in the second row of the table, the assignment of the scale score of 2 would lead us to accurately predict scientific responses to the two easier items and a nonscientific response to the hardest. In each of the four scale types we could accurately predict all the actual responses given by all the respondents.

The mixed types in the table present a problem, however. The first mixed type (– + –) was scored 1 on the index to indicate only one scientific response. If 1 were assigned as a scale score, however, we would predict that all respondents in this group had chosen only the easiest item (+ – –), thereby making two errors for each such respondent. Scale scores are assigned, therefore, with the aim of minimizing the errors that would be made in reconstructing the original responses given. Table 14–6 illustrates the index and scale scores that would be assigned to each of the response patterns in our example.

As mentioned above, the original index scoring for the four scale types would be maintained in the construction of a Guttman scale, and no errors would be made in reproducing the responses given to all three items. The mixed types would be scored differently, however, in an attempt to reduce

Table 14-6.   Index and Scale Scores

	Response Patterns			Number of Cards	Index Scores	Scale Scores*	Total Scale Errors
Scale Types:	+	+	+	116	3	3	0
	+	+	−	127	2	2	0
	+	−	−	92	1	1	0
	−	−	−	48	0	0	0
Mixed Types:	−	+	−	18	1	2	18
	+	−	+	14	2	3	14
	−	−	+	5	1	0	5
	−	+	+	7	2	3	7

*Note: This table presents one common method for scoring "mixed types," but the reader should be advised that other methods are also used.

errors. Note, however, that one error is made for each of the respondents in the mixed types. In the first mixed type we would erroneously predict a scientific response to the easiest item for each of the 18 respondents in this group, making a total of 18 errors.

The extent to which a set of empirical responses form a Guttman scale is determined in terms of the accuracy with which the original responses can be reconstructed from the scale scores. For each of the 427 respondents in this example, we will predict three questionnaire responses, for a total of 1,281 predictions. Table 14–6 indicates that we will make 44 errors using the scale scores assigned. The percentage of *correct* predictions is called the *coefficient of reproducibility:* the percentage of "reproducible" responses. In the present example, the coefficient of reproducibility is 1,237/1,281 or 96.6 percent.

Except for the case of perfect (100 percent) reproducibility, there is no way of saying that a set of items does or does not form a Guttman scale in any absolute sense. Virtually all sets of such items *approximate* a scale. As a rule of thumb, however, coefficients of 90 percent or 95 percent are the commonly used standards in this regard. If the observed reproducibility exceeds the level set by the researcher, he will probably decide to score and use the items as a scale.[2]

One concluding remark should be made with regard to Guttman scaling: It is based on the structure observed among the *actual data under examination.* This is an important point that is often misunderstood by researchers. It does not make sense to say that a set of questionnaire items (perhaps developed and used by a previous researcher) constitute a Guttman scale. Rather, we can say only that they form a scale within a given body of data being analyzed.

[2]The decision as to criteria in this regard is, of course, arbitrary. Moreover, a high degree of reproducibility does not insure that the scale constructed in fact measures the concept under consideration, although it increases confidence that all the component items measure the same thing. Finally, the reader should be advised that a high coefficient of reproducibility is more likely when few items are involved.

Scalability, then, is a sample-dependent, empirical question. While a set of items may form a Guttman scale among one sample of respondents, there is no guarantee that they will form such a scale among another sample. In this sense, then, a set of questionnaire items in and of themselves never form a scale, but a set of empirical observations may.

14.4   Typologies

We shall conclude this chapter with a short discussion of typology construction and analysis. Recall that indexes and scales are constructed to provide ordinal measures of given variables. We attempt to assign index or scale scores to respondents in such a way as to indicate a rising degree of prejudice, religiosity, conservatism, and so forth. In these regards, we are dealing with single dimensions.

Often, however, the researcher wishes to summarize the intersection of two or more dimensions. He may, for example, wish to examine political orientations separately in terms of domestic issues and foreign policy. The four-fold presentation in Table 14–7 describes such a typology.

Table 14-7.   A Political Typology

Domestic Policy	Foreign Policy Attitudes	
Attitudes	Conservative	Liberal
Conservative	A	B
Liberal	C	D

Persons in cell A of the table are conservative on both foreign policy and domestic policy; those in cell D are liberal on both. Respondents in cells B and C are conservative on one and liberal on the other. It should be noted that for purposes of analysis, each of the cell types might be represented by an IBM card punch (A = 1, B = 2, C = 3, D = 4) and could be easily manipulated in examining the typology's relationship to other variables.

Frequently, the researcher arrives at a typology in the course of his attempt to construct an index or scale. The items that he felt represented a single variable appear to represent two. In the present example, the researcher may have been attempting to construct a single index of political attitudes but discovered—empirically—that foreign and domestic politics had to be kept separate.

In any event, the researcher should be warned against a difficulty inherent in typological analysis. Whenever the typology is used as the *independent variable*, there will probably be no problem. In the example above, the researcher might compute and present the percentages of persons in each cell who say they normally vote for the Democratic Party. He could then easily examine the effects of both foreign and domestic policy attitudes on voting behavior.

It is extremely difficult to analyze a typology as a *dependent variable,* however. If the researcher wants to discover why respondents fall into the different cells of the typology, he is in trouble. This becomes apparent when we consider the ways in which he might construct and read his tables. Assume, for example, that he wants to examine the effects of sex on political attitudes. With a single dimension he could easily determine the percentages of men and of women who have been scored conservative and liberal on his index or scale. With a typology, however, he would have to present the distribution of the men in his sample among types A, B, C, and D. Then he would repeat the procedure for the women in the sample and compare the two distributions. Let us suppose that 80 percent of the women are scored as type A (conservative on both dimensions) as compared with 30 percent of the men. Moreover, suppose that only 5 percent of the women are scored as type B (conservative only on domestic issues) compared with 40 percent of the men. It would be incorrect to conclude from an examination of type B that men are more conservative on domestic issues than women, since 85 percent of the women, compared with 70 percent of the men, have this characteristic. The relative sparsity of women in type B is due to their concentration in type A. It should be apparent that an interpretation of such data would be very difficult in anything other than description.

Ultimately, the researcher will probably examine the two political dimensions separately. This is even more likely if the dependent variable has more categories of responses than was the case in the example of sex.

The reader should not take the preceding comments to indicate that typologies should always be avoided in survey analysis. Often they provide the most appropriate device for understanding the data. The reader should be warned, however, against the special difficulties involved in using typologies as dependent variables.

Summary

This chapter has been addressed to the logic and construction of indexes and scales. These techniques are very frequently used in survey analysis and are extremely valuable. Good composite measures such as indexes and scales have the following advantages:

1. Where single indicators (for example, responses to a questionnaire item) may produce a biased measurement of the variable under examination, a composite measure constructed from several different indicators may solve this problem.

2. Composite measures can provide a broader range of variation on the variable. Where a single dichotomous item would provide only two levels of intensity (for example, high and low), the combination of five such items could result in the creation of an index or scale ranging from a low of 0 to a high of 5. If the composite measure is properly constructed, it will provide for greater explanatory power in the analysis.

3. Scales can provide an efficient technique for data reduction. An extensive set of questionnaire responses may be summarized in the form of a single scale score without losing much of the original information.

Additional Readings

Lazarsfeld, Paul F., and Morris Rosenberg (eds.), *The Language of Social Research* (New York: The Free Press, 1955), sec. I.

Oppenheim, A. N., *Questionnaire Design and Attitude Measurement* (New York: Basic Books, Inc., Publisher, 1966).

Selltiz, Claire, *et al., Research Methods in Social Relations* (New York: Holt, Rinehart & Winston, Inc., 1959), chap. 10.

Chapter Fifteen

The Elaboration Model

This chapter is devoted to a perspective on survey analysis that is referred to variously as "the elaboration model," "the interpretation method," "the Columbia school," or "the Lazarsfeld method." This varied nomenclature derives from the fact that the method we shall be discussing aims at the *elaboration* on an empirical relationship among variables in order to *interpret* that relationship in the manner developed by Paul Lazarsfeld at Columbia University.

The elaboration model is used to understand the relationship between two variables through the simultaneous introduction of additional variables. It was developed primarily through the medium of contingency tables, but later chapters of this book will show how it may be used with other statistical techniques.

It is my firm belief that the elaboration model offers the researcher the clearest picture of the logic of survey analysis that is available. Especially through the use of contingency tables, this method portrays the logical processes of scientific analysis. Moreover, if the reader is able to fully comprehend the use of the elaboration model using contingency tables, he should be in a far better position to use and understand more sophisticated statistical techniques.

15.1 History of the Elaboration Model

The historical origins of the elaboration model are especially instructive for a realistic appreciation of scientific research in practice. During World War II, Samuel Stouffer organized and headed a special social research branch within the United States Army. Throughout the war, this group conducted a large number and variety of surveys among American servicemen. Although the objectives of these studies varied somewhat, they generally focused on the factors affecting soldiers' combat effectiveness.

Several of the studies examined the issue of morale in the military. Since morale was believed to affect combat effectiveness, the improvement of morale would increase the effectiveness of the war effort. Stouffer and his research staff, then, sought to uncover some of the variables that affected morale. In part, the group sought to confirm, empirically, some commonly accepted propositions. Among them were the following:

1. Promotions surely affected soldiers' morale, and it was expected that those soldiers serving in units with low promotion rates would have relatively low morale.

2. Given racial segregation and discrimination in the South, it was expected that Negro soldiers being trained in Northern training camps would have higher morale than those being trained in the South.

3. Those soldiers with more education would be more likely to resent being drafted into the army as enlisted men than would those soldiers with less education.

Each of these propositions made sense logically, and common wisdom held each to be empirically true. Stouffer decided to test each empirically. To his surprise, none of the propositions was confirmed.

First, soldiers serving in the Military Police—where promotions were the slowest in the Army—had fewer complaints about the promotion system than did those serving in the Army Air Corps—where promotions were the fastest in the Army. This finding was derived from responses to a question asking whether the soldier believed the promotion system to be generally fair.

Second, Negro soldiers serving in Northern training camps and those serving in Southern training camps seemed to differ little if at all in their general morale.

Third, the less educated soldiers were more likely to resent being drafted into the Army than were those with greater amounts of education.

Faced with data such as these, many researchers would have no doubt tried to hide the findings, as a poor reflection on their scientific abilities. Others would have run tests of statistical significance and then tried to publish the results. Stouffer, instead, asked *Why?*

Stouffer found the answer to this question within the concepts of "reference group" and "relative deprivation." In the simplest overview, Stouffer suggested that soldiers did not evaluate their positions in life in accord with absolute, objective standards, but on the basis of their relative position vis-à-vis others around them. The people they compared themselves with were their "reference group," and they felt "relative deprivation" if they did not compare favorably in that regard.

Within the concepts of "reference group" and "relative deprivation," Stouffer found an answer to each of the anomalies in his empirical data. Regarding promotion, he suggested that soldiers judged the fairness of the promotion system on the basis of their own experiences relative to others around them. In the Military Police, where promotions were few and slow, few soldiers knew of a less-qualified buddy who had been promoted faster than they had. In the Army Air Corps, however, the rapid promotion rate meant that many soldiers knew of less-qualified buddies who had been promoted faster than seemed appropriate. Thus, ironically, the MP's said the promotion system was generally fair while the Air Corpsmen said it was not.

A similar explanation seemed appropriate in the case of the Negro soldiers. Rather than simply comparing conditions in the North with those in the South, they compared their own status—as Negro soldiers—with the status of the Negro civilians around them. In the South, where discrimination was at its worst, they found being a soldier somewhat insulated them from adverse cultural norms in the surrounding community. Whereas Southern Negro civilians were grossly discriminated against and denied self-esteem, good jobs, and so forth, Negro soldiers had a slightly better status. In the North, however, many of the Negro civilians they encountered were holding down well-paying defense jobs. And with discrimination less severe, being a soldier did not help one's status in the community.

Finally, "reference group" and "relative deprivation" seemed to explain the anomaly of highly educated draftees accepting their induction more willingly than was true of those with less education. Stouffer reasoned as follows:[1]

1. A person's friends will, on the whole, have about the same educational status as the person himself.

2. People with less education will be more likely to engage in semiskilled, production-line occupations and farming than will be the case for those with much education.

3. During wartime, many production-line industries and farming were declared vital to the national interest; production-line workers in those industries and farmers would be exempted from the draft.

4. A person with little education was more likely to have friends who were in draft-exempt occupations than would be the case for the person with more education.

5. The draftee of little education would be more likely to feel discriminated against than would the draftee with more education, by virtue of each comparing himself with his friends.

---

[1]Samuel A. Stouffer *et al.*, *The American Soldier* (Princeton, N.J.: Princeton University Press, 1949), vol. I, pp. 122 ff., esp. p. 127.

These were the explanations that Stouffer suggested to unlock the mystery of the three anomalous findings. Because they were not part of a preplanned study design, he lacked empirical data for testing them, however. Nevertheless, Stouffer's logical exposition provided the basis for the later development of the elaboration model: understanding the relationship between two variables through the controlled introduction of other variables.

The formal development of the elaboration model was the work of Paul Lazarsfeld and his associates at Columbia University. In a methodological review of Stouffer's Army studies, Lazarsfeld and Patricia Kendall presented hypothetical tables that would have proved Stouffer's contention regarding education and acceptance of induction had the empirical data been available.[2]

Kendall and Lazarsfeld began with Stouffer's data showing the negative association between education and acceptance of induction (see Table 15-1).

Table 15-1.   Summary of Stouffer's Data on
Education and Acceptance of Induction

	Hi Ed	Low Ed
Should *not* have been deferred	88%	70%
Should have been deferred	12	30
	100%	100%
	(1731)	(1876)

Tables 15-1, 15-2, 15-3, 15-4 are modified with permission of the Macmillan Company from *Continuities in Social Research: Studies in the Scope and Method of "The American Soldier"* by Robert K. Merton and Paul F. Lazarsfeld. Copyright 1950 by The Free Press, a Corporation.

Following Stouffer's explanation, Kendall and Lazarsfeld created a hypothetical table, compatible with the empirical data, to show that education was related to whether one had friends who were deferred. In Table 15-2, we note that 19 percent of those with high education reported having friends who were deferred, as compared with 79 percent among those with less education.

Stouffer's explanation next assumed that soldiers with friends who had been deferred would be more likely to resent their own induction than would those who had no deferred friends. Table 15-3 presents the hypothetical data from Kendall and Lazarsfeld that would have supported that assumption.

The hypothetical data presented in Tables 15-2 and 15-3 confirm the linkages that Stouffer had specified in his explanation. First, soldiers with low education were more likely to have friends who were deferred than was true

[2]Patricia L. Kendall and Paul F. Lazarsfeld, "Problems of Survey Analysis," in Robert K. Merton and Paul F. Lazarsfeld (eds.), *Continuities in Social Research: Studies in the Scope and Method of "The American Soldier"* (New York: The Free Press, 1950), pp. 133–196.

Table 15-2. *Hypothetical Relationship between Education and Deferment of Friends*

		Hi Ed	Low Ed
Friends deferred?	Yes	19%	79%
	No	81	21
		100%	100%
		(1731)	(1876)

Table 15-3. *Hypothetical Relationship between Deferment of Friends and Acceptance of One's Own Induction*

	Friends Deferred?	
	Yes	No
Should not have been deferred	63%	94%
Should have been deferred	37	6
	100%	100%
	(1819)	(1818)

of those with less education. And, second, having friends who were deferred made a soldier more likely to think he should have been deferred. Stouffer had suggested that these two relationships would clarify the original relationship between education and acceptance of induction. Kendall and Lazarsfeld created the hypothetical table that would confirm that ultimate explanation (see Table 15-4).

Table 15-4. *Hypothetical Data Relating Education to Acceptance of Induction through the Factor of Having Friends Who Were Deferred*

	Friends Deferred		No Friends Deferred	
	Hi Ed	Lo Ed	Hi Ed	Lo Ed
Should not have been deferred	63%	63%	94%	95%
Should have been deferred	37	37	6	5
	100%	100%	100%	100%
	(335)	(1484)	(1426)	(392)

Recall that the original finding was that draftees with high education were more likely to accept their induction into the Army as fair than was true of those with less education. In Table 15-4, however, we note that level of education has no effect on the acceptance of induction among those who report having friends deferred: 63 percent say they should not have been deferred among *both* educational groups. Similarly, educational level has no significant effect on acceptance of induction among those who reported having no friends deferred: 94 and 95 percent say they should not have been deferred.

On the other hand, among those with high education the acceptance of induction is strongly related to whether or not one's friends were deferred: 63 percent versus 94 percent. And the same is true among those with less education. The hypothetical data in Table 15-4, then, support Stouffer's contention that education affected acceptance of induction only through the medium of having friends deferred. Highly educated draftees were less likely to have friends deferred and, by virtue of that fact, were more likely to accept their own induction as fair. Those with less education were more likely to have friends deferred and, by virtue of that fact, were less likely to accept their own induction.

It is important to recognize that neither Stouffer's explanation nor the hypothetical data denied the reality of the original relationship. As educational level increased, acceptance of one's own induction also increased. The nature of this empirical relationship, however, was interpreted through the introduction of a third variable. The variable, deferment of friends, did not deny the original relationship; it merely clarified the mechanism through which the original relationship occurred. This, then, is the heart of the elaboration model and of multivariate analysis.

Having observed an empirical relationship between two variables, the researcher seeks to understand the nature of that relationship through the effects produced by introducing other variables. Mechanically, he accomplishes this by first dividing his sample into subsets on the basis of the *control* or *test* variable. For example, having friends deferred or not is the control variable in our present example, and the sample is divided into those who have deferred friends and those who do not. The relationship between the original two variables is then recomputed separately for each of the subsamples. The tables produced in this manner are called the *partial tables* and the relationships found in the partial tables are called the *partial relationships.* The partial relationships are then compared with the initial relationship discovered in the total sample.

15.2   The Elaboration Paradigm

This section presents guidelines for the reader to follow in the understanding of an elaboration analysis. To begin, we must know whether the test variable is antecedent (prior in time) to the other two variables or whether it is intervening between them, as these suggest different

logical relationships in the multivariate model. If the test variable is intervening, as in the case of education, deferment of friends, and acceptance of
induction, then the relationships of Figure 15-1 are posited.

Figure 15-1

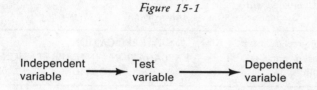

The logic of this multivariate relationship is as follows: The independent
variable (educational level) affects the intervening test variable (having
friends deferred or not), which in turn affects the dependent variable (accepting induction).

If the test variable is antecedent to both the independent and dependent
variables, a very different multivariate relationship is posited (see Figure
15-2).

Figure 15-2

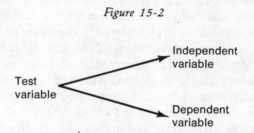

In this second situation, the test variable affects both the independent and
dependent variables.[3] Because of their individual relationships to the test
variable, the independent and dependent variables are empirically related to
each other, but there is no causal link between them. Their empirical relationship is merely a product of their coincidental relationships to the test variable.
(Subsequent examples will further clarify this.)

Table 15-5 is a guide to the understanding of an elaboration analysis. The
two columns in the table indicate whether the test variable is antecedent or
intervening in the sense described above. On the left side of the table is
indicated the nature of the partial relationships as compared with the original
relationship between the independent and dependent variables. In the body
of the table are given the technical notations assigned to each case.

---

[3]Realize, of course, that the terms "independent variable" and "dependent variable" are, strictly speaking,
used incorrectly in the diagram. In fact, we have one independent variable (the "test variable") and two
dependent variables. The incorrect terminology has been used only to provide continuity with the preceding
example.

Table 15-5.   The Elaboration Paradigm

Partial Relationships Compared with Original	Test Variable	
	Antecedent	Intervening
Same relationship	REPLICATION	
Less or none	EXPLANATION	INTERPRETATION
Split*	SPECIFICATION	

*One partial the same or greater, while the other is less or none.

Replication

Whenever the partial relationships are essentially the same as the original relationship, the term "replication" is assigned to the result, regardless of whether the test variable is antecedent or intervening. The meaning here is essentially the same as common sense would dictate. The original relationship has been replicated under test conditions. If, in our previous example, education still affected acceptance of induction both among those who had friends deferred and those who did not, then we would say the original relationship had been replicated. Note, however, that this finding would not confirm Stouffer's explanation of the original relationship. Having friends deferred or not would not be the mechanism through which education affected the acceptance of induction.

Researchers frequently use the elaboration model rather routinely in the hope of replicating their findings among subsets of the sample. The researcher who discovered a relationship between education and prejudice, for example, might introduce such test variables as age, region of the country, race, religion, and so forth, to test the stability of that original relationship. If the relationship were replicated among young and old, among persons from different parts of the country, and so forth, he might thereby conclude that the original relationship was a genuine and general one.

Explanation

Explanation is the term used to describe a spurious relationship: an original relationship that is "explained away" through the introduction of a test variable. Two conditions are required for this. The test variable must be antecedent to both the independent and dependent variables, and the partial relationships must be zero or significantly less than was found in the original. Three examples make this clear.

There is an empirical relationship between the number of storks in different areas and the birthrates for those areas. The more storks in an area, the higher the birthrate. This empirical relationship might thereby lead one to assume that the number of storks affects the birthrate. An antecedent test variable "explains away" this relationship, however. Rural areas have both more storks and higher birthrates than is true of urban areas. Within rural areas, there is no relationship between the number of storks and the birthrate; nor is there a relationship within urban areas.

Second, there is a positive relationship between the number of fire trucks responding to a fire and the amount of damage done. If more trucks respond, more damage is done. One might assume from this, then, that the fire trucks themselves cause the damage. An antecedent test variable, however, explains away the original relationship: the size of the fire. Large fires do more damage than small ones, and more fire trucks respond to large fires than to small ones. Looking only at large fires, the original relationship would vanish (or perhaps reverse itself); and the same would be true looking only at small fires.

Finally, there is an empirical relationship between the region of the country in which a medical school faculty member attended medical school, and his attitude toward Medicare.[4] To simplify matters, only the East and the South will be examined. Of faculty members attending Eastern medical schools, 78 percent said they approved of Medicare, compared with 59 percent of those attending Southern medical schools. This finding makes sense in view of the fact that the South seems generally more resistant to such programs than the East, and medical school training should presumably affect a doctor's medical attitudes. This relationship is explained away through the introduction of an antecedent test variable: the region of the country in which the faculty member was raised.

Of faculty members raised in the East, 89 percent attended medical school in the East, and 11 percent in the South. Of those raised in the South, 53 percent attended medical school in the East and 47 percent in the South. Moreover, the area in which faculty members were raised is related to attitudes toward Medicare. Of those raised in the East, 84 percent approved of Medicare, as compared with 49 percent of those raised in the South.

Table 15-6 presents the three-variable relationship among region in which raised, region of medical school training, and attitudes toward Medicare.

Those faculty members raised in the East are quite likely to approve of Medicare, regardless of where they attended medical school. By the same token, those raised in the South are relatively less likely to approve of Medicare, but, again, the region of their medical school training has little or no effect. These data indicate, therefore, that the original relationship between region of medical training and attitudes toward Medicare was spurious; it was

---

[4]Earl R. Babbie, *Science and Morality in Medicine* (Berkeley: University of California Press, 1970), see esp. p. 181.

Table 15-6.   *Region of Origin, Region of Schooling,*
and Attitudes toward Medicare

Percent Who Approve of Medicare		Region in Which Raised	
		East	South
Region of Medical School Training	East	84	50
	South	80	47

Source: Babbie, 181.

only due to the coincidental effect of region of origin on both region of medical training and on attitudes toward Medicare. When region of origin is *held constant* as we have done in Table 15-6, the original relationship disappears in the partials.

Interpretation

Interpretation is similar to explanation, except for the time placement of the test variable and the implications that follow from that difference. The earlier example of education, friends deferred, and acceptance of induction is an excellent illustration of interpretation. In the terms of the elaboration model, the effect of education on acceptance of induction is not explained away; it is still a genuine relationship. In a real sense, educational differences *cause* differential acceptance of induction. The intervening variable, deferment of friends, merely helps to interpret the mechanism through which the relationship occurs.

Note an important point here. The researcher might have begun his analysis with the observation that having friends deferred made draftees less willing to accept their own induction as fair. In the attempt to better understand this original finding, he might have introduced education as an antecedent test variable. Had he done this, however, he would have found that the relationship between friends being deferred and acceptance of induction was *replicated* among the highly educated and among the lesser educated soldiers (see Table 15-4). He would have also noted that highly educated soldiers were less likely to have friends deferred, but the original relationship would not have been explained away.

As a final example of interpretation, it has been observed by researchers in the past that children from homes with working mothers are more likely to become delinquent than those whose mothers do not work. This relationship may be interpreted, however, through the introduction of "supervision" as a test variable. Among children who are supervised, delinquency rates are not affected by whether or not their mothers work. The same is true among those who are not supervised. It is the relationship between working mothers and lack of supervision that produced the original relationship.

Specification

Sometimes the elaboration model produces partial relationships that differ significantly from each other. For example, one partial relationship may look very much like the original two-variable relationship, while the second partial relationship is near zero. This situation is referred to as *specification* in the elaboration paradigm. The researcher has specified the conditions under which the original relationship occurs.

In a study of the sources of religious involvement, Glock and his associates discovered that among Episcopal church members, involvement decreased as social class increased.[5] This finding is reported in Table 15-7, which examines mean levels of church involvement among women parishioners at different levels of social class.

Table 15-7. *Social Class and Mean Church Involvement among Episcopal Women*

	Social-Class Levels				
	Low 0	1	2	3	High 4
Mean Involvement	.63	.58	.49	.48	.45

Source: Glock *et al*, 85.

Glock interpreted this finding in the context of others in the analysis, and concluded that church involvement provides an alternative form of gratification for those people who are denied gratification in the secular society. This explained why women were more religious than men, why old people were more religious than young people, and so forth. Glock reasoned that people of lower social class (measured by income and education) had fewer chances to gain self-esteem from the secular society than was the case for people of higher social class. To illustrate this, he noted that social class was strongly related to the likelihood that a woman had ever held an office in a secular organization (see Table 15-8).

Glock then reasoned that if social class was related to church involvement only by virtue of the fact that lower-class women would be denied opportunities for gratification in the secular society, the original relationship should *not* hold among women who were getting gratification. As a rough indicator

[5]Charles Y. Glock, Benjamin B. Ringer, and Earl R. Babbie, *To Comfort and to Challenge* (Berkeley: University of California Press, 1967), p. 92.

Table 15-8.   Social Class and the Holding of Office
in Secular Organizations

	Social Class Levels				
	Low 0	1	2	3	High 4
Percent who have held office in a secular organization	46	47	54	60	83

Source: Glock *et al*, 92.

of the receipt of gratification from the secular society, he used the variable regarding the holding of secular office. In terms of this test, then, social class should be unrelated to church involvement among those who had held such office (see Table 15-9).

Table 15-9.   Church Involvement by Social Class and
Holding Secular Office

	Social Class Levels				
Mean Church Involvement	Low 0	1	2	3	High 4
Have held office	.46	.53	.46	.46	.46
Have not held office	.62	.55	.47	.46	.40

Source: Glock *et al*, 92.

Table 15-9 presents an example of a *specification*. Among women who have held office in secular organizations, there is essentially no relationship between social class and church involvement. In effect, the table specifies the conditions under which the original relationship holds: among those women lacking gratification in the secular society.

The term "specification" is used in the elaboration paradigm regardless of whether the test variable is antecedent or intervening. In either case, the meaning is the same. The researcher has specified the particular conditions under which the original relationship holds.

Refinements to the Paradigm

The preceding sections have presented the primary logic of the elaboration model as developed by Lazarsfeld and his colleagues. Morris Rosenberg has offered an excellent presentation of the paradigm described above, and he goes beyond it to suggest additional variations.[6]

[6]Morris Rosenberg, *The Logic of Survey Analysis* (New York: Basic Books, Inc., Publishers, 1968).

Rather than reviewing the comments made by Rosenberg, it might be useful at this point to consider the logically possible variations. Some of these comments may be found in Rosenberg's book, others were suggested by it.

First, the basic paradigm assumes an initial relationship between two variables. It might be useful, however, for a more comprehensive model to differentiate between positive and negative relationships. Moreover, Rosenberg suggests the application of the elaboration model to an original relationship of *zero*—with the possibility that relationships will appear in the partials.

Rosenberg cites as an example of this a study of union membership and attitudes toward having Jews on the union staff.[7] The initial analysis indicated that length of union membership did not relate to the attitude: Those who had belonged to the union less than four years were as willing to accept Jews on the staff as were those who had belonged to the union for longer than four years. The *age* of union members, however, was found to *suppress* the relationship between length of union membership and attitudes toward Jews. Overall, younger members were more favorable to Jews than were older members. At the same time, of course, younger members were less likely to have been in the union as long as the old members. Within specific age groups, however, those in the union longest were the most supportive of having Jews on the staff. Age, in this case, was a *suppressor variable,* concealing the relationship between length of membership and attitudes toward Jews.

Second, the basic paradigm focuses on partials being the same or weaker than the original relationship, but does not provide guidelines for specifying what constitutes a significant difference between the original and the partials. Every researcher using the elaboration model will frequently find himself making an arbitrary decision as to whether a given partial is significantly weaker than the original. This, then, suggests another dimension to the paradigm.

Third, the limitation of the basic paradigm to partials that are the same as or weaker than the original neglects two other possibilities. A partial relationship might be *stronger* than the original. Or, on the other hand, a partial relationship might be the reverse of the original—negative where the original was positive.

Rosenberg provides a hypothetical example of this by first suggesting that a researcher might find working-class respondents in his study more supportive of the civil-rights movement than middle-class respondents.[8] He further suggests that *race* might be a *distorter variable* in this instance, distorting the true relationship between class and attitudes. Presumably, black respondents would be more supportive of the movement than whites, but blacks would also be overrepresented among working class respondents and

---

[7] *Ibid.,* pp. 88-89.
[8] *Ibid.,* pp. 94-95.

underrepresented among the middle class. Middle-class black respondents might be more supportive of the movement than working class blacks, however; and the same relationship might be found among whites. *Holding race constant,* then, the researcher would conclude that support for the civil-rights movement was greater among the middle class than among the working class.

All these new dimensions further complicate the notion of specification. If one partial is the same as the original, while the other partial is even stronger, how should the researcher react to that situation? He has specified one condition under which the original relationship holds up, but he has also specified another condition under which it holds even more clearly.

Finally, the basic paradigm focuses primarily on dichotomous test variables. In fact, the elaboration model is not so limited—either in theory or in use—but the basic paradigm becomes more complicated when the test variable divides the sample into three or more subsamples. And the paradigm becomes more complicated yet when more than one test variable is used simultaneously.

These comments are not made with the intention of faulting the basic elaboration paradigm. To the contrary, my intention is to impress upon the reader that the elaboration model is not a simple algorithm—a set of procedures through which analysis is accomplished. The elaboration model is a logical device for assisting the researcher in the understanding of his data. A firm understanding of the elaboration model will facilitate a sophisticated survey analysis. It does not suggest which variables should be introduced as controls, however, nor does it suggest definitive conclusions as to the nature of elaboration results. For all these things, the researcher must look to his own ingenuity. Such ingenuity, moreover, will come only through extensive experience. By pointing to the oversimplifications in the basic elaboration paradigm, I have sought to bring home the point that the model only provides a logical framework. Sophisticated analysis will be far more complicated than the examples used to illustrate the basic paradigm.

At the same time, the elaboration paradigm is a very powerful logical framework. If the reader fully understands the basic model, he will be in a far better position for understanding other techniques such as correlations, regressions, factor analyses, and so forth. The next chapter will attempt to place such techniques as partial correlations and partial regressions in the context of the elaboration model.

15.3   Elaboration and Ex Post Facto
             Hypothesizing

Before leaving the topic of the elaboration model, one further word is in order regarding its power in connection with an unfortunate sacred cow in the traditional norms of scientific research. The reader of methodological literature will find countless references to the fallacy of *"ex post facto hypothesizing."* The intentions of such injunctions are correct, but the inexperienced researcher is sometimes led astray.

When the researcher observes an empirical relationship between two variables and then simply suggests a reason for that relationship, this is sometimes called ex post facto hypothesizing. He has generated an hypothesis linking two variables after their relationship is already known. We will recall from an early discussion in this book, that all hypotheses must be subject to disconfirmation. Unless the researcher (or theorist) can specify empirical findings that would disprove his hypothesis, it is essentially useless. It is reasoned, therefore, that once the researcher has *observed* a relationship between two variables, any hypothesis regarding that relationship cannot be disproved.

This is a fair assessment in those situations in which the researcher does nothing more than dress up his empirical observations with deceptive hypotheses after the fact. Having observed that women are more religious than men, he should not simply assert that women will be more religious than men because of some general dynamic of social behavior and then rest his case on the initial observation.

The unfortunate spin-off of this injunction against ex post facto hypothesizing is in its inhibition of good, honest hypothesizing after the fact. Inexperienced researchers are often led to believe that they must make all their hypotheses before examining their data—even if this means making a lot of poorly reasoned ones. Furthermore, they are led to ignore any empirically observed relationships that do not confirm some prior hypothesis.

Surely, few researchers would now wish that Sam Stouffer had hushed up his anomalous findings regarding morale among soldiers in the Army. Stouffer noted peculiar empirical observations and set about hypothesizing the reasons for those findings. And his reasoning has proved invaluable to subsequent researchers.

There is a further, more sophisticated, point to made here, however. Whereas anyone can generate hypotheses to explain observed empirical relationships in a body of data, the elaboration model provides the logical tools for *testing* those hypotheses within the same body of data. A good example of this may be found in the earlier discussion of social class and church involvement. Glock explained the original relationship in terms of social deprivation theory. If he had stopped at that point, his comments would have been interesting but hardly persuasive. He went beyond that point, however. He noted that if the hypothesis were correct, then the relationship between social class and church involvement should disappear among those women who were receiving gratification from the secular society—those who had held office in a secular organization. This was then subjected to an empirical test. Had the new hypothesis not been confirmed by the data, he would have been forced to reconsider.

These additional comments should further illustrate the point that data analysis is a continuing process, demanding all the ingenuity and perseverance the researcher can muster. The image of a researcher carefully laying out hypotheses and then testing them in a ritualistic fashion results only in ritualistic research.

For the reader who is concerned that the strength of ex post facto proofs is less than the traditional kinds, let me repeat the earlier assertion that "scientific proof" is a contradiction in terms. Nothing is ever proved *scientifically*. Hypotheses, explanations, theories, or hunches can all escape a stream of attempts at disproof, but none can be proved in any absolute sense. The acceptance of a hypothesis, then, is really a function of the extent to which it has been tested and not disconfirmed. No hypothesis, therefore, should be considered sound on the basis of one test—whether the hypothesis was generated before or after the observation of empirical data. With this in mind, the researcher should not deny himself some of the most fruitful avenues available to him in data analysis. He should always try to reach an honest understanding of his data, develop meaningful theories for more general understanding, and not worry about the manner of reaching that understanding.

Additional Readings

Glock, Charles Y., *Survey Research in the Social Sciences* (New York: Russel Sage Foundation, 1967), chap. 1.

Hyman, Herbert, *Survey Design and Analysis* (New York: The Free Press, 1955).

Rosenberg, Morris, *The Logic of Survey Analysis* (New York: Basic Books, Inc., Publishers, 1968).

Stouffer, Samuel A., *Social Research to Test Ideas* (New York: The Free Press, 1962).

16.1 *Descriptive Statistics*

Data Reduction
Measures of Association

16.2 *Inferential Statistics*

Univariate Inferences
Tests of Statistical Significance

Chapter Sixteen

The Proper Uses of Statistics

Many people are intimidated by empirical research because they feel uncomfortable with mathematics and statistics. And indeed, many research reports are filled with a variety of semispecified computations. The role of statistics in survey research is very important, but it is equally important to see that role in its proper perspective.

Empirical research is first and foremost a *logical* operation rather than a mathematical one. If a person is fully conversant with the logic of science, he will be able to understand and use the appropriate mathematics. Mathematics is merely a convenient and efficient language for accomplishing the logical operations inherent in good data analysis. Statistics is the applied branch of mathematics especially appropriate to a variety of research analyses.

This chapter will consider two types of statistics: *descriptive* and *inferential*. Descriptive statistics is a medium for describing survey data in manageable forms. Inferential statistics, on the other hand, permits the researcher to draw conclusions from his sample survey data to apply to the population from which the sample was drawn.

16.1 Descriptive Statistics

Data Reduction

It is useful to begin the discussion of descriptive statistics with a brief look at the raw-data matrix produced by a typical survey.

Table 16-1 presents such a raw-data matrix.

For our purposes, it will be useful to think of the variables in Table 16-1 as punch-card columns. Each column represents a coded set of data. Column V_3, for example, might represent the respondent's sex: 1 for male and 2 for female. The "persons" in the left column of Figure 16-1 are the several survey respondents.

This raw-data matrix contains all the original coded information that the researcher collects from his respondents. It is worth noting, moreover, that the survey researcher often sees his data in just this form. If the survey questionnaires are coded on transfer sheets for keypunching, those sheets

Table 16-1. Typical Raw-Data Matrix

						Variables				
	V_1	V_2	V_3	V_4	V_5	V_6	V_7	V_8	$V_9 \cdots V_n$
Person 1	2	5	1	4	3	3	9	2	$7 \cdots 6$
Person 2	3	2	1	1	8	5	9	1	6　1
Person 3	1	3	2	3	2	5	3	7	5　2
Person 4	2	1	2	2	5	2	7	4	4　3
$\vdots$									
Person n	1	3	1	2	4	4	6	7	$1 \cdots 4$

form a raw-data matrix like the one in Table 16-1. And after keypunching the data, the researcher often has the computer list his data file, and the result is a raw-data matrix.

Recalling the earlier discussion of univariate analysis in Chapter 13, we note that the raw-data matrix has the advantage of representing all the available information. If the reader of a research report were provided with the raw-data matrix, he would have all the information available to the researcher himself.

The prime difficulty of such a data matrix is that it is a very inefficient presentation of the data. Imagine for a moment a matrix containing perhaps 200 variables for each of 2,000 respondents. Such a matrix would contain nearly half a million entries. Neither the researcher nor the reader would be able to sift through so many numbers to recognize meaningful patterns in them.

Descriptive statistics provide a method of reducing large data matrices to manageable summaries to permit easy understanding and interpretation. Single variables can be summarized by descriptive statistics and so can the associations among variables.

Chapter 13 discussed the various methods of summarizing univariate data: frequency distributions in either raw numbers or percentages, either grouping the data into categories or leaving them ungrouped; averages such as the mean, median, or mode; and measures of dispersion such as the range, the standard deviation, and so forth. The reader should keep in mind the inherent trade-off between summarization and the maintenance of the original data. The prime goal of univariate descriptive statistics is efficiency: The maximum amount of information should be maintained in the simplest summary form. We shall turn now to an extension of those concerns in an examination of the descriptive statistics available for summarizing associations among variables.

Measures of Association

The association between any two variables may also be represented by a data matrix, this time produced by the joint frequency distributions of the two variables. Table 16-2 presents such a matrix.

Table 16-2. *Association between Variables as a Data Matrix*

	Variable X						
	X_1	X_2	X_3	X_4	X_5	X_6	$X_7 \cdots X_n$
Y_1	35	27	26	12	15	7	2 $\cdots$ 0
Y_2	38	48	38	22	35	13	8 3
Y_3	32	41	75	64	46	22	17 10
Y_4	28	45	63	80	79	45	33 32
Y_5	20	35	53	90	103	87	76 24
Y_6	23	12	76	80	99	165	132 98
Y_7	5	8	43	60	73	189	237 128
$\vdots$	$\vdots$	$\vdots$					$\vdots$
Y_n	1	3	8	13	12	32	45 $\cdots$ 98

The data matrix presented in Table 16-2 provides all the necessary information for determining the nature and extent of the relationship between variables X and Y. The column headings in the Table represent the values of variable X, while the row headings represent the values of variable Y. The numbers in the body of the matrix represent the number of respondents having a particular response pattern. For example, 35 persons have the response pattern $X_1 Y_1$, 43 persons are $X_3 Y_7$.

Like the raw data matrix presented in Table 16-1, this one gives the reader more information than he can easily comprehend. The careful reader will note that as values of variable X increase from X_1 to X_n, there is a general tendency for values of Y to increase from Y_1 to Y_n, but no more than a general impression is possible. A variety of descriptive statistics permit the summarization of this data matrix, however. Selecting the appropriate measure depends initially on the nature of the two variables.

We shall turn now to some of the options available to the researcher for summarizing the association between two variables. This discussion and those to follow are taken largely from the excellent statistics textbook by Linton C. Freeman.[1]

Each of the measures of association to be discussed in the following sections is based on the same model—*proportionate reduction of error* (PRE). The logic of this model is as follows. First, let's assume that the researcher is asked to "guess" respondents' attributes on a given variable, for example, whether they answered "yes" or "no" to a given questionnaire item. To assist him, let's assume further that the researcher knows the overall distribution of responses in the total sample—say, 60 percent said "yes" and 40 percent said "no." The researcher would make the fewest errors in this process if he always guessed the *modal* (most frequent) response: "yes."

[1]Linton C. Freeman, *Elementary Applied Statistics*, (New York: John Wiley & Sons, Inc., 1968).

Second, let's assume that the researcher knows the empirical relationship between the first variable and some other variable: say, sex. Now, each time we ask the researcher to guess whether a respondent said "yes" or "no," we shall tell him whether the respondent is a man or a woman. If the two variables are related to each other, the researcher should make fewer errors the second time. It is possible, therefore, to compute the PRE due to knowing the relationship between the two variables: the greater the relationship, the greater the reduction of error.

This basic PRE model is modified slightly to take account of different levels of measurement—nominal, ordinal, or interval. The following sections will consider each level of measurement and present one measure of association appropriate to each. The reader should realize that the three measures discussed are only an arbitrary selection from among many appropriate measures.

Nominal Variables.   If the two variables consist of nominal data (for example, sex, religious affiliation, race), lambda (λ) would be one appropriate measure. As discussed above, lambda is based on the researcher's ability to "guess" each respondent's value on one of the variables: the PRE achieved through knowledge of respondents' values on the other variable. A simple, hypothetical example will illustrate the logic and method of lambda.

Table 16-3. *Hypothetical Data Relating Sex to Employment Status*

	Men	Women	Total
Employed	900	200	1,100
Unemployed	100	800	900
Total	1,000	1,000	2,000

Table 16-3 presents hypothetical data relating sex to employment status. Overall, we note that 1,100 respondents are employed, while 900 are unemployed. If the researcher were to predict whether or not respondents were employed, knowing only the overall distribution on that variable, he would always predict "employed," since this would result in fewer errors than always predicting "unemployed." Nevertheless, this strategy would result in 900 errors out of 2,000 predictions.

Let's suppose that the researcher had access to the data shown in Table 16-3 and that he was told each respondent's sex prior to making his prediction of employment status. His strategy would change in that case. For every man, he would predict "employed," while for every woman, he would predict "unemployed." In this instance, he would make 300 errors—the 100 unemployed men and the 200 employed women—or 600 fewer errors than would have been made in ignorance of respondents' sexes.

Lambda, then, represents the reduction in errors as a proportion of the errors that would have been made on the basis of the overall distribution of responses. In this hypothetical example, lambda would equal .67: 600 fewer errors divided by 900 errors based on the total distribution of employment status alone. In this fashion, lambda provides a measure of the statistical association between sex and employment status.

If sex and employment status were statistically independent of one another, we would have found the same distribution of employment status for men and women. In this case, knowing respondents' sexes would not have affected the number of errors made in predicting employment status, and the resulting lambda would have been zero. If, on the other hand, all men were employed and all women were unemployed, the researcher would have made no errors in predicting employment status, knowing sex. He would have made 900 fewer errors (out of 900) and lambda would have been 1.0— representing a perfect statistical association.

Lambda is only one of several measures of association appropriate to the analysis of two nominal variables. The reader is referred to Freeman[2] for discussion of other appropriate measures.

Ordinal Variables. If the variables being related were ordinal in nature (for example, social class, religiosity, alienation), gamma (γ) would be one appropriate measure of association. Like lambda, gamma is based on the researcher's ability to guess values on one variable by knowing values on another. Instead of guessing exact values, however, gamma is based on the ordinal arrangement of values. For any given pair of respondents, the researcher guesses that their ordinal ranking on one variable will correspond (positively or negatively) to their ordinal ranking on the other. Gamma is the proportion of pairs that fit this pattern.

Table 16-4. *Hypothetical Data Relating Social Class to Prejudice*

Prejudice	Lower Class	Middle Class	Upper Class
Low	200	400	700
Medium	500	900	400
High	800	300	100

Table 16-4 presents hypothetical data relating social class to prejudice. An inspection of the table will indicate the general nature of the relationship between these two variables: as social class increases, prejudice decreases. There is a negative association between social class and prejudice.

[2]*Op. cit.*

Gamma is computed from two quantities: (1) the number of pairs having the same ranking on the two variables and (2) the number of pairs having the opposite ranking on the two variables. The pairs having the same ranking are computed as follows: The frequency of each cell in the table is multiplied by the sum of all cells appearing below and to the right of it—with all these products being summed. In the present example, the number of pairs with the same ranking would be 200(900 + 300 + 400 + 100) + 500(300 + 100) + 400(400 + 100) + 900(100) or 340,000 + 200,000 + 200,000 + 90,000 = 830,000.

The pairs having the opposite ranking on the two variables are computed as follows: The frequency of each cell in the table is multiplied by the sum of all cells appearing below and to the left of it—with all these products being summed. In this example, the numbers of pairs with opposite rankings would be 700(500 + 800 + 900 + 300) + 400(800 + 300) + 400(500 + 800) + 900(800) or 1,750,000 + 440,000 + 520,000 + 720,000 = 3,430,000.

Gamma is computed from the numbers of same-ranked pairs and opposite-ranked pairs as follows:

Gamma = (same – opposite) ÷ (same + opposite)

In the present example, gamma would equal: (830,000 – 3,430,000) divided by (830,000 + 3,430,000) or –.76. The negative sign in this answer indicates the negative association suggested by the initial inspection of the table. Social class and prejudice, in this hypothetical example, are negatively associated with one another. The numerical figure for gamma indicates that 61 percent more of the pairs examined had the opposite ranking than had the same ranking.

Note that while values of lambda vary from 0 to 1, values of gamma vary from –1 to +1, representing the *direction* as well as the magnitude of the association. Since nominal variables have no ordinal structure, it makes no sense to speak of the direction of the relationship. (A negative lambda would indicate that the researcher had made more errors in predicting values on one variable while knowing values on the second than he made in ignorance of the second.)

Gamma is only one of several measures of association appropriate to ordinal variables. Again, the reader is referred to Freeman[3] for a more comprehensive treatment of this subject.

Interval or Ratio Variables.   If the variables being associated are interval or ratio in nature (for example, age, income, grade point average, and so forth), one appropriate measure of association would be

---

[3] *Op. cit.*

Pearson's product-moment correlation (r). The derivation and computation of this measure of association is sufficiently complex to lie outside the scope of the present book, so only a few general comments will be made.

Like both gamma and lambda, r is based on guessing the value of one variable on the basis of knowing the other. For continuous interval or ratio variables, however, it is unlikely that the researcher would be able to predict the *precise* value of the variable. But on the other hand, predicting only the ordinal arrangement of values on the two variables would not take advantage of the greater amount of information conveyed by an interval or ratio variable. In a sense, r reflects *how closely* the researcher can guess the value of one variable through his knowledge of the value of the other.

To understand the logic of r, it will be useful to consider the manner in which a researcher might hypothetically "guess" values that respondents have on a given variable. With nominal variables, we have seen that the researcher might always "guess" the modal value. This is not an appropriate perspective for interval or ratio data, however. Instead, the researcher would minimize his errors by always guessing the mean value of the variable. While this would produce few if any perfect guesses, the extent of his errors would be minimized.

In the computation of lambda, we noted the number of errors produced by always guessing the modal value. In the case of r, "errors" are measured in terms of the sum of the squared differences between the actual value and the mean. We shall refer to this later as the *total variance*.

To improve his "guessing," the researcher constructs a *regression line* (see Chapter 17), stated in the form of a regression equation that permits the estimation of values on one variable from values on the other. The general format for this equation is $Y' = a + b(X)$, where a and b are computed values, where X is a given value on one variable, and Y' is the estimated value on the other. The values of a and b are computed in such a way as to minimize the differences between actual values of Y and the corresponding estimates (Y') based on the known value of X. The sum of squared differences between actual and estimated values of Y is called the *unexplained variance,* in that it represents errors that still exist even when estimates are based on known values of X.

The *explained variance* is the difference between the total variance and the unexplained variance. Dividing the explained variance by the total variance produces a measure of the *proportionate reduction of error* corresponding to the similar quantity in the computation of lambda. In the present case, this quantity is the correlation *squared*: r^2.

In practice, the researcher will compute r rather than r^2, since the product-moment correlation can take either a positive or negative sign, depending on the direction of the relationship between the two variables. (Computing r^2 and taking a square root would always produce a positive quantity.) The reader is referred to Freeman[4] or any other standard statistics textbook for the method of computing r, although it is anticipated that most readers using this measure will have access to computer programs designed for this function.

One final comment is in order in this brief discussion. Although r is based on a regression model, r is a *symmetrical* measure. (Gamma is also symmetrical, but lambda is not.) We shall see in the next chapter that predicting values of Y from values of X produces a different equation than predicting values of X from values of Y. Thus, while the linear regression model is asymmetrical, the computation of r is such as to produce a symmetrical solution.

Mixed Types of Variables.   Often, the researcher will find that his interest lies in the association between two variables that differ in type: one ordinal variable and one nominal variable. A variety of special statistics are appropriate to these different possibilities, and the reader is encouraged to examine Freeman[5] for the appropriate statistics for his particular situation.

This is an opportune point for a general comment regarding types of variables and the appropriateness of statistical measures. A quick review of the social scientific research literature will yield countless examples of statistical measures applied to data that do not meet the logical requirements of the measures. The computation of Pearson's r for ordinal data is perhaps the most typical example. One's response to this practice seems largely a matter of personal taste. The person who argued against it would be correct on statistical grounds: Correlation coefficients assume interval data and ordinal data do not meet that criterion. On the other hand, it is my personal orientation to accept, and even to encourage, the use of whatever statistical techniques help the researcher (and the reader) to understand the body of data under analysis. If the computation of r from ordinal data serves this purpose, then it should be encouraged. However, I strongly object to (and discuss in the next section) the practice of making statistical inferences on the basis of such computations. The researcher is justified in bending the rules if it helps him understand his data, but he must be aware of the implications of bending those rules.

16.2   Inferential Statistics

Sample surveys are seldom if ever conducted for the sole purpose of describing the particular sample of respondents studied. In

---

[4] *Op. cit.*
[5] *Op. cit.*

most instances, the ultimate purpose is to make assertions about some larger population. Frequently, then, the researcher will wish to interpret his univariate and multivariate sample findings as the basis for *inferences* about the population from which the sample was selected.

This section will examine the statistics available to the researcher for making such inferences and the logical bases for them. We shall begin with univariate data and move to multivariate.

Univariate Inferences

The opening sections of Chapter 13 dealt with methods for presenting univariate data. Each summary measure was intended as a method for describing the sample studied. Now we have come to the point of using those measures to make broader assertions about the population. This section is addressed to two univariate measures: percentages and means.

If 50 percent of a survey sample say they have had a cold during the past year, the researcher's best estimate of the similar proportion of the total population from which the sample was drawn is 50 percent. (This assumes a simple random sample, of course.) It is rather unlikely, nonetheless, that *precisely* 50 percent of the population has had a cold during the year, however. If a rigorous sampling design for random selection has been followed, however, the researcher will be in a position to estimate the expected range of error when the sample finding is applied to the population.

Chapter 5 on sampling theory covered the procedures for making such estimates, so they will be only reviewed here. In the case of a percentage, the quantity $\sqrt{pq/n}$, where p is a percentage and q equals $1-p$, and where n is the sample size, is called the *standard error*. As noted in Chapter 5, this quantity is very important in the estimation of sampling error. Since the researcher may be 68 percent "confident" that the population figure falls within plus or minus one standard error of the sample figure, he may be 95 percent "confident" that it falls within plus or minus two standard errors, and 99.9 percent "confident" that it falls within plus or minus three standard errors.

Any statement of sampling error, then, must contain two essential components: the *confidence level* (for example, 95 percent) and the *confidence interval* (for example $\pm$ 5 percent). If 50 percent of a sample of 1,600 respondents say they have had a cold during the year, the researcher might say he is 95 percent confident that the population figure is between 47.5 percent and 52.5 percent.

Recognize in this example that we have moved beyond simply describing the survey sample into the realm of making estimates (inferences) about the larger population. In doing this, the researcher must be wary of several assumptions.

First, the sample must be drawn from the population about which inferences are being made. A sample taken from a telephone directory cannot legitimately be the basis for statistical inferences to the population of a city.

Second, the inferential statistics assume simple random sampling, which is virtually never the case in sample surveys. The statistics assume sampling with replacement, which is almost never done; but this is probably not a serious problem. Although systematic sampling is used more frequently than random sampling, this probably presents no serious problem if done correctly. Stratified sampling, since it improves representativeness, clearly presents no problem. Cluster sampling does present a problem, however, as the estimates of sampling error may be too small. Quite clearly, street-corner sampling does not warrant the use of inferential statistics. Also assumed is a 100 percent completion rate. This problem increases in seriousness as the completion rate decreases.

Third, the inferential statistics are addressed to sampling error only; they do not take account of *nonsampling* errors. Thus, it might be quite correct to state that between 47.5 percent and 52.2 percent of the population (95 percent confidence) would *say* that they had had a cold during the previous year, but their reports might be essentially worthless. The researcher could confidently guess the proportion of the population who would report colds, but not the proportion who had had one. Whereas nonsampling errors are probably larger than sampling errors in a respectable sample design, the researcher should be especially cautious in generalizing from his sample findings to the population.

Tests of Statistical Significance

What constitutes a *significant* association between two variables? This question, like many, has no reasonable answer. Nevertheless, it is frequently answered in an unreasonable manner.

There is no scientific answer to the question of whether a given association between two variables is "significant," strong, important, interesting, or worth reporting. Perhaps the ultimate test of significance rests with the researcher's ability to persuade his audience (present and future) of the association's significance.

At the same time, there is a body of inferential statistics that may assist the researcher in this regard: the body of *parametric tests of significance*. As the name suggests, "parametric" statistics are those that make certain assumptions about the parameters describing the population from which the sample is selected.

Although tests of significance are widely reported in survey literature, the logic underlying them is rather subtle and is often misunderstood. Tests of significance are based on the same sampling logic that has been discussed elsewhere in this book. To understand the logic of these tests, let's return for a moment to the concept of sampling error in regard to univariate data.

Recall that a sample statistic normally provides the best single estimate of the corresponding population parameter, but that it is seldom the case that the statistic and the parameter precisely correspond. Thus, the researcher reports the probability that the parameter falls within a certain range (confidence interval). The degree of uncertainty within that range is due to normal sampling error. The corollary of such a statement is, of course, that it is *improbable* that the parameter would fall outside the specified range only as a result of sampling error. Thus, if the researcher estimates that a parameter (99.9 percent confidence) lies between 45 percent and 55 percent, he says by implication that it is *extremely improbable* that the parameter is actually, say, 90 percent if his only error of estimation is due to normal sampling. This is the basic logic behind tests of significance.

Given a specified degree of association between two variables, tests of significance represent the likelihood that such an association could be due only to normal sampling error in the case where there is *no association* between the variables in the population. In a sense, the researcher assumes no association in the population (called the *null hypothesis*) and then asks whether his measured association in the sample could be due only to sampling error. If the measured association could not reasonably be attributed to sampling error, he will then assume that an association exists between the variables in the population.

There is a corollary to confidence intervals in tests of significance: representing the probability of the measured association being due only to sampling error. This is called the *level of significance.* Like confidence intervals, levels of significance are derived from a logical model in which several samples are drawn from a given population. In the present case, we assume that there is no association between the variables in the population, and then ask what proportion of the samples drawn from that population would produce associations at least as great as those measured in the empirical data. Three levels of significance are frequently used in survey reports: .05, .01, and .001. These mean respectively, that the chances of obtaining the measured association as a result of sampling error are 5/100, 1/100, and 1/1,000.

Researchers who use tests of significance normally follow one of two patterns in this regard. Some prefer to specify in advance the level of significance that they will regard as sufficient. If any measured association is statistically significant at that level, they will regard it as representing a genuine association between the two variables. In other words, they are willing to discount the possibility of it resulting from sampling error only.

Other researchers prefer to report the specific level of significance for each association, disregarding the conventions of .05, .01, and .001. Rather than reporting that a given association is significant at the .05 level, they would indicate that it was significant at the .023 level; indicating the chances of it having resulted from sampling error as 23 out of 1,000.

Chi-square is a frequently used test of significance in survey research.

It is based on the *null hypothesis:* the assumption that there is no relationship between the two variables in the total population. Given the observed distribution of values on the two separate variables, the researcher computes the conjoint distribution that would be expected if there were no relationship between the two variables. The result of this operation is a set of *expected frequencies* for all the cells in the contingency table. The researcher then compares this expected distribution with the distribution of cases actually found in the sample data, and he determines the probability that the discovered discrepancy could have resulted from sampling error alone. An example will illustrate this procedure.

Let's assume that a researcher is interested in the possible relationship between church attendance and sex among the members of a particular church. To test this relationship, he has selected a sample of 100 church members at random. Assume further that he finds his sample is made up of 40 men and 60 women. And, finally, assume that 70 percent of his sample reports having attended church during the preceding week, while the remaining 30 percent say they did not.

If there were no relationship between sex and church attendance, then we should expect 70 percent of the men in the sample to have attended church during the preceding week and should expect that 30 percent did not. Moreover, we should expect the same proportional results from women. Table 16-5 (Section A) presents the expected frequencies based on this model. Thus, we should expect that 28 men and 42 women would have attended church, while 12 men and 18 women would not have attended church.

Table 16-5. A Hypothetical Illustration of Chi-Square

Section A. expected cell frequencies

	Men	Women	Total
Attended church	28	42	70
Did not attend church	12	18	30
Total	40	60	100

Section B. observed cell frequencies

	Men	Women	Total
Attended church	20	50	70
Did not attend church	20	10	30
Total	40	60	100

Section C. (Observed - expected)^2 / expected

	Men	Women
Attended church	2.29	1.52
Did not attend church	5.33	3.56

$x^2 = 12.70, p = .001$

Section B of Table 16-5 presents the hypothetically observed cell frequencies discovered among the sample of 100 church members. We note that 20 of the men report having attended church during the preceding week, while the remaining 20 say they did not. Among the women in the sample, 50 attended church and 10 did not. Comparing the expected and observed frequencies (Sections A and B), we note that somewhat fewer men attended church than expected, while somewhat more women than expected attended.

Chi-square is computed as follows. For each cell in the tables, the researcher (1) subtracts the expected frequency for that cell from the observed frequency, (2) squares in this quantity, and (3) divides the squared difference by the expected frequency. This procedure is carried out for each cell in the tables, and the several results are added together. (Section C of Table 16-5 presents the cell-by-cell computations.) The final sum is the value of chi-square: 12.70 in the example.

The value that we have now computed provides an indication of the overall discrepancy between the observed conjoint distribution in the sample and the distribution that we should have expected if the two variables were unrelated to one another. Of course, the mere discovery of a discrepancy does not prove that the two variables are related, since normal sampling error might produce discrepancies even when there was no relationship in the total population. The magnitude of the value of chi-square, however, permits us to estimate the probability of this having happened.

To determine the statistical significance of the observed relationship, we must utilize a standard table of chi-square values. This will require one additional value: the *degrees of freedom*. In the case of chi-square, the degrees of freedom is computed as follows: the number of rows in the table, minus one, is multiplied times the number of columns, minus one. This may be written as $(r - 1)(c - 1)$. In the present example, we have two rows and two columns (discounting the *totals*), so the degrees of freedom equals 1.

Turning to a table of chi-square values, we find that for one degree of freedom and random sampling from a population in which there is no relationship between two variables, 10 percent of the time we should expect a chi-square of at least 2.7. Thus, if we selected 100 samples from such a population, we should expect about 10 of those samples to produce chi-squares equal to or greater than 2.7. Moreover, we should expect chi-squares of at least 6.6 in 1 percent of the samples. Chi-square values of 10.8 should be expected in only .1 percent of the samples. Thus, the lower the computed chi-square value, the more probable it is that the value could be attributed to sampling error alone. The higher the chi-square value, the less probable it is that it could be due to sampling error alone.

In the present, hypothetical, example, the computed value of chi-square is 12.70 If there were no relationship between sex and church attendance in the whole church member population and a large number of samples had been selected and studied, then we would expect a chi-square of this magnitude in fewer than .1 percent of those samples. Thus, the probability of obtaining a chi-square of this magnitude is less than .001, if random sampling has been used and there is no relationship in the population. We report this finding by saying the relationship is statistically significant "at the .001 level." Since it is so improbable that the observed relationship could have resulted from sampling error alone, we are likely to reject the null hypothesis and assume that there is a relationship between the two variables in the total population of church members.

Most measures of association can also be tested for statistical significance in a similar manner. Standard tables of values permit the researcher to determine whether a given association is statistically significant and at what level. Any standard statistics textbook provides instructions on the use of such tables, and we shall not pursue the matter further here.

Tests of significance have the advantage of providing an objective yardstick against which to estimate the significance of associations between variables. They assist the researcher in ruling out associations that may not represent genuine relationships in the population under study. The researcher who uses or reads reports of significance tests should remain wary of several dangers in their interpretation.

First, we have been discussing tests of *statistical* significance; there are no objective tests of *substantive* significance. Thus, the researcher may be legitimately convinced that a given association is not due to sampling error, but he may be in the position of asserting without fear of contradiction that two variables are only slightly related to one another. Recall that sampling error is an inverse function of sample size; the larger the sample, the smaller the expected error. Thus, a correlation of, say, .1 might very well be significant (at a given level) if discovered in a large sample, whereas the same correlation between the same two variables would not be significant if found in a smaller sample. Of course, this makes perfectly good sense if one understands the basic logic of tests of significance: in the larger sample, there is less chance that the correlation could be simply the product of sampling error. In both samples, however, it might represent a very weak and essentially useless finding.

Second, tests of significance are based on the same sampling assumptions as were assumed in the computation of confidence intervals. To the extent that these assumptions are not met by the actual sampling design, the tests of significance are not strictly legitimate.

Third, the researcher should be wary of applying tests of significance to data that represent a total population rather than a sample. If, for example, he has surveyed *all* the undergraduates at State University and discovered a correlation of .3 between two variables, he should not report that the association is significant at the .001 level. Since he has not sampled, there is *no* chance that the association could be due to sampling error. The association between the two variables as measured in the population is *precisely* a correlation of .3—whether that degree of association is a *substantively significant* one, whether it is important, cannot be answered through any objective test. (It should be noted that some researchers feel a test of significance in such a case indicates the probability that the relationship is a general one over time—that it describes State University undergraduates over time and not just the particular student body matriculating at the time of the survey.)

As is the case for most topics covered by this book, I have a personal prejudice. In this instance, it is against tests of significance. My objection is not with the statistical logic of those tests, since it is sound. Rather, I am concerned that such tests seem to mislead more than they enlighten. My principal reservations are the following:

1. Tests of significance make sampling assumptions that are virtually never satisfied by actual survey designs.

2. They assume the absence of nonsampling errors, which is a questionable assumption in most actual empirical measurements.

3. In practice, they are too often applied to measures of association that have been computed in violation of the assumptions made by those measures (for example, product-moment correlations computed from ordinal data).

4. Statistical significance is too easily misinterpreted as "strength of association," and/or substantive significance.

At the same time, I feel that tests of significance can be a valuable asset to the researcher—useful tools for the understanding of data. My view in this regard is perhaps paradoxical. While the above comments suggest an extremely conservative approach to tests of significance—use them only when all assumptions are met—my general perspective is just the reverse. I would encourage the researcher to use any statistical technique—any measure of association or any test of significance—on any set of data if it will help him to understand his data. If the computation of product-moment correlations among nominal variables and the testing of statistical significance in the context of uncontrolled sampling will meet this criterion, then I would encourage such activities. I say this in the spirit of what Hanon Selvin has referred to as "data-dredging" techniques. Anything goes, if it leads ultimately to the understanding of data and of the social world under study.

The price that must be paid for this radical freedom, however, is the inappropriateness of strict, statistical interpretations. The researcher would not be able to demonstrate the ultimate importance of his finding solely on the basis of his correlation being significant at the .05 level. Whatever the avenue to discovery, empirical data must ultimately be presented in a legitimate manner, and their importance must be argued logically.

Summary and Conclusions

This chapter has focused on a variety of statistical techniques that can be used to assist the researcher in the interpretation of his data. We have examined *descriptive* and *inferential* statistics, applied to univariate and multivariate data. In each instance, I have attempted to lay out the basic logic upon which the techniques are based, and the assumptions that each makes.

The chapter has ended with a discussion of statistical significance and this is an appropriate ending point, as the ultimate goal of all analysis is the discovery of "significant" associations. A variety of statistical tests offer the researcher important tools to be used in the discovery of significant associations, but none of these is more than a tool. Tools are effective only to the extent that they are used properly and with imagination.

The researcher should continually ask himself, "What does it all mean?" If, in a very large sample, he discovers that sex is associated with a given attitude at the .05 level of significance, he must ask whether that is important. Does it really matter that 48 percent of the men and 50 percent of the women hold that attitude? Perhaps it does, but the researcher must ask the question and must persuade his readers on grounds other than statistical significance. If 100 percent of the respondents scored "very high" on some index are prejudiced against blacks, but such people represent .5 percent of the total population, the researcher must ask himself whether that finding has any ultimate significance. In some instances, he may decide that the specific finding has no practical significance but that it points to a more general dynamic that has both theoretical and practical importance.

The varieties of questions, answers, and interpretations in this regard are clearly too great to permit the formulation of cookbook rules of any real value. The researcher must learn to grapple with such problems, however, if his research is to have any significance.

Additional Readings

Freeman, Linton C., *Elementary Applied Statistics* (New York: John Wiley & Sons, Inc., 1968).

Kish, Leslie, *Survey Sampling* (New York: John Wiley & Sons, Inc., 1967).

Meuller, John H., and Karl F. Schuessler, *Statistical Reasoning in Sociology* (Boston: Houghton Mifflin Company, 1961).

Morrison, Denton E., and Ramon E. Henkel, *The Significance Test Controversy: A Reader* (Chicago: Aldine-Atherton, Inc., 1970).

Chapter Seventeen

Complex Modes of Analysis

For the most part, this book has focused on rather rudimentary forms of data manipulation in survey analysis. I have suggested that the logic of data analysis can be most clearly seen through the use of contingency tables and percentages. The elaboration model of analysis was presented in this form.

The preceding chapter has dealt with some other statistical techniques that may be applied to survey data—especially within the context of contingency tables. Now we shall move one step further and consider briefly a few more complex methods of data analysis and presentation. Each of the techniques examined in this chapter will be presented from the logical perspective of the elaboration model. Four methods of analysis will be discussed: regression analysis, path analysis, factor analysis, and smallest-space analysis. The reader should realize that these four techniques represent only an arbitrary selection from among the many that are available to the survey analyst.

17.1 Regression Analysis

At several points in this text, I have referred to the general formula for describing the X association between two variables: $Y = f(X)$. Recall from Chapter 12 that this formula is read "Y is a function of X," meaning that values of Y can be explained in terms of variations in the values of X. Stated more strongly, we might say that X causes Y, so the value of X determines the value of Y. Regression analysis provides a method for determining the specific function relating Y to X.

The regression model can be seen most clearly in the case of a perfect linear association between two variables. Figure 17-1 is a scattergram presenting in graphic form the conjoint values of X and Y as produced by a hypothetical survey.

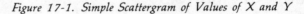

Figure 17-1. Simple Scattergram of Values of X and Y

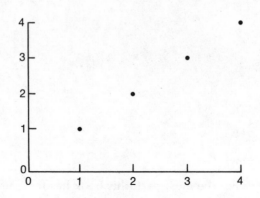

A quick perusal of Figure 17-1 indicates that for the four cases in our survey, the values of X and Y are identical in each instance. The person with a value of 1 on X also has a value of 1 on Y, and so forth. The relationship between the two variables in this instance could be described by the equation $Y = X$; this would be the *regression equation.* Since all four points lie on a straight line, we could superimpose that line over the points; this would be the *regression line.*

The regression model has important descriptive uses. The regression line offers a graphic picture of the association between X and Y. And the regression equation is an efficient form for summarizing that association. The regression model has inferential value as well. To the extent that the regression equation correctly describes the *general* association between the two variables, it may be used to predict other sets of values. If, for example, we know that a new respondent has a value of 3.5 on X, we would predict the value of 3.5 on Y as well.

In practice, of course, surveys are seldom limited to four cases, and the associations between variables are seldom as clear as the one presented in Figure 17-1. A somewhat more realistic example is presented in Figure 17-2.

Two observations may be made regarding Figure 17-2. As was the case in our previous example, we note that the values of Y generally correspond to those of X; and as values of X increase, so do values of Y. At the same time, however, the association is not nearly as clear as was the case in Figure 17-1.

While it is not possible on Figure 17-2 to superimpose a straight line that will pass through all the points in the scattergram, an approximate line could be constructed. This line would provide the *best* possible linear representation of the several points.

The statistical procedures for computing the regression line can be found in any standard statistics text, so we shall consider only the *logic* of that procedure here. Assume for the moment that we have drawn through the scattergram a line that seems to represent fairly closely the general pattern of the points. This line would permit us to roughly predict values of Y on the basis of values of X.

Figure 17-2. Complex Scattergram of Values of X and Y

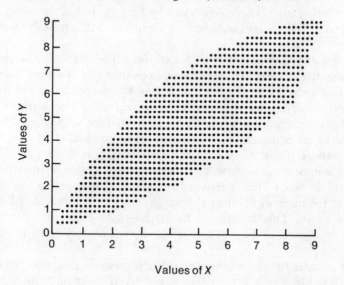

Figure 17-3. Measuring Distances Between Points and Regression Line

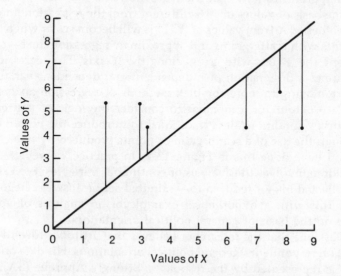

For a given value of X, we could locate that value on the approximate regression line and determine the value of Y at that point on the line. Since the several points clearly do not lie directly on the line, however, it is clear

that we shall make errors in most predictions of Y on the basis of X. For all those cases with values of X equal to 2 in Figure 17-2, we note that the actual values of Y range between 1 and 4. Given our approximate regression line, then, it is possible to measure the errors in predicting each value of Y from each value of X; these errors can be represented as distances along the Y axis between the points and the line. Figure 17-3 illustrates this with fewer points.

The linear regression line is the straight line that has the property of minimizing the *squared distances* between points and the line—as measured along the Y axis. Thus, the regression line is referred to as the *least-squares line*. The line having this property, then, provides the best summary description of the association between X and Y. Moreover, any straight line can be expressed as an equation, as was the case in Figure 17-1.

The general form of the regression equation is $Y = a + bX$. In this equation, a indicates the value of Y when $X = 0$. (Note in the equation that for $X = 0$, $Y = a$.) This is referred to as the *Y-intercept*. In the equation, b represents the number of units change in Y for every increase of *one* unit in the value of X. This is referred to as the *slope*. Note that in the simpler example in Figure 17-1, $a = 0$ and $b = 1$, which reduced the equation to $Y = X$.

Let's assume for the moment that the regression equation for the points in Figure 17-2 is $Y = 2 + 1.3X$. For every given value of X, then, we would be able to estimate the value of Y. If X equals 23, then we would estimate Y as $2 + 1.3(23) = 31.9$.

It is important to note that the regression line that best predicts values of Y on the basis of values of X is different from the regression line that best predicts values of X from values of Y. This will become clear when the reader experiments with scattergrams and approximate regression lines—comparing errors along the Y axis with errors along the X axis. The regression model, then, assumes a designation of independent and dependent variables.

Before moving to more complex methods of regression analysis, it will be useful to detour for a moment to consider the logic of scattergrams in normal survey conditions. It is traditional to introduce the notion of regression through the use of a scattergram of points produced by two continuous variables. I have done this in Figure 17-2. In practice, however, survey research seldom involves the analysis of continuous variables: typically survey data is collected in—or reduced to—a limited set of answer categories. Let's illustrate this with a hypothetical example of an analysis of approval of Medicare on the basis of general political orientations.

Let's assume that the researcher believes that attitudes toward Medicare are based on respondents' general political orientations. His data on Medicare attitudes is represented by the responses: Strongly Approve (SA), Approve (A), Disapprove (D), and Strongly Disapprove (SD). His data on general political orientations are represented by respondents' self-characterizations as

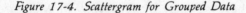

Figure 17-4. Scattergram for Grouped Data

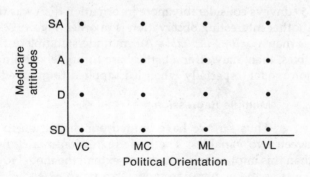

Very Conservative (VC), Moderately Conservative (MC), Moderately Liberal (ML), and Very Liberal (VL). The scattergram of points produced by these variables is presented in Figure 17-4.

Clearly, Figure 17-4 tells us nothing about the association between political orientations and attitudes toward Medicare, since the points are evenly distributed with no apparent pattern. This is due to the fact that each point represents more than one respondent; since the data are grouped, the individual points have been "piled up" on top of each other.

Figure 17-5 is more useful. The several points have been replaced by numbers: representing the number of respondents giving a particular re-

Figure 17-5. Scattergram of Grouped Data with Frequencies

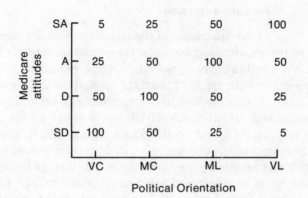

sponse pattern. For example, we discover that 100 "very conservative" respondents said they "strongly disapproved" of Medicare; 50 "moderately conservative" respondents "approved" of Medicare.

Figure 17-5 conveys considerably more information than was the case for Figure 17-4. Another interesting observation is in order. Figure 17-5 is nothing more or less than a *contingency table.* A firm understanding of the logic of contingency tables, then, may offer a better base for understanding the logic of the regression model, especially when it is applied to grouped data.

Multiple Regression

Thus far, we have limited our discussion to the linear regression between two variables. The basic regression model, however, is more general than this implies. It is possible to extend the model to more than two variables, just as the elaboration model can be so extended.

In the discussion of the elaboration model, we recall that some dependent variables may be affected by more than one independent variable. By constructing more complex contingency tables, the researcher can determine the joint contribution of several independent variables to the prediction of values on the dependent variable.

If, for example, the researcher believes that both age and education affect prejudice, he could construct tables appropriate for testing this. Presumably, he would find that the oldest respondents having the least education would be the most prejudiced, while the youngest respondents having the most education would be the least prejudiced. This would show him the joint effects of age and education on prejudice.

Multiple regression is based on the same logic. Although it is difficult to present a regression line in more than two dimensions, the multiple regression equation can be presented: $P = a + bE + cA$, where P is prejudice, E is education, and A is age. If more independent variables were involved, the equation would simply be extended to take those into account.

Partial Regression

In the discussion of the elaboration model, special attention was paid to the relationship between two variables when a third, test, variable was held constant. Thus, we might have examined the effect of education on prejudice with age held constant: testing the independent effect of education. To do this, we would have computed the tabular relationship between education and prejudice separately for each age group.

Partial regressions are based on this same logical model. The equation summarizing the relationship between two variables is computed on the basis of the test variable(s) remaining constant. As in the case of the elaboration model, this may then be compared with the "uncontrolled" relationship between the two variables to further clarify the nature of the overall relationship.

Curvilinear Regression

Up to now, we have been discussing the association among variables as represented by a straight line—though in more than two dimensions. The regression model is even more general than this implies.

The reader with a knowledge of geometry will already know that curvilinear functions can also be represented by equations. For example, the equation $X^2 + Y^2 = 25$ describes a circle with a radius of 5. Raising variables to powers greater than 1 has the effect of producing curves rather than straight lines. And from the standpoint of empirical research, there is no reason to assume that the relationship among every set of variables will be linear. In some cases, then, curvilinear regression analysis can provide a better understanding of empirical relationships than can any linear model.

Although curvilinear functions are more difficult to identify and interpret in contingency tables, our previous discussion of scattergrams and tables suggests the possibility of a contingency table similar to the one presented in Figure 17-6.

Figure 17-6. Curvilinear Relationship in a Contingency Table

	X_1	X_2	X_3	X_4	X_5	X_6	X_7
Y_4	100	50	0	0	0	50	100
Y_3	0	100	25	0	25	100	0
Y_2	0	50	100	0	100	50	0
Y_1	0	25	50	100	50	25	0

The data presented in Figure 17-6 roughly describe a curvilinear relationship between X and Y. All persons having the value of X_1 also have the value of Y_4. As we move across the table to X_4, we note the tendency for decreasing values of Y; then the values of Y increase again as we move past X_4 until we discover that all persons with X_7 are also Y_4. Thus the relationship is a curvilinear one, not adequately represented by any straight line.

Curvilinear regression analysis would provide a neater summary of the relationship apparent in Figure 17-6. Moreover, the regression equation would permit one estimate of Y values from X values.

The potential of curvilinear regression analysis is very great, although this has scarcely been approached in survey practice. Most collections of points representing the coincidence of two variables could be perfectly represented by an equation. With normal survey data, however, such an equation would be complex indeed, involving variables raised to very high powers. Such a complex equation might have little practical value, and its theoretical value might be minimal as well.

Recall that a regression line serves two functions. It describes a set of sample observations, and it provides a general model of the relationship between two variables in the population from which the sample was selected. A very complex equation might result in a rather erratic line that would indeed pass through every individual point. In this sense, it would perfectly describe the sample observations. There would be no guarantee, however, that such a line would adequately predict new observations, or that it in any meaningful way represented the relationship between the two variables in general. Thus, it would have little or no inferential value.

Earlier in this book, we discussed the need for balancing detail and utility in data reduction. The researcher attempts to provide the most faithful, yet also the simplest, representation of his data. This is essentially the same problem facing the researcher using regression analysis. He wishes to represent his data in the simplest fashions (thus, linear regressions are most frequently used), but in such a way as to best describe the actual data. Curvilinear regression analysis adds a new option to the researcher in this regard, but it does not solve his problems altogether. Nothing does that.

Cautions in Regression Analysis

The use of regression analysis for statistical inferences makes certain assumptions of which the researcher should be aware. These are the same ones assumed by correlational analysis: concerning simple random sampling, the absence of nonsampling errors, and continuous interval data. Since survey research never completely satisfies these assumptions, the reader should use caution in assigning ultimate meaning to the results of regression analyses.

As indicated earlier, however, I would encourage the use of these techniques—even though they may not be statistically justified—in any situation in which their use assists the researcher in understanding his data and, by extension, the world around him.

17.2   Path Analysis

Path Analysis offers another graphic presentation of the interrelations among variables. It is based on regression analysis, but it can provide a more useful graphic picture of relationships among several variables than is possible through other means.

Path analysis is a *causal* model for understanding relationships between variables. It assumes that the values on one variable are caused by the values on another, so it is essential that independent and dependent variables be distinguished in path analysis.

By way of an introduction to path analysis, let's consider the simple case of two variables causally related. X is the independent variable and Y the dependent. We might describe this causal relationship by the graphic notation of Figure 17-7a. We may improve the communicative value of the diagram by adding to the arrow the standardized regression coefficient describing the strength of their empirical relationship, as shown in Figure 17-7b. This is called the *path coefficient* in path analysis.

In a sense, path analysis represents a closed system of analysis. Whereas the present example is based on the explanation of variance in variable Y, path analysis aims at explaining *all* of that variance. Clearly, however, X is probably not sufficient for that purpose. Since we know how much of the variance in Y is explained by X, however, it is possible to compute the *unexplained variance* as a residual. To close the analytical system, the path analyst posits a hypothetical variable that combines all the remaining explanatory variables. This variable (R) is added to the path diagram, as shown in Figure 17-7c.

Figure 17-7. Causal Relationship Between Two Variables

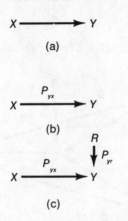

Figure 17-8. Path Diagram for Three Variables

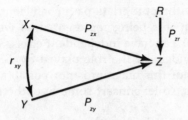

Clearly, the path analysis describing the relationship between only two variables is little more than a different presentation of the standardized regression coefficient describing their relationship. As additional variables are added to the model, however, the special value of path analysis becomes clearer. Note the example (Figure 17-8) in which independent variables X and Y are seen as causes of the dependent variable Z.

This latest diagram differs from the earlier one in several fashions. First, the notation P_{zx} represents the *partial* relationship between Z and X with Y held constant. The notation P_{zy} represents the partial relationship between Z and Y with X held constant. In other words, the arrow connecting X and Z represents the causal effect of X on Z *independent* of the effects of Y, and so forth.

Second, note that the relationship between the two independent variables has also been indicated in the diagram. This arrow has two heads, to indicate that there is no causal direction implied in the relationship. Finally, P_{zr} still represents the hypothetical relationship between Z and all the residual explanatory variables.

The power of path analysis becomes even clearer when we add a new variable—an intervening variable between the independent variables and the dependent variable. For this purpose, let's designate the independent variables as X and Y, the intervening variable as I, and the dependent variable as Z (see Figure 17-9).

Figure 17-9. Path Diagram for Four Variables

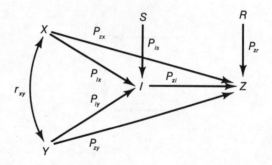

This more complex example provides even more paths between variables. To begin, both X and Y are believed to causally affect I, and these are represented as paths with appropriate path coefficients. And I is believed to causally affect Z, with this being represented as well. At the same time, however, both X and Y can have independent effects on Z—independent of each other and independent of the role played by I.

The interpretation of this diagram is not possible without knowing the actual path coefficients, so let's insert some hypothetical figures (see Figure 17-10).

In the latest diagram, it is clear that the strongest predictor of Z is the intervening variable, I. Looking further in the diagram, we note a strong partial relationship between Y and I, and, at the same time, a rather weak partial relationship between Y and Z. This suggests that Y primarily affects Z through the intervening variable. X on the other hand, shows a rather strong direct relationship with Z, with a weaker relationship between X and

Figure 17-10. Hypothetical Path Diagram

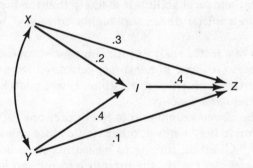

I. Here we would conclude that X affects Z directly more than working that effect through the intervening variable.

Even this rather simple example should indicate the general complexity of path analysis. As additional variables are added to the diagram, its interpretation becomes more difficult. At the same time, the reader should have noted a striking similarity between the interpretation of a path diagram and the use of the multivariate elaboration model. In the latter case, the researcher compares partial tables to determine the effect of control variables on the initially observed association between two other variables. The path analyst does this through the use of standardized regression coefficients arranged in a logical schematic. The basic logic is the same.

17.3   Factor Analysis

Factor Analysis represents a different approach to multivariate analysis. Its statistical basis is sufficiently complex and sufficiently different from the foregoing discussions as to suggest a very general discussion here.

Factor analysis is used to discover patterns among the variations in values of several variables. This is done essentially through the generation of artificial dimensions (factors) that correlate highly with several of the real variables and that are independent of one another.

Let's suppose for the moment that our data file contains several indicators of respondents' prejudice. Each of the questionnaire items should provide some indication of prejudice, but none of them would give a perfect indication. All of these items, moreover, should be highly intercorrelated empirically. In a factor analysis of the survey data, it is likely that an artificial dimension would be created that would be highly correlated with each of the items measuring prejudice. Each respondent would essentially receive a value on that artificial dimension, and the value assigned would provide a good predictor of responses given to the questionnaire items on prejudice.

Suppose now that the same questionnaire contained several indicators of respondents' mathematical ability. It is likely that the factor analysis would also generate an artificial dimension highly correlated with each of those items.

The output of a factor analysis program consists of columns representing the several factors (artificial dimensions) generated from the observed relations among variables plus the correlations between each variable and each factor—called the *factor loadings*.

Pursuing the above example, it is likely that one factor would more or less represent "prejudice" while another would more or less represent "mathematical ability." Questionnaire items measuring prejudice would have high loadings on (correlations with) the prejudice factor and low loadings on the mathematical ability factor. Questionnaire items measuring mathematical ability would have just the opposite pattern.

In practice, however, factor analysis does not proceed in this fashion. Rather, the variables are input to the program, and a series of factors with appropriate factor loadings are the output. The researcher must then determine the meaning of a given factor on the basis of those variables that load highly on it. The generation of factors, however, has no reference to the meaning of variables, only their empirical associations. Two criteria are taken into account: (1) a factor must explain a relatively large proportion of the variance found in the study variables; and (2) every factor must be more or less independent of every other factor.[1]

There are a number of advantages in factor analysis. First, it is an efficient method for discovering predominant patterns among a large number of variables. Instead of the researcher being forced to compare countless correlations —simple, partial, and multiple—to discover those patterns, factor analysis can be used for this task.

Second, factor analysis presents data in a form that can be interpreted by the reader and/or researcher. For a given factor, the reader can easily discover the variables loading highly on it, thus noting clusters of variables. Or, he can easily discover which factors a given variable is or is not loaded highly on.

Factor analysis has disadvantages as well. First, as noted above, factors are generated without any regard to substantive meaning. Often the researcher will find factors producing very high loadings for a group of substantively disparate variables. He might find, for example, that prejudice and religiosity have high positive loadings on a given factor with education having an equally high negative loading. Surely the three variables are highly correlated, but what does the factor represent? All too often, inexperienced researchers will be led into naming such factors as "religio-prejudicial lack of education," or with a similarly nonsensical name.

Second, factor analysis is often criticized on basic philosophical grounds. Recall an earlier discussion which stated that to be legitimate an hypothesis must be disconfirmable. If the researcher is unable to specify the conditions

---

[1] *Note:* This is not true of all factor analytical methods (for example, *oblique* solutions).

under which his hypothesis would be disproven, his hypothesis is in reality either a tautology or useless. In a sense, factor analysis suffers this defect. No matter what data are input, factor analysis produces a solution in the form of factors. Thus if the researcher were asking "Are there any patterns among these variables," the answer will always be "yes." This fact must also be taken into account in evaluating the results of factor analysis. The generation of factors by no means insures meaning.

My personal view of factor analysis is the same as presented in regard to other complex modes of analysis. It can be an extremely useful tool for the survey researcher. Its use should be encouraged whenever such activity may assist the researcher in his understanding of a body of data. As in all cases, however, the researcher must maintain an awareness that such tools are only tools and never magical solutions.

17.4 Smallest-Space Analysis

Smallest-space analysis (SSA) is rather different from the previously discussed methods of multivariate analysis; and, while it is still relatively new, it appears to hold considerable potential for the understanding of survey data.

Smallest-space analysis is based on the correlations between variables. Any measure of association may be used for this purpose, although we shall use Pearson's r in the examples to follow. Let's begin with a simple correlation matrix describing the associations among variables: A, B, and C (Table 17-1).

Table 17-1

	A	B	C
A	x	.8	.2
B		x	.5
C			x

Now let's plot these three variables as points on a plane, letting the distance between two points represent the *inverse* of the correlation between the two variables. That is, if two variables are highly correlated, they will be close together; if they are weakly correlated, they will be farther apart. The following diagram would satisfy this design.

$$A \quad B \qquad C$$

Since A and B are the most highly correlated variables, they have been placed relatively close together. The next highest correlation is between B and C, and the distance between these two points is the next shortest.

Finally, the correlation between A and C is the weakest of the three correlations, and the distance between A and C is the longest distance in the diagram.

Now let's enlarge our correlation matrix by adding variable D (Table 17-2).

Table 17-2

	A	B	C	D
A	x	.8	.2	.1
B		x	.5	.3
C			x	.9
D				x

It is still possible to plot these four points in such a fashion that the distance between two points corresponds to the inverse of the correlation between the two variables. It should be noted, however, that the distances do not *equal* the inverse of the correlations. The metric distances are irrelevant, thus SSA is referred to as a *nonmetric* technique. However, the *rank order* of distances between points should be the inverse of the rank order of correlations. The diagram in Figure 17-11 would satisfy the latest correlation matrix.

Figure 17-11. Smallest Space Analysis: Four Variables

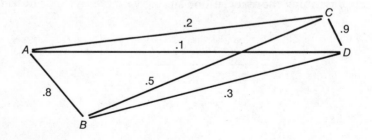

To clarify the new diagram, the points have been connected by lines, which in turn have been labeled with the correlations between the pairs of variables. An examination of the diagram will indicate that the longest distance (AD) corresponds to the weakest correlation. The shortest distance (CD) corresponds to the strongest correlation. The same is true for all other distances and correlations. (An understanding of plane geometry will help to explain how the diagram was constructed.)

Many readers will have already realized that there are some correlation matrices that could not be represented in accordance with the rules laid down. This is especially true as more and more variables are added. Given such a situation, SSA permits the researcher to move in two different directions.

First, SSA is not limited to two dimensions (although this textbook essentially is). Like multiple regressions, SSA can employ an unlimited number of geometric dimensions. As a general guideline, n variables can be plotted perfectly in SSA format within n-1 dimensions. Thus, any two variables can be plotted on a line, any three can be plotted on a plane, any four can be plotted in three dimensions, and so forth. As we have seen in other contexts, however, such liberties can lead the researcher into uninterpretable situations.

The second solution to this problem lies in the familiar area of compromise. Perhaps the researcher cannot plot six variables perfectly within two dimensions (which would be easily read), but he may be able to come close. Thus, it may be possible to plot the points in such a manner that they more or less satisfy the correspondence of rankings between correlations and distances.

At this point, and with the addition of many variables generally, hand tabulations and hand-drawn diagrams become too difficult. But this is the sort of task that the computer handles easily. Computer programs now exist to generate SSA diagrams from an input in the form of a correlation matrix. The researcher must specify the number of dimensions desired in his solution, and the computer works on that basis. In addition to the diagram, moreover, the computer provides a summary statistic called the *coefficient of alienation*. While this statistic has no commonsensible interpretation, it represents the extent to which the SSA diagram violates the rules of correspondence between distances and correlations. The lower the coefficient, the better the fit of the diagram to the rules.

The computer output from an SSA program will look something like the configuration shown in Figure 17-12.

Figure 17-12. Sample Smallest-Space Analysis Results—Hypothetical

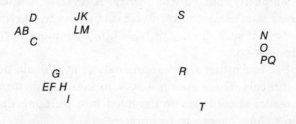

Since each of the letters in this diagram represents a survey variable, the diagram would be interpreted in terms of the observed clustering of variables. For example, we note that variables *J, K, L,* and *M* are closely clustered, and *A-B-C-D* forms another cluster, with both of these clusters being rather distant from the cluster *N-O-P-Q*.

The reader will note from the previous section of this chapter that SSA is quite similar to factor analysis, and it is sometimes referred to as a nonmetric factor analysis.

Summary

This chapter has touched on a few of the more complex modes of analysis appropriate to survey data. I have attempted to present each of these within the same general logical perspective that informed the discussion of the elaboration model. In some cases, the logical parallels are quite clear.

Hopefully, the reader will now have a little better understanding of the variety of analytical techniques available to the survey researcher. The present discussion has been far from exhaustive. Numerous other methods have not been discussed, and more are being developed all the time.

I would encourage researchers to experiment with any or all of these techniques. Much is to be gained from the use of several different techniques on the same body of data, permitting a comparison of the conclusions to be drawn from each. I believe this procedure will best satisfy the researcher's basic goal of understanding the nature of his data.

I have made no attempt to conceal my personal biases in the area of survey analysis. I have grave reservations about many of the complex modes of analysis, but these do not apply to the methods themselves, only to the ways they are often used. Survey analysis is an extremely difficult skill to acquire; it requires great logical sophistication, a mass of practical experience, and a continuing willingness to spend hours, weeks, or years in the full understanding of a set of empirical data.

Many inexperienced researchers complain that the elaboration model, using contingency tables, is a difficult method of analysis. There are no clear guidelines for interpreting elaboration table results. I agree with this conclusion completely. Some of the more complex summary techniques offer the illusion of simplicity, but not the reality. A regression equation or a factor loading seems much simpler to interpret, and the inexperienced researcher may conclude that such devices provide him with more truth per man-hour. This is pure illusion.

It is not so much that elaboration analysis is difficult, but that scientific analysis is difficult. There are no easy solutions to this problem, only hard ones. The reader should not be deceived into thinking that any mode of analysis can reduce science to technology.

Additional Readings

Borgatta, Edgar F., (ed.), *Sociological Methodology, 1969* (San Francisco: Jossey-Bass, Inc., Publishers, 1969), esp. chaps. 1 and 2 on path analysis.

Ezekiel, Mordecai, and Karl A. Fox, *Methods of Correlation and Regression Analysis* (New York: John Wiley & Sons, Inc., 1967).

Harmon, Harry H., *Modern Factor Analysis* (Chicago: University of Chicago Press, 1967).

18.1 Some Basic Considerations

Audience
Form and Length of Report
Aim of the Report

18.2 Organization of the Report

Purpose and Overview
Review of the Literature
Study Design and Execution
Analysis and Interpretation

18.3 Guidelines for Reporting
Analyses

Chapter Eighteen
The Reporting of Survey Research

Thus far in this book, we have considered the variety of activities that comprise the *doing* of a survey. Now we turn to an often neglected subject: reporting the survey to others. Unless the survey is properly communicated, all the efforts devoted to the preceding steps will go for naught.

Before proceeding further on this topic, I should suggest one absolutely basic guideline. Good social scientific reporting requires good English (unless you are writing in a foreign language). Whenever we ask the "figures to speak for themselves," they tend to remain mute. Whenever we use unduly complex terminology or construction, communication is reduced. Every researcher should read and reread (at approximately three-month intervals) an excellent small book by William Strunk, Jr., and E. B. White, *The Elements of Style.* If he does this faithfully, and if even 10 percent of the contents rub off, he stands a rather good chance of making himself understood and his findings perhaps appreciated.

Scientific reporting has several functions, and it is a good idea to keep these in mind. First, the report communicates to an audience a body of specific data and ideas. The report should provide those specifics clearly and with sufficient detail to permit an informed evaluation. Second, the scientific report should be viewed as a contribution to the general body of scientific knowledge. While remaining appropriately humble, the social scientist should always regard his research report as an addition to what we know about social behavior. Finally, the report should serve the function of stimulating and directing further inquiry.

18.1 Some Basic Considerations

Despite these general guidelines, different reports serve different purposes. A report appropriate for one purpose might be wholly inappropriate for another. This section of the chapter deals with some of the basic considerations in this regard.

Audience

Before drafting his report, the researcher must ask himself who he hopes will read it. Normally, he should make a distinction between fellow scientists and laymen. If written for the former, he may make certain assumptions as to their existing knowledge and may perhaps summarize certain points rather than explaining them in detail. Similarly, he may appropriately use more technical language than would be appropriate for an audience of laymen.

At the same time, the researcher should remain always aware that any science is composed of factions or cults. Terms and assumptions acceptable to his immediate colleagues may only confuse other scientists. This applies with regard to substance as well as techniques. The sociologist of religion writing for a general sociology audience, for example, should explain previous findings in more detail than would be necessary if he were addressing an audience of other sociologists of religion.

Form and Length of Report

I should begin this subsection by saying that my comments apply both to written and verbal reports. These two forms, however, will affect the nature of the report.

It is useful to think about the variety of reports that might result from a research project. To begin, the researcher may wish to prepare a short *research note* for publication in an academic or technical journal. Such reports should be approximately one to five pages in length (double-spaced, typed) and should be concise and direct. In a short amount of space, the researcher will not be able to present the state of the field in any detail, and his methodological notes must be somewhat abbreviated as well. Basically, he should tell the reader why he feels a brief note is justified by his findings, and then tell what those findings are.

Often, researchers must prepare reports for the sponsors of their research. These may vary greatly in length, of course. In preparing such a report, however, the researcher should bear in mind the audience for the report— scientific or lay—and their reasons for sponsoring the project in the first place. It is both bad politics and bad manners to bore the sponsor with research findings that have no interest or value to him. At the same time, it may be useful to summarize the ways in which the research has advanced basic scientific knowledge (if it has).

Working papers or monographs are another form of research reporting. Especially in a large and complex project, it will be useful for the researcher to obtain comments on his analysis and the interpretation of his data. A working paper constitutes a tentative presentation with an implicit request for comments. Working papers can also vary in length, and they may present all of the research findings of the project or only a portion of them. Since the researcher's professional reputation is not at stake in a working paper, he should feel free to present tentative interpretations that he cannot altogether justify—identifying them as such and asking for evaluations.

Many research projects result in papers delivered at professional meetings. Often, these serve the same purpose as working papers. The researcher is able to present findings and ideas of possible interest to his colleagues and ask for their comments. Although the length of professional papers may vary depending on the organization of the meetings, the reader is strongly encouraged to say too little rather than too much. Whereas a working paper may ramble somewhat through a variety of tentative conclusions, conference participants should not be forced to sit through a verbal unveiling of the same. Interested listeners can always ask for more details later, and uninterested ones can gracefully escape.

Probably the most popular research report is the article published in an academic journal. Again, lengths vary and the researcher should examine the lengths of articles previously published by the journal in question. As a rough guide, however, 25 typed pages is as good as any. A subsequent section on the organization of the report is primarily based on the structure of a journal article, so I shall say no more at this point, except to indicate that student term papers should be written on this model. As a general rule, a term paper that would make a good journal article would also make a good term paper.

A book, of course, represents the most prestigious form of research report. It has all the advantages of the working paper—length, detail—but it should be a more polished document. Since the publication of research findings as a book gives those findings an appearance of greater substance and worth, the researcher has a special obligation to his audience. Although he will still hope to receive comments from his colleagues, possibly leading him to revise his ideas, he must realize that other readers may be led to accept his findings uncritically.

Aim of the Report

Earlier in this book, we considered the different purposes of survey research projects. In preparing his report, the researcher should keep these same differences in mind.

Some reports may focus primarily on the *exploration* of a topic of interest. Inherent in this aim is the tentativeness and incompleteness of the conclusions. The researcher should clearly indicate to his audience the exploratory aim of the study and point to the shortcomings of the particular project. An important aspect of an exploratory report is to point the way to more refined research on the topic.

Most studies have a *descriptive* purpose, and the research reports from such studies will have a descriptive element. The researcher should carefully distinguish for the reader those descriptions that apply only to the sample and those that are inferred to the population. Whenever inferential descriptions are to be made, the researcher should give his audience some indication of the probable range of error in those descriptions.

Many reports have an *explanatory* aim; the researcher wishes to point to causal relationships among variables. Depending on the probable audience for his report, the researcher should carefully delineate the rules of explanation that lie behind his computations and conclusions; and, as in the case of description, he must give his readers some guide to the relative certainty of his conclusions.

Finally, some research reports may have the aim of *proposing action.* For example, the researcher of prejudice may wish to suggest ways in which prejudice may be reduced, on the basis of his research findings. This aim often presents knotty problems for the researcher, as his own values and orientations may interfere with his proposals. While it is perfectly legitimate for his proposals to be motivated by personal values, he must insure that the specific actions he proposes are warranted by his data. Thus, he should be especially careful to spell out the logic by which he moves from empirical data to proposed action.

18.2   Organization of the Report

Although the organization of reports differs somewhat on the basis of form and purpose, it is possible to suggest a general format for presenting research data. The following comments apply most directly to a journal article, but with some modification they apply to most forms of research reports.

Purpose and Overview

It is always helpful to the reader if the researcher begins with a brief statement of the purpose of the study and the main findings of the analysis. In a journal article, this may sometimes be accomplished in the form of an abstract.

Some researchers find this difficult to do. For the researcher, his analysis may have involved considerable detective work, with important findings revealing themselves only as a result of imaginative deduction and data manipulation. He may wish, therefore, to lead the reader through the same exciting process, chronicling the discovery process with a degree of suspense and surprise. To the extent that this form of reporting gives an accurate picture of the research process, I feel it has considerable instructional value. Nevertheless, many readers may not be interested in following the entire research account, and not knowing the purpose and general conclusions in advance may make it difficult for them to understand the significance of the study.

An old forensic dictum says: "Tell them what you're going to tell them; tell them; and tell them what you told them." Researchers would do well to follow this dictum in the preparation of research reports.

Review of the Literature

Since every research report should be placed in the context of the general body of scientific knowledge, it is important for the researcher to indicate where his report fits in that picture. Having presented the general purpose of his study, he should then proceed to bring the reader up to date on the previous research in the area, pointing to general agreements and disagreements among the previous researchers.

In some cases, the researcher may wish to challenge previously accepted ideas. He should carefully review the studies that have led to the acceptance of those ideas, and then indicate the factors that have not been previously considered or the logical fallacies present in the previous research.

When the researcher is concerned to resolve a disagreement among previous researchers, he should organize his review of the literature around the opposing points of view. He should summarize the research supporting one view, then summarize the research supporting the other, and finally suggest the reasons for the disagreement.

To an extent, the researcher's review of the literature serves a bibliographic function for readers, indexing the previous research on a given topic. This can be overdone, however, and the researcher should avoid an opening paragraph that runs three pages, mentioning every previous study in the field. The comprehensive bibliographic function can best be served by a bibliography at the end of the report, and the review of the literature should focus only on those studies that have direct relevance to the present study.

Study Design and Execution

A research report containing interesting findings and conclusions can be very frustrating when the reader is unable to determine the methodological design and execution of the study. The worth of all scientific findings depends heavily on the manner in which the data were collected and analyzed.

In reporting the design and execution of a survey research project, the researcher should always include the following: the population, the sampling frame, the sampling method, the sample size, the data collection method, the completion rate, and the method of data processing and analysis. The experienced researcher is able to report these details in a rather short space, without omitting anything required for his reader's evaluation of the study.

Analysis and Interpretation

Having set the study in the perspective of previous research and having described the design and execution of it, the researcher should then proceed to present his data. The following major section will provide further guidelines in this regard. For now, a few general comments are in order.

The presentation of data, the manipulations of those data, and the researcher's interpretations should be integrated into a logical whole. It is frustrating to the reader to discover a collection of seemingly unrelated analyses and findings with a promise that all the loose ends will be tied together later on in the report. Every step in the analysis should make sense—at the time it is taken. The researcher should present his rationale for a particular analysis, present the data relevant to it, interpret the results, and then indicate where that result leads next.

Summary and Conclusions

Following the forensic dictum mentioned earlier, it is essential to summarize the research report. The researcher should avoid reviewing every specific finding, but he should review all of the significant ones, pointing once more to their general significance.

The report should conclude with a statement of what the researcher has discovered about his subject matter and where future research might be directed. A quick review of recent journal articles will probably indicate a very high frequency of the concluding statement: "It is clear that much more research is needed." This is probably always a true conclusion, but it is of little value unless the researcher can offer pertinent suggestions as to the nature of that future research. He should review the particular shortcomings of his own study and suggest ways in which those shortcomings might be avoided by future researchers.

18.3   Guidelines for Reporting Analyses

The presentation of data analyses should be such as to provide a maximum of detail without being cluttered. The researcher can accomplish this best by continually examining the following aims.

Data should be presented in such a way as to permit recomputations by the reader. In the case of percentage tables, for example, the reader should be able to collapse categories and recompute the percentages. He should be given sufficient information as to permit him to percentage the table in the opposite direction from the researcher's presentation.

All aspects of the analysis should be described in sufficient detail to permit a secondary analyst to replicate the analysis from the same body of data. This means that he should be able to create the same indexes and scales, produce the same tables, arrive at the same regression equations, obtain the same factors and factor loadings, and so forth. This will seldom be done, of course, but if the report is presented in such a manner as to make it possible, the reader will be far better equipped to evaluate the report.

As a final guide to the reporting of methodological details, the reader should be in a position to completely replicate the entire study independently. He should be able to identify the same population, select the same size sample in the same manner, collect his data in the same manner, execute the same analyses, and see if he arrives at the same conclusions. It should be recalled from an earlier discussion that replicability is an essential norm of science generally. A single study does not prove a point; only a series of studies can begin to do this. Unless studies can be replicated, there can be no meaningful series of studies.

I have previously mentioned the importance of integrating data, analysis, and interpretations in the report. A more specific guideline can be offered in this regard. Tables, charts, and figures should be integrated into the text of the report—appearing near that portion of the text discussing them. Sometimes students describe their analyses in the body of the report, and place all the tables in an appendix at the end. This procedure greatly impedes the reader. As a general rule, it is best to (1) describe the purpose for presenting the table, (2) present it, and (3) review and interpret it.

Be explicit in drawing conclusions. Although research is typically conducted for the purpose of drawing general conclusions, the researcher should carefully note the specific basis for such conclusions. Otherwise he may lead his reader into accepting unwarranted conclusions.

Point to any qualifications or conditions warranted in the evaluation of conclusions. Typically, the researcher himself is in the best position to know the shortcomings and tentativeness of his conclusions, and he should give the reader the advantage of that knowledge. Failing to do this can misdirect future research and result in the waste of research funds.

I will conclude with a point made at the outset of this chapter, as it is extremely important. Research reports should be written in the best possible literary style. Writing clearly is easier for some people than for others, and it is always harder than writing poorly. The reader is again referred to the Strunk and White volume. Every researcher would do well to follow this procedure. Write. Read Strunk and White. Revise. Reread Strunk and White. Revise again. This will be a difficult and time-consuming endeavor, but so is science.

Summary

A perfectly designed, carefully executed, and brilliantly analyzed survey will be altogether worthless unless the researcher is able to communicate his findings to others. This chapter has attempted to provide some general and specific guidelines toward that end. The best guides are logic, clarity, and honesty. Ultimately, there is probably no substitute for practice.

Additional Readings

Strunk, William, Jr., and E. B. White, *The Elements of Style* (New York: The Macmillan Company, 1959).

H. W. Fowler, *A Dictionary of Modern English Usage* (New York: Oxford University Press, 1965).

Franklin, Billy J., and Harold W. Osborne (eds.), *Research Methods: Issues and Insights* (Belmont, Calif.: Wadsworth Publishing Co., Inc., 1971), part 8.

Part Four

Survey Research in Social and Scientific Perspective

For the most part, this book has been addressed to the skills of doing survey research. In that regard, every attempt has been made to place this particular research method within the context of science in general. The remainder of the book is stimulated by the belief that even this perspective is not sufficiently broad.

The prefatory remarks that opened the book took note of the ways in which survey research affects the lives of us all, whether *we* do surveys or not. It is not sufficient, therefore, to regard survey research solely as a neutral, scientific technique. Rather, the reader should be sensitized to the *social* context in which surveys are conducted.

Chapter 19 is devoted to a discussion of research ethics as they relate to survey methods. Following a discussion of general ethical guidelines in survey research, I have provided a series of illustrations of research situations in which ethical issues are involved. While few of the situations can be unequivocally regarded as ethical or unethical, I believe that a considered examination of them will make the reader more sensitive to the knotty ethical problems that survey researchers often face.

Chapter 20 reviews some of the different ways in which survey findings are used. In addition, the chapter provides a checklist of questions the reader might follow in examining and evaluating a survey report published by someone else. (And, of course, the checklist might serve as a reasonable guide in the preparation of such a report.)

Finally, Chapter 21 concludes the book with an overview of the scientific and social context of survey research. Hopefully, this short chapter will round out the reader's view of this single research method and better enable him to conduct and use meaningful research efforts.

Chapter Nineteen   The Ethics of Survey Research

A theoretically oriented textbook on survey research methods would provide the student with only an ideal image of how surveys should be conducted. In the previous portions of this book, I have sought to impress upon the reader that a variety of administrative and practical concerns impinge upon the research process, so that it is not always possible to live up to the ideal model. The enlightened survey researcher should be aware of those additional constraints and be able to balance administrative and scientific factors so as to arrive at the best possible compromise.

This chapter is addressed to another nonscientific constraint—the ethics of research. These ethical concerns are not a part of the scientific method. Nevertheless, they comprise a set of norms that scientists in most disciplines are obliged to follow. In many instances, these ethical norms directly conflict with scientific procedures, just as administrative concerns do. The researcher should, therefore, be aware of the possible conflicts so as to ultimately conduct the most scientific, ethical research.

Science in and of itself is amoral. The law of gravity and the correlation between education and prejudice are neither moral nor immoral. Scientists, however, are not amoral, and neither are those who may use the results of scientific inquiry. Thus, scientific research may be conducted and/or used for either moral or immoral purposes. And, of course, one man's morality is another man's immorality. These are lessons that the nuclear physicists learned a quarter of a century ago—lessons that social scientists are still learning today.

There is no way of insuring that all scientists will always be motivated by ethical concerns when they engage in scientific research. Nor is there any way to insure that scientific findings will be used only for ethical purposes. It is possible, however, to point to a set of more or less agreed upon ethical norms relating to the execution of research. This chapter will present some of the more common ethical problems that appear in survey research and will suggest ethical solutions to them that do not seriously endanger the "scientific" quality of the research itself.

19.1   Voluntary Participation

Survey research almost always represents an intrusion into the lives of people. The interviewer's knock on the door or the arrival of a questionnaire in the mail signals the beginning of an activity that the respondent has not requested and one that may require a significant portion of his time and energy. Moreover, the survey often requires the respondent to reveal personal information about himself—attitudes and personal characteristics—that may be unknown to his friends and associates. Yet survey research requires that the respondent reveal such information to a complete stranger.

Other professionals, such as physicians and lawyers, also require such information. Their requests may be justified, however, on the grounds that the information is required for them to serve the personal interests of the respondent. The survey researcher can seldom make this claim. Like the medical scientist, he can only argue that the research effort may ultimately help all mankind.

A major tenet of medical research ethics is that experimental participation must be *voluntary*. (Interestingly, the indictment of Nazi medical experimentation was based not so much on the cruelty of the experiments—such research is often unavoidably cruel—but on the fact that prisoners were forced to participate.) The same norm applies to survey research. No one should be forced to participate in a survey. This norm is far easier to accept in theory than to apply in practice, however.

Again, medical research provides a useful parallel. Many experimental drugs are tested on prisoners. In the most rigorously ethical cases, the prisoners are told the nature—and the possible dangers—of the experiment; they are told that participation is completely voluntary; and they are further instructed that they can expect no special rewards—such as early parole—for participation. Even under these conditions, it is often clear that volunteers are motivated by the belief that they will personally benefit from their cooperation.

When the instructor in an introductory sociology class asks his students to fill out a questionnaire that he hopes to analyze and publish, he should always impress upon them that their participation in the survey is completely voluntary. Even so, it should be clear that most students will fear that nonparticipation will somehow affect the grades they receive in the course. In such a case, the instructor should be especially sensitive to the implied sanctions, and make special provisions to obviate them. Perhaps he might leave the room while the questionnaires are completed and dropped in a box. Or, he might ask students to return the questionnaires by mail, or put them at a box near the door upon arriving at the next meeting of the course.

In this particular situation, the instructor should be encouraged, if it is appropriate, to involve his students in the processing and analysis of the data, thereby providing them with a learning experience valuable to them personally. They would, of course, receive appropriate credit in any published report on the study. (This should not be used as a method of obtaining cheap labor.)

Participation in surveys must be voluntary, but this goes directly against a scientific concern. If statistical techniques are to be used legitimately in the analysis of survey data, then every member of the random sample should participate. Even with less rigorous statistical plans, the researcher will desire a high completion rate in order to insure a reasonably representative sample. Thus, while the researcher cannot ethically require participation, he will typically do everything possible to obtain it.

In an interview survey, interviewers will typically be trained to persuade uncertain respondents. "It will only take a few minutes," "The results of the study will be valuable to people living in this area," and "May I come back at a more convenient time" are all important phrases in the interviewer's vocabulary. The fortunate research director will discover some interviewers who are more persuasive than others, and these will probably be assigned to follow up on the sample members who refused the initial request. (Experience has shown an eight-month-pregnant interviewer is more successful than the average in this regard.) Clearly the line between ethical persuasion and coercion is a fuzzy one.

In a mail survey, the researcher will normally execute follow-up mailings to those members of the sample who have not responded to earlier requests. Usually, the follow-up mailings are accompanied by special appeals for cooperation, and again the line between persuasion and coercion is not always clear.

19.2   No Harm to Respondents

Survey research should never injure the respondents who have volunteered to cooperate with the researcher. Perhaps the clearest instance of this norm in practice concerns the revealing of information that would embarrass the respondent or endanger his home life, friendships, job, and so forth. This is discussed more fully in the next section.

It is also possible for the respondent to be harmed in the course of an interview, however, and the researcher should be aware of this and guard against it. Even with the most professional (that is, neutral) interviewer, the respondent may feel extremely uncomfortable about reporting deviant behavior, attitudes he feels are unpopular, or demeaning personal characteristics such as low income, the receipt of welfare payments, and the like.

Often, surveys force the respondent to face aspects of himself that he does not normally consider. In retrospect, a certain past behavior may appear to him as unjust or immoral. The interview, then, may be the source of a continuing personal agony for him. Perhaps he will begin thinking that he is not as religious as he feels he ought to be, and this will continue to bother him.

There is no way in which the researcher can insure against all these possibilities. At the same time, some questionnaire items are more likely to produce such reactions than others, and the researcher should be sensitive to this. If a given item seems likely to produce unpleasant reactions for the respondent, the researcher should have the firmest scientific grounds for asking it. Unless it is vital to his research aims, he should not ask it. If the item is both essential and sensitive, then he will find himself in an ethical nether world and may himself be forced to do some personal agonizing.

Although it often goes unrecognized, respondents can be harmed by the analysis and reporting of data. Every now and then, respondents read the books published from the surveys they participated in. A reasonably sophisticated respondent will be able to locate himself in the various indexes and tables. Having done this, he may find himself characterized—though not identified by name—as bigoted, unpatriotic, irreligious, and so forth. At the very least, this is likely to trouble him and threaten his self-image. Yet the whole purpose of the research project may be to explain why some people are prejudiced while others are not.

The present author conducted a survey some years back of church-women. Ministers in a sample of churches were asked to distribute questionnaires to a specified sample of members, collect them, and return them to the research office. One of these ministers read through the questionnaires from his sample before returning them, and then proceeded to deliver a hell-fire and brimstone sermon to his congregation, saying that many of them were atheists and going to hell. Even though he could not know or identify the respondents who gave particular responses, it seems certain that many respondents were personally harmed by the action.

Like voluntary participation, not harming respondents is an easy norm to accept in theory, but it is often difficult to insure in practice. Sensitivity to the issue and experience with its applications, however, should improve the researcher's batting average.

19.3   Anonymity and Confidentiality

The clearest case involving the protection of the respondent's interests and well-being concerns the protection of his identity. If revealing his survey responses would injure him in any way, adherence to this norm becomes all the more important. Two techniques—*anonymity* and *confidentiality*—assist the researcher in this regard, although the two are often confused.

Anonymity

A respondent may be considered *anonymous* when the researcher himself cannot identify a given response with a given respondent. This means that an interview survey respondent can never be considered anonymous, since an interviewer collected the information from an identifiable respondent. (This assumes that standard sampling methods were followed.) An example of anonymity would be the mail survey in which no identification numbers are put on the questionnaire prior to its return to the research office.

Of course, anonymity complicates any follow-up plans for increasing response rates. If the researcher does not know who among his sample have failed to reply, he cannot contact them only. As an alternative, however, he could mail again to all members of the original sample, asking those who had already replied to ignore the second appeal; or he could employ the postcard technique discussed in Chapter 8.

Despite the difficulties attendant upon insuring anonymity, there are some situations in which the researcher may be advised to pay the necessary price. In a recent study of drug use among university students, the researchers decided that they specifically did not want to know the identity of respondents. There were two reasons for this. First, they felt that honestly assuring anonymity would increase the likelihood and accuracy of responses. Second, they did not want to be in the position of being asked for the names of drug offenders. In the few instances in which respondents volunteered their names, such information was immediately obliterated on the questionnaires.

Confidentiality

In a *confidential* survey, the researcher is able to identify a given person's responses but essentially promises that he will not. In an interview survey, for example, the researcher would be in a position to make public the income reported by a given respondent, but the respondent is assured that this will not be done.

There are a number of techniques whereby the researcher can better insure his performance on this guarantee. To begin, interviewers and others with access to respondent identifications should be trained in their ethical responsibilities. As soon as possible, all names and/or addresses should be removed from questionnaires and replaced by identification numbers. A master identification file would be created linking numbers to names—to permit the later correction of missing or contradictory information—but this file would not be available except for legitimate purposes.

Whenever a survey is confidential rather than anonymous, it is the responsibility of the researcher to make that fact clear to the respondent. The use of the term "anonymous" to mean "confidential" should never be tolerated.

Inferred Identity

Even in a truly anonymous survey, it is sometimes possible to identify a given respondent. This is particularly true with open-ended questions. If the respondent lists his occupation (or his father's occupation) as "President of ABC Company," the cat is out of the bag. Sometimes the multivariate analysis of closed-ended questions will permit the identification of a given respondent.

Since this is always a possibility in any survey, anonymous or not, the researcher cannot rule it out altogether. He should never attempt to make such identifications, however, and should insure that his research workers do not make such attempts. And, moreover, he should never report aggregated data in such a way that will permit readers to make such identifications. It is for this reason that the United States Census Bureau will not report aggregated data containing fewer than 15 cases per cell in a table.

Hidden Identification

Occasionally some researchers conduct surveys in which respondents are insured anonymity when in fact they are identifiable. Sometimes the return address of the research office contains a "box number" with that number being different for each respondent. On occasions, researchers have entered identification numbers under the stamps placed on return envelopes. Probably some have written numbers with lemon juice.

I suspect that in virtually all cases—and they are probably few—the researchers have attempted to maintain the confidentiality of the data and have made no attempt to harm respondents. (It is my impression that those researchers most convinced of their personal morality are the most willing to engage in this practice.)

Whatever the motivations or scientific value, I am personally repelled by such practices and feel they should not be tolerated. If a survey is confidential rather than anonymous, the respondent should be so informed.

Finally, all surveys should be at least confidential.

19.4   Identifying Purpose and Sponsor

Often the researcher faces the dilemma that knowledge of his survey's purpose and/or sponsor may affect the answers respondents will provide. In more extreme cases, it may affect the likelihood of cooperation. If the interviewer introduces herself as being engaged in a study of prejudice, it stands to reason that the respondent will be rather careful not to sound prejudiced. Or if the study is identified as being sponsored by the welfare office, a recipient's responses are likely to be modified somewhat to guard against the loss of benefits. If the local university is in particularly bad repute among the population—say, as a result of student demonstrations—a university-sponsored study may face severe opposition and produce a low completion rate.

Almost any specification of purpose and/or sponsor will have some effect on completion rates and on the answers given by those who participate. These considerations, of course, affect the scientific quality of the data and the conclusions to be drawn from their analysis. Yet, deceiving the respondent as to the study's purpose and/or sponsor raises an ethical issue.

It is my general feeling that the researcher is obliged to be honest with his respondents with regard to both the sponsor and the auspices of the study. If the study is being conducted by a university research office on behalf of the state government, all this should be spelled out in the interviewer's introduction (or in the introductory letter accompanying a self-administered questionnaire). Moreover, I am especially wary of fictitious organizations—research office names made up for purposes of a particular study.

It should be noted that honesty in this regard has a practical value as well as being more ethical. Whenever the researcher attempts to deceive his respondents as to the sponsor or auspices of a study, he runs the risk that the truth will become known during the study. In such a case, there is a good chance that the study will receive such notoriety as to suffer more than one openly conducted by an unpopular research agency or sponsor.

Honesty with regard to purpose is more difficult, as a given survey will often serve a variety of analytical purposes. Thus, the researcher cannot be completely honest with respondents since he cannot fully anticipate the uses that the survey will serve. And, of course, a precise statement of the primary purposes of the study will probably affect responses more than will disclosure of the sponsor.

In view of these concerns, I tend to be somewhat more liberal than in the case of sponsorship. The following guidelines seem appropriate. (1) The researcher should tell nothing about the purpose of the study that is likely to affect the reliability of responses. (2) At the same time, he should tell respondents whatever he can about purposes where such information will not likely affect responses. (3) Explanations of purpose should be kept general rather than specific. (4) The researcher should *never* offer fictitious reasons for the study.

19.5   Analysis and Reporting

Just as the researcher has ethical obligations to respondents, so he has ethical obligations to his readers in the scientific community.

As these latter norms are not often considered in the ethical realm, a few comments are in order.

In any rigorous survey, the researcher should be more familiar with the technical shortcomings of the study than anyone else, and he should make these shortcomings known to his readers. If, near the conclusion of the study, he discovers that a particular subset of the population was omitted from sampling, he should disclose this fact. If he believes that several respondents misunderstood a questionnaire item, he should apprise the reader of this fact. Any defect in the study design or analysis that will have any possible effect on the conclusions drawn should be noted openly.

Negative findings should be reported if they are at all related to the analysis being reported. There is an unfortunate myth in scientific reporting that only positive discoveries are worth reporting (and journal editors are sometimes guilty of this as well). From the standpoint of the scientific community, however, it is often as important to know that two variables are not related to each other as to know that they are. Sometimes—as in *The American Soldier*—the lack of expected correlations can be even more useful. Researchers must learn that there is no embarrassment inherent in nonrelationships.

Similarly, researchers should not fall victim to the temptation to "save face" by describing empirical findings as the products of preplanned analytical strategy when this is not the case. It is simply a fact of life that many findings arrive unexpectedly—even though they seem patently obvious in retrospect. Embroidering such events with descriptions of fictitious hypotheses is both dishonest and tends to mislead inexperienced researchers into thinking that all scientific inquiry is preplanned.

If an unexpected association between variables appears, it should be presented as unexpected. If the entire analytical strategy was radically restructured during the course of the study, the reader should be let in on the secret. This is especially beneficial since other researchers should be aware of the fact that another—seemingly functional—strategy is not appropriate to the subject matter. Science generally progresses through honesty and is retarded by ego-based deception.

19.6   Ethics—Relevant Illustrations

The ethics of survey research—or of any scientific research—are not clear-cut. In this chapter, I have pointed to relatively few firm guidelines, and most of those are subject to debate, since they represent my own personal orientations.

My primary concern has been to make the reader more *sensitive* to ethical issues in survey research. It will be far more important if the reader is able to recognize ethical considerations in real research situations than if he simply memorizes a set of ethical norms. With this in mind, the chapter concludes with the description of several research situations—most of them real, some hypothetical—which I believe have no clearcut solutions, but I hope that the reader will be able to recognize the ethical issues in them.

1. An instructor in introductory sociology asks his students to complete questionnaires that he will then use for the analysis of a research problem of interest to him.

2. In a proposed study of attitudes among new law school graduates, an agreement is made with the state bar association to include a questionnaire in the bar exam materials. Completion of the questionnaire will be a requirement for licensing.

3. The university contracts to conduct a survey for the local city government. Since the city government is in general disfavor with the public, interviewers are instructed to say only that they are doing the study for a group of university researchers.

4. The researcher's analysis of his data has produced so many surprises that his initial hypotheses have been wholly displaced by the findings that have appeared in his hectic and often confused analysis. The final conclusions are such that he is ashamed for not having begun with hypotheses appropriate to them. To save face, he writes his report as though he had.

5. After an interview study of deviant behavior, law enforcement officials demand that the investigator identify for them those respondents who reported participating in looting during a recent riot. Rather than be an accomplice after the fact, the investigator complies.

6. At the completion of his analysis, the researcher discovers that 25 of the 2,000 interviews were falsified by the interviewers. He chooses to ignore the fact in his report.

7. A person who was not selected in the sample for a survey contacts the researcher and insists on being interviewed. The interview is conducted, and the questionnaire is then discarded.

8. Researchers obtain a list of right-wing radicals they wish to study. Questionnaires are sent to this group with the explanation that they have been "selected at ramdom."

9. Race matching is considered essential for a study of racial prejudice. This means, however, that in the large city being studied, black interviewers will be working under generally poorer conditions than white interviewers.

10. *A college instructor administers an hour exam to both sections of his course. The overall performance of the two sections is essentially the same. The grades of one section are artificially lowered, however, and the instructor berates them for performing so poorly. His purpose is to test the effect of such berating. He then administers the same final exam to both sections, and he discovers that the unfairly berated section performs more poorly. His hypothesis is confirmed.*

11. *A researcher in higher education wishes to examine the effect of various background factors on academic achievement. To measure achievement, he obtains students' grade point averages from the university administration.*

12. *Respondents are assured that a questionnaire they are asked to complete is anonymous. In fact, a serial number has been placed inconspicuously on the questionnaire to permit the analysis of other information collected about the respondents from other sources.*

13. *In a study of sexual behavior, the investigator wants to overcome respondents' reluctance to report what they will consider deviant behavior. Thus, he uses the following item: "Everyone masturbates now and then; about how often do you masturbate?"*

14. *Respondents are told that a survey is being conducted simply to determine how people felt about a series of public issues. In fact, the researcher is interested in determining sources of opposition to a particular issue.*

15. *A researcher discovers that 85 percent of the university student body smoke marijuana regularly. Publication of this finding will probably create a furor in the community. Since he is not planning to analyze drug use in depth, he decides to ignore the finding.*

16. *A researcher is contracted to conduct a study and prepare a report for the sponsor regarding a particular topic. He finds the data provide an opportunity to examine a related issue, although one that the sponsor is not concerned with. He uses project funds to cover the costs of analysis and typing for a paper, which he then delivers to a professional association meeting.*

17. *To test the extent to which respondents may try to save face by expressing attitudes on matters they are wholly uninformed about, the researcher asks for attitudes regarding a fictitious issue.*

18. *A research questionnaire is circulated among students as part of their university registration packet. Although students are not told they must complete the questionnaire, the hope is that they will believe they must, thus insuring a higher completion rate.*

Summary and Conclusions

The requirements of *scientific* research sorely tax the researcher's imagination and ingenuity. Practical, administrative constraints further complicate matters by often ruling out the ideal research procedures. Ethical concerns are likely to place an additional burden on the researcher. Having discovered that he has neither the time nor the money to execute the best possible study, the researcher may arrive at a brilliant compromise that is both administratively feasible and scientifically sound only to discover that it violates ethical concerns.

As repeated throughout this book, good scientific research is often difficult; ethical, scientific research may be harder yet, but the researcher cannot afford to give up on any of these concerns. He must conduct research that is scientifically sound, administratively feasible, and ethically defensible. He must not hurt people in the attempt to help them.

Additional Readings

American Association for Public Opinion Research, "Code of Professional Ethics and Practices," printed in *Public Opinion Quarterly* (Fall 1960).

Sjoberg, Gideon, *Ethics, Politics, and Social Research* (Cambridge, Mass.: Schenkman Publishing Co., Inc., 1967).

Chapter Twenty   The Uses of Survey Research

This book began with the observation that survey research is one of the most widely used research methods in the social sciences today. This chapter will review some of the different uses to which surveys are put and suggest some guidelines for the use of survey data.

20.1   Common Types of Survey Uses

For the most part in this book, we have looked at survey research as it is used by academic social scientists. It serves as an effective tool for collecting and analyzing data that may help the scientist understand the world around him. It may be used for an original inquiry into a particular substantive area, and it is especially appropriate to careful replication of prior studies. In this regard, survey methods may be used in the academic quest for knowledge and understanding.

Other surveys, often conducted by university faculty, have a more directly practical orientation. With increasing frequency, governmental agencies—local, state, and federal—commission surveys aimed at collecting and analyzing data of immediate policy relevance. For example, a local government may commission a survey of its population for purposes of determining the local unemployment rate—possibly with the aim of obtaining federal funding to reduce unemployment. Sometimes, such a study may be formally initiated by the government agency and conducted on a contractual basis by university faculty members and/or a survey research center. In other instances, informal inquiries may indicate that a given faculty member sees general, theoretical implications in the data that might be collected, and he may initiate a proposal for funding of the survey. The data, then, are analyzed in such a manner as to meet the policy needs of the agency and also to elaborate on the theoretical concerns of the researcher.

Survey research methods are used very frequently for political purposes. Sometimes the mass media commission political polls during campaigns, hoping to recoup their expenditures through increased readership and, in turn, increased advertising revenues. Or, more frequently perhaps, political candidates commission political polls in order to determine how well they are doing overall and to gain a better understanding of their particular strengths and weaknesses. More than once, in recent years, an aspiring candidate for office has terminated his campaign on the basis of a poor showing in the political polls.

A great deal of survey research is done in connection with product marketing. Survey methods are fairly appropriate for obtaining insights into the probable consumer response to a new product or for learning more about the nature of consumer support for a competitor's product. More complex surveys in marketing research seek to understand the basic nature of consumption and purchasing patterns. As a general rule, the well-known national polling companies earn their financial support through consumer research and engage in public opinion polling only to achieve or maintain visibility. Political polls, in such cases, are similar to the "loss leader" in a supermarket.

20.2   Combining Survey Research with Other Methods

It has been repeated frequently throughout this book that survey research is only one method of social scientific inquiry. Some of the other methods have been touched on briefly from time to time. It bears repeating once more that wherever possible, survey should be used in conjunction with those other methods.

Every individual research method carries certain limitations as to the kinds of data, variables, and analytical approaches that it permits. Few interesting research problems, however, can adequately be examined within such constraints. Thus survey data should be supplemented with other forms of data whenever appropriate and possible.

Most social phenomena ought to be examined within an historical context. A cross-sectional survey of specialization among physicians, for example, will be more meaningful if the survey data are accompanied by data reporting the extent of specialization among physicians over time. A survey report on voting intentions in a given community would be more useful to the reader if accompanied by a report on the voting behavior of the community in previous elections.

By the same token, the researcher might do well to initiate a variety of research methods in examining a particular phenomenon. In studying the nature of religiosity among a group of church members, for example, he might administer a standardized, closed-ended questionnaire for one source of data. At the same time, he could conduct in-depth, unstructured interviews with a smaller sample of respondents from the group or engage in some participant observation among the group. These different methods would yield different types of data; and, taken together, they should provide a more comprehensive understanding of the phenomenon under study.

Because of the similarities of procedures, survey research and content analysis should be easily applied to many research problems. Following an interest in political decision making in a community, a researcher might conduct a survey of voters, seeking to learn their sources of information, and also conduct a content analysis of the local mass media.

Some hypotheses may be framed and initially tested in an experimental situation and then replicated by survey. Thus, the researcher might look for the sources of prejudiced views under rigorously controlled experimental conditions, thereby ruling out extraneous variables, and then examine the manner in which the observed effects are represented in the real world.

The list of possibilities could go on and on. Unfortunately, few researchers employ a variety of methods in their inquiries. Rather, they tend to develop a special expertise in a single method and then apply it to whatever research problem interests them. And increasingly, the single method used is survey research even when it is not the best possible method for the particular problem area.

20.3　　　　Multiple-Purpose Surveys

As hinted at previously, a given survey can serve more than one purpose. We have already noted how a university faculty member may conduct a survey under governmental funding for the dual purpose of providing policy-relevant data and examining more general, theoretical issues.

Frequently, a survey designed for a specific purpose carries a number of unrelated "riders." A person who is interested in obtaining only a single datum may persuade the project director to include a questionnaire item that will generate it. In the case of commercial polls, such riders may be added for a fixed fee per item, say $1,500 for a single questionnaire item. The person requesting the rider, then, obtains his information at a cost significantly less than an entire survey would have entailed, and, moreover, he will be in a position to analyze that single item in relation to any others collected in the same survey.

A given survey may serve several purposes after the fact as well. Survey data may be collected for a particular purpose, but the same data may be subjected to secondary analysis—for different purposes—by other researchers later on. As noted previously in this book, the development of data archives throughout the country have greatly facilitated this; and this capability represents one of the particular advantages of survey research.

20.4   The Ethical Use of Survey Data

It is by now an accepted adage that a scientist can seldom insure that the products of his research will be used only for good and moral purposes. J. Robert Oppenheimer, among others, has attested to this in physics, and it is true of all science. The scientist's dilemma in this regard is compounded by the scientific norm regarding the openness of data. Each scientist operates under a normative obligation to share his findings with the scientific community, which means sharing them with nonscientists as well.

Survey research findings and data can be put to uses that the original researcher might find immoral or misleading. Thus the political researcher may find that voters are particularly susceptible to a given emotional appeal. Such a finding is valuable to those who would understand political decision making from a scientific standpoint, but it might also be exploited by an unscrupulous political candidate. Or a researcher might find a given racial or ethnic group more likely to engage in a certain form of deviant, perhaps illegal, behavior. This too would be interesting from a scientific standpoint, but it could also serve as the basis for public discrimination against that group.

Somewhat differently, whereas the researcher is under a scientific obligation to make his data available for secondary analysis, he is in no position to control (or even monitor, perhaps) the quality of analysis to which they are subjected. Throughout this book, we have examined the various sampling and nonsampling errors to which survey data are subject. We have seen that a slight change in the wording of a questionnaire item can produce quite different responses. A well-reasoned interpretation of survey data usually requires time and careful scrutiny. Yet the original researcher who releases his data for secondary analysis will probably see them hastily analyzed and incorrectly reported at some point. This is especially likely if the substantive issues covered by the data are controversial.

All the above notwithstanding, data should be made available for secondary analyses. Moreover, it would seem unwise in the long run for the original researcher to exercise controls over the analyses of such data, for this would go against the openness of science. Indeed, a variety of analyses should be encouraged, even when the original researcher tends to disagree with the analytical approach proposed, or even the value orientations of the secondary analysts. The original researcher can partially guard against misinterpretations in the following ways, however.

First, he might retain total control over the data for a certain period of time. This is well accepted in practice. The original researcher has invested considerable time and money in the collection of his data, and it is quite just that he have the first opportunity to analyze and report them. His analyses should be extensive and careful. Not only should the grace period give him an opportunity to prepare the first reports from the data, but it should also permit him to gain a detailed understanding of his data. During this period, he should come to understand which of his questionnaire items provide good indicators of general concepts and which are defective. Before releasing the data for secondary analyses, he should prepare a methodological report on the study, indicating not only the manner in which the study was conducted, but also pointing to special strengths and weaknesses in the data.

Second, the original researcher might request that secondary analysts provide him with a copy of reports prepared from his data. This should not mean that the original researcher has veto power over publications, but that he should be aware of the uses being made of his data. A conscientious secondary analyst may delay publication until the original researcher has had an opportunity to react and to point out any possible misinterpretations of the data.

Finally, the original researcher may wish to challenge any serious misuses of his data in secondary analyses. It should be made clear that he can do this effectively only if he has taken advantage of the grace period to understand those data fully. Otherwise, he will read a report on his data, sense that the conclusions are incorrect, spend considerable time reanalyzing the data in an attempt to discover the shortcomings of the secondary analyses, and finally challenge the conclusions long after they have been either forgotten or fully accepted.

It should be clear that all this is more easily and effectively accomplished if the original researcher truly understands his data and has published a good methodological report. Finding an incorrect conclusion published by a secondary analyst, he will know immediately why it is incorrect, and he may be able to point to a section of his own methodological report which shows why such a conclusion would be unfounded. Spending all his time belatedly challenging secondary analysts, however, is unsatisfying from both scientific and professional standpoints.

In viewing and perhaps speaking to the uses and subsequent analyses of his data, the researcher should be careful to keep separate scientific and moral concerns, although he may address himself to both. If he feels that his own research findings are being used for immoral purposes, he should challenge such uses *on moral grounds*. If the uses or analyses are subject to scientific challenge, he should make his criticism within the logic of science. If both are appropriate, he may be more persuasive by using a scientific challenge. An example should illustrate this point.

For years, it has been widely believed that the black American family was generally matriarchal—dominated primarily by the wife-mother. This belief, moreover, has been substantiated by a variety of survey data, in which black respondents reported that the wives/mothers in their own families made the more important decisions and had the greatest power within the family.

For the most part, these data have been accepted at face value, with

discussions of them being in moral/philosophical terms. Antiblack conservatives have used the data to substantiate the belief that black American males
are inherently weak and submissive. Such supposed character flaws have
been used as explanations for the relatively deprived status of blacks in
American society. Liberals, on the other hand, have taken the data as an
indication of the ways in which the black American family has been weak-
ened by discrimination and, more specifically, by inhumane welfare regula-
tions, which often require that a father desert his family in order to obtain
government support for them. These opposing arguments have been expressed for years, without changing the opinions of persons in either camp.

More recently, Herbert Hyman and John Reed took a more careful scientific look at the data in question.[1]   In reviewing each of the surveys in
question, it seemed true that black respondents attested to the matriarchal
elements in their own families. But Hyman and Reed went beyond this
observation to examine the white respondents in the same surveys. *Black and
white responses were virtually identical.* Thus, if the black American family is a
matriarchy, then so is the white American family. This scientific observation,
then, may lead some people to question whether the questionnaire items
measure matriarchy in a meaningful way, whereas no amount of moralistic
objection could have this effect.

20.5   Guide to Reading Survey Reports

This textbook is intended as a guide to the consumers of
survey research as well as to those who will actually conduct surveys. In this
regard, it will be useful to conclude this chapter with a checklist of questions
a reader might ask himself whenever he reads a published report of a survey
project. The answers to such questions should assist him in evaluating the
significance of the findings reported.

1. What general topic does the researcher wish to examine?

2. What was his motivation in designing and executing the study?

*3. Is the researcher's main purpose one of exploration, description, explanation, or
a combination of these?*

4. What general population are the findings meant to represent?

*5. What was the sampling frame used for purposes of selecting a sample to represent
that population?*

---

[1]Herbert H. Hyman and John Shelton Reed, "Black Matriarchy Reconsidered: Evidence from Secondary
Analysis of Sample Surveys," *Public Opinion Quarterly* (Fall 1969), pp. 346–354.

6. *How was the sample actually selected?*

7. *How many respondents were initially selected in the sample and how many actually participated?*

8. *To what extent is sampling error likely to affect the results of the survey?*

9. *How were the data collected? Was the data collection method appropriate to the population and the subject matter of the study?*

10. *When did the data collection take place and how long did it take?*

11. *How were specific variables measured in the analysis? How were questionnaire items worded and/or how were responses combined into composite measures of variables? Does a given response pattern—imagining the orientations of persons giving it—reflect our common sensible interpretation of the summary term associated with the response pattern (for example, "very religious")?*

12. *Have composite measures been validated in such a way as to further ensure their adequate representation of the variables under consideration?*

13. *Are the methods of analysis used in the report appropriate both to the subject matter and the form of the data collected?*

14. *How strong are the associations discovered among variables? What do associations of that strength mean in understanding the real world?*

15. *Has the researcher adequately presented the logic of associations discovered empirically? Has he presented plausible reasons for those associations?*

16. *Has the researcher adequately tested for alternative explanations? Has he tested the possible spuriousness of the relationships?*

17. *Do the empirical relationships suggest further analyses that the researcher has neglected?*

18. *Could an independent reader replicate the survey on the basis of information presented in the report?*

While these questions will not provide an exhaustive critique of all survey reports, they indicate the kinds of questions that a critical reader should ask and that the conscientious researcher should anticipate in the framing of his report.

Additional Readings

Fellin, Phillip, Tony Tripodi, and Henry J. Meyer (eds.), *Exemplars of Social Research* (Itasca, Ill.: F. E. Peacock Publishers, Inc., 1969).

Lazarsfeld, Paul F., William H. Sewell, and Harold L. Wilensky (eds.), *The Uses of Sociology* (New York: Basic Books, Inc., Publishers, 1967).

Tripodi, Tony, Phillip Fellin, and Henry J. Meyer, *The Assessment of Social Research* (Itasca, Ill.: F. E. Peacock Publishers, Inc., 1969).

21.1 *Social Implications of Survey Research*

21.2 *Scientific Implications of Survey*

Research

21.3 *Educational Implications of Survey Research*

Chapter Twenty-One

Survey Research in Social and Scientific Perspective

For the reader who has come this far in the book, it should be clear that I have a special fondness for survey research. While it is surely only one of several research methods available to the social scientist, it has some very special advantages. It has important implications for society, for science, and for education. I shall conclude the present book with a brief consideration of each of these.

21.1   Social Implications of Survey Research

Survey research is appropriate to the study of countless social problems. Unemployment, for example, is an important social problem for people who are unemployed and for the society as a whole. While government officials, working with economists, can take positive steps to alleviate the problem of unemployment, such steps must be based on concrete knowledge about the problem. A sample survey would be an excellent method for determining the extent of unemployment in a given locality—or nationally —and for describing the characteristics of the unemployed. When it comes to detailed counting and describing, survey research is usually unexcelled.

Nor is survey research limited to the description of *hard data*. Prejudice can be measured; so can poor health and alienation. While the measurement of *soft data* is typically more difficult, survey research, by the specificity of its methods, affords the greatest possibility of continuity and progress in such research. While a given measurement of prejudice, for example, may not be altogether satisfactory to all readers, each will know exactly *how* prejudice was measured. The utility and the shortcomings of such a measurement can be evaluated through a careful, logical analysis of the data at hand, and subsequent studies can replicate and/or modify the methods of measurement.

There is a tendency at the present time for more humanistically inclined people—especially students, perhaps—to reject quantitative studies of human social behavior. It is frequently asserted that quantification of human relations dehumanizes them. I think this is a grossly incorrect conclusion, which results from equating humanitarianism with humanism.

If everyone always regarded human relations only in an aggregated, quantitative fashion, then such relations would probably be dehumanized in the process, and whatever innate humanitarian instincts are in man would have been lost. But even the most dedicated scientists do not act this way. Even the most deterministic, quantitative social scientist does not conduct his personal life wholly in such terms.

More important, however, social problems that require a strong moral foundation and compassion for their solution also typically require some firm data. Sometimes such data may assist moral persuasion, but this is not the only value of such data. Even if all men were in moral agreement on the need to solve a given problem, *how* to solve it becomes a pragmatic issue usually requiring data. A broad consensus on the need to cure cancer is not sufficient for the solution of the problem, and the same is true for social problems. And when moral consensus does not exist, firm empirical data become all the more important.

Survey research can serve another, different social function in a democratic society. Public opinion polls can serve the purpose of a quasi referendum. Where elections may occur only every two years or so, public opinion polls provide a continual monitor of public attitudes on issues. Officials need not wait for election day to find out how well they have represented their constituents. Like everything else, of course, this can be misused. Some elected officials try to give the impression of following the public mandate without really doing so. In an important sense, elected officials should not always cater to public opinions when they feel that such opinions are illfounded and unwise. In any event, however, a firm knowledge of public opinion on issues is better than ignorance of it.

In summary, survey research can potentially serve a wide range of social goals. There is no guarantee that such goals will be served, and surveys may often contribute to improper, even immoral, actions. But like a scalpel, survey research is a tool, not a moral philosophy. It will be used morally only if moral people learn how to use it.

21.2   Scientific Implications of Survey Research

Part One of this book was addressed to the logic of science in general, social science in particular, and survey research within that context. As pointed out earlier, survey research is especially well adapted to the basic logic of scientific inquiry. The specificity of operation that survey demands permits the careful delineation of scientific logic in practice.

All the critical decisions relating to measuremert and association that are inherent in all research must be made specific within a survey format. Whereas the participant observer has a certain latitude for acting on impressions, the survey researcher must convert even such impressions into clear empirical operations. While the participant observer, then, can conclude that a given person is unquestionably more radical politically than another, the survey researcher might agree but would be forced to specify the empirical indicators of radicalism so conceived.

As a result of this, the survey researcher always knows exactly what decisions he has made and how he made them. If his ultimate analysis seems incorrect or misleading, he will be able to evaluate and perhaps modify those earlier decisions, and reanalyze his data with as much precision as before. And of course, subsequent analysts can do the same with the given body of empirical data.

As noted in the earlier discussion of the elaboration model, the survey researcher is able to conduct a rigorously logical analysis of his data. He may work out the logical implications of a given interpretation and then test those implications empirically. While ex post facto hypothesizing is normally regarded as unsound in science, the survey format permits this activity in a rigorous and often fruitful manner.

Finally, the permanence of survey data are important for science. At one point in time, a set of survey data may be analyzed and found to support a general theoretical perspective. If the theory is subsequently displaced by another, the original survey data may be reanalyzed to determine whether they support the new theory. And the new theoretical understanding may suggest a more refined test of the old theory that was not considered in the original analysis of the data.

21.3   Educational Implications of Survey Research

In sociology at least, graduate methodology courses typically focus on survey research methods. There is a good reason for this, I think, and it is not a function of the popularity of survey research only.

Because survey research is so explicit in its application of scientific logic under actual field conditions, it provides an excellent pedagogical device for methodological instruction. All research methods face the problems of sampling, conceptualization and measurement, data collection, and analysis and interpretation, but survey research deals with each of these problems head on. As a result, training in survey research can give a student the best introduction to the scientific logic underlying such problems and the logical solutions to them.

The student who fully understands the logic of survey design and analysis should be excellently equipped to learn other social research methods. If he is to learn and conduct participant observation, for example, he will probably be more attuned to the problems of sampling and measurement than a person with no survey training. This is not to say that he will conduct participant observation with all the formal rigor of a survey or that he should necessarily, since the survey format has shortcomings, but that he will do *better* participant observation.

Conclusion

Survey research has a very great social, scientific, and educational potential. The popularity and extensive use of the method, however, does not mean that the potential is being realized.

Survey research will achieve scientific excellence to the extent that excellent scientists understand and use it. It will serve useful social purposes to the extent that people empowered to solve social problems understand how to use it effectively. It will serve as a moral instrument to the extent that moral people employ it wisely.

A textbook such as the present one can provide only some assistance in understanding the logic and practical skills of survey research. The use of that logic and those skills rests with the reader.

Appendix A. Table of Random Numbers

10480	15011	01536	02011	81647	91646	69179	14194	62590	36207	20969	99570	91291	90700
22368	46573	25595	85393	30995	89198	27982	53402	93965	34095	52666	19174	39615	99505
24130	48360	22527	97265	76393	64809	15179	24830	49340	32081	30680	19655	63348	58629
42167	93093	06243	61680	07856	16376	39440	53537	71341	57004	00849	74917	97758	16379
37570	39975	81837	16656	06121	91782	60468	81305	49684	60672	14110	06927	01263	54613
77921	06907	11008	42751	27756	53498	18602	70659	90655	15053	21916	81825	44394	42880
99562	72905	56420	69994	98872	31016	71194	18738	44013	48840	63213	21069	10634	12952
96301	91977	05463	07972	18876	20922	94595	56869	69014	60045	18425	84903	42508	32307
89579	14342	63661	10281	17453	18103	57740	84378	25331	12566	58678	44947	05585	56941
85475	36857	53342	53988	53060	59533	38867	62300	08158	17983	16439	11458	18593	64952
28918	69578	88231	33276	70997	79936	56865	05859	90106	31595	01547	85590	91610	78188
63553	40961	48235	03427	49626	69445	18663	72695	52180	20847	12234	90511	33703	90322
09429	93969	52636	92737	88974	33488	36320	17617	30015	08272	84115	27156	30613	74952
10365	61129	87529	85689	48237	52267	67689	93394	01511	26358	85104	20285	29975	89868
07119	97336	71048	08178	77233	13916	47564	81056	97735	85977	29372	74461	28551	90707
51085	12765	51821	51259	77452	16308	60756	92144	49442	53900	70960	63990	75601	40719
02368	21382	52404	60268	89368	19885	55322	44819	01188	65255	64835	44919	05944	55157
01011	54092	33362	94904	31273	04146	18594	29852	71585	85030	51132	01915	92747	64951
52162	53916	46369	58586	23216	14513	83149	98736	23495	64350	94738	17752	35156	35749
07056	97628	33787	09998	42698	06691	76988	13602	51851	46104	88916	19509	25625	58104

Abridged from *Handbook of Tables for Probability and Statistics*, Second Edition, edited by William H. Beyer (Cleveland: The Chemical Rubber Company, 1968.) Reproduced by permission of the publishers, The Chemical Rubber Company.

```
48663 91245 85828 14346 09172 30168 90229 04734 59193 22178 30421 61666 99904 32812
54164 58492 22421 74103 47070 25306 76468 26384 58151 06646 21524 15227 96909 44592
32639 32363 05597 24200 13363 38005 94342 28728 35806 06912 17012 64161 18296 22851
29334 27001 87637 87308 58731 00256 45834 15398 46557 41135 10367 07684 36188 18510
02488 33062 28834 07351 19731 92420 60952 61280 50001 67658 32586 86679 50720 94953

81525 72295 04839 96423 24878 82651 66566 14778 76797 14780 13300 87074 79666 95725
29676 20591 68086 26432 46901 20849 89768 81536 86645 12659 92259 57102 80428 25280
00742 57392 39064 66432 84673 40027 32832 61362 98947 96067 64760 64584 96096 98253
05366 04213 25669 26422 44407 44048 37937 63904 45766 66134 75470 66520 34693 90449
91921 26418 64117 94305 26766 25940 39972 22209 71500 64568 91402 42416 07844 69618

00582 04711 87917 77341 42206 35126 74087 99547 81817 42607 43808 76655 62028 76630
00725 69884 62797 56170 86324 88072 76222 36086 84637 93161 76038 65855 77919 88006
69011 65795 95876 55293 18988 27354 26575 08625 40801 59920 29841 80150 12777 48501
25976 57948 29888 88604 67917 48708 18912 82271 65424 69774 33611 54262 85963 03547
09763 83473 73577 12908 30883 18317 28290 35797 05998 41688 34952 37888 38917 88050

91567 42595 27958 30134 04024 86385 29880 99730 55536 84855 29080 09250 79656 73211
17955 56349 90999 49127 20044 59931 06115 20542 18059 02008 73708 83517 36103 42791
46503 18584 18845 49618 02304 51038 20655 58727 28168 15475 56942 53389 20562 87338
92157 89634 94824 78171 84610 82834 09922 25417 44137 48413 25555 21246 35509 20468
14577 62765 35605 81263 39667 47358 56873 56307 61607 49518 89656 20103 77490 18062

98427 07523 33362 64270 01638 92477 66969 98420 04880 45585 46565 04102 46880 45709
34914 63976 88720 82765 34476 17032 87589 40836 32427 70002 70663 88863 77775 69348
70060 28277 39475 46473 23219 53416 94970 25832 69975 94884 19661 72828 00102 66794
53976 54914 06990 67245 68350 82948 11398 42878 80287 88267 47363 46634 06541 97809
76072 29515 40980 07391 58745 25774 22987 80059 39911 96189 41151 14222 60697 59583

90725 52210 83974 29992 65831 38857 50490 83765 55657 14361 31720 57375 56228 41546
64364 67412 33339 31926 14883 24413 59744 92351 97473 89286 35931 04110 23726 51900
08962 00358 31662 25388 61642 34072 81249 35648 56891 69352 48373 45578 78547 81788
95012 68379 93526 70765 10592 04542 76463 54328 02349 17247 28865 14777 62730 92277
15664 10493 20492 38391 91132 21999 59516 81652 27195 48223 46751 22923 32261 85653
```

16408	81899	04153	53381	79401	21438	83035	92350	36693	31238	59649	91754	72772	02338
18629	81953	05520	91962	04739	13092	97662	24822	94730	06496	35090	04822	86774	98289
73115	35101	47498	87637	99016	71060	88824	71013	18735	20286	23153	72924	35165	43040
57491	16703	23167	49323	45021	33132	12544	41035	80780	45393	44812	12515	98931	91202
30405	83946	23792	14422	15059	45799	22716	19792	09983	74353	68668	30429	70735	25499
16631	35006	85900	98275	32388	52390	16815	69298	82732	38480	73817	32523	41961	44437
96773	20206	42559	78985	05300	22164	24369	54224	35083	19687	11052	91491	60383	19746
38935	64202	14349	82674	66523	44133	00697	35552	35970	19124	63318	29686	03387	59846
31624	76384	17403	53363	44167	64486	64758	75366	76554	31601	12614	33072	60332	92325
78919	19474	23632	27889	47914	02584	37680	20801	72152	39339	34806	08930	85001	87820
03931	33309	57047	74211	63445	17361	62825	39908	05607	91284	68833	25570	38818	46920
74426	33278	43972	10119	89917	15665	52872	73823	73144	88662	88970	74492	51805	99378
09066	00903	20795	95452	92648	45454	09552	88815	16553	51125	79375	97596	16296	66092
42238	12426	87025	14267	20979	04508	64535	31355	86064	29472	47689	05974	52468	16834
16153	08002	26504	41744	81959	65642	74240	56302	00033	67107	77510	70625	28725	34191
21457	40742	29820	96783	29400	21840	15035	34537	33310	06116	95240	15957	16572	06004
21581	57802	02050	89728	17937	37621	47075	42080	97403	48626	68995	43805	33386	21597
55612	78095	83197	33732	05810	24813	86902	60397	16489	03264	88525	42786	05269	92532
44657	66999	99324	51281	84463	60563	79312	93454	68876	25471	93911	25650	12682	73572
91340	84979	46949	81973	37949	61023	43997	15263	80644	43942	89203	71795	99533	50501
91227	21199	31935	27022	84067	05462	35216	14486	29891	68607	41867	14951	91696	85065
50001	38140	66321	19924	72163	09538	12151	06878	91903	18749	34405	56087	82790	70925
65390	05224	72958	28609	81406	39147	25549	48542	42627	45233	57202	94617	23772	07896
27504	96131	83944	41575	10573	08619	64482	73923	36152	05184	94142	25299	84387	34925
37169	94851	39117	89632	00959	16487	65536	49071	39782	17095	02330	74301	00275	48280
11508	70225	51111	38351	19444	66499	71945	05422	13442	78675	84081	66938	93654	59894
37449	30362	06694	54690	04052	53115	62757	95348	78662	11163	81651	50245	34971	52924
46515	70331	85922	38329	57015	15765	97161	17869	45349	61796	66345	81073	49106	79860
30986	81223	42416	58353	21532	30502	32305	86482	05174	07901	54339	58861	74818	46942
63798	64995	46583	09785	44160	78128	83991	42865	92520	83531	80377	35909	81250	54238

82486	84846	99254	67632	43218	50076	21361	64816	51202	88124	41870	52689	51275	83556
21885	32906	92431	09060	64297	51674	64126	62570	26123	05155	59194	52799	28225	85762
60336	98782	07408	53458	13564	59089	26445	29789	85205	41001	12535	12133	14645	23541
43937	46891	24010	25560	86355	33941	25786	54990	71899	15475	95434	98227	21824	19585
97656	63175	89303	16275	07100	92063	21942	18611	47348	20203	18534	03862	78095	50136
03299	01221	05418	38982	55758	92237	26759	86367	21216	98442	08303	56613	91511	75928
79626	06486	03574	17668	07785	76020	79924	25651	83325	88428	85076	72811	22717	50585
85636	68335	47539	03129	65651	11977	02510	26113	99447	68645	34327	15152	55230	93448
18039	14367	61337	06177	12143	46609	32989	74014	64708	00533	35398	58408	13261	47908
08362	15656	60627	36478	65648	16764	53412	09013	07832	41574	17639	82163	60859	75567
79556	29068	04142	16268	15387	12856	66227	38358	22478	73373	88732	09443	82558	05250
92608	82674	27072	32534	17075	27698	98204	63863	11951	34648	88022	56148	34925	57031
23982	25835	40055	67006	12293	02753	14827	23235	35071	99704	37543	11601	35503	85171
09915	96306	05908	97901	28395	14186	00821	80703	70426	75647	76310	88717	37890	40129
59037	33300	26695	62247	69927	76123	50842	43834	86654	70959	79725	93872	28117	19233
42488	78077	69882	61657	34136	79180	97526	43092	04098	73571	80799	76536	71255	64239
46764	86273	63003	93017	31204	36692	40202	35275	57306	55543	53203	18098	47625	88684
03237	45430	55417	63282	90816	17349	88298	90183	36600	78406	06216	95787	42579	90730
86591	81482	52667	61582	14972	90053	89534	76036	49199	43716	97548	04379	46370	28672
38534	01715	94964	87288	65680	43772	39560	12918	86537	62738	19636	51132	25739	56947

*Appendix B. Estimated Sampling Error for a Binomial (95%
Confidence Level)*

How to use this table: Find the intersection between the sample size and the approximate percentage distribution of the binomial in the sample. The number appearing at this intersection represents the estimated sampling error, at the 95% confidence level, expressed in percentage points (plus or minus).

Example: In a sample of 400 respondents, 60% answer "Yes" and 40% answer "No." The sampling error is estimated at plus or minus 4.9 percentage points. The confidence interval, then, is between 55.1% and 64.9%. We would estimate (95% confidence) that the proportion of the total population who would say "Yes" is somewhere within that interval.

| Sample size | ---------- BINOMIAL PERCENTAGE DISTRIBUTION --- | | | | |
	50/50	60/40	70/30	80/20	90/10
100	10	9.8	9.2	8	6
200	7.1	6.9	6.5	5.7	4.2
300	5.8	5.7	5.3	4.6	3.5
400	5	4.9	4.6	4	3
500	4.5	4.4	4.1	3.6	2.7
600	4.1	4	3.7	3.3	2.4
700	3.8	3.7	3.5	3	2.3
800	3.5	3.5	3.2	2.8	2.1
900	3.3	3.3	3.1	2.7	2
1000	3.2	3.1	2.9	2.5	1.9
1100	3	3	2.8	2.4	1.8
1200	2.9	2.8	2.6	2.3	1.7
1300	2.8	2.7	2.5	2.2	1.7
1400	2.7	2.6	2.4	2.1	1.6
1500	2.6	2.5	2.4	2.1	1.5
1600	2.5	2.4	2.3	2	1.5
1700	2.4	2.4	2.2	1.9	1.5
1800	2.4	2.3	2.2	1.9	1.4
1900	2.3	2.2	2.1	1.8	1.4
2000	2.2	2.2	2	1.8	1.3

Index